D1458338

THE SCOTTISH MOUNTAINEERING CLUB JOURNAL 2022

MacLeod's Maidens, Duirinish, Skye. Photo: John Sanders.

THE SCOTTISH MOUNTAINEERING CLUB JOURNAL 2022

Edited by Graeme Morrison

Volume 50

No. 213

THE SCOTTISH MOUNTAINEERING CLUB

THE SCOTTISH MOUNTAINEERING CLUB JOURNAL 2022
Volume 50 No 213

Published by the Scottish Mountaineering Club 2022

ISSN 0080-813X
ISBN 978-1-907233-29-6

Typeset by Noel Williams

Printed and bound by Novoprint S.A., Barcelona, Spain.

Distributed by Cordee Ltd, 11 Jacknell Road, Hinckley, LE10 3BS.

CONTENTS

Helen G.S. Forde: 'Old Man of Hoy, showing Detail of Top Corner'
mixed media, 88×106cm.

WINTER OUT WEST

by Neil Adams

MY FIRST FORAY TO ARDGOUR was with Ally Fulton in January 2009. With hindsight, this was quite an adventurous choice – we had both been winter climbing for a few years but hadn't ventured too far outside the honeypot venues. This particular weekend, the weather had been wild across the country, loading most slopes with windslab that deterred us from the usual destinations. South appeared to be the only safe aspect so I scoured the guidebook for south-facing winter crags accessible in a day-trip from Glasgow. I didn't find many options, but did notice that the South Wall on Garbh Bheinn had some low-grade summer routes that might be worth trying in winter. In the absence of any better ideas, we decided to give it a try.

A few hours later we were racing north, our enthusiasm to catch the first ferry restrained by treacherous driving conditions across Rannoch Moor. Once aboard, we realised for the first time what a magical little journey the Corran ferry is. Despite only taking a few minutes, it feels like a portal to a different realm.

We took the 'short and brutal' approach to Garbh Bheinn, which was exactly as pleasant as one would expect in deep snow, emerging on the ridge in a blizzard. Inevitably it took us a little while to locate the crag, but when we did, we were delighted to see it encrusted in rime. The line of the summer Severe *Sgian Dubh* looked like the most obvious winter option. The first chimney felt hard, but Ally succeeding in grovelling his way up it after I backed off. I led the second pitch, with lovely, steep, positive climbing leading to a little niche just below easy ground. We topped out in a proper Scottish hoolie, grateful for our goggles and anxious to get down as quickly as we could.

In the meantime, a well-meaning local had spotted Ally's car first thing in the morning, then passed it again as daylight faded. Concerned that we might be in trouble, they called the police. They somehow got hold of Ally's flatmate who reassured them: 'Don't worry – they're never off the hill before dark.' Nevertheless, when we returned to the car the police were waiting for us to check we were OK. It was an unusual end to a memorable day.

I returned to the west-coast peninsulas occasionally over the next few years, but not in winter. My first trip to the Ardnamurchan Ring crags in the spring of 2012 opened my eyes to the quality of the rock climbing in the far west. Eventually I returned to Garbh Bheinn to do some of the classic summer rock climbs and the excellent mountaineering ridges on the east flank of the mountain, as well as walking some of the nearby hills. I came to appreciate what wonderful terrain Ardgour has: beautiful, rough, unforgiving and seemingly always deserted.

I had always intended to return in winter but it somehow never reached

The busiest day in Ardgour's winter climbing history? Pete Hoang making the FWA of Gralloch (left), and Damien Granowski, Tim Miller & Callum Johnson making the FWA of Scimitar (right). Photo: Neil Adams.

the top of the priority list until 2020. In that season, Tim Miller and Jamie Skelton made the first of their many sorties to Garbh Bheinn, making the first winter ascent of *Butterknife* (an excellent summer HS and winter VI). A week later, Tim and I were both hosts on the MS–SMC–BMC–AC winter meet. There was much debate about where to go on the final day of the meet, as increasingly stormy weather had raised the avalanche risk across the country, leading to conditions reminiscent of my first Garbh Bheinn trip many years previously. With that in mind, I suggested Garbh Bheinn to Tim and Callum Johnson. We and our guests reconfigured into two teams of three, lightening the load on exhausted legs for the walk-in. Tim, Callum and visiting Polish climber Damian Granowski made the first winter ascent of *Scimitar* (summer VS and winter VII,8), an excellent-looking line cutting through both tiers. I had been paired with Canadian superstar Pete Hoang all week; he was well and truly out of my league, so by the end of the week I had resorted to pointing him at hard routes and trying to scrape my way up the crux pitches as second. In this spirit, I spotted what looked like appealing pick-width cracks on a direct version of the summer E2 *Gralloch*, and suggested Pete give it a go. This starts immediately left of *Scimitar*, causing probably the only crag congestion in the history of Ardgour winter climbing. Pete took a short, inverted fall low-down, lowering to the ground for a second go on which he dispatched the route smoothly in a single 50m pitch. It was only when Czech guest Lukáš Klingora and I attempted to second it that I realised quite how hard this pitch was. The pick-width cracks turned out to be blind seams, so the crux section relied on a series of strenuous and delicate stein-pulls. I fell twice from this section, struggling to maintain the load on the stein in the right direction while making a very long reach to the next placement. Higher up, the icy corner I assumed would bring respite turned out to have more tenuous, run-out climbing. I've never climbed a Tech 10 pitch before, but I guessed this would warrant IX,10 overall; I would be interested to hear the views of any strong climbers who repeat it.

It was around this time that I was starting to work on the SMC's new *Scottish Winter Climbs West* guidebook.[1] In thinking about what to include in the far west, it struck me that Ardgour and its neighbouring peninsulas have a lot in common with the Arrochar area. The crags are similarly turfy, are at roughly the same elevations and share a maritime climate. In a decent winter, the Arrochar crags see scores of ascents while Ardgour may only see a couple. In part this is because of Arrochar's proximity to the central belt, but surely it means there is huge untapped potential in Ardgour?

My hopes of investigating further that season were cut short by the pandemic. The next winter, my partner Claire and I were both working from home full-time. To enable progress on the book to continue, we decided to move to Fort William for the season. Given the lock-downs that followed, this turned out to be a fortunate decision. We ended up living just south of the town with views across Loch Linnhe to Ardgour, deepening my fascination with the place. The cold winter brought those crags into climbable (and, crucially, photographable) condition for a month or more. It felt inappropriate to push one's grade on hard or dangerous routes during the Covid restrictions, but this period allowed me to team up with a few local climbers to explore some of the lesser-known venues at more modest levels of difficulty.

One such venue was Creach Bheinn and its eastern top Maol Odhar, which lie just south of Glen Tarbert across the road from Garbh Bheinn. Two glens run up to the north side of this mountain, leading to Coire nam Frithallt to the east and Coire an Dubh-Alltan to the west. Both now have well-made hydro tracks running about halfway up to the crags, easing access at the expense of aesthetics. I first visited the crags to explore and take photographs for the book, and *Voodoo Buttress*, a good-looking Grade V in Coire nam Frithallt, caught my attention. I returned a few days later to climb it with Helen Rennard. Helen led the long first pitch up a ramp to the base of a steep corner that provided a short, spicy crux pitch. Above, as is so often the case, a complex-sounding description turned out to mean 'Follow the line of least resistance to the top,' taking in some

---

[1] Published by the Scottish Mountaineering Club in April 2022. See the Reviews section of this *Journal*. – Hon. Ed.

Helen Rennard on Voodoo Buttress in Coire nam Frithallt, just below the summit of Maol Odhar, the eastern top of Creach Bheinn in Morvern. This crag is just across the road from Garbh Bheinn and easily accessed by a new hydro track.
Photo: Neil Adams.

spectacular positions. It was a great route and whetted my appetite for more.

I visited a few other off-the-beaten-track venues through the season, including the crag on Stob Coire a' Chearcaill, the view of which had always intrigued me from the A82. At the same time, Tim Miller and Jamie Skelton were hoovering up the first winter ascents of the more feasible-looking routes on the South Face of Garbh Bheinn, and Simon Richardson and Robin Clothier were developing another venue in the Creach Bheinn area, Mad Man's Crag. The venue that most grabbed my attention was Sgùrr Ghiubhsachain, at the northern end of Ardgour just south of Glenfinnan and east of Loch Shiel. It is a beautiful, wild place with a gorgeous outlook over the hills of Glenfinnan, northern Ardgour and Moidart. The previous summer, I had done the classic scrambling circuit from Fersit, up the North-North-East Ridge of Sgùrr Ghiubhsachain and across to Sgùrr Craobh a' Chaorainn. In summer, the most exciting scrambling feels a little contrived as one has to seek out the difficulties, but it struck me that it would make an excellent winter mountaineering circuit via the line of least resistance. Along the way, I spotted an attractive-looking buttress left of the ridge, too vegetated for worthwhile rock climbing but with lots of winter potential. Scouring the *Journal*, I found that Steve Kennedy and Andy MacDonald had done one line on the mountain (*Bestial Devotion*, III,4) but I interpreted the description as being on the Loch Shiel (NW) face; so as far as I knew, this buttress was untouched.

My first winter visit was with Kevin Hall. We cycled in from Fersit

Helen Rennard on the North-North-East ridge of Sgùrr Ghiubhsachain, a worthwhile Grade I in its own right as well as an aesthetic approach to Jacobite Buttress. Photo: Neil Adams.

along the side of Loch Shiel and approached the crag via the NNE ridge. We climbed two of the most obvious lines: firstly a groove running up from the left toe of the buttress, finishing up a corner left of the steepest ground; and secondly a steep chimney branching out of a diagonal fault on the right side of the buttress. Since the top of the crag is in sight of the Jacobite memorial at Glenfinnan, we settled on a Jacobite theme for the route names: *The Uprising* and *The Young Pretender* respectively. Both were good Grade IVs and worth repeating.

I went back a couple of weeks later with Helen Rennard. The approach was made more exciting by ice on the track, resulting in us both falling off our bikes simultaneously mid-conversation, which would have been hilarious for any on-lookers. We had decided to explore the Loch Shiel side of the mountain in search of the existing route, but after much scrambling around had only found one line worth climbing, an unremarkable Grade II/III gully which we called *Chasing Wild Geese*. We came back round to the Jacobite buttress and climbed the diagonal fault on the right, out of which *The Young Pretender* had branched, which gave a surprisingly good Grade III,4. It was only later, after corresponding with Steve, that we realised this was the line they had climbed – it was just about recognisable in hindsight!

Ali Rose also added a couple of lines to the right-hand side of the crag: *White Rose* (III,4) and *Flora* (II). However, the wall between the routes I did with Kevin Hall remained unclimbed. It looked steep and hard, but there were some cracks and grooves that looked as if they might offer a way through.

Neil Adams on the FA of Raising the Standard on Sgùrr Ghiubhsachain.
Photo: Nathan Adam.

I returned to try this with Nathan Adam and Garry Campbell in January 2022. Persistent drizzle at Glenfinnan dampened our moods as we set off, but the weather cleared as we approached. Arriving at the crag, it seemed that our gamble had paid off: the wall was white and the turf frozen. Nathan led a good introductory pitch up a turfy groove with some tricky, unprotected moves straight off the ground. From there, I stepped right and climbed a series of grooves that cut through the steep wall. These were surprisingly accommodating, with positive hooks and plentiful gear, though the climbing was steep and sustained with sloping footholds. Eventually the angle eased, and I reached a perfect block belay. Garry led a relatively straightforward pitch up a turfy groove to the top.

The route turned out quite a bit easier than I had expected. We debated the grade, eventually settling on V,7: it is too well-protected to warrant Grade VI, but a bit trickier than most V,6s. Whatever the grade, it's a cracking route and deserves some repeats. Sticking with the Jacobite theme, we called it *Raising the Standard*.

Considering how close Ardgour is to the honeypots of Fort William and Glen Coe, I'm amazed how rarely these crags are visited and how many unclimbed lines remain. I hope the new book opens more climbers' eyes to the quality and variety of climbing here.

NIGHT

by Ian Crofton

Blood-red the Sun may set behind black mountain peaks ...
– Keats, 'Walking in Scotland'.

MOST CLIMBERS DO MOST of their climbing, sensibly, in daylight. But some of the best climbing days are highlighted by the night at either end, heralded by sunset, seen off by the dawn, punctuated by the cold wonders of moon and stars. Night, at least from the astronomical perspective, might be better regarded, not as a period of time – not night-time – but as a space. Night is a space with clearly defined boundaries, the half-sphere of darkness formed by the shadow the earth casts. Wherever we are on the planet, we enter this space as the ground we stand on rotates eastward, away from the sun. I'd never thought of this until I read Mark Vanhoenacker's book *Skyfaring*, an account of the life and experiences of an airline pilot. There is of course a hint of the spatial nature of the division in Genesis (1:4–5):

> And God saw the light, that it was good: and God divided the light
>   from darkness.
> And God called the light Day, and the darkness he called Night.

All climbers will have memories of their favourite sunsets from some high point – although only in the Himalaya are we likely to get anywhere near as high as an airline pilot, a position of vantage from where it might just be possible to get some slight impression of the curvature of the earth. I've never experienced anything like that, not even as a passenger in an airliner.

My most memorable mountain sunset, seen from the summit of Ben Nevis, was bracketed by two kinds of darkness: the gloom of thick, dank cloud, and the deeper darkness of a January night. We'd camped by the Allt a' Mhuilinn, some way below the CIC Hut, and set off in misty conditions to find the foot of Observatory Ridge. We found the ridge all right, but after a bit of foraging found no snow or ice on the lower rocks, so left it for another day. Now surrounded by thick cloud, we plodded up Observatory Gully. Then, just a few hundred feet before the top, a bit below the start of Gardyloo Gully, the gloom suddenly fell away beneath our feet, and we found ourselves in light. We were breathless, like new-born babies yearning to make a first cry, to take a first look at a new world.

Without at first realising what was happening, we'd emerged through the ceiling of the cloud, which spread out below us in an even white carpet as far as the horizon. To the north-east, only the shoulders of Càrn Mòr Dearg and Aonach Mòr, patched with snow and bathed in golden sunlight, were visible above the blanket. As the sun began its downward curve unseen behind us, the shadow of the Ben itself crept eastward across the cloud towards them.

Looking out of Gardyloo Gully, as the Ben spreads its shadow over a sea of clouds, 24 January 1987.   Photo: Ian Crofton.

That early in the season there was still an ice pitch in Gardyloo Gully. I would have roped up, but I was carrying the rope, and Bob was ahead and already half-way up. I had no choice but to follow unroped. No doubt the exposure sharpened my appetite for the feast ahead.

Deep in the gully we were still in shade, but as we negotiated the steep névé next to the cornice and pulled over the top, we found ourselves

On the top of Scotland as day turned to night.   Photo: Ian Crofton.

suddenly in a different world, a world confined to the summit plateau, a world in which the snow was gold and shaped by blue shadows, a world bounded to the south and west by a great sea of cloud, spread out before us. There was no sign of the mountains of the Mamores or the peaks of Glen Coe. All had been submerged into the gloomy sub-nebular world, leaving us alone in glory on the top of Scotland.

We were not quite alone. A few other figures were dotted in the vicinity of the summit, lingering as we lingered, reluctant to leave these realms of gold. Like Cortez and his men in that sonnet by Keats, as they first gazed upon the Pacific Ocean, we

> Look'd at each other with a wild surmise
> – Silent, upon a peak in Darien.

We watched and waited as the sunset worked through its quiet drama. Blue and green, the components of the spectrum with the shorter wavelengths, had long been scattered to invisibility by molecules and particles in the air as the beams of the sun, slipping down towards the horizon, pierced the earth's atmosphere more and more tangentially. We were left with the longer wavelengths of red and orange, mixed together into gold, warm in colour only as by now the temperature had begun to plummet.

With no breath of wind, we were oblivious to the cold, intent on waiting for the final act of the drama to unfold. Then, just as the sun dipped below the far western edge of the cloud field, we thought we saw it: the green flash. Green flashes, or green rays, are a rarity, seen for only a second or two, as green light from the sun's spectrum is refracted over the horizon.

We had heard of the phenomenon, we were looking out for it, staring into the setting sun, so I cannot to this day be absolutely sure that we did in fact see it. Soon enough it was time to turn our backs and make our way carefully down into the cloud-filled darkness, descending the CMD Arête, and from there into Coire Leis.

The next day the Ben was still wrapped in cloud, with no hint of the golden world we'd entered only hours before. We decided to go exploring up the right side of Glover's Chimney. Wandering about in the mist, somewhat lost, we ended up doing what turned out to be the first ascent of *Beam Me Up, Scotty*.

Green flashes are rarely seen. Almost as rarely witnessed, in my own experience, is that more nocturnal of phenomena, the Northern Lights. My first experience of the aurora was on Skye in the hot summer of 1976. By August, the bogs had become so dry they crunched underfoot. My companion was not a climber so I found myself doing some long solos such as *Pinnacle Ridge* on Sgùrr na Gillean and *Amphitheatre Arête* on Sròn na Cìche. I can't now recall where precisely we were camped on our last night on the island, but we faced north looking over alternating strips of land and sea. Late in the evening something caught my eye. Along the far northern horizon, beyond Raasay and Trotternish, there was a low band of pale greenish light, shimmering like a silken curtain. I blinked in disbelief. Opening my eyes I found it was still there, stretching from east to west, quietly, unshowily drifting and glimmering. This I have since learnt is a subdued version of the aurora known as the northern dawn. It was like a great wave breaking far away, on the distant north shore of the world.

It was many years before I saw the version of the aurora that I had seen in picture books as a child, the version known as the streamers or the merry dancers. One cold winter's night, a night when the temperature dropped to −20°C, we were drinking in a bar in Kincraig, next to the bunkhouse where we were to spend the night. The bunkhouse was not heated, and had a concrete floor, but the bar had both heat and carpets, so we stayed till closing time.

Pitched out at last into the darkness we found a great span of the sky high above us swirling with looping and swooping shows of light. Unlike the northern dawn I'd seen on Skye, the motion was quick and dramatic – although still monochromatic, rather than the full palette of pinks, yellows and greens of the picture books. These dancers, *na fir-chlis*, the lively ones, as they once would have been known in Speyside when Gaelic was still spoken here, were merry indeed – although it is possible that 'merry' may be a corruption of 'mirrie', meaning 'shimmering'. The old Gaelic saying:

> When the merry dancers play
> They are like to slay

suggests that the Gaels regarded the aurora as a portent of violence. To us the dancers in their cold beauty seemed neither malevolent nor kindly, merely lofty and indifferent – which is what the aurora is, a silent show that results when energetic charged particles of the solar wind become trapped in the magnetic fields above the poles. The particles then interact in the upper atmosphere with scattered atoms and molecules, which emit the lights we see. Recovering our breath we turned on our heels and battered on the door of the bar to rouse the staff to witness what they were missing. They thanked us for it.

Green rays and merry dancers are rare harbingers and denizens of night. Even rarer are comets. In April 1997 I was lucky enough to be staying at the CIC Hut when Comet Hale-Bopp was hanging brightly in the northern sky above the Allt a' Mhuilinn, framed by the great cliff of Càrn Dearg on one side and the long shoulder of Càrn Mòr Dearg on the other. That day we'd successfully climbed Observatory Ridge, the lower half bare rock, although occasionally verglassed, the upper half in full winter fig, sometimes subject to falling lumps of ice as the sun hit the upper part of the Orion Face. A couple of days before, I'd looked up at the same comet above London, its tail blazing across the sky, undimmed by a million streetlights. The last time Hale-Bopp had been so close to our planet was more than four thousand years before. Its passage had been remarked by the scribes of ancient Egypt.

The year before I saw the comet from the CIC, Bob Reid and Bob Appleyard made the first ascent of *Hale-Bopp Grooves*, not far from *Beam Me Up, Scotty*. Advance publicity for the comet was by then already in full flow. I watched them finish the route from the top of Number Three Gully Buttress. The Ben's penchant for astronomical nomenclature persisted.

More common night-time spectacles include shooting stars, though when someone sees one I'm usually looking the other way. More reliable, when up in the Scottish hills in winter, or bivouacking in summer high in the Alps, far away from the light pollution of the cities, is the bowl of the stars above one's head. The creamy trail of the Milky Way never ceases to astonish, boggling the mind with its myriad of stars, and the knowledge that one is looking into the centre of our galaxy. It is at such times that one remembers that we live on a small rock orbiting just one of a hundred billion suns in our own galaxy, which in turn is just one of a hundred billion galaxies thought to be scattered thinly through the universe. *'Le silence éternel de ces espaces infinis m'effraie,'*[1] Pascal said, observing the heavens.

Homelier by far is our closest companion in the night sky – the moon. Whether full or new, high above us or low on the horizon, waxing or waning, silver or gold, in a clear sky or glimpsed through rags of wind-torn cloud, the moon is always a welcome sight. It is a particular friend to the climber who finds himself or herself caught on the wrong side of dusk on a short winter's day. Even with less than half a moon a headtorch may not be necessary. If there's snow on the ground, no torch will be

---

[1] 'The eternal silence of these infinite spaces terrifies me.'

needed at all. On one such day, in a December long ago, I and a companion reached the top of Black Spout Buttress on Lochnagar. It was long after sunset. But the sun might as well have still been up, it was so bright by moonlight. It was the first time I remember ever experiencing moon-shadows. As we wandered round the rim of the plateau, I wondered at my shady double following me across the snow. To the east the moon glinted off distant snowfields. The far hills seemed to glow in cold clear light. To the south, somewhere on the Firth of Tay, a lighthouse winked.

Nature is not always so kind to the benighted climber. A few Decembers earlier I had found myself on the last pitch of *D Gully Buttress* on the Buachaille. Up till then the climb had been straightforward and fun. Now I was faced by a blank slab. There was no ice, just a smattering of powder. The pick of my old axe was straight. There was, as far as I could see, no possibility of further progress. Reluctantly but inevitably we made the decision to retreat. Darkness fell soon after. Route-finding down that complex face of the Buachaille was not easy. If there was a moon, I'm not sure it helped. At times we were in D Gully, at times on Curved Ridge, at times in Easy Gully, at times who knows where. It seemed to take forever. My greatest worry was not whether we were going to get down, but that we were going to get down very late, and that my mother would be worried sick.

Of course it would have been sensible to abseil, but we were too impoverished to sacrifice any gear. By the time we got back to the car (borrowed from my father for the day) it was nine o'clock. The straps of my crampons were balled with frozen snow. I had to hold the buckles in my bare hands for some minutes before the ice thawed, and I could remove my boots and embark on the long drive back to Edinburgh. But first I had to stop at the public 'phone box at the head of the Glen Etive road and make a difficult call home.

At least we weren't benighted. I've only ever once suffered that ignominious fate. It resulted from an excess of hubris. It was to be my fifth season in the Alps, my second with Bob Reid. My ambitions were high. Too high, as it turned out. For our first climb, we chose the Aiguille des Pèlerins. And not by the normal route, but by the South-West Ridge, a D+ with several pitches of V.

Although we were rock-climbing fit, we weren't acclimatised. We left our small tent on the Plan d'Aiguille before dawn, and cramponed up the snow of the steep Pèlerins glacier. At the start of the route proper we changed into rock boots, so our sacks were not only carrying crampons and axes, but also our big boots. Unaccustomed to the altitude, and with heavy loads on our backs, we strained and thrutched up the gnarly, unforgiving granite, pitch after pitch.

It must have been late afternoon by the time we gasped our way to the summit. Then we set off down the ordinary route on the South Face. Except we went wrong somewhere, and found ourselves on far more difficult ground than we'd expected. As the light began to go, we at last

The author starting up the Southwest Ridge of the Aiguille des Pèlerins in the summer of 1985. It was the beginning of what was to prove a long day, and a long night.
Photo: Bob Reid.

realised our mistake. Bob started to lead back up the face. After about thirty feet he found he could see nothing. It was useless, he said. He lowered off and joined me on a rocky ledge.

There was no choice. We would have to sit it out there until the light returned in the morning. We began to sort ourselves out for the night, each crouched on our own little perch. There wasn't room to lie down. We sat on a rope each, with our feet in our sacs, and with our orange polythene survival bags pulled over our heads. We tore out holes to breathe through. I had a rounded rock beside me, which I leant my head against, my Dachstein mitts cushioning my cheek. Despite my exhaustion, I didn't sleep. This was more to do with the discomfort of my cramped position than the cold, although it was cold enough.

Very many hours later, a glimmering of grey light began to seep into the unknown world around us. There was not the drama, the golden glory of a typical Alpine dawn, rather a slow, reluctant lessening of the dark. And as the drape of night was gradually withdrawn we could see that only a hundred feet or so of straightforward scrambling below our ledges would lead us back down to the Pèlerins glacier. If we'd continued down by headtorch, we'd have found ourselves off the mountain soon enough.

Back at our campsite on the Plan later that morning, I lay myself down flat-out in the shade of a big boulder, trying to recover lost sleep. My limbs ached, my head swam, the sun beat down. No dreams or comfort came. My brain and body must have known it was day, not the time for sleep, however much that sleep was needed. My clock had been too badly disrupted, my dials swivelled the wrong way, my rhythm broken.

I didn't completely recover in that whole holiday. A couple of days later, climbing the long ladders up from the Mer de Glace to the Couvercle Hut, I found my heart beginning to race. I could feel it beating fast in my throat. Even when I stopped to rest it would not slow down. It persisted all that night at the hut, and the next day, when we took a look at the East Face of the Aiguille du Moine and decided we weren't up to it. Even the straightforward South Face of L'Evêque the following day proved a struggle. My heart and my breath only settled down again once I was back down in the valley.

Failure to acclimatise gently must take some of the blame. My heart has never raced like that since, nor had it before, even at higher altitudes. Back in Glasgow the cardiologists tested me, and said they'd never had anyone run so long and fast on their treadmill. They could find nothing wrong with my heart. I suspect the fact that my cycle of sleeping and waking had been so badly shattered must take much of the blame. My internal clock, dictating sleep, had been overridden by cold and discomfort on the ledge. The external stimulus of complete darkness had also been totally ignored. And the following day I'd attempted to override the external stimulus of sunlight and warmth and tried to sleep.

I have since learnt that such irregularities in sleep patterns can play havoc with all kinds of key body processes in addition to heart rate, from core temperature and cell regeneration to hormone production and brain-wave activity. Jet-lag is a well-known manifestation of this. It is even worse for professional pilots, who frequently traverse a number of time-zones and regions of day and night while still awake in the course of a single flight. This results in fatigue, which may in turn lead to misjudgments. People who work nightshifts for long periods can also

The author on the Plan de l'Aiguille, unsuccessfully attempting to reconcile day and night after descending the next morning from the unplanned bivouac on the Aiguille des Pèlerins. Photo:Bob Reid.

suffer all kinds of harmful consequences, from cancer and diabetes to heart attacks and obesity. This is partly because many genes are programmed to be active at specific times of day, partly because many organs have their own unchanging clock, and are confused if the brain is running to a different time.

So there is much to be said for paying attention to the changing light. When you're out on the hill and the sun begins to sink, it's perhaps time for you too to think of sinking, descending valley-wards. Of course after a short winter day you can linger and enjoy the glories of sunset, the half-light of moonlight, the quarter-light of stars. You might see meteors, merry dancers, planets and satellites, even a comet. But don't for ever reverse your day and night, your sleeping and your waking hours. It was not for nothing that the God of Genesis divided the light from darkness, not for nothing that Europe's emergence from superstition and barbarism is called the Enlightenment, not for nothing that Goethe, one of that movement's late great figures, on the edge of death and eternal night, exclaimed '*Mehr Licht!*' We are not bats or owls, worms or moles, fitted by eons of evolution to thrive in the dark. We are, in contrast, evolved to fear the dying of the light, and so for long ages we lit fires and set dogs to guard our camps from nocturnal predators.

But as we've evolved, we've also come to learn that the beauty of the light is only seen in its full brilliance when framed by the darkness of the night that surrounds it.

EASTERN PROMISE:
THREE SKI-TOURS IN THE CAIRNGORMS

by Finlay Wild

WITH THE SNOW LINE RISING in Lochaber at the tail-end of the 2020–21 winter I made more frequent forays east to the high Cairngorm plateaux, where snow conditions were still good. Nowhere else in Britain is there so much continuously high terrain, and the possibilities for long ski-tours are well known. I was keen to combine lightweight 'skimo' race kit with my running and mountaineering fitness to see what was possible in the 'Gorms.

Cairngorms 4000ers

First I had a great outing on the 4000ers loop, the classic ski-round of the five Munros exceeding 4000 feet: Cairn Gorm, Ben Macdui, Cairn Toul, Sgòr an Lochain Uaine and Braeriach. The weather and snow conditions were both ideal, and it was a really sociable day bumping into friends along the way. Good snow cover meant it was easy to ski right to the river in the Lairig Ghru from Ben Macdui's summit, a long run with fantastic views and atmosphere. Up around the corries of Braeriach the snow was firm and fast, allowing the kind of easy, quick movement that displays the true efficacy of skis. As expected, after the Chalamain Gap there was a fair bit of jogging on foot to get back down to the snow gates where I had started, the road beyond being closed for the season. While satisfied with a fantastic day out on the 'Five Tops', my appetite was whetted for some longer missions, and I began planning.

Cairngorms Eight Tops

The Cairngorms Eight Tops is a loop around the eight highest Munros in the region – the 4000ers plus Ben Avon, Beinn a' Bhùird and Beinn Mheadhoin. My dad Roger Wild made what was perhaps the first completion in 2010 in a time of 27 hours[1] and then again in 2013 in 22 hours.[2] He used long Nordic skis with three-pin bindings and leather boots. Having already been amazed by how my race skis could eat up the miles, I wanted to try the Eight Tops myself. As well as the advantage conferred by lighter kit, the downhills would be easier and quicker as my skis lock into alpine mode for descents, unlike Nordic skis which are free-heel and harder to control.

I liked the idea of starting and stopping the clock on Cairn Gorm summit. For a ski-tour it made sense – maximising the use of snow – and had a logical simplicity and aesthetic appeal. After an early start I cycled up the closed ski-road and slowly skinned up Cairn Gorm to get in

---

[1] See R. Wild, 'Cairngorms Six & Eight Tops Ski-Tours', *SMCJ*, 41/202 (2011), 365–70.

[2] See R. Wild, 'Cairngorms Ski-Tours Update,' *SMCJ*, 42/204 (2013), 461–4.

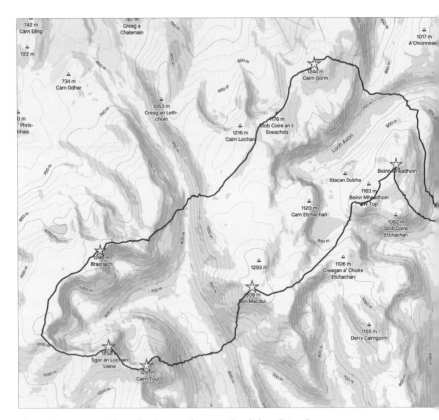

The Eight Tops tour. The author's circuit began and ended on Cairn Gorm.

position. When I set off from the summit cairn at 05.39 on Monday 15 March it was dark, and not brilliant weather – windy and clagged in. By GPS I skied fairly directly down to The Saddle and was able to pick my way towards the outflow of Loch Avon in the growing half-light, only taking skis off for a short way when descending heather. Climbing around the northern shoulder of Beinn Mheadhoin I was able to traverse quickly on skis almost to the top of the Lairig an Laoigh. Now it was daylight but clag remained on the summits as I traversed the Mòine Bhealaidh (Yellow Moss) eastward, eventually climbing into cloud as I ascended Beinn a' Bhùird's North Top. The snow conditions were really fast, and I skated and poled around to reach the descent to the Sneck. Always wild and remote, today it seemed a lonely place, and I went on foot up an exposed wind-stripped ridge for a while before transferring back to skis. Ben Avon's summit, Leabaidh an Daimh Bhuidhe, is a huge tor, and in the wind and clag I was glad to turn back west after scrambling up the hoared rock.

After retracing my tracks to Beinn a' Bhùird I descended back to the

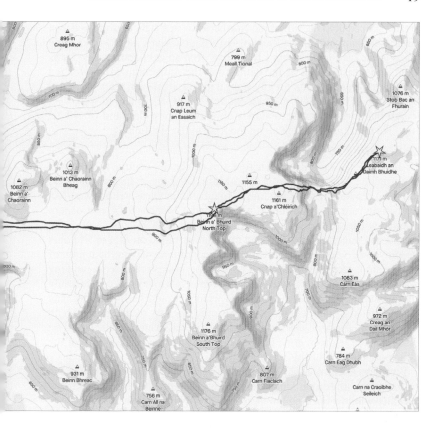

huge expanse of the Yellow Moss, then made fast progress back to the Lairig an Laoigh. Skinning up Beinn Mheadhoin there were early signs that the weather might improve, and I got a good view from its summit tor across the snowy expanses. Crossing the frozen outflow of Loch Etchachan I ascended into thin mist for the pull up to the day's highest peak, Ben Macdui. Shortly after leaving the summit, however, I emerged from the mist and found surprisingly good skiing as the views into the Lairig Ghru opened up. Skiing all the way to the river, I boulder-hopped across and filled my water bottle. Where previously I had cramponed up steep Coire an t-Sabhail towards Cairn Toul, today I was able to skin the whole way on a thin layer of soft, grippy snow. Now in the sun, I skied firm descents from Cairn Toul and Sgòr an Lochain Uaine before traversing around the impressively corniced cliffs of Braeriach back into the clag.

From Braeriach's summit I descended to the col before Sròn na Lairig and then more steeply to the Pools of Dee. Tiring, I skinned and then booted up the March Burn back on to the plateau from where it was a steady skin back to the rim of the Northern Corries, which I followed past Coire Domhain and Coire Raibert. Arriving back at Cairn Gorm's large cairn in the clag once again, I felt it had been an exhilarating day. I was tired and satisfied but at the same time the momentum of prolonged motion meant that I didn't really want it to end. However, after 54km and 9hr 19min 41s with 3500m of ascent, my legs were content to stop.

All that remained was to slowly ski down Coire Cas, and freewheel my bike uneventfully back along the road to the Hayfield.

Cairngorms 18 Munros

In July 1988, Mark Rigby on foot linked the 17 central Cairngorms Munros in a 120km loop from Glen More. Over the years the round has gained a reputation for being tough, rough and pathless, with fewer than 30 people repeating the run. It also gained a Munro, Sgòr an Lochain Uaine, when Munro's Tables were updated in 1997. In 2010 John Fleetwood undertook the first and only winter round on foot in 54 hours despite some very difficult weather and conditions. Given the nature of the terrain it seemed obvious that an attempt on skis made sense, and my success on the Eight Tops gave me the confidence to try this considerably bigger outing. I had often wondered what it would be like to do 'The Rigby' on skis, but of course there was only one way to find out. As both a runner and a skier I was probably more excited to attempt the round on ski; it had never been done before and seemed an ideal showcase of the skis' potential and utility.

Five days after my Eight Tops tour I was back at the Hayfield and trying to get some afternoon sleep before my attempt. There was a narrow weather-window opening but there had already been some thaw since my last tour. Although Rigby had started and stopped the clock at the Norwegian Stone in Glen More, for my skiing version it didn't seem to make sense to stick to this rule. The snow-line often doesn't reach glen level here and it seems much better to start on Cairn Gorm, maximising time on skis and allowing a sporting finish back there again many hours later. How many hours, I had no real idea. Rigby took 22 hours and Paul Raistrick brought this down to 19.5 hours (both on foot, in summer). I hoped to get round in under 24 hours.

After repeating the steady ascent to Cairn Gorm summit I chatted to a few skiers who were camping by the weather station, then once again set off for The Saddle by GPS in the dark. When I left at midnight exactly (on 20 March 2021) the weather was clear and calm, and descending I felt a mix of excitement and apprehension. While not disastrous, it quickly became apparent that the snow-cover below about 900m had taken a hit in the recent warm spell. After picking my way down to The Saddle I then alternated walking and skinning as I linked patches of snow on the way up A' Choinneach. Cover improved and I skinned firm consolidated snow to Bynack More's summit, sometimes turning my torch off to experience travelling solely by starlight in this silent special world.

In descent I aimed for the Fords of Avon via a traverse back around the east side of A' Choinneach. In better cover this would have been relatively straightforward, but it was awkward trying to find the most profitable snow runnels in the dark, and they often didn't run directly in the direction I wished to travel – a factor that would slow me down several times during the tour. After passing the deserted refuge I arrived at the river to find I would indeed be fording the Avon. Barefoot with my lycra suit rolled up above my knees, I waded through and then stood with numb, throbbing feet on the snowy opposite bank. Carefully drying feet and replacing socks, boots and skis, I was able to continue south. In a few hundred metres I had to repeat the whole operation to cross the river draining the Lairig an Laoigh. This second cold therapy might have been avoidable by making an initial detour to cross the Avon further east, although perhaps the river is deeper there and I did not want to be finding this, to my detriment, alone at 2 a.m.

Getting back into a rhythm I ascended Beinn a' Chaorainn, although its summit had been thawed down to the boulderfield by the recent hot sun. From here my route was down to the Yellow Moss, which was simple enough but less direct than five days ago owing to the snow-loss. Linking snowy patches I eventually attained high ground and Beinn a' Bhùird's minimalist cairn. Now very familiar with this stretch I quickly negotiated the Sneck and Ben Avon, pausing briefly to watch the lights of Aberdeenshire to the east. Returning west I descended back onto the Yellow Moss but this time turned southward and skated a section of the firm Allt an Aghaidh Mhilis in growing dawn light, before a more awkward ascent to Beinn Bhreac's bare summit. After a flat section and a water fill-up I climbed from the head of the Lairig an Laoigh to Beinn Mheadhoin's beautiful tor, the rock free of hoar this time. Though it was now clear and sunny, a strengthening wind had developed that was an early sign of problems to come.

The aller-retour to Derry Cairngorm was on good snow, although again the pattern of a short walk across boulders to the melted-out summit cairn was repeated. I was feeling good, keeping a steady pace and fuelling sensibly. Coire Sputan Dearg looked brilliant in the sunlight; I passed by and up to Ben Macdui. On looking back at my photographs I can see it was still a nice day at this point, and I felt as though I was looking right across Scotland from the top of its snowcap. The descent of Allt Clach nan Tàillear was firm and fast but although I was able to remain on ski for large sections of it, the ridge out to Càrn a' Mhàim had melted considerably since my last view of it five days earlier. This was made up for, however, by a thin tongue of snow I was able to descend from near the summit 400m vertically all the way to the path in the Lairig Ghru, a section I had been slightly concerned about when planning my route.

Now nine Munros in – Cairn Gorm would be counted last – I had a five-minute break at the Corrour bridge to adjust my rucksack, replenish water and take stock. Up Coire Odhar I was able to skin but the ridge to Bod an Deamhain (The Devil's Point) was bare of snow, giving a short break from

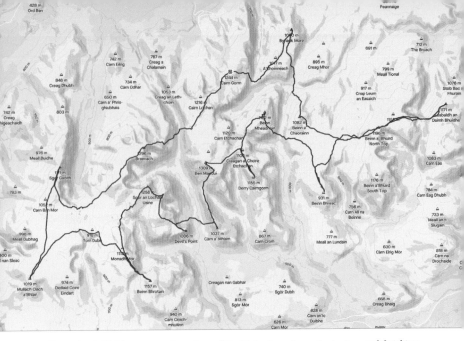

The author's 18 Munros tour (a variant of the Rigby Round), again starting and finishing on Cairn Gorm.

carrying a sack and skis which I left at the col. Skirting Stob Coire an t-Saighdeir I climbed Cairn Toul into strong wind. After the short hop to Sgòr an Lochain Uaine I left the corrie rim to ski south-west to the col near Loch nan Stuirteag. The now mild ambient temperature together with strong sun was starting to affect the snow, making it softer and slower, and the wind was tiring me. Monadh Mòr's gentle top seemed to drag on, but the connection to Beinn Bhrotain via the col overlooking Coire Cath nam Fionn was exciting, with some skiing close to the edge.

On returning to Monadh Mòr things got difficult, as I was forced to skin and pole downhill because of the soft snow and strong head-wind. Mullach Clach a' Bhlàir looked a long way off and indeed it is, but made worse by the need for a circuitous arc to the north via Tom Dubh to avoid a significant drop into the Eidart's deep glen. (In retrospect I think I should have taken the direct line, descending and crossing the Eidart.) When finally I turned more to the south, my skins were sopping in the soft afternoon snow and a change to my spare set aided progress. After a long, gentle climb to Mullach Clach a' Bhlàir I now skied north for another long stint, crossing the Great Moss towards Sgòr Gaoith. The wind was strengthening, dark high clouds starting to encroach; I was tired but still confident and resolute.

On Sgòr Gaoith the cloud came in. I sat down by the perched summit looking into Glen Einich: only two more hills to go. Rounding the head of the glen on the high ground to the south I started the long climb to Braeriach's plateau. Somewhere near Càrn na Crìche I ascended into whiteout and then it started raining persistently. The GPS batteries died but I had spares – just an inconvenience. I hadn't brought heavy-duty waterproofs so gradually became saturated. Moving along I wasn't cold, but stopping wasn't really an option. I chain-ate a few gels and caffeine chews to sharpen me up; this wasn't a place to make any mistakes. After some careful progress through the whiteness I arrived at Braeriach's summit, just able to make out the dull doom of the Coire Bhrochain cliffs. From here it was a short way east to where I could drop to the Lairig Ghru, and once there it was great finally to see a bit more sharply.

The snow around the March Burn had receded quite a lot since my Eight Tops visit, and I was able to boot uphill just north of the burn on steep grass slopes. Back in the whiteout my goggles were dripping and I could only just make out an occasional ski track as I made my way with the wind back to the head of Coire Domhain. Visibility was still terrible and the light was fading; it would be dark again before long. A sodden skin tried to escape but I was too tired and too close to let it bother me. I stuck it back on the ski and willed it to stay there. The final climb to Cairn Gorm from near Point 1141 was not fast, but on completing it I arrived at the cairn, closing my 105km loop (with 6000m ascent) in 18hr 50min 43s. With just enough light left I scooted down through the damp ski area, out from the cloud, and down to the Hayfield to sleep.

The most memorable outings are usually our longest days. The days when, on setting out, the outcome is uncertain are seldom forgettable. Moving through that arctic landscape the pleasure was in just doing, journeying. The snow was stable and safe, but it became too warm and soft, slowing me down. The strong wind was draining, and very poor weather in the last few hours was clearly not ideal. Snow cover was fairly thin below around 850m and some exposed or sun-baked spots even higher were bare. Snow stability, cover and weather will rarely all align perfectly for this sort of journey, surely the longest day-tour on skis in Britain. Earlier in the season there had been far more lower-level snow, but this route would have been too laborious with all the trail-breaking and avalanche caution required. Setting out, I never really had any doubts that this would make an incredible ski route in the right conditions. But knowing that is nothing compared with actually finding out.

SCOTLAND'S SEMI-PERENNIAL SNOW PATCHES

by Iain Cameron

WHETHER IT IS THE EXPERTISE of a butcher or a baker, of a haberdasher or a watchmaker, people prize continuity. An inherited skill-set, passed from generation to generation, inspires confidence in the customer. And although in this country the profession of outdoors guiding or leading is too young in general terms to have such pedigree, I can think of one hill-going pursuit where knowledge and experience have been passed down, in direct lineage, for over 100 years.

The subject to which I refer is the study of Scotland's long-lasting snow patches. It is esoteric research, to be sure, but a topic that many folk will have seen discussed or written about in various media of late. The reasons for its rise in prominence are probably threefold: an increase in awareness of the outdoors; the use of social media; and the influence of climate change on our national discourse. To understand this subject properly, however, we need to wind the clock back well over 100 years, to the start of the twentieth century.

Readers of the *Journal* will probably need little introduction to the man who first studied patches of snow on Scotland's hills with something resembling scientific rigour. Seton Gordon is a name so familiar to anyone with even a passing interest in the Scottish outdoors that it hardly needs explained who he was. A self-taught naturalist *par excellence*, Gordon wrote on a huge variety of outdoor topics. Bird-watching, especially the golden eagle, was his speciality, but in many of his books he would turn to the discipline of snow-patch study. His fascination with those doughty relics of our glacial past was lifelong and encompassed any hill where the snow endured past a date when one might *expect* it to last. For example, during research for my own book on this subject (reviewed elsewhere in this *Journal* by Greg Strange) I came across letters to a local paper in Berwickshire where Gordon had noted snow in June on The Cheviot of Northumberland in 1951. For decades Gordon would record the various patches of snow that endured, especially on his beloved Cairngorms, from one year to the next. Though he never published on the subject specifically, he would pass on his knowledge, first-hand, to the man who came after him.

In the pantheon of Scottish outdoor greats, Adam Watson is surely near the top. Together with Seton Gordon, Hamish MacInnes, Dick Balharry and John Muir, Watson sits deservedly at the top table. In a career spanning over 65 years, he wrote an almost bewildering number of books, papers, and reviews. His membership of the SMC spanned an equally remarkable 64 years, from 1954 until his death in January 2019.[1] Despite his impressive array of post-nominal letters, Watson's first and most

---

[1] For an obituary see *SMCJ*, 47/210 (2019), 299–304. See also A. Watson, 'Warmer Climate & Scottish Snow', *SMCJ*, 39/196 (2005), 51–9. – HON. ED.

enduring love was snow; specifically, patches of snow. As a young boy he would marvel at summer wreaths that hugged the ridges of the high Cairngorms, sketching them to send as letter attachments to Seton Gordon. The two became correspondents and acquaintances from the 1930s until Gordon's death in 1977. Among the letters between the two was information on patches of snow, recalling specific locations where they had been known to persist the longest.

My own epiphany on snow patches came at an equally early age to Watson's. As a nine-year-old boy I looked from my parents' house across to hills in the far distance.

> One hill, many miles distant, towered higher than the others. It rose from behind two smaller hills and the summit cone sat atop two large shoulders which jutted out horizontally in pleasing symmetry. On that beautiful May morning, sitting on this distant peak's south-facing slope, gleaming prominently in the early sunshine, was a large patch of what seemed to be brilliant-white snow. I couldn't understand how it had endured. I stood for a moment and looked at it. 'It can't be,' I said to myself, doing a double take.

This experience was to have a profound effect on me, for reasons that all these years later I am still unable to articulate adequately. Such are the vicissitudes of youth. Many years later, in a tale almost identical to Adam Watson's contacting of Seton Gordon, I wrote to the former. I had some information that I felt he might find useful, from my own observations made over the years. In his first written reply to me, he concluded by saying:

> I am interested to come across a snow enthusiast, as there are so few of us! Best wishes and keep in touch, Adam Watson.

I was delighted. Here was I, a grunt who had left school at 16 with barely a qualification to my name, receiving positive feedback and genuine warmth from one of the country's most respected and best-known scientists. From that day until his death in January 2019 we kept in regular contact, seeing each other fairly frequently and speaking on the 'phone. I hoovered up the knowledge and experience that practically dripped from his person, keen to imbibe as much of it as possible. My own enthusiasm was a match for his, maybe, but my knowledge of the upland environment was not – and could never be – anything like his.

That initial contact was back in 2005. At that time Adam – along with Davie Duncan and John Pottie – wrote the annual 'snow patch' paper that appears in the Royal Meteorological Society's *Weather* journal. After a couple of years of contributions from me, Adam asked me to become co-author, which I was immensely proud of. In 2011 he suggested that perhaps I'd like to have a stab at being lead author. Though more than capable himself of continuing the role, he wisely surmised that he wasn't going to be around for ever, and that new blood was needed. My first attempt at writing a draft was returned with so much red pen from Adam

Adam Watson, FRSE (1930–2019).   (All photos are by the author.)

that I thought perhaps I was not cut out for such an endeavour, but he suggested that I persist. And, like a dog with a bone, persist I did.

Over the years the red penning got less and less, to the point where in 2017 there was hardly any. The master had imparted sufficient knowledge to the callow apprentice, who was ready now to take up this particular mantle. I consider it a great honour that the last published piece featuring Adam's name was printed beside my own in the 2018 snow-patch paper. Since his passing I have sought to be as diligent and judicious as possible when writing the paper, imagining that I still need to send him it for comment. His spectre looms large and always will so long as I'm involved in writing the annual report. The 100 years of knowledge, passed down and entrusted to me as custodian, will I hope be passed to an equally enthusiastic apprentice in the years to come.

Most people reading this will need little introduction to patches of snow in summer. Those who frequent the high cliffs of Ben Nevis's north-east face or the Ben Macdui and Cairn Gorm plateau between June and September will be well used to seeing large remnants of the previous winter's snow clinging limpet-like to the hollows and shaded gullies above 3000 feet. But it surprises and interests those urbanites with little appetite for outdoor pursuits, when I tell them that snow in Scotland can be found almost always, if one knows where to look.

This genuine interest found a particular nationwide focus in early October 2021 after I announced via social media that Scotland's most enduring patch of snow was on the cusp of melting completely for the third time in five years, having done so the same number of times in the

The 'Sphinx' snow patch in Garbh Choire Mòr, 6 October 2021.

previous 300 years.[2] The wreath to which I refer, Braeriach's 'Sphinx',[3] became, at least for a while, the world's best known snow patch. This was in large measure owing to the climate conference, COP26, being held in Glasgow. Reporters on the hunt for a local climate-change story latched on to it. For almost a month, barely a day went by without my 'phone ringing or my inbox pinging, asking me to give an interview or offer a comment. The Sphinx had, quite literally, gone global.

'Can we get a film crew to it?' was a question put to me about half-a-dozen times, most memorably by American-based CNN. After I had explained the process of getting to Garbh Choire Mòr, the Cairngorms' most isolated corrie and the place where the Sphinx reposes, the various news agencies in search of a piece-to-camera were happy to settle for a photograph of me standing wistfully at the location.

Another question I had to bat away constantly was: 'Is the Sphinx's more frequent disappearance due to climate change?' As I say to absolutely everyone who asks this, I am not even an academic, let alone a climatologist. Like Seton Gordon and Adam Watson before me, I have not studied snow patches in a professional capacity. We did it and do it as amateurs. We simply collect the data and then publish it via the Royal Meteorological Society for others to extrapolate and pontificate as they deem appropriate. That being said, it is hard to believe that climate change

---

[2] Snow at Garbh Choire Mòr has disappeared since the eighteenth century a total of seven times (1933, 1959, 1996, 2003, 2006, 2017 & 2018).

[3] So called because of the rock climb above it, *The Sphinx*, first attempted in the 1940s. See *Cairngorm Club Journal*, 15/83 (1942–43), 229–230.

Snow patch on Aonach Mòr, 19 September 2020.

is not playing a part in the semi-perennial patches of snow in Scotland becoming less reliable than in days gone by.

It is not just Ben Nevis[4] and Braeriach that can hold year-round patches of snow on our highest hills. As recently as 2015, small relics endured on Beinn Dearg near Ullapool, as well as on the Grey Corries and the Mullardoch Munros. Instances like these have always been rare, though, and are now becoming exceptional. Snowy winters followed by cold springs are set to be features of history.

Another notable feature of modern snow-patch observation is watching the potential 'changing of the guard'. Though the Sphinx remains the benchmark, in the last few years its position as our most durable patch of snow has been put under threat by another on the Nevis range, at Aonach Beag. This historically little-studied wreath endured in 2018 and 2021 when the Sphinx did not. 2018 was the first time in recorded history the Sphinx was not the last to melt. For it to happen twice in four years suggests something is afoot. The Aonach Beag patch is something of an enigma, sitting just on the 3000-foot contour – well below the altitude at which patches of snow normally survive. Time will tell if it emerges as our most resilient.

Though it is gratifying to see the number of people interested in this subject increase dramatically in the last ten years (a Facebook page I set up on the subject has over 4000 members), stubbornly few can be relied upon to put on a pair of boots and venture to the often extremely

---

[4] Observatory Gully and Point-Five Gully *tend* to hold snow from one year to the next, but even these patches are becoming less reliable.

challenging locations where the snow sits. There are about 30 or 40 who might go to a particular patch in summer, but when push comes to shove, in late September when there are but a handful of wreaths left, only about ten people will actually visit the most inaccessible places. Perhaps more worryingly, most of them are at least middle-aged. It is to be hoped that the avid watchers of these patches will not suffer the same apparent fate, and slowly and quietly disappear in the succeeding decades with little more than a whimper.

Iain Cameron is lead author of the annual snow-patch paper that appears in the Royal Meteorological Society's 'Weather' journal. He is also the author of a recent book on the subject, 'The Vanishing Ice' (Vertebrate Publishing, 2021); see Greg Strange's review on p.352.

THE SIGNS

The signs are all in Gaelic now
But you never hear it in the shop.
Ravens croak and buzzards mew,
Herons screech with anger
When disturbed;
Their language is not threatened
By the Saxon race.
I wonder what the Gaelic is
For 'Passing Place'?

P.J. Biggar

Ewan Paterson leading the penultimate pitch of Trapeze (E1,5b) on Aonach Dubh.
Photo: Stuart McLeod.

THE REUNION

by Mike Dixon

THE DRIVE NORTH WAS FAST, risky but liberating. The 'phone call two nights ago had come completely out of the blue. He wondered if Phil really would turn up.

With their elegant sweeps but isolated ruggedness, the Southern Highlands always flattered on a clear night. The mountains were the constants, the reliable ones, he thought, even if every so often they snuffed out the odd person. Humans were the mysteries. Memories of Phil kept intruding: bivouacs, epics, evading bandits in Bolivia, car crashes. In retrospect, it was one of the most intense relationships he'd had with another person.

The moon tracked the car's progress as it negotiated the bends and climbed to the edge of Rannoch Moor. Cigar smoke coiled out of the half-open window as he admired the mythic silhouettes against the star-spangled sky. Smoking was a rare luxury these days; the sanctimonious lectures he received from his kids were more of a deterrent than the threat of cancer. We've all got our demons, not just Phil, he thought.

As he approached the Clachaig his mind flipped back to the first time he'd met Phil. Sweaty pre-Gore-Tex jackets, hairy fleeces, breeches; the toilet floor awash in a mixture of dodgy plumbing and even dodgier aims; Phil holding court about the climb he'd done that day. He was never short of self-confidence, an arrogant bastard in the eyes of many, which made it even sweeter for his detractors when his world fell apart. He'd received just one letter from Phil in all the time he'd been away. The whole tone of it had been very strange. He was relieved there was no address on it, and he never shared the contents with anyone. At the time he wondered if he ever wanted to see Phil again.

Entering the chalet behind the hotel he was greeted with indifference. The kids were absorbed in their smart 'phones. His wife was chatting to a friend staying in the adjacent chalet. He was reminded of the times when they couldn't keep their hands off each other following even a short separation. Their relationship now was solid and financially secure. He still needed to climb.

Escaping to the bar, he broke the news of the surprise visitor to his reunion cronies. It was not received well. No need to hand out the party poppers for Phil's big entrance.

'Didn't he move to Ireland?'

'You mean after his release?'

A silence ensued.

'He was your best friend, Dave, wasn't he?'

'Yeh. We've shared a lot over the years.'

The group were muted again, staring at their pint glasses. Dave continued: 'You can't write people off just like that. … He did his time. Give him a break.'

Some sneered. A few privately admired the way he defended him.

'He's still a mate.'

On cue, Phil walked in.

Dave went straight over and steered him to a quieter corner away from the eyes of the group, then proceeded to the bar. The three-piece band was murdering Sweet Home Alabama as he returned with two pints.

'Cheers.'

'Just what I need,' Phil replied, taking a long drink. 'I've had one hell of a hitch to get here. Left Killybegs yesterday morning.'

'Where are you staying tonight?'

'I was planning on putting the tent up just along the road.'

'Those days are over, I'm afraid. You'll get fined and moved on. I'll help you carry your stuff over to the campsite later.'

An awkward gap followed.

'It's been a long time Dave.'

'Too long. How was Ireland?'

'Some good times, some not so. I was the caretaker in a hostel in Galway, climbed on The Burren and the Aran Islands, did quite a bit of soloing – anonymous out there. Then I met this American woman, but I couldn't tell lies …' His rigid body language could not be thawed by the alcohol, his eyes were darting about the busy room. '… so I moved up to Donegal and started again. But you miss the old places. That's why I'm back.'

Before leaving him later at the campsite Dave asked, 'Where are you going to base yourself next?'

'Don't know yet; one day at a time. Anyway,' he smiled, 'who knows what might happen to us tomorrow?' The smile unnerved Dave.

When he returned to the chalet the news had leaked back to his wife.

'What's that weirdo doing back here?'

'He's trying to move on. He's had a tough time …'

'Tough time! No one forced him to do what he did! You've got two kids sleeping next door. Now I hear you're going climbing with him! He's not stable!' She twisted the two ends of a tea towel in opposite directions as if she was preparing to strangle someone. 'Don't bring him near here! All the others think you're mad!'

There was no point in arguing; he went outside. The west face of Aonach Dubh was faintly illuminated in a silvery wash. Dave felt unsure about climbing with him the next day. When he woke at around 3 a.m. he twitched the curtains to stare up at the pulsing moon. 'It'll be OK,' he tried to convince himself.

He was just as fit as Dave remembered.

'Do you still keep in touch with your family, Phil?'

'The last time was via my solicitor. That was to tell me my daughters wanted no more contact.'

Dave wondered how he himself would have sustained all these body-blows.

'It's good of you to come out with me today,' said Phil awkwardly. 'I haven't had much luck with climbing partners.'

There were new mannerisms that made Dave feel apprehensive. Sometimes Phil failed to respond to questions or comments, even innocuous ones. He talked to himself in brief snatches. Just when Dave thought he should make some excuse to get out of the climb, there were flashes of wit and swagger and the old Phil was right back there with him.

'This'll be a great route to finish on, Dave! You have to know when to call it a day.'

'Call it a day? I'd like a pint for everyone I've heard say that.'

Phil turned and looked directly at him: 'This will be my last route. For you too perhaps.' Dave felt a chill despite the warm day, and thought of his family. He called for a rest and sat on a smooth rock to take stock.

They tied on. They should really have been on this route together fifteen years ago. It had been a shared ambition during that summer. They both had wanted to lead the crux and had argued in a friendly way about it, waiting for the other to give in. Phil had studiously avoided him for weeks when he'd climbed it without him.

'Hell, we're not married!' Dave had joked at the time. But for Phil it had been an act of betrayal. The fact that Dave had not led the crux on the day did nothing to appease Phil.

Dave remembered the key pitch vividly. It looked most improbable from below, and was extremely exposed with sparse protection. From a leader's point of view the long arc of rope behind you made you wonder why you'd bothered to carry up a rack of gear. You might as well be soloing.

On the walk up to the crag Dave offered the crux to Phil, a generous act as it was the best pitch on the climb. They laughed about their past squabbles over this. 'I'll even things up for you later,' he winked at Dave.

From the comfortable ledge he watched Phil climb diagonally up a wall just short of vertical on small, flat holds. He paused at its right edge below a band of overhangs at the top of the wall.

He bawled something out, unintelligible to Dave, before swinging round the hanging arête. Dave's body tensed with this outburst, but he was relieved to be still paying out the rope to his now out-of-sight partner. He imagined him on the wildly exposed undercut section that led up to the next belay ledge. What was all that shouting about?

Dave waited for the rope to be taken in and absorbed the whole setting. The peak cast a shadow over the opposite hillside as if asserting its superiority. He felt vulnerable and alone now with Phil hidden round the arête. One more pitch after this, and they'd be coiling the rope. He had been unnerved by Phil's scream but not by his climbing. He was sure Phil wouldn't pack in climbing; he'd climbed the crux pitch immaculately. Dave felt vindicated. Climbing was cathartic for them both. All the real madness was down in so-called civilisation.

'When you're ready!'

Dave climbed to the arête, his feet and fingers moulding precisely round the holds. It felt like an out-of-body experience as he floated effortlessly upwards, savouring the audacity of the pitch and its situation.

His rhythm was broken by a request to stop before the swing round the arête. It was a dynamic move, the type he made all the time on the climbing wall. The whooshing sound of something falling behind him and clanking into the gully 300 feet below him shattered his concentration. It sounded like the metallic clatter of a rack of gear.

'What was that? What's happening, Phil? ... Can I climb?'

An unwelcome loop of slack hung below the knot on his harness.

'Take in!'

Bridged out, his hamstrings were tiring. Pride caused him to keep quiet. All of a sudden the slack was pulled in and he could continue. But the fluidity had gone.

Dave's chalked fingers played with all the possible combinations of holds on offer. He seemed to be missing something; he needed his right middle fingers to find more of a purchase for the swing. Dave's focus was disturbed by the onset of manic laughter that reverberated round the gully wall. Anger and fear swelled in him, and he decided to trust the holds he had in his grasp. Sweat was oozing from his fingertips. Thoughts of a fall flashed across his mind.

'Take in, Phil!' His higher voice-register revealed anxiety.

Once he'd committed himself he soon reached better holds and the angle lay back just enough to allow him to rest. He shook out his arms while his eyes focused on Phil, thirty feet above him, nonchalantly stacking the rope on the meagre belay ledge.

But there was something alarmingly wrong. The rope wasn't being taken in through a belay device. There was no gear hanging from Phil's harness loops, no slings round his shoulders. He wasn't even belayed.

'What are you doing!' yelled Dave.

'I'm giving you the chance to savour the lead of this pitch too! Take care.'

Phil smiled then turned his back on him and started climbing the final pitch. There was no gear in place between them. They were both effectively soloing, but tied to the same rope. Dave's tongue was paralysed.

At ground level the next moves would have been a formality, but in the circumstances Dave couldn't convince himself.

Concentrate! Focus! Climb!

He moved up, trying to ignore the figure climbing simultaneously above him. If he could just get to the ledge he knew he could untie from Phil and either continue genuinely solo or be rescued from there. The final fifteen feet up to the ledge looked very thin and there was nothing in his memory banks to reassure him.

The laughter started again. Dave's right calf began to shake …

'Back already?' his wife remarked as he entered the chalet just before midday.

'I just didn't fancy climbing today. Something didn't feel right.'

'I'm glad you changed your mind. Where's himself?'

'I took him to the campsite and helped him pack up. Then I dropped him by the roundabout at the hitching spot.'

'Where's he going?'

'Who knows? … He said to somewhere he can properly escape the past.'

'There's no such place.'

MOUNTAINEERING IN HYPERBOREA: LAND BEYOND THE NORTH WIND

by Iain Young

I HAD KNOWN FOR YEARS that a gaping omission from my winter climbing CV was doing something in the farthest north. With only an attempt to climb on Foinaven in the earliest 1980s and one winter route on Beinn Dearg, I felt I needed to do something if only to convince myself that it is, as many people seemed to suggest, all too far, all too unpredictable, and altogether too much hassle. After all, there's always something to do in the Cairngorms whatever the winter is like. Then one fine day John Higham and I visited the Cadh' a' Mhoraire on Beinn Mòr Coigach. From a starlit start, we tramped in over iron-hard bogs and were treated to a new route on solid turf, perfect stone, névé, and views to the north that went on forever. We named it *Hyperborea*.[1] We didn't see a cloud and we didn't see a soul. I was hooked.

Beinn Lair — night

A big, orange sun was hovering just above the Minch. Adorned with all the usual clouds, and all the usual beams of fleeting light. Nothing outstanding, just another west-coast sunset. But something else made it special: it was February, John and I were on the top of Beinn Lair, and we were a very, very long way from the car.

The day had started pleasantly enough, cycling past Kernsary in the barking dark, losing our way in the trees, wading through ice-crusted mud, and walking for what seemed like forever below enormous cliffs that do go on for ever. Beinn Lair is big, maybe even the biggest. There would be a lifetime of winter climbing there if we only had a lifetime of winters left. Lunching early under some suitably enormous boulders, we chose a line above, which went as far as we could see without looking as difficult as we might imagine. It started with some icy grooves, then we stretched the ropes for pitch after pitch on turf and runnerless schist. The scale was Alpine, the atmosphere uniquely Scottish. The final belay was taken by wrapping the rope round the cairn on the little 830m top, and now here we were enjoying the show.[2] Just a long dark walk, another cycle, a night drive, closed snow-gates, a crawl into bed at five, and a six o'clock alarm separated me from the commute to work. A twenty-four-hour day, mostly spent in the dark.

We always meant to go back sometime for *Marathon Ridge*. But then an Andy Nisbet team of four beat us to it. Slightly disappointing, though perhaps no surprise, and at least it saved us the walk.

---

[1] *Hyperborea*, IV, 5, on Beinn Mòr Coigach; *SMCJ*, 42/203 (2012), 166.

[2] *Glaodh an Iar* (Call of the West), III, on Beinn Lair; *SMCJ*, 49/212 (2021), 168.

Stac Pollaidh — sunshine and stars

A fine weather forecast and a road-closing dump of snow on the Wednesday made Coigach an obvious choice for a long weekend, even though February was rather late in the season for low-lying routes. Late arrival meant that Plan A was put on hold, and we searched about for something far less arduous for Day One. Stac Pollaidh was selected: a short walk and a straightforward route. Intrigued that a Diff climbed by Walker and Inglis Clark in 1906 on the West Buttress had apparently never had a winter ascent, we headed up there as first light turned Cùl Beag's west face into a miniature Eigerwand. Starting from the lowest rocks below Baird's Pinnacle (home of a full-value VS) we climbed moderate ground to a belay in the brèche between pinnacle and mountain. From there we moved a bit right then back left via an awkward step around a prow, to gain slabs and the midway snow-slopes. Upwards we followed the most aesthetic and logical-looking route on the junction between the west and south faces. More slabs, grooves and cracks to a move rightwards and a final pull on to the summit ridge. None of this had looked remotely like 'Diff' country from below, nor felt anything like it whilst climbing. The last pitch involved a couple of very, very tenuous moves laybacking on tools off a rounded edge before the sanctuary of a well frozen blob of turf was reached.[3] So tenuous that I fell off seconding, for only the second time in my winter climbing career – yes, I know, this means I can't really be trying.

Deep, deep powder and no footprints on the summit. We could almost have been in Greenland. We have never really been minded to award stars for these routes in the far north-west. Why would we, when the landscape is the headline and the climbing the support act? But this one was better than *Eagle Ridge*!

Garbh Choireachan — the sea, the sea

After we came down from Stac Pollaidh in the gloaming, and with the route having been unexpectedly taxing, the next day demanded something guaranteed to be suitably mellow. With snow to sea level, we kicked Plan A's can even further down the road and headed instead for the direct west ridge of Garbh Choireachan.[4] Fun, turfy, low-commitment, and unremarkable winter climbing. But what a situation! These crags sit at the top of a hillside that pretty much drops in an unbroken sweep of rock, heather, and deer-grass straight down to the sea. The sight of John climbing from below, silhouetted against an unbelievably blue ocean, was a bit surreal – more Longhaven than Lochnagar despite the snow.

On our hitting the main ridge, the summit beckoned to the north, but beer in the afternoon sun looking upon the sparkling water around Tanera

---

[3] *Western Buttress Edge*, VI, 7, on Stac Pollaidh; *SMCJ*, 44/207 (2016), 159.

[4] *West Ridge Direct*, III, 5, on the Garbh Choireachan of Beinn Mòr Coigach; *SMCJ*, 44/207 (2016), 159.

Iain Young on Western Buttress Edge, Stac Pollaidh. Photo: John Higham.

More tempted to the west. So west it was. The next day was again cold, calm, and very, very sunny. We went rock-climbing on the coast.

Na Tuadhan — an undiscovered country
On any fine day on Conival, a descending hillwalker will see an obvious and attractive ridge-line dropping north-east from the summit of Na Tuadhan. Surely an obvious objective for any winter climber? Few can have looked, however, for the ridge remained untouched. As it lay in one of the snowiest parts of the whole area, we chose to head up there on a day when there was hardly a speck of snow in Coigach.

Not knowing how hard the climbing was going to be, we carried ropes and rack all the way in and climbed the slopes to the col, cramponed across on steep, white, iron-hard turf, and gained the crest of the ridge. This turned out to be disappointingly ill-defined, so it was a ropeless winter scramble to the headwall, through which one and a half pitches gained the summit. For a change the day was only half-done so we decided to return to Inchnadamph in a big loop by picking up the path down from Loch na Cuaran. The plateau here is Munroless, Corbettless, Grahamless, and I imagine almost always climberless. We enjoyed sun-soaked, blowing powder, easy going on moss and quartzite blocks, and views of mountains that promised adventures to come. A great day to be alive.

And then we came across the headstone and little crosses that mark the graves of the aircrew of an Avro Anson that crashed here in a snowstorm in 1941. A thought-provoking spot, especially since it's not only a crash-site, but also a cemetery. In the days that followed we decided on *Headstone Rib*[5] as a name for our route; but I confess I still feel a little uneasy and hope the name doesn't prompt the type of punning competition that gives us all so much fun elsewhere.

Cùl Mòr — dawn and difficulty
Cùl Mòr is one of those hills that saves its best for those prepared to work, unlike Stac Pollaidh, which brazenly flaunts everything to any passing tourist. And Cùl Mòr is remarkably complex, the rest of it nothing at all like the Elphin side. Two of its more pronounced ridges appeared inviolate in winter and both promised days in remote country.

Suilven going all pink and orange in the dawn enlivened the approach to the north-east ridge. Bypassing Coire Gorm, we traversed on and on past the start of the summer scramble and around towards the Assynt coast until the way upwards looked interesting. A line of shallow chimneys and grooves led to the summit of the first major pinnacle, a down-climb on its west side, then the next pinnacle, the Old Man, or Bod a' Mhadhail, was bypassed to the left and the final rock band climbed by a turfy

---

[5] *Headstone Rib*, III, 4, on Na Tuadhan of Beinn an Fhuarain (improbably 'Beinn an Fhurain' on OS map – Hon. Ed.); *SMCJ*, 45/208 (2017), 149.

Cùl Beag reflected in the waters of Lochan Dearg a' Chùil Mhòir. Photo: Iain Young.

groove.[6] The snowy arête from here to the western top provided a fine end in the dying of the light and the rising of the wind. Even more fun, because I have this super-long sling that I occasionally drape around enormous blocks for runners. John hates wrapping it up again. Feeling mischievous, I managed to use it several times that day.

On the Coigach flank, *Table Rib* drops towards the wilds of Gleann Laoigh. We had talked about this as a possible objective for a few years, but the southerly aspect and low start meant we needed to wait for a cold snap, snow to low levels in the west, and an early-season day when the sun doesn't get too high. These conditions arrived in early 2020, and for a change first light saw us just leaving the car park. Having to leave the path for another battle with deep, snowy heather was more than made up for by sunrise reflections of Cùl Beag and Stac Pollaidh, viewed from the little sandy beach on a mirror-still Lochan Dearg a' Chùil Mhòir. Then down and round under Creag nan Calman and up a gully to the start of the 'slimy slabs'. These were dribbling with (unusable) ice and gave us a few nerve-wracking moments on the way to the ridge-line. The turf wasn't always fully frozen and there were no runners (for these slabs catch all the morning sun going). Above, a 400m combination of short technical sections on much improved turf, the odd hook move and much moving together led to the sting in the tail and the top of the Table.[7] As to the grade, as always there was some discussion: maybe III, 4 we thought, but who knows – so is *Chimney Ridge* on Cha-no, and that's just a few metres

---

[6] *North-East Ridge*, III, 4, on Cùl Mòr; *SMCJ*, 46/209 (2018), 134.

[7] *Table Rib*, III, 4, on Cùl Mòr; *SMCJ*, 48/211 (2020), 159.

long. At the other end of the scale, so is *Tower Ridge*, which I've soloed, but I would not have soloed this! Best take all of these grades with a pinch of salt.

Canisp — enthusiasm

Same year, different winter, and another mountain. I have a soft spot for Canisp. It is often coupled with Suilven in pictures, when it always looks less interesting, less dramatic, and somehow less appealing. But a long, high-altitude walk up the southern edge of the hill to a picnic on top makes for a very fine summer's day with outstanding views (of Suilven of course), and for a surprisingly long walk from the road. A broken buttress drops northwards from the summit shelter, and I'd long felt it would make a worthwhile objective when the snowline was high.

And so just before Lockdown 2, we navigate the approach swamp in the dark, heads down and striking a steady rhythm, gaining height. Eventually, John decides to ask, 'When do we traverse round to the start?' My response, 'We don't, we drop down from the summit ...', doesn't seem to go down too well. But sure enough, it is easier that way: from the north-west ridge there's a convenient snow gully to drop into, a short traverse back to the crest of our rib and then some straightforward, blocky scrambling back to the shelter and a sandwich.[8] 'That was great, time to head down for tea,' says I. John's response, 'No, no; still time to drop down again and climb that little buttress on the other side of the gully ... ,' doesn't go down too well with me this time; but I acquiesce.[9] His enthusiasm knows no bounds.

Conival — tactics and names

And on past another lockdown lock-in till the start of 2022. The New Year period had been one of record warm temperatures, but then the winds turned northerly, we got snow and gales, followed by a brief ridge of high pressure. I was in the north-west, John was free and is always keen, so we decided to go high, turfy, and sheltered from the remaining wind. The south-west flank of Conival had intrigued me for years – driving north over Knockan on a winter morning, or looking north-east on a dawn approach to Cùl Mòr, you can't help but be attracted to its long, broken spurs catching the early sun. The South Ridge of Conival itself doesn't appear to have had a winter ascent until 1968, and one of the spurs had already been climbed and named *Explorers' Ridge* by Eve and John Mackenzie in 2013, but I knew from summer walks that there was another, steeper-looking line so that became the plan.

The long walk up Gleann Dubh and on to the Bealach Trallgil was eased by going Alpine-style – one 60m 7.3mm rope to be used singly (unnervingly thin when you're leading) and a tiny rack – but it's still a

---

[8] *North Rib*, II/III, on Canisp; *SMCJ*, 49/212 (2021), 154.
[9] *One Too Many*, II, on Canisp; *SMCJ*, 49/212 (2021), 154.

John Higham on pitch 2 of the rock band, Geologists' Ridge, Conival. Photo: Iain Young.

long way in fresh snow. The ridge itself was mostly easy climbing in fine situations, but it kept us in suspense until we had completed two much steeper pitches through the obvious barrier wall. Above that we relaxed and enjoyed the views, although as always the summit was further away than imagined. Late light on Ben More Assynt, Breabag, and the increasingly familiar hills to the west got us back to Gleann Dubh before fading torches lit us back to the car.

I enjoy the route-naming process. For this one, we reflected that two famous geologists, Ben Peach and John Horne, used to stay at Inchnadamph (there is a memorial to them there) while they did their seminal mapping for the Geological Survey in the late nineteenth century. Our route[10] crossed several major thrust faults associated with the Moine Thrust, John and I are both geologists by background, and so *Geologists' Ridge* seemed an appropriate companion to *Explorers' Ridge*.

Yet another mountain — the gift that keeps on giving

Sometime and somewhere in the middle of all of this, back on schist again, another snow-to-the-road day and another new crag to visit. We think this one should be reasonably quick to get to; John has even been before and soloed an unreported, easy gully or two (you could probably say the same of many cliffs in the Highlands). Turns out that today at least it's slow; pathless trail-breaking through deep heather and deeper snow. This is hard work, and dawn turns remarkably quickly into late morning. The cliff duly appears, and a superb, steep, central groove-line, with icicles dribbling down an overhung right wall, is revealed. Not enough ice for today though, so we scurry away left and up something short, turfy, and as yet unreported. 'We'll be back,' we say. But we haven't been. Yet.

And we still haven't seen a soul.

---

[10] *Geologists' Ridge*, IV, 4, on Conival; submitted to *SMCJ*, 50/213 (2022). (For a description and diagram, see New Routes section, p.190. – HON. ED.)

SCOTTISH MOUNTAINEERING ARCHIVES

by Robin N. Campbell

THIS ARTICLE IS INTENDED as a short guide to archives available to historians of Scottish mountaineering. It is not by any means comprehensive, but based only on the writer's limited knowledge. Individual clubs and persons will have material that I know little or nothing about, and my hope is that on reading this guide others may be encouraged to make good its deficiencies.

I will begin by reviewing archives held by other organisations, before moving on to our own SMC collections. The National Library of Scotland in Edinburgh (NLS) holds pride of place, and its spacious Special Collections Reading Room on the 15th floor looks out over the jumbled streets and buildings of the Old Town to the inspiring heights of Arthur's Seat. Gaze from its windows and you are confronted at once with history and mountaineering. The bulk of the SMC archives are held here, but in addition there are substantial archives deriving from many prominent mountaineers: **Louis Baume** (Acc.11022),[1] **James H.B. Bell** (Acc.9960), **Hamish M. Brown** (Acc.13940), **Thomas Graham Brown** (Acc.4338), **Charles Howard-Bury** (Acc.11359), **Una May Cameron** (Acc.10384, Acc.12651 & Acc.10480), **George Ingle Finch** (Acc.8338 & Dep.345), **Peter Hodgkiss** (Acc.13445),[2] **Benjamin Hutchison Humble** (Acc.13846), **Donald Bertram McIntyre** (Acc.13760), **Harry MacRobert** (Acc.14275), **William Hutchison Murray** (Acc.13936, with many subdivisions), **Janet Adam Smith** (Acc.13396 & Acc.13861), **Thomas Weir** (Acc.13059), **James Mann Wordie** (Acc.12559). Each of these Accessions is an inventory of material – documents and photographs. While most of the accession files may be inspected online via the NLS website,[3] for others it is necessary to visit the Reading Room to consult them. Although occasional items may be included in NLS's Digital Gallery, in general images or transcriptions of material are not available online – only the inventories referred to by accession numbers, as above.

In addition to mountaineers' archives, there are three other sorts of archive that can assist research:

1. Those deriving from people who have written about mountaineering, notably the large collection of material from **Ronald W. Clark** (Acc.9589), author along with Edward C. Pyatt of the fundamental historical text *Mountaineering in Britain*

---

[1] About the British Antarctic Survey Expedition to South Georgia, 1955–56.

[2] Mainly concerning the Ernest Press.

[3] To inspect an accession file, simply insert the file code, e.g. 'Acc.11538', into the Library Search box.

(Phoenix House, 1957), and of several other books relevant to mountaineering history;

2. Those deriving from collectors of mountaineers' papers, e.g. **Robert Wylie Lloyd** (MSS.6337–6346); and

3. Those deriving from the books of climbers' bothies, huts and hotels – **Glenbrittle House** (Acc.13985), **Glen Brittle Post Office** (Acc.12050).

Some university libraries hold mountaineering archives in their Special Collections departments. Aberdeen University holds some **Cairngorm Club** archives and **Ronald Burn**'s diaries and incoming correspondence; Dundee University has **Grampian Club** archives; and St Andrews University has the very large nineteenth-century collection of correspondence and papers of **James D. Forbes**, many of which deal with exploration in Scotland, Norway and the Alps. In addition, the St Andrews Photo Library contains a comprehensive collection of early mountain postcard photographs, the nineteenth-century photographic collections of **John E.A. Steggall**, and the later photographic archives of **Robert Moyes Adam** and of **Hamish M. Brown**, all of which contain many mountain photographs. Online catalogues for all of these University collections are available. Strathclyde University holds our own SMC Library, but this contains very little in the way of archival material. Perhaps the most interesting is a copy of the original William Douglas Guide to the Cuillin (*SMCJ* Volume 9) which is heavily annotated by **William Naismith**.

Municipal libraries also hold some mountaineering archives. I identify here only the few that I know about. Edinburgh Central Library has two notebooks of material relating to the Cuillin collected by **William Douglas**; these are held in the Scottish Library, catalogued XDA910 A8981/2x. The A.K. Bell Library in Perth holds the archives of **The Munro Society**, for which there is a detailed catalogue. Highland Council Archive (online catalogue available) holds the climbing diaries of **Colin V. Dodgson**, covering the lengthy span of 1927–1990.

The Alpine Club Library in London holds the wonderful diaries of **William N. Ling**, as well as some interesting correspondence from **Harold Raeburn** to **Geoffrey Young**, and some material from other Scottish members. Ling's diaries consist of 21 volumes detailing expeditions from 1893 until 1952, the year of his death, in which dates and companions are always carefully recorded. As Ling attended every meet of the SMC apart from one year when he had bad influenza, his diaries are a very valuable historical resource. Ling's Will clearly intended his diaries to go to SMC rather than the Alpine Club. I do not complain about this, however, because we might easily have lost them in the chaos of our various Library moves, or to theft. We have a facsimile copy, and those who are interested can apply to me, or my successor in office, for help.

Lastly, before turning to our own archives, the heroic efforts of **Stuart**

Pedlar should be acknowledged. He has photographed every page of every visitors or climbers book relating to the Cuillin of Skye, and freely distributed the digital files to me and other interested parties. That is, the books of **Sligachan Hotel**, **Glenbrittle House**, **Glen Brittle Post Office**, **Cuillin Cottage** and the **Coruisk Hut**. The Sligachan books are still held by the hotel in its museum, apart from the original Climbers Book, which was donated to the SMC by the departing proprietor in 1903, and is now in NLS.

Our own Archives are located in NLS, and in the premises of our Image Custodian and of our Archivist. In addition, other Club Officers retain recent papers and correspondence necessary to carry out their work. The process of Loan Deposit in NLS began around 1970 when the then Librarian – Robin Gall Inglis – worried by losses from the Library, deposited a large amount of material. When the Club appointed an Archivist in the 1990s – Donald McIntyre – there was a further removal of manuscript material from our Library into NLS. Since I took over from Donald in 1997, I have continued to deposit all significant manuscript material in NLS. More recently, with the advent of easy digital photography and computer storage, I have copied much of the deposited material to digital files before depositing it. Printed photographs, whether on glass, film or paper, are also properly regarded as Archives, because, even if not unique, impressions are few in number, and the originals from which paper and glass photographs were printed are usually lost or destroyed. Long before our current Image Custodian – David Stone – joined the Club in 2006, I had recruited him to the task of cataloguing and digitising the **A.E. Robertson Collection** of 4000-plus photographs, which had been looked after for many years by Graham and Maude Tiso. Once appointed, David began the daunting task of cataloguing and scanning our equally large **General Collection** of photographs. In the coming year, we hope to secure agreement to deposit these physical photographs in NLS, together with album material described below, as an addition to our existing Loan Deposit. Although the two forms of archive – handwritten texts and printed photographs – are managed separately by different Officers of the Club, their content overlaps strongly, and we have constantly found that the textual material is essential to an understanding of the photographs, and that the photographs often help us to better understand (and sometimes correct) the textual material, and of course they animate it. This was obvious to our Edwardian members **William Inglis Clark**, **William Douglas**, **William Ling**, **Harry MacRobert**, **Hugh Munro**, **Norman Nelmes**, and **James R. Young**, who put together personal histories in the form of annotated albums of photographs. The early Club also compiled a series of annotated albums of photographs recording its meets, of which Albums No 2 and No 3 survive, and Slide Custodians compiled a further eight albums. We also have post-WWI albums compiled by **Percy Donald**, **John Dow** and **Sandy Harrison** (digital copies only in the latter two cases). MacRobert's albums have been donated to NLS by his family, and these and the others mentioned have been catalogued and digitised by David Stone, whose 20 years of effort in gathering, organising and digitising these photographs and albums deserve our highest gratitude and praise.

The bulk of our present deposited material is described in Acc.11538. Broadly, it consists of

1. Club papers such as books of Minutes and Accounts, Membership Lists, Library Catalogues and Members' Application Forms;

2. Visitors and Climbs books from Bothies, Howffs, Huts and Hotels, including very early Climbs books from the **Clachaig** and **Sligachan Hotels**;

3. A complete run of Munroist Completion Letters from 1971 to date;

4. Grangerised Volumes 3 to 7 of our *Journal* in which incoming correspondence and some Club papers are interleaved. These were assembled by our second Editor, William Douglas. His Volume 2, which didn't reach our Library or was taken from it, was generously acquired from the book market by NLS (Acc.9623);

5. Papers of individual members – diaries, notebooks, lists of climbs, photograph albums, etc. While many of these are described in Acc.11538, some early members' papers were described in separate accession files – **William Docharty** (Acc.6334) and **Alan Garrick** (Acc.11401) – and the previous Curator of Manuscripts Olive Geddes chose to describe most of the later-deposited members' papers in separate accession files – **Arthur W. Russell** (Acc.12690), **Iain Smart & Malcolm Slesser** (Acc.13310), **F. Campbell Allen** (Acc.13313), **Alastair Cram** (Acc.13170), **Alex C.D. Small** (Acc.13368), **William D. Nicoll** (Acc.13874), **Edward Zenthon** (Acc.13576) and **Iain H. Ogilvie** (Acc.14269). Ogilvie's diaries cover a great range of Club history, from 1920 to 1990. Of the very many sets of members' papers described in Acc.11538, there are substantial deposits from **J. Logan Aikman**, **James H.B. Bell**, **John Dow**, **Ben Humble**, **William Ling**, **Harold Raeburn**, **A.E. Robertson** and historical gold in the form of **Hugh Munro**'s annotated copy of his Tables and his Card Index of Munros and Tops, and an unpublished book-length manuscript by our first Editor **Joseph G. Stott** which describes the pre-SMC-formation activities of the Edinburgh 'Tramps' – *'Tir nam Beann', a Record of Rambles and Scrambles among the Bens and Glens of Scotland.*

As mentioned earlier, both Image Custodian and Archivist retain a considerable amount of material on their premises, but this is too miscellaneous to describe here. In a purgatorial state, deposited in NLS but not yet accessioned, are two important manuscripts – a book-length collection of expeditions recorded by **Ernest Alexander MacLagan 'Sandy' Wedderburn**, and a large collection of diaries by **Pat Bell** (née Style). Mrs Bell was wife to James H.B. Bell and a prominent member of the Ladies Scottish Climbing Club. Her diaries are a valuable record in their own right but also shed important light on James Bell's activities at home and abroad. Although not yet accessioned, it should be possible to consult these two deposits by applying to the Manuscripts Department at NLS.

East Face of Mount Godwin-Austen (K2) in 1909. Photo: SMC Image Archive.

I hope that this brief review of Scottish Mountaineering archives may encourage members and others to undertake research into its history, or simply to better understand the nature of the footsteps that they are following when venturing among the corries, crags, ridges and summits of Scotland's mountains. Text objects are never particularly exhibitable, so I have chosen to illustrate this review with one of our photographic treasures, a magnificent print of a photograph of the forbidding East Face of Mount Godwin-Austen or K2, taken in 1909 by Prince Luigi Amedeo, Duke of the Abruzzi, but almost certainly made in the studio of Vittorio Sella. The print was sent by the Duke to the celebrated mountaineer Tom Longstaff, who in turn presented it to the SMC in 1959, suitably mounted and framed. No doubt several such prints were made, but ours, thanks to its shining provenance through the Prince and Dr Longstaff, is – like all true archives – unique and irreplaceable.

MISTRAL

by David Almond

'A VIOLENT, COLD, NORTH-WEST WIND' seemed an appropriate definition as we set off up the track in a howling, freezing gale. I was excited to be back at my favourite winter climbing venue after the madness of the previous two years, even if my excitement was tempered by knowledge of the exacting approach up the ridiculously steep flank of Còinneach Mhòr. Indeed I was more concerned about possible failure on the walk-in than failure on the route, as I was on the waiting list for hip surgery. My partner Dave Keogh was doing the stressing for both of us about failure on the route. Dave had been training hard in the build-up to winter and he wanted a route that would test him. Having read accounts by two previous ascensionists and corresponded with them, we knew that *Mistral* on Beinn Eighe's West Central Wall wasn't going to be a push-over.

The route had originally been climbed as a summer E1,5b and had its first winter ascent by the formidable team of Davison and Nisbet back in 1991. Nineteen years later Erick Baillot and Dave Kerr made a valiant attempt, ending up lost in the complicated and confusing ground of Pitch 3. One month later James Higgins and Graeme Briffett took up the challenge, only to find themselves lost at the same point as Baillot and Kerr. It took James three years before he ventured back with Malcolm Bass, when armed with the knowledge from his previous attempt he made the second winter ascent. Three years later Ben Silvestre and Rocio Siemens, after recent successful ascents of *Blood, Sweat & Frozen Tears* and *Boggle* – both graded VIII,8 – fought their way up *Mistral* and suggested a more likely VII,8 grading, reinforcing James Higgins's verdict.

I had had a really bad start to this adventure as I had driven across from Roybridge in the late evening, arriving at Beinn Eighe on the front edge of a snowstorm. As I relaxed after a stressful drive, I realised my boots, axes, crampons, and hard shells were still at Roybridge! I spent the next six hours driving through the night and the snowstorm, to arrive back at the car park in time for one hour of sleep. We then missed the river crossing in the storm and squandered an hour before finding the line up the scree slope of Còinneach Mhòr. Then came the worst conditions underfoot I have ever experienced, with knee-deep power on unfrozen scree. After a search we found the abseil point and dropped in. Staring up at the maze of V-grooves and overhanging roofs we headed up 'to climb the obvious V-groove' as the guidebook described the start. I soon realised we had done Pitch 1 of *Bruised Violet* (VIII,8), which didn't enthuse Dave. We traversed the ledges and found *Mistral* but it was far too late for an attempt, so we abseiled into West Central Gully to have the joy of a chest-deep wade up Fuselage Gully back to the bags, before descending to the car thoroughly exhausted.

David Almond high on the crux pitch of Mistral, West Central Wall, Beinn Eighe.
Photo: Dave Keogh.

Two days later we were back. This time it was a leisurely drive and six hours of sleep, followed by an easy walk-in kicking steps in névé all the way up, on a calm day with good visibility. We managed to take a better line on the abseil and were at the base of the route for ten o'clock. The first pitch was a lovely introduction to the route and felt like ice climbing in Europe, followed by an awkward chimney pitch with a potential nasty fall to a flat ledge, which Dave quickly dispensed with. I followed, finding it particularly difficult, and remember thinking: 'If that pitch was that hard, how tough is the crux pitch going to be!'

The crux pitch started with a steep bulging wall that immediately had me working hard on marginal hooks. This relented on one of the big ledges, which is great for recovery but means you are back to ground-fall territory once more. The pitch carried on up a wild overhang on small hooks requiring a big swinging move to the right, calling for total commitment, protected by a hand-placed Bulldog that I managed to retrieve by pulling it up after me. Another bulging wall led to an overhanging roof that took some very technical moves on vertical ground, with cramping arms and muscles fading, to gain a big, seated belay ledge and a well-received breather. Dave moved on into the dark up the final huge chimney that offered muscular, awkward climbing. We emerged from the chimney into a moonlit and starlit vista of snow-capped mountains, with lights twinkling in the far distance.

Previously I had climbed *Blood, Sweat & Frozen Tears* on this wall, which is the line of the abseil, so no route-finding problems there. The abseil is somewhat committing as Erick Baillot noted after his attempt, and it is a very complicated cliff, so unless you are a regular there it's going to be difficult to find your way, especially coming in from the top. Like Erick and James before us, we struggled with the route-finding, taking two attempts before succeeding. It is the sort of route you embark on and end up thinking 'What a sandbag!' I knew that Ben and James had both found it difficult although they were strong and going really well at the time, so did fully expect to have a fight on my hands.

The epic nature of this mountain (and especially this particular wall), the early start, the brutal walk-in, the very long pitches of steep climbing and the inevitable late finish with a walk-out in the dark, combined with the feeling of remoteness and the grandeur of the scenery make success hard-won and all the sweeter. My hip held out and I had another fabulous experience on this fantastic mountain.

I have certainly done easier VIII,8 routes in my time, so *Mistral* is another demonstration of the *avant-garde* nature of Davison and Nisbet's climbing at the time. It has only taken 20 years for us to catch them up!

ACCIDENT & AFTERMATH

by Brian Shackleton

A falling stone may come at any man ...
— W.H. Murray, 'Mountaineering in Scotland'.

MOUNTAINEERING IN ITS VARIOUS FORMS, whether in Scotland or further afield, is an activity where risk and uncertainty of outcome remain part of the intrinsic appeal. In an increasingly structured world, we seek escape from everyday life in mountaineering's essential simplicity, especially when it takes us to inspiring places. For many of us, walking, climbing and skiing in the mountains have become cherished activities that we would find it difficult to live without. We accept the particular challenge of climbing summer rock or winter ice-lines in the knowledge that poor decision-making can have serious consequences. As well as the risks that we try to manage whilst climbing, there are also those beyond our control that we mitigate through planning and by continuous assessment whilst we are out. As we gain experience, we may think that we can better manage risk or simply avoid danger by being more risk-averse, but does such an approach really work in practice?

Improvements in equipment and techniques, along with more reliable maps and information on routes, do encourage us to remain active in climbing (and sports generally) for longer than previous generations. Even with a lifetime's experience, however, some risks remain unmitigated. Prolonged and frequent activity make it likely that at some time we will encounter death or injury to our contemporaries or ourselves. This is sadly borne out by observing that three of the past Presidents of the SMC in recent times have lost their lives in mountaineering accidents in later life, as have several other Club members from my generation. Having climbed with them in Scotland and elsewhere, I accept this as an ever-present reminder of the risks that many of us face as we live longer and seek to remain active.

So, what has been my own experience of injury or accident? Having been hillwalking and skiing from an early age, perhaps I am fortunate to have escaped relatively unscathed in over 65 years of these pursuits, especially in the case of skiing. In over 45 years of climbing, however, the story has been different. In this article I initially look back on accidents in which I have had some involvement, before describing my recovery from a serious accident in 2020. In my final paragraphs I do not set out to judge the actions of myself or others, but merely reflect on my own experience and how I have managed to progress towards recovery, at times without certainty of the eventual outcome.

Early accident encounters

It was January 1983, and Graeme Morrison and I were at the CIC Hut as guests on an SMC winter meet. On the Sunday we had a long day on Tower Ridge, finishing in the dark and returning late to the Hut in poor conditions; but, as we descended from Coire Leis, we could see much activity around the Hut, so hurried down as best we could. Tragically, SMC member Gerry Smith had fallen whilst descending after a climb and the rescue team had just recovered his body. Though not personally involved in the incident, seeing Gerry laid on the stretcher made a lasting impression on me, having returned from a testing day on the Ben, especially after breakfasting with him in the Hut that morning. As we returned to Fort William in the late evening, the clouds over the Ben parted and the moonlight shone down, picking out Gerry's solitary car at the Allt a' Mhuilinn dam, a haunting image that has remained with me to this day.

The first occasion I was involved in a serious accident was in August 1992 near the summit of L'Evêque above Arolla in the Swiss Alps. One of our Ferranti MC party[1] was hit by rocks dislodged from above by climbers who had taken the wrong line having just overtaken us below the summit rocks. This was before the days of mobile 'phones, and two of us had a long wait with the casualty whilst others descended to summon help from the Vignettes Hut and a helicopter eventually came from the valley. The casualty spent the rest of the holiday in hospital with back injuries before returning home to recover and eventually resuming her hill-going. This incident left me wary of others when there is loose rock around.

The second occasion was in July 1994 in Glen Coe when climbing on the Rannoch Wall of Buachaille Etive Mòr with Mark Litterick. We were on our third route of the day, *Whortleberry Wall*, having already climbed *Red Slab* and *Line Up*. As Mark prepared to follow me across the poorly protected traverse pitch, the ledge he was on collapsed and he took a massive pendulum swing across the wall, hitting rock on the return swing and seriously injuring his knee-joint. With help from others, the casualty was lowered to the foot of the wall and first aid administered, but his injury necessitated further help and Mark was evacuated by helicopter to the Belford Hospital in Fort William. The lesson was that even parts of the Glen Coe crags that are frequently climbed may not be as reliable and sound as one might hope.[2]

Over the following years, I counted myself fortunate to suffer little more than the odd cut or bruise as a result of falling ice or small stones, despite taking a big leader-fall at Creag Dubh in July 1993 and being struck by rockfall whilst abseiling from a peak in Greenland in May 1998. On

---

[1] The Ferranti Mountaineering Club, founded in 1955 and based in Edinburgh, had frequent trips to the Alps over the years. The author, Graeme Morrison and Mark Litterick all served terms as president and subsequently joined the SMC.

[2] Following this July 1994 accident, Bill Murray (then Honorary President of the Ferranti MC) wrote to Mark commenting that he himself had experienced loose and unsound rock on that part of the Rannoch Wall.

Hogmanay 2000, however, I was less lucky when climbing *Quartzvein Scoop* on Beinn Udlaidh, again with Mark Litterick.[3] While we waited for what seemed an eternity for the parties ahead to complete the route, the wind was rising and accumulating a lot of new snow in the exit funnel. By the time I reached this point on the second pitch, it was clear I was in a hazardous position, and I should not have continued as far as I had from the cave at the top of Pitch 1. The top slope then came down on top of me, but when the snow cleared I had not been swept off but instead found myself hanging by one axe and only able to use one foot to kick into the slope. I was able to construct a belay and bring up Mark to complete the climb, now cleared of the drifted new snow, and I managed to hobble very slowly with the help of walking poles and so get off the hill. Initially I thought I had had a lucky escape but it turned out I had ruptured the Achilles' tendon in my left ankle, so spent most of winter 2001 in plaster, though I did recover sufficiently to go on the SMC Greenland expedition that July.

A serious accident in 2020

More than 45 years after settling in Edinburgh, and with hillwalking, climbing and skiing remaining important to me and giving a continuing thread to my life, I move forward to the start of summer 2020. In common with everyone else, I was relieved that the initial lockdown to control the Covid-19 pandemic had been lifted, and we could travel to the hills again from 2 July. Helen and I then enjoyed two trips to the granite peaks of Arran and had outings to local crags as well as to Dunkeld, so we felt confident in planning a weekend's climbing in August, starting in Glen Coe and perhaps moving on to Ardgour. Glen Coe was busy, and we had to park quite far down the glen, so it was early afternoon before we were under the East Face of Aonach Dubh and scrambling to the foot of *Archer Ridge*. I had climbed this route several times before, and suggested that Helen should take the first pitch, which I knew offered good though spaced protection. This brought us to the steeper part of the climb, which can be tackled directly or to the right before cutting back up left to the crest. I opted on this second pitch for the original route to the right, but confess to finding the climbing quite taxing with a combination of steepness, somewhat rattling flakes, and poor protection.[4] Most probably I was still rusty after the lockdown break, so was relieved to reach the

---

[3] The Beinn Udlaidh incident is described by the author in a note called 'Hogmanay 2000' in *SMCJ*, 37/192 (2001), 712–15.

[4] In *Classic Rock*, this part of *Archer Ridge* (V. Diff.) is described as follows: 'The wall is a steep, reddish chunk of rock, equipped with an alarming number of blocky holds and wobbly spikes. It is quite steep and gives awkward, out-of-balance climbing. It is difficult to find the best line. The actual holds are big enough, if you can trust them, and it is partly the absence of runners and the exposure which combine to make this feel more like Severe climbing.' The route is today graded Severe.

belay stance back on the crest not far below the top of the route. It was a sultry afternoon, and with our plan being to go on to Ardgour we were both anxious to complete the route without delay, so I opted to go right again to avoid the steep step above the belay. Above the niche on the right I encountered a short broken wall and, having placed the only runner I could find low-down on the wall, I worked my way upwards towards a parapet at the top of the wall.

It is not clear to me what happened next, except that I was suddenly aware of falling backwards along with a lot of rock debris. I landed on my back in the niche to the right of Helen's stance but supported by the rope from the runner. With difficulty I tied to a bight in the rope from Helen's stance to be independent of the runner that was holding me, and we assessed the situation. It was clear I had a serious injury in the vicinity of my right hip or lower pelvis as well as multiple cuts and bruises to my hands and face, so assistance was urgently needed. It was fortunate that Helen could get an emergency 'phone signal, but with only an intermittent link and frequent cut-offs it took repeated calls to get the message across. Nevertheless, the helicopter arrived before the mountain rescue team, and I was winched off and flown directly to Raigmore Hospital in Inverness. I can only surmise that the assessment of my predicament by the helicopter crew was that time could be all-important and, on balance, it was better to get me to hospital and not wait for help to put me on a stretcher. The Glencoe MRT arrived a bit later and helped Helen abseil to the base of the East Wall of Aonach Dubh, before accompanying her safely back to the road.

I spent four nights in the High Dependency Unit at Raigmore, before being transferred to Edinburgh Royal Infirmary for a further 16 nights, having been found to have fractures to my pelvis and my back. Fortunately there was no displacement of the fractured bones, and as a result no surgery was required whilst I was in hospital. I had also injured my spleen but this was not so bad as to require anything other than time for healing to take place. I was allowed to leave hospital once fitted with a back-brace and able to demonstrate that I could move around on crutches, given that the pelvic fractures were on my right side and I could still put some weight on my left leg. I counted myself fortunate that my injuries were not more serious, that the fractures had not been displaced in any way, and that I was able to move around on crutches and therefore to return home. The prospects were encouraging for a good standard of recovery, but there would be a long road to follow before I would find out how everything would turn out and whether I could climb or ski again.

Good fortune

The foundations for recovery from a serious accident are likely to be laid in the initial period following the incident, starting with the rescue itself. My own evacuation to hospital took place in a few hours without further aggravation of my injuries. Today we are most fortunate to be able to call for help using mobile 'phones from many locations, though this cannot be relied upon from a remote spot, which is likely to be the case in a mountainous area. Thereafter, evacuation may also be possible by helicopter if weather conditions and the terrain allow. I count myself fortunate on both counts, because help was summoned quickly and I was lifted directly into the rescue helicopter. If my evacuation had been delayed to await the mountain rescue teams and had then taken place by stretcher over many hours, the greatly extended time before reaching hospital might have made all the difference, especially if I had suffered more serious internal injuries.

At Raigmore

Once evacuated to Raigmore, my recollection of detail on my arrival and initial examination are not at all clear, presumably owing to sedation. I had been given morphine when the helicopter first arrived and I can only assume this continued in some form before and after I reached Raigmore. By the early hours of Sunday morning I had been placed in Raigmore's High Dependency Unit on a special spinal bed whilst an assessment was made of the best course of action. Looking back, this was undoubtedly when a number of key decisions were made, especially about my back injuries and whether surgery might be necessary, since this would have required transfer to a specialist unit in Aberdeen. In the meantime I was told to keep still and avoid any movement whatsoever. In the event, the decision was taken that there would be no surgery, and over the next day or so several specialists explained to me the nature of the injuries affecting my back, my pelvis and my spleen. I was also aware of the many cuts and bruises to my hands and face as a result of the rockfall that had accompanied my fall, though none required any stitches.

After a day or so, I was given the OK for quite limited movement including taking food and drinks unaided, and I started to reflect on what had happened, realising that I was perhaps lucky to have survived such injuries. My thoughts also turned to the more mundane matter of the appointments and commitments I would need to cancel, and I was able to convey this to Helen by way of a to-do list from my diary. News of my accident spread quickly, and replying to texts and e-mails soon became a distraction from my woes and a welcome source of encouragement.

The care I received at Raigmore was excellent, and I am very grateful for the vital part this played in setting me on the long road to recovery. After four days at Raigmore the decision was made that I could be moved to the Royal Infirmary in Edinburgh to continue my treatment and to recover in a location closer to home.

Royal Infirmary

On arrival in Edinburgh I was allocated to the High Trauma orthopaedic ward, but it was as well that the ambulance crew remained with me and insisted on precautions in transferring me from the trolley to the bed, there being no awareness that I had a very recent back injury. Having spent four nights in a specialist spinal bed, the standard hospital bed seemed inappropriate, and I recall being somewhat concerned about this.

Around halfway through my 16-night stay in the Royal, I was fitted with a back-brace to make for easier movement in and out of bed and as a precursor to using crutches. After two weeks flat on my back I had become amazingly weak, and found it exhausting to simply sit up and swing my legs out of bed. I felt dizzy and nauseous so had to leave it to a second day and then a third day before progressing to standing with a zimmer frame. Finally, on Day 3, I was able to progress to crutches and, with my back protected by the brace, was subsequently encouraged by the physiotherapists to start moving around the ward and contemplate a timescale for release from hospital.

For the last six nights at the Royal I was in a general orthopaedic ward with a focus on satisfying the criteria for discharge. One of the last obstacles was the removal of the catheter and regaining the routine of regular toilet visits. Another was to demonstrate an ability to self-inject one of the drugs I was taking to quell my stomach against a cocktail of painkillers. Arrangements were also made for support at home, to help me wash and to help prepare breakfast and an evening meal. Since the back brace was to stay on for at least 12 weeks and I needed help to wash when my back was unsupported, I would have carers visiting from the time of my discharge on 4 September until just after Christmas, some 15 weeks later!

At home

The best part of being home from hospital was being able to sleep without extraneous disturbance. My pelvic injuries remained uncomfortable for several more weeks, however, and I needed an elaborate array of pillows at night, as well as pillows and foam pads that let me sit down around the house during the day. I re-learnt how to move about on crutches, having been reliant on them previously when recovering from the Achilles' tendon injury in 2001 and from hip surgery in 2011. The difference now was the presence of the back-brace, which restricted upper body movement and transformed simple tasks into major challenges even with the help of a 'handy hand' (a device resembling a litter-picker). Other mobility aids also helped ease me back to some sort of normality. With time I regained independence through preparing meals by myself and carrying out everyday tasks with increasing confidence, until finally I felt ready to go out for short street-walks on my own.

Return to the hills

As the summer of 2020 moved into autumn, though still on crutches, I moved to a routine of at least two daily walks together with physio exercises, and started to regain strength. Around this time I began to compare my progress with my recovery from the Achilles' tendon injury

The author on Blackford Hill with his crutches. Photo: Helen Brown.

in 2001 and from the hip operation in 2011, and realised that this would be a much longer convalescence, given the more serious nature of the injuries. A notable milestone, however, was a visit on crutches to the top of Blackford Hill in November, and then progression from crutches to walking poles, opening the prospect of some easy hillwalking which I achieved on 11 December with an ascent of Carnethy Hill in the Pentlands, just under four months since the fall on Aonach Dubh.

Though finally signed off by the neurosurgical unit in late December and cleared to progressively dispense with the back-brace, I continued to wear it as a precaution outside into January 2021, before dispensing with it altogether just as snow started to blanket the Pentland Hills.

Snow and the onset of winter provided added encouragement for scenic outings, at a time when a second national lockdown limited travel to within a few miles of the Edinburgh city boundary. During January and February the snowy Pentlands provided the perfect setting for not just accessible winter walking but also ski-touring at times on untracked powder snow, with views in all directions under a bluebird sky. I was initially wary of venturing back on skis so soon after the all-clear for my back, but was very quickly reassured to find skiing in many ways easier than walking in such conditions. The freedom to move unfettered in a winter landscape seldom seen so close to Edinburgh, after many months of restricted physical movement, together with the joy and satisfaction that this brought, will forever stay with me.

Return to climbing

The second lockdown in the early part of 2021 dispelled any thoughts of resuming rock climbing, because climbing walls were all closed and even the local crags around Edinburgh remained out-of-bounds until 16 April. A probable benefit, however, was that my general strength and fitness were much improved by regular hillwalking and I was far better prepared physically for climbing than if I had attempted an earlier return. When eventually I went to the Ratho climbing wall and the Hawkcraig at Aberdour, I stuck to easy or very familiar routes and always put mileage ahead of improvement in grade. This approach served me well going into summer, and I took full advantage of the fine weather to make visits to the far north-west, the Ardnamurchan Ring crags, Glen Nevis, the Lakes and Northumberland, in addition to the local Edinburgh crags, and I gradually felt both confidence and ability returning as the weeks and months passed. Avoiding anything too ambitious in terms of multi-pitch climbing, I enjoyed repeating after many years the *Great Ridge* on Garbh Bheinn, the *Cioch Nose* in Applecross and somewhat by chance, the *Western Buttress Edge* on Stac Pollaidh during the remarkably settled summer that we enjoyed in 2021.

Reflections

As I pen this piece in the spring of 2022, the winter of 2021–22 is now over, but despite a somewhat mixed season I have enjoyed a few good winter climbing days in the Northern Corries and spent a weekend at the CIC Hut as well as doing some Scottish skiing when conditions allowed. As international travel was progressively opened up following the pandemic, there was a trip to Calpe in Spain to sport-climb in October 2021, a couple of downhill skiing trips to France and Andorra during the 2021–22 season and a short ski-touring trip to Austria in April 2022. The uncertainties of outcome following the fall in August 2020 are finally behind me, and I feel both fortunate and relieved to be able to enjoy once again all the activities in the places that are important to me.

I have recovered to the extent that I am now unaware of the injuries I suffered in the accident and have regained a reasonable level of strength and stamina, such that I can do a full day on the hill or indeed several days in succession on the likes of a ski-tour. Mentally, I have the confidence to return to multi-pitch traditional rock climbing more frequently this summer, having put in the practice last summer on shorter routes and indoors on the climbing wall over the past winter, but I may extend my wary approach from last summer by keeping at least a grade in hand and being especially wary of poor climbing conditions or suspect rock.

Looking to the future, I can envisage mountaineering days in the company of others of similar mind for quite some time to come, even if this means being more risk-averse than previously. I am only too aware that I have been fortunate in making a good recovery from a serious accident that might have turned out differently. In part, however, the positive outcome has resulted from correct decisions in the immediate aftermath of the accident, rather than from good fortune alone. My recovery has been helped by a measured and gradual approach and avoiding any temptation to fast-track any improvement. The national lockdown that limited travel may have played a positive part in my recovery whilst having the opposite effect on others who were limited and frustrated by the constraints. Finally, there is the natural determination within us all to overcome adversity, to remain positive and not give up when doubts creep in. Messages of support, throughout my time in hospital and afterwards at home, were an inspiration to me to maintain this determination and belief, and for this I am most grateful.

I have been able to return to the hills and mountains across the seasons to keep a connection that remains an important part of my existence. The wild and high places have already shaped a great part of my life, and it matters to me that this connection should continue. Were it denied, I would surely lose a part of my very soul and the cornerstone of what living means to me. My life's journey can, however, continue in the way that I have chosen with so much yet to explore. The words of Nan Shepherd in the final chapter of *The Living Mountain* when looking back on her life may resonate with many of us, when we reflect on our own lives.

> But as I grew older, and less self-sufficient, I began to discover the mountain in itself. Everything became good to me, its contours, its colours, its waters and rocks, flowers and birds. This process has taken many years, and is not yet complete. Knowing another is endless. And I have discovered that man's experience of them enlarges rock, flower and bird. The thing to be known grows with the knowing.[5]

The opportunities and benefits, both physical and mental, that a connection with the hills and mountains provides, are indeed endless.

---

[5] Nan Shepherd, *The Living Mountain*, Chapter XII.

VIGNETTES:
IAIN, TWO DAVES & GAVIN THE HAMSTER

by Helen Rennard

In 23 years of winter climbing my companions have included some formidable figures. Not least was Andy Nisbet, who endured his inside leg being scaled by my hamster, Gavin. But here are my impressions of just three: Dave MacLeod, Iain Small and Dave Almond.

Dave MacLeod

I'm still not entirely sure how I ended up climbing with Dave – a world-famous climber who has done routes ten E-grades harder than anything I've ever led. I had the gall to ask him, I suppose. And we go out together only in winter, when the chasm between our respective abilities isn't quite so great and when other factors come into play. It is an uneven climbing partnership, with Dave leading all of the hard pitches, but I get up these behind him and the dynamic works for us. In this way we have together done a number of hard new winter routes, first winter ascents and repeats: *Southern Freeze* (IX,9 – FWA) on The Cobbler; *Red Dragon* (VIII,9), *Night Fury* (IX,9) and *Cloudjumper* (VIII,9), all new routes on Ben Nevis; *Tarbh Uisge* (IX,8 – FWA) on Stob Coire nam Beith; *Rose Innominate* (IX,9 – FWA) on Number 2 Gully Buttress of Aonach Dubh, together with Andy Nelson; and the second winter ascent of *Mammoth* (IX,9) on The Brack (Greg Boswell and Guy Robertson having made the first winter ascent of this in 2010).

On our initial outings I worried that I was going to make an idiot of myself in front of Dave, and I did go through a series of 'firsts': 'I'm going to have to go for a wee on a belay ledge next to Dave MacLeod,' for instance. But he's surprisingly easy-going and relaxing to be around in winter, and these fears quickly dissipated. I say 'surprisingly' because I wasn't expecting one-and-a-half-hour tea breaks at the CIC before climbing as standard. There have been a number of star-struck fans asking for autographs and selfies in the Hut. It's an interesting experience walking up to the north face with Dave when every other person you pass does a double-take and whispers 'Is that …?' There's a lot of basking in reflected glory on a day out with him. There's also a lot of being in awe at how long he can hang on while hammering in Bulldogs and Peckers on tenuous overhanging ground.

Southern Freeze back in 2016 was a memorable day: extremely cold, deep snow on the walk-in, and a very hard (for me) climb with a few moves that seemed so ridiculous that I laughed out loud at one point (with the safety of a rope above). The most impressive thing that day was that Dave fuelled himself entirely on one hard-boiled egg. He climbed in his fruit boots (not being too sure what winter grade an E3,5c would equate

Dave MacLeod on Southern Freeze on the Cobbler's South Peak.
Photo: Helen Rennard.

to) and I remember he had them strapped on the outside of his rucksack walking in, one in a Lidl carrier bag and the other in a Tesco. The bags were rustling in the wind and I caught myself thinking, 'He looks like a right punter.' We were back two days later to climb *Mammoth*. All of this was done while I was signed off work with a stress-related back problem. This was made worse by extended sitting (which I did at work) but eased by being upright and moving, and therefore I went climbing. Explaining this at a disciplinary hearing a month later, with photos and a write-up from Dave's blog spread on the table between me and senior management, was not the easiest of experiences.

Another particularly memorable day out with Dave – for really quite bizarre reasons – was on *Red Dragon*. This was a new VIII,9 on the East Flank of Tower Ridge. We finished late (after our extended tea-break on the way up) and got back to the Hut in the dark. I had spent all day fretting about Gavin, who had escaped seven days previously while in the care of two climbing friends who were staying. (They shall remain nameless, although one is a Piolet d'Or winner.) As intrepid as Gavin was, seven days missing was starting to push it. Over the course of the day, Dave was very polite in listening to my endless chat about him – 'Do you think he might still be alive?' 'Where do you think he is?' – whilst simultaneously trying to concentrate on climbing Tech 9 moves.

Back at the Hut at 8 p.m. came a text from my neighbour to say he had heard scratching in the wall cavity beneath his living-room window, and that he '… might know where Gavin is.' Overcome with relief, I announced to a packed hut – none of whom knew any of the back story, other than Dave – 'He's been found! They've found Gavin!' As you might expect, people assumed there'd been a mountain rescue. There was more than a little puzzlement when I explained the reality.

Gavin was rescued the following morning and lived happily for another year. My thanks to Dave for his offer of drilling into the side of my neighbour's house with his Hilti for the rescue mission – ultimately not required, but much appreciated nonetheless.

Iain Small

I've only climbed with Iain a handful of times, but he ranks alongside Dave Mac as someone you feel a bit self-conscious climbing in front of. He's incredible to watch and his grace and precision are astonishing. I remember chatting about Iain to a guest called Magnus on a BMC winter meet. Magnus said:

Before I came to Scotland I had read all about Simon Richardson and he was my hero. Then I got to climb with Iain Small on this meet and he is now my new hero (sorry, Simon!). He does not make any wasted movement – every movement he does make is progression up the climb.

As with Dave, I'm not really sure how climbing with Iain ever came about, other than that I must have asked him at some point.

The biggest winter day I've had out with Iain was on *The Moth Direct* (VIII,8) on Creag Meagaidh, along with Dave Mac too. This is a 380m route up the Pinnacle Buttress and the original line was first climbed by Guy and Es Tressider in March 2005. The direct part of the route was the first pitch, up a dribble of ice below a roof before stepping left to pull

Iain Small on the crux first pitch of The Moth Direct (VIII,8), Creag Meagaidh. Photo: Dave MacLeod.

through the roof. Iain led this with ease and without a single bit of fuss. I followed with some difficulty, cursing the fact I hadn't used my arms much recently. (I'd done the winter Tranter a few weeks before, but the build-up to that was all about legs.) I spent most of that day wondering what I was bringing to that climbing trio and failed to identify anything beyond 'belay chat' – though perhaps the value of chat on belays on a big serious route is not to be underestimated. And it definitely did feel serious: at one point the three of us did an 80m pitch on 70m ropes (ice lines, too, which are never overly reassuring when you're only attached to one of them). This section was Grade V icy face-climbing with effectively no gear.

I recall Iain and Dave having a chat higher up about how 'this kind of climbing makes you unfit.' I understand that they were referring to rock-climbing fitness and finger strength, with the spring rock season not far away, but at that moment I was doing my best to get up the damn thing. I was not in the least bit worried about it making me unfit!

Dave Almond

My winter climbing partnership with Dave Almond got off to a shaky start when we struggled to find Coire an Lochain in the mist on our first outing, but we persisted and have since got up some cracking routes together. Dave is the only person I know who took up winter climbing when he became a parent. His reasoning was to find an activity safer than

Dave Almond, minus a fully functioning bicep, on the crux pitch of En Garde (IX,9), Stob Coire nan Lochan. Photo: Helen Rennard.

what he had been doing up to that point (motorbike racing), now that he had parental responsibilities. Known as 'The Almondator' by his climbing friends, he comes up to Scotland from Liverpool three or four times every winter for five-day hits, maintaining an astonishing level of psyche throughout – so much so that friends talk of being 'Almondated' if they've partnered him on one of these trips. Climbers who have heard of Dave but have never met him tend to assume he's some young upstart – based on what he climbs and his attitude, I presume. It always surprises them when I tell them his actual age.

Dave A isn't interested in climbing anything below Grade VII – which is fair enough given the amount of training he does and the limited time he has in Scotland – and we've done some hard routes together including: *En Garde* (IX,9) in Glen Coe with Rich Kendrick – Dave led the crux about six weeks after tearing his long head bicep tendon; *Omerta* (IX,9) in Coire an t-Sneachda with Simon Frost – a brilliant lead by Dave on the crux pitch; *Babes in the Wood* (IX,8) in Sneachda – the only time I have ever heard Dave shout 'Watch me!'; *Happy Tyroleans* (IX,9?) and *The Gathering* (VIII,9, also with Simon) in Coire an Lochain; *Sake* (VIII,9) on the Ben – the second and possibly last ascent, because a large number of blocks subsequently fell off the bottom section when Iain, Murdoch Jamieson and Andy Inglis were attempting it; *Knuckleduster Direct* (VIII,8) on the Ben, also with Dave Mac; *The Godfather* (VIII,8) on Beinn Bhàn; and many others. *The Godfather* is probably my favourite day out with Dave, as things were more balanced on that occasion; Dave generally leads a lot of the pitches but on that day we alternated. I had seconded Dave Mac up a few IXs earlier that winter, so this was a step down and felt not too bad by comparison!

I have never met anyone with quite the mindset of Dave A. He doesn't seem to get scared and thrives in highly stressful situations. He was a paratrooper when younger, which fits. My list of anecdotes about his mental fortitude is endless and would fill an entire article. 'Pass me the rack' is what he says when the balance has tipped from a fun day out to something suddenly more serious. He's the man you want to be with when you're climbing to get off the mountain. We once retreated from near the top of the Shelterstone Crag on a February night when a front arrived early. We were soaked through and our ropes got stuck. I was glad Dave was there. As with Dave Mac and Iain, it feels a privilege to go winter climbing with Dave A.

Climbing with the Daves and Iain has given me the opportunity to get up some amazing climbs in outrageous situations, and I'm thankful to all of them for letting me come along for the experience.

NO CAVE, NO CRAG, NO LADY

by Phil Gribbon

I HADN'T BEEN THERE FOR YEARS, even decades, but now with time to fill came the chance to go and gaze at the scene of some youthful activities.

I was alone, but anyhow there was now no way that I was capable of any sort of athleticism on the face of the overreaching crag. The idea was to go and stand below a simple route that I may have done, and conjure an image of being up there either quite glad of the rope from above or belayed hopefully from below, in a manner of speaking. Those had been the days before the craggy face was punctured and pitted with an interminable array of helpful boltware to provide that feeling of up-in-the-air and face-to-face with the unrelenting and impenetrable realm of the harsh Mother Earth turned to stone.

It is quite remarkable how the feel of just doing some sequence of moves on a climb can be remembered as if it had been the learned re-enactment of a peculiar slow gymnastic display or a studiously implemented sequence of predestined moves on a chess board, all preformed on a beautiful natural arrangement of heaps and hollows and crimps and cracks and drilled into the brain in a hurried mental imprint of those few brief moments of some long-forgotten times. Does it matter exactly what were my points of contact, with fingertips tentatively stroking the rock and shoe-toes lurking on quirks of weathered geology, the mind always debating the next move but drifting onward with slow and craven consideration?

Half a century has slipped by since an outing on this sun-warmed rock, with the backwards glance to the ground hiding below, the long curving stride out from the rippled slab and round the exposed edge to a wall-shuffle across to a secure stance on another route altogether – or that's the way I think it was. Pause to bring my second over, lean back and gaze across the trees radiant in flush of spring green, down to where the big river idles its way to the distant sea. This realm of assorted crags close to the Highland fault was just the place to visit for the first tentative meander up rocks at the start of another climbing season.

That is what I would be able to imagine when I stood gazing dreamily up at the cliff; but I had to get there first. Nowadays there is a regular car park with gravel spread across a cleared space surrounded by trees, reached by a motorable track well decorated with dips that drag down the front suspension for a good solid bump. Today the car park was full but deserted, with no sign of the walking public who must have gone off to follow the track up to the lochs nestling in the low hills.

I was munching my lunch piece with radio on and no need to hurry, when a strange trio of hurrying figures appeared like silent wraiths out of nowhere and thrust themselves into the green bracken wall in front of me. The leader seemed to know where he might be going, while a big faceless one trailing in the rear was shrouded under a broad-brimmed safari-style hat and carried what looked like a real chunky camera. Why was the small one stuck there in the middle so poorly dressed for a cool, damp, grey autumnal day like this? Was that a mere mortal maiden I had glimpsed? She appeared as a slight, agile, scurrying figure wrapped in a flimsy colourless gauze of faded muslin that looked as fragile as a gossamer haze on a frosted spider's web. Was this her induction journey to the realm of dutiful offerings where the flying heroes took to thin air as they were rejected by the perforated crag? Of course, the rational explanation had to be that they were off to re-enact some prearranged fashion shots of a young damsel of high birth who would be doomed to spend her days incarcerated deep in a mouldy cavern; or perhaps they wanted to get photographs to prove that there were fairies at the bottom of the crag; or could it just be they had planned an unusual venue for a ceremonial photo-shoot?

Okay, let's get out and go to look at that unseen crag. The tree barrier looked uninviting. There were too many tall trees, all straight as ramrods, but planned planting had made sure that any excess of old drab conifers would yield to a bright gaggle of the hybrid Japanese larches that helped to keep any forest gloom at bay. When the path had first been trodden the tiny saplings began reaching for the sky, but now it was a stroll under a high reticulated canopy of branches keeping the sky away. There once had been a watery trickle coming down through a sturdy old beech-wood but it wasn't there now, and neither were the jagged blocks of toppled boulders that enclosed the cavernous feature known as Lady Charlotte's Cave, she having been the daughter of the laird of a big but long-obliterated Georgian mansion down by the river. Going online one views an archway constructed in broken rough schist with a trickle of water spilling off a rock beside a highly unattractive folly. I have no recollection, however, of having ever seen this once-popular place of solace and peace. Perhaps it was a romantic niche where the lady could spend her idle hours and meditate on her possible fate as a lonely spinster ordained to pursue a life of gentle pastimes, as she waited for some eligible bachelor suitor to enter her life.

I looked up the slope with my eyes fixed on the place where I knew the crag had to be. It had vanished from sight. Not a trace of craggy rock could be seen, the whole extensive wall of the cliff having retreated from view. To blame was a massive barrier arranged in a ranked stockade of tightly packed conifers, each pushing a leader-tip ever higher to tickle the clouds covering the dull autumn sky. The crag had hidden itself behind a brazen and formidable green curtain of fir trees.

There was little to be gained by trying to penetrate higher into a tangled jungle where all was unrecognisable, and the present had claimed the past.

Quit, don't bother going up any further. You know what the crag looks like, and need not relive that inglorious climbing outing when we preformed like bashful amateurs despite being more than competent exponents of scrabbling up those rocky and flawed features scattered across the face of the wee crags.

Nevertheless, just halt a moment and have a dreamy uncomplimentary moment going back to the past years. Chris Doake and I had found ourselves standing below the south end of the crag one sunny summer afternoon, after bringing our American visitor Jim Renny out at his request to sample some of our local delights. His climbing background had turned out to be the stretch of broken blocky cliffs known as the Gunks in upstate New York, where belay points were hammered into the cracks and one would proceed with a drapery of nuts on wires hanging like six-guns from a waist belt. Being a visitor with no gear to his name but having expressed a wish to lead the wide crack at this short end of the crag he needed the use of our sparse and motley collection of sometimes bought, left behind to be removed and extracted, or borrowed but never yet returned gear. He took the assortment, rattled them about, weighed up each one's usefulness, and took one or two bits before handing the rest back with an unspoken look of disdain. Off he went and never used any of our offerings. We were quite impressed because he did it wearing ordinary everyday domestic shoes while we who were familiar with the route followed in the tennis shoes or bendy boots that were the height of our style in those days.

Now, that crack had a neighbour in the shape of a blank slabby shield followed by a rightward-trending, outward-inclining wee wall which together with that slab turned out to lack discernible holds for any sensible progression. I don't remember if he made it but he probably did, while my mind refuses to recall how dismal was our failure to follow him, or whether we even tried.

Today's alternative to crag viewing was just to keep stumbling along these unfamiliar squelchy tracks and find the thin pond promoted as an admirable piece of water in the direction billed on the car-park signpost. Get there, and it lay close to the more traditional set of climbs worked out on some more amenable and diminutive craggy bits

Ah, those warm summer days when one wandered across the hillside with one of these routes enjoyed and then the descent to try for another one and maybe yet another, but please be careful and don't stand on the zigzagged adder coiled asleep on the dust of the sun-soaked path.

I walked back, thinking again of that fleeting feminine vision in the car park. Perhaps I had imagined seeing a wee girl with the two big guardian males being wafted off to some strange rendezvous in the forest, or was she being taken to be incarcerated in the clammy cave?

Just forget it. Today there had surely been no cave, no crag, and no lady? Really, do you believe that!

HAROLD RAEBURN IN LAKELAND

by Mike Jacob

IN LAST YEAR'S *JOURNAL*, Robin Campbell described some of Harold Raeburn's climbing activities outwith Scotland and included a brief account of his time in the English Lake District.[1] Living, as I do, a stone's throw across the Solway from Lakeland, it happens that I have an interest in this topic and am thus able to add a bit more flesh to the bones. Even so, this has to be an incomplete picture as only a few of Raeburn's personal diaries and notebooks survived his death, and so the main source of information is the unique collection of W.N. Ling's diaries that Robin referenced. To those readers unfamiliar with the geography of the Lake District I can only express my sympathy.

Raeburn's first visits, in the early 1890s, were spent fell-walking. His trips coincided with the so-called 'golden age' of rock-climbing that was pioneered by a small group of adventurers (including the magisterial Norman Collie) during the last two decades of the nineteenth century. Although Raeburn was not one of these pioneers, he most certainly was an adventurer, with a record of solitary explorations on the wild Shetland sea-cliffs in search of birds' eggs. Once he became aware of them, how could he possibly have failed to be challenged by Lakeland's test-piece rock-climbs, all concentrated in a relatively compact and easily accessible area?

The total number of rock-climbers in Britain at that time was very low, the sport being the preserve of a prosperous minority with time on their hands. It was inevitable that they would meet each other at the inns and hotels they patronised and would exchange details of the latest routes. Although the thrilling new sport of rock-climbing was perceived by the disapproving 'old guard' as mere rock-gymnastics and highly risky, not a single life was lost until September 1903, when four climbers fell to their deaths on Scafell Pinnacle.

At Christmas 1897 Raeburn made a short visit to the Wasdale area because he was unable to attend the SMC's New Year Meet at Fort William. He was following a recommendation by W.W. Naismith, who had made a similar trip with W. Douglas at Whitsuntide 1896 and had delighted in the warm, dry conditions, ideal for rock-climbing. They had met up with four English members of the SMC, namely Messrs Barrow, Brunskill, Priestman, and Squance. Naismith wrote a short account of the visit for the *SMC Journal*.

> Now that we have seen this climbers' El Dorado with our own eyes, we both confirm heartily all that has been said or sung in its praise. Indeed, the half was not told us. As compared with Sligachan, Wastwater Hotel has a great advantage in being placed in the middle

[1] R.N. Campbell, 'Harold Raeburn – His Pilgrimages Abroad', *SMCJ*, 49/212 (2021), 20–37.

of the best climbing ground, instead of on the edge of it; and as most of the finest climbs are within an hour or an hour and a half of the hotel, one can enjoy a grand day's scrambling, and get back in time for tea, and have a swim in the 'beck' before dinner 'forbye'.

He described the routes that they had climbed on Pillar, Scafell and Great Gable.

> One of these, the *Arrowhead Arête*, is narrower than anything I ever saw in Scotland. ... During our visit a party descended for the first time the steep and difficult chimney in the Scafell cliffs, called *Collier's Climb*, Mr O.G. Jones being 'last man'. The same brilliant cragsman on the previous day made the first ascent of a vertical crack over sixty feet high in the north side of the Kern Knott.[2]

Raeburn had caught a train from Penrith to Keswick on Christmas Eve (not possible now as the branch line closed in 1972) and then walked through Borrowdale and over Styhead Pass to reach the distant valley of Wastdale (or Wasdale as it is now more usually spelt). He wrote:

> A couple of most enjoyable days were spent in sampling Great Gable and the Pillar Rock ... a climber is sure of a hearty welcome from the first-rate climbers and thorough sportsmen who make Wastdale Head Hotel their Headquarters at Christmas or Easter.

It was probably on this occasion that he met the pioneering Abraham brothers (George and Ashley) from Keswick and O.G. Jones himself. Jones was staying at the hotel for the final week of December but it is unclear whether Raeburn was also a guest or whether he boarded at one of the other establishments at the head of the valley – Row Farm Guest House or Burnthwaite Farm – which were often used by climbers. One of the climbs that he repeated was the famous Napes Needle on Great Gable, first soloed by W. Haskett Smith in 1886. Raeburn found the top part sufficiently difficult to require help, in the form of the head of an ice-axe used as a supplementary foothold.

In 1900, after his summer fortnight in the Dolomites with W. Douglas, Raeburn repeated his trip to Wasdale, this time in November and in the company of Henry Lawson. He described how

> ... leaving Edinburgh by the 2 p.m. express to Carlisle, one can dine on board and be deposited at Keswick in time to walk up to the head of Borrowdale by nine the same night. This we did, and were surprised to find how quickly and easily the nine miles walk was reeled off.

They climbed on the high, extensive Gable Crag on the northern side of Great Gable, finding the rock smeared in ice, and then made their way over the mountain to the Napes crags. They descended *Eagle's Nest Ridge* to reach Napes Needle, which they climbed, before an ascent of *Needle Ridge*. On the Needle, Raeburn gained some assistance from Lawson's shoulder at the awkward spot where he had previously used the ice-axe

---

[2] Using a top-rope; but in 1897 Jones repeated the climb in conventional fashion. Today *Kern Knotts Crack* is graded in the FRCC guide as VS,4c.

Early image of Napes Needle. The circled climbers are on the original Wasdale Crack route. Photo: FRCC Abraham archive.

for aid. Modern climbers might scoff at these antics, but it must be remembered that, at that time, climbers used nailed boots (leather-soled boots with projecting metal 'nails' of various patterns such as tricounis, studs and clinkers). Although these were ideal for damp or lichenous rock with small incut holds, they were hopeless for the sort of friction climbing to be found on the final moves to the top of the Needle (now graded Hard

Glover, Ling, Raeburn & Lawson at Seathwaite in November 1900.
Photo: Ling's Diary, Alpine Club Library, London.

Severe). Interestingly, following a suggestion by O.G. Jones in his book *Rock-Climbing in England*, Harold experimented with *Kletterschuhe*, felt-soled or rope-soled shoes also known as *scarpetti* in the Italian Dolomites. He tried them on Edinburgh's Salisbury Crags as well as in the Lake District and thought that 'although they undoubtedly render climbing both easier and safer' they wore out too quickly and were unsuitable for damp conditions.

The following day, 18 November, they were joined by William Ling and George Glover, English members of the SMC who in July 1899 had made the first ascent of *Engineer's Chimney*, a deep cleft (VS) on Gable Crag. Ling was a grain merchant who lived at Wetheral and worked in Carlisle, and it is around this time that he and Raeburn began their great climbing partnership, having first met, it would seem, at the SMC's Yacht Meet in 1897. It is also possible, as Raeburn was a brewer by trade, that they had a professional relationship. They subsequently climbed together regularly both at home and abroad and forged a formidable partnership. Ling wrote:

> … left Seathwaite at 8.30 on one of the few fine days of this month. On reaching Scawfell we found all white with fog crystals and the rocks all glazed, and a cold N. wind blowing. Many of the more difficult climbs were out of the question, so we tackled Deep Ghyll which proved quite sporting in ice. Raeburn and Glover were not content until they had done Professor's Chimney and the short route of the Pinnacle, Lawson and I going on to the summit for the view, which was very extensive in the strong sunlight. We descended by the

N. Climb and hastened back to Seathwaite 3 p.m. and left at 4 p.m. to catch the evening train from Keswick.

Two other leading English climbers of the period, William Cecil Slingsby and Godfrey A. Solly, were well known to Harold Raeburn, as they were also members of the SMC; indeed, Solly was President from 1910 to 1912. Slingsby was a spirited Yorkshire squire who completed many Alpine routes but whose greatest love was the exploration of the mountains of Norway, where he eventually accumulated over 50 first ascents to his name. In 1892, Solly made the outstanding first ascent of *Eagle's Nest Ridge Direct* on Great Gable, and in 1894 he accompanied Collie and J. Collier on the first winter ascent of Tower Ridge on Ben Nevis. Membership of the SMC was based on a candidate's record of ascents rather than on nationality or domicile (although women were debarred) and it was not unusual for English climbers to join the SMC; indeed, about 13% of the Club's original members came from south of the Border. Raeburn joined the Club in December 1896, having been proposed by W. Douglas and seconded by W. Naismith, and he served twice as a committee member and, later, as Vice-President, 1909–11.

In October 1901, Ling records that he was joined by Glover, J.H. Bell and Raeburn for a wet day on Great Gable. Rock-climbing was curtailed but they ascended *Doctor's Chimney* on the gloomy Gable Crag and then descended the left-hand branch of Central Gully in the mist. (This was also the year when Raeburn joined the Edinburgh Skating Club and when the new Raeburn brewery opened at Craigmillar.)

In October 1903, Ling and Raeburn repeated a couple of Lakeland's hardest rock-climbs. After days of continuous rain, they were fortunate to have fine weather for their walk from Seathwaite Farm to Styhead Tarn and thence to the Napes cliffs on Great Gable, where they ascended *Arrowhead Ridge* (VD). They then descended the top part of *Eagle's Nest Ridge*, where Raeburn put on his *Kletterschuhe* and, in Ling's words, 'went down to prospect', with his friend giving him a top-rope: '… I paid out 70ft of rope and then he returned, coming up without the slightest assistance.' Solly regarded the Direct start as having such a narrow margin of safety that 'no-one should climb it unless he had previously reconnoitered it with a rope from above.' Undaunted, Raeburn now accepted the challenge of leading the Direct route. They descended a gully to reach the foot of the climb and roped up.

> Then Raeburn started off to the left to the very edge of the arête. The holds are minute but the rock is good and he was very soon in the Eagle's Nest. A pull up on the hands to a platform higher up is the next proceeding and then comes a nasty bit, very sensational with scanty holds sloping the wrong way. However, they did not seem difficult to my leader who simply romped up. I followed in boots with the security of the rope but there is no doubt that *Kletterschuhe* are the correct footgear for the climb. It is very straight up and sensational and is only justifiable under good conditions, such as we had.

Solly's ascent of this route has been described as the nineteenth-century equivalent to Johnny Dawes's first ascent of the terrifying *The Indian Face* on Clogwyn Du'r Arddu in 1986 and it was the first British climb to be given a grading of VS. To lead this climb without protection required nerves of steel and a cool head as well as technical ability. Clearly, Raeburn possessed all of these. It remains a stunning and airy line, although these days it can be protected with small wires. It was the scene of a tragedy in 1927 when the very experienced C.D. Frankland was fatally injured in a fall that was suspected to have been caused by a broken hold.

Then the pair traversed to the foot of Kern Knotts where Ling took a belay at the foot of *Kern Knotts Crack*.

> Then, half-kneeling, I took Raeburn on my shoulder and straightened up. He then mounted onto my head (the *scarpetti* were quite soft) and pulled up into the crack above. He ascended some distance and I followed. I tried hard to get up by myself but it was no use …

and Ling had to accept the help of the rope. They then made their way back to Seathwaite after a capital day's work.

Raeburn made regular rock-climbing trips to the Lake District but it has proved impossible to catalogue the details, particularly for the next few years. We do know he was there in October 1906 with Ling and T.E. Goodeve, climbing the *Keswick Brothers'* route in icy conditions on Scafell and descending *Collier's Climb*. Ling wrote that '… over the last bit Goodeve was lowered first, I followed and was pulled in by him, and Raeburn came last with the rope hitched.' Although Raeburn usually spent his winter months in Scotland, during January 1907 he visited Great End with the same party where they ascended an icy *South-East Gully* in snowy conditions.

One of his regular venues was Pillar Rock in Ennerdale, perhaps a bit reminiscent of one of Glen Coe's big crags. The altitude and northerly aspect of the climbs here – particularly in anything but the most benign of weather conditions – add a serious feel to any undertaking, and the summit of the Rock can only be reached by the use of hands as well as feet. In the early days, on the summit of Pillar Rock was a double tin box where climbers would deposit their cards. L.J. Oppenheimer recorded that this was blown away in a storm and the cards distributed about the nearby fells. It was replaced, however, by a book in which climbers recorded their names, and some assiduous research by Stephen Reid shows that Raeburn was there on 5 May 1907, on his own.

Unusually, Raeburn gives no details about his climbs, but it was perhaps on this occasion that he made a solo descent of the *North-West Climb* (VS), maybe with the purpose of an inspection prior to a later ascent. But more about this later.

Raeburn's signature appears again on 21 October 1907 (with Natalia Yovitchitch and a Miss Brown). They ascended by *Central Jordan Climb* (VD) and descended the *Old West Route* (M). Raeburn often climbed with

*Pages 4 & 5 of the
Pillar summit book.
FRCC archives.*

Natalia (whose middle name was Rutherford after her great-grandfather
Robert Rutherford), and there has been speculation about a possible
romantic relationship. This seems unlikely, however, as she was born in
1882 and was therefore 17 years younger than Raeburn.

The last entry in the book is dated 11 July 1908, after an ascent of the
North-West Climb in wet conditions. Ling describes this ascent in gripping
detail.

What a difference there is between a delightful ascent of warm, dry
rocks and the same climb in cold, wet, intimidating conditions. The
notional grade counts for nothing as your resolve chills and you lose trust
in the holds. Imagine, then, that you have no nuts, no camming devices,
no nylon ropes, no harness, no helmet – just a thick, hawser-laid natural-
fibre rope knotted round your waist, and the rocks 'greasy and slippery'.

> Raeburn called me and I traversed along to him. Standing on a small
> ledge where, however, I had good handholds, I gave him a shoulder
> but it was no good. The rocks were impossible and he returned … .
> After some time he called and I followed with the two sacks. It was
> extremely steep but I climbed up to a square corner with a sloping
> floor. This was overhanging above and it was necessary to traverse to
> the right … . There was practically no hold and I should have been
> off if it had not been for the rope. I had to go back and reconsider.

With the assistance of the rope, Ling managed 'with great exertion' to
reach Raeburn's position.

> How he got up this place I do not know, nor is it a place to be repeated.
> The final overhanging chimney was now above us, but we preferred
> to traverse round the corner, a very delicate piece of balancing, & then
> up a narrow crack, an ingenious variation.

After five hours on the rope, they emerged on the top of Low Man.

Ling's summary was that 'the wet state of the rocks had made the climb much more difficult and dangerous' and that neither of them wished to repeat the climb. They finally reached the Wasdale Head Hotel at 6.30, thoroughly 'wet through'. They walked over the fells back to Keswick the following day.

On 11 October, Ling and Raeburn, accompanied by Ruth Raeburn and Mr & Mrs J.H. Bell, had another wet outing when they climbed *Oblique Chimney* (VD) on Gable Crag. The following year, 1909, Ruth, who was eight years younger than Harold, again accompanied her brother, Ling and F.S. Goggs on an ascent of Scafell's *Moss Ghyll* on 5 September.

The climbing club historically linked with Lakeland is the Fell and Rock Climbing Club (FRCC), formed by aficionados in 1906, and Harold Raeburn was invited to represent the SMC at their third annual dinner at Coniston on 20 November, 1909. After the Great War, Raeburn was made an honorary member of the FRCC.

Harold Raeburn (Vice-President of the SMC at the time) was called upon by George Seatree (President of the FRCC) to propose the toast. In the *FRCC Journal* it was recorded that Raeburn received loud and warm applause for his speech, during which he commented on the compact nature of the Lake District and said that the SMC was not quite in the same happy position because of the relative inaccessibility of the Scottish mountains and the 'sporadic' nature of their climbs.

FRCC Dinner at Coniston, November 1909.
Back Row: *H.Lee, L. Rottenburg, F. Botterill, S.H. Gordon, J. Rogers, J. Coulton, R. Gregson, W.B. Brunskill, C. Yeomans, H.B. Lyon, G. Turner.*
3rd Row: *W. Wilson, J. Randal, Dr. T. Burnett, H. Bishop, C. Grayson, J.R. Corbett, L.J. Oppenheimer, W.C. Slingsby, W.A. Woodsend, A. Craig, J. Hanks.*
2nd Row: *P.S. Minor, J.C. Woodsend, G. Thorpe, C.B. Phillip, George Seatree (holding ice-axe), Harold Raeburn, W.T. Palmer, J.Ritson.*
Front Row: *E. Scantlebury, George Abraham, J.R. Whiting, D Leighton, F. Clitheroe, Godfrey Solly, R. Domony, H. Harland, Ashley Abraham.*
Photo: Alan Craig, by courtesy of the FRCC.

He went on to say that he had a deep regard for the Lake District and, indeed, it was the location of his first introduction to climbing for its own sake. In those days he was a hillwalker (which he hoped he always would be) and knew nothing about rock-climbing. One day, on the top of Great Gable, he met a clergyman and asked him if he knew anything about the Needle Rock. Encouraged by the response, Raeburn made his solitary way down [possibly to Sty Head Pass at the head of Wasdale and then by the Gable Traverse] to find the famous Napes Needle. It was getting near dusk but he attempted it anyway, succeeding as far as the shoulder below the top-block where, he was bound to confess, the rest of the way looked rather unattractive. He dithered, it was getting darker and a nearby raven seemed to be croaking 'Don't, don't!' so he took the bird's advice and climbed down, somewhat chastened by the experience. All this occurred several years before his ascent in 1897. Raeburn also commended the FRCC on the quality of their journal, which appeared with great regularity, contained a large amount of valuable material and was finely illustrated, and which he rated the best of all such publications. In conclusion, he proposed the following tribute.

> You are a young club, only three years old. My club is practically of age and I am very glad indeed to be able to convey to you – a baby, but a very active baby – the fraternal greetings of an elder brother and I shall convey to the members of my own club when I meet them, the very cordial way in which you have received me. I wish long life and prosperity to the Fell Walking & Rock Climbing Club of the English Lake District.

The following winter 1909–10 Raeburn had his serious accident on Stùc a' Chroin (see *SMCJ*, 40/199 (2008), 45), where he suffered debilitating injuries, from which his recovery took several months. The accident did not, however, curtail his summer Alpine season nor, later, another formidable excursion to the Lake District with W. Ling and G. Sang. On this occasion, in October, after catching trains from Edinburgh to Penrith and Keswick and hiring cycles, Raeburn's account for Sunday 23rd says:

> L. proposes to take us to Raven Crag. Went up the slopes of Glaramara … right up to Great End almost … Sprinkling Tarn to Styhead …to Kern Knotts …we did not try the crack … went along to Napes … there Sang led up the top stone very well, a horrid wind blowing. I also went up. I had a look at … traverse which has no nail marks on it. It could be done fairly well in Kletters but would be best tried with a rope thrown over … came down the long side of it and then Sang led up the Needle Arête. *[At this point Ling left the party, presumably to return home.]* S. and I went down the Eagle Nest Ridge Ord. … went down to Wastdale Head Hotel having a look first at the Church … Gaspard expected back tomorrow, detained by train disorganisation owing to Paris Strike. Weather had been fine in Dauphiné and a lot of the big peaks going well in Sept.

Joseph Gaspard was a French alpine guide who was engaged by the

Wasdale Head Hotel in 1901 to take beginners up the easier climbs 'for a moderate charge'. Fred Botterill, describing some days in the spring of 1909, said that Gaspard was insatiable, doing three and four climbs in the day:

> We tell G. we are exhausted and suggest we should accompany him on alternate days and so tire him out. On the day before he leaves we do six climbs, but with no such result, and we learn with joy that he afterwards fell into the sea, a victim to nailed boots and Seascale's mossy pier.

The notorious Furggen ridge, the south-east ridge of the Matterhorn, was first climbed, in September 1909, by a party that included a certain J. Gaspard, who may well have been the one-and-same man.

Raeburn was meticulous in recording, often in the margins of his journals, all sorts of small details, usually relating to time. For example, the following morning:

> Breakfast promised for 7 not ready till 7.50. Left 8.30 and crossed footbridge … Brown Tongue in 45 mins … 10.20 foot of Deep Gill. Mists swirling round summits and crags … Scafell cliffs look very severe … I surprised a fox. It was within 1 yard, a big and very light yellow beast. It was watching a shepherd and his dog on the other side of the cirque. Fine moraines here, one might easily expect to see a little glacier clinging round the base of the crags of Scafell and the Pikes.

They climbed *Slingsby's Chimney* from Steep Gill with mist swirling round, Raeburn remarking:

> It seemed a good deal easier than when I did it alone and I understand new holds have been found and developed since that date.

They then descended *Moss Ghyll*, Raeburn commenting that this was his first descent after two previous ascents, considering it much easier and safer coming down, although the Collie Step, an infamous hold chipped by Norman Collie with an ice-axe on the first ascent, was perhaps a little harder coming down; then went to the top of Scafell, taking ten minutes to go both up and down Broad Stand before returning, over the hills, to Seathwaite and thence to Keswick, where they missed the train. It cost them 35 shillings (£1.75) to hire a motor-car to enable them to drive the 18 miles to Penrith to catch the train home to Edinburgh. All the fine detail of times of ascent has been used to suggest that Raeburn was rather obsessive, but it was by no means an unusual practice. G. Winthrop Young did exactly the same in his own journals, for example recording times for each stage of his ascent of the West Face of the Zinal Rothorn in 1910, and it merely suggests a yardstick to gauge personal performance over the years.

It is claimed[3] that Raeburn also stayed, when in the beautiful valley of Buttermere, at Lower Gatesgarth, the holiday home of Arthur Cecil Pigou

---

[3] Quoted in *Menlove* by Jim Perrin, p.147.

(1877–1959). It is thought that Raeburn explored on Eagle Crag, Birkness Combe – one of Cumbria's biggest cliffs and, with its promise of large raptors, an attraction that Raeburn could scarcely ignore. The two gully lines – *Birkness Gully* (S) and the longer *Birkness Chimney* (HS) – were recorded as first ascents for N. Sheldon and L.J. Oppenheimer (standing near Raeburn in the Coniston photo, above) in 1903. Oppenheimer would be yet another victim of the Great War, and his name is on the FRCC memorial plaque on top of Great Gable, along with 19 others.

Pigou, the son of an army officer, began lecturing at Cambridge University in 1901 and was awarded the chair of Political Economy in 1908. Like Geoffrey Young, he worked as a driver for the Friends' Ambulance Unit during the Great War. He was a proficient mountaineer who played host to many climbing visitors to Lakeland – including, over the years, Geoffrey Winthrop Young, John Menlove Edwards and Wilfrid Noyce – and Lower Gatesgarth was an ideal base, with its private beach, stone-flagged hall and billiards table. The idiosyncratic Professor Pigou, who thought that the common failing of politicians, women and Americans was their incapacity for intellectual integrity, appreciated the beauty of mountains and men, as proclaimed by the photographs round his rooms. Conventional honours were regarded with humorous contempt: during the War he had acquired various medals and ribbons, which he used to confer on visitors to reward achievements, such as *distinguished incompetence*, in hill-walking and rock-climbing.[4]

In a diary entry for Saturday 14 September 1912, Raeburn describes another visit to the Lake District which started when he 'left [Edinburgh] with motorcycle on board coal train for Carlisle.' He then rode the motorcycle to the Buttermere Hotel, where he rendezvoused with Ling. Unfortunately, he doesn't give any details about his motorbike. By 1901, they were in production at the famous British companies of Norton, Ariel, Matchless and Royal Enfield, followed in 1902 by Triumph, so it could have been any of these. They were very primitive and temperamental machines, prone to breakdown, more akin to bicycles with engine-power as early photographs reveal. On 15 September they made their way to Pillar Rock on 'a beautiful day'. Their target was *North-East Climb* (MS), first climbed by the Abraham brothers a few months earlier and already ascended a couple of times by Ling. Raeburn described it as 'a very good and ingenious climb'. Ling describes how [near the top of the route] 'after doing the wall above the groove we went straight up the corner instead of taking the usual route'.

At this point the pair separated as Ling had to return to Buttermere and Raeburn decided to solo some other climbs. A normal person would feel a knot of apprehension in the stomach as they tried to decide on the wisdom of proceeding. Being on your own at this point is a true test of character for, when doubt starts to niggle, there is no-one to turn to for

[4] 'Arthur Cecil Pigou (1877–1959)' by D. Champernowne in *Journal of the Royal Statistical Society, Series A (General)*, 122/2 (1959), 263–5.

The lines of North-East Climb and North-West Climb on Pillar Rock. The right-hand finish to North-West Climb was pioneered by Raeburn and Ling on 11 July 1908, avoiding Oppenheimer's Chimney. Photo: Stephen Reid.

discussion and reassurance. The first few feet of climbing might seem reasonable but, as the ground recedes below your feet, your courage is tested tenfold as an invisible wall of fear bars your progress. Now, you stand or fall entirely on your own resolve and route-finding decisions and, hesitant and unsure, it is only too easy to find multiple reasons to avoid the challenge. Never have you felt so alone or in need of a word of encouragement. How you miss the welcome sight of a rope, that friendly umbilicus of safety! The battle now is within your mind. To press on requires uncommon will-power and a steely control of nerve, and Harold Raeburn, conditioned by many such solitary cliff-ramblings, was, in this sense, on familiar territory. Although solo climbing was roundly condemned by the traditionalists as extremely foolhardy, Raeburn would have been highly aware of both his own abilities and the risks that he was taking; but the raised level of danger also brought the heightened rewards of absolute concentration and total elation – powerful drugs indeed. He records that he ascended the *West Climb*, by which he probably meant that, from the top of Low Man, he joined what is now called the *Old West Route* (M) to the summit of High Man.

The topography of Pillar Rock is complicated, and route-finding downwards is not straightforward, particularly in mist: it requires competence and experience, as apparently encouraging descent-lines end above vertical gullies. *Walker's Gully*, for example, is not a route of descent for walkers but was named after a youth called Walker who plunged down it to his death on Good Friday, 1883. Raeburn was familiar with the terrain, however, and chose to down-climb *Central Jordan Climb* (first climbed by Haskett Smith in 1882 and now graded Very Difficult) to reach the Shamrock traverse and rejoin the High Level Traverse, before taking the Black Sail Pass to Wasdale.

Also staying at the legendary Wasdale Head Hotel were Siegfried Herford, a rising rock-climbing star, H.B. Gibson and W.B. Brunskill among others. Raeburn wrote:

> They all have rather more than a respect for the N.W. however. Had heard of my descent alone and seemed to think it a bit risky. It was not of course as I did it.

Raeburn must have been referring to an earlier solo descent but what did he mean by the initials NW? It could have been either Botterill's 1906 *North-West Climb* or the easier *New West Climb*. So I asked Stephen Reid, who has an unrivalled knowledge of the mountain and its history, for his opinion. He told me that *New West Climb* was never abbreviated to NW and, even if Raeburn himself had done so, it was highly unlikely that Herford and company would have had 'more than a respect' for it. Having done the route several times himself, Stephen is sure that Raeburn did indeed descend the *North-West Climb*, one of the hardest routes of the day. It should be remembered that climbers were very aware of, and comfortable with, the necessity to be able to down-climb to extricate themselves from tricky situations, and Raeburn himself wrote in his book that

> for the expert, climbing down is easier, much quicker, and very much less fatiguing. If the climb is steep and difficult, climbing down is also much safer, as a rope can be used for security.

It is open to conjecture whether or not he was able to use a rope for security, but in Stephen's opinion this would have required at least 100 feet of rope.

As for risk, some might question Raeburn's logic and the dogmatic nature of his assertion. The assessment of risk is a very personal business and he was accustomed to solitary wanderings on dangerous ground, something perhaps that was not appreciated by the others. These climbs were, however, on a steep, isolated rock-face and any slip would inevitably have resulted in a fatal fall.

This was one of his last visits to the Lake District before the First World War intervened. Although Raeburn's outings were restricted by the war, he did still manage some visits to the Lake District. In August 1915, Ling and Raeburn visited Gable Crag again. They rejected *Smuggler's Chimney* (VS) as 'wet and slimy' before climbing to the Westmorland Cairn

> by a steep chimney and face with excellent rock. Then we went down the ordinary Eagle's Nest climb *[Eagle's Nest Ridge via the West*

Chimney, HD], lunched and then went up the Abbey Ridge
*[presumably Abbey Buttress, VD, first ascent 1909 by F. Botterill &
J. De Vere Hazard]*. This is extremely steep but the rock is fine.

They then went down to Wasdale for tea and met G. Bower.

The following year, in September, Raeburn made an attempt on
Birkness Chimney (HS) having approached Buttermere by rowing up
Crummock Water with a party that included his sister Ruth. It ended in
retreat but, with R.P. Bicknell, he climbed the strenuous *Birkness Gully*
(S), which was 'wet and difficult'.

During July 1917, Ling and Raeburn enjoyed good weather for more
rock-climbing.[5] Interestingly, Ling records that Raeburn led *Jones's Route*
from Deep Ghyll (S) 'easily in rubbers', presumably an early use of
plimsolls. Later, during August, they were back in Buttermere, climbing
on the immaculate Grey Crag with a party of nine others.

Raeburn returned to the Lake District on at least one occasion in 1918,
as a letter to Godfrey Solly indicates.

18 Bruntsfield Avenue
Edinburgh
9th Feb, 1920.

Dear Solly,
I have yours with Meldrum's application form for the S.M.C. which I
have signed with pleasure and return herewith. I climbed with him in
Skye in 1913 and also met him in 1918 when he led the ascent of the
Engineer's chimney on Gable. I consider him one of the very best rock
climbers I know. In normal and former times of course his Scottish
snow climbs or rather lack of them would bar him, but I do not think
the Committee will bother about that for a year or two at any rate.[6] If
he tackles Nevis at Easter under your auspices he begins high up on
Scottish Snow. I do not know if I shall be at the meet. Everything
depends upon the Himalayan Expedition.

I am
Yours sincerely
Harold Raeburn.

On one of these later visits to Lakeland, Harold met a young woman
called Mabel M. Barker. She wrote[7] in the *Pinnacle Club Journal* of how
she yearned to realise her 'wild and impossible dream' of rock-climbing.
She was an extremely keen fell-walker but 'met with no rock climbers in
those days. I knew that they existed, but they were as the gods, and far
beyond my ken.' Then,

… once, in an inn, I don't know when or where, I met a Mr. Raeburn,
and he, finding that I knew the fells, told me a thrilling yarn about a

[5] For details see '100 Years Ago' in *SMCJ*, 45/208 (2017), 225–30.

[6] Bernard Meldrum's application to join the SMC was successful.

[7] *Pinnacle Club Journal*, No 5, (1932–34).

rock climb. Now I know that this was an incident on the first ascent of Central Buttress.[8] Which of us would have been the more surprised, I wonder, to know that I myself should feel those rocks one day, make, in fact, in two hours, with C.D. Frankland, its fourth ascent? *[Climbed by them in August 1925.]*

On 19 October 1919, Raeburn, Ling and W. Crowder climbed *Stack Ghyll* (VS) on the 400 to 500-foot Warnscale face of Haystacks, another of the area's hardest climbs, which I imagine is rarely climbed in summer these days. The first ascent had been made in December 1900 by Oppenheimer and party, at a time when chimneys and gullies, rather than open faces, were the focus of attention. Ling describes the first pitch as 'very hard' and led by Raeburn 'in stockings ... seven pitches in all, all giving good climbing with much variety.' This was another remarkable *tour de force* by the 54-year-old Raeburn, particularly his lead of the final pitch on dubious rock. This was akin to soloing, given the equipment (or lack of it) at the time, but he seemed to thrive in these situations. It demonstrates his physical fitness and driven nature at an age when many people are starting to lose their resolve.

This would appear to be Raeburn's swansong in the Lake District. In summary, the facts speak for themselves: Raeburn was a climber of quite exceptional ability, drive and commitment which took him from Edinburgh – via Shetland, his native Scottish mountains, the Lake District, Norway, the Alps and the Caucasus – all the way to Everest.

Acknowledgements:

I am extremely grateful for the photos and other help that I received from Stephen Reid, Mike Cocker and Deborah Walsh, all members of the FRCC.

Sources:

SMC and FRCC Journals and archives.
Ling's Diaries (Alpine Club archive).
Raeburn, H., *Mountaineering Art* (London: T. Fisher Unwin Ltd, 1920).
Oppenheimer, L.J., *The Heart of Lakeland* (Manchester: Sherratt & Hughes, 1908; reprinted by Ernest Press, 1988).
Hankinson, A., *The First Tigers* (Keswick: Melbecks Books, 1984).
Rigby, P. & Reid, S.J. (eds), *Guide to Gable and Pillar* (Colne: FRCC, 2007).

---

[8] *Central Buttress* on Scafell was first climbed in April 1914 by a party led by Siegfried Herford, fresh from a trip to Skye, and it immediately became the most difficult rock-climb in Britain. The 'incident' refers to the key pitch of the climb, the Great Flake, where, by threading a rope behind a chockstone, a rope cradle was devised. In this the second man, George Sansom, sat and, by using his shoulders as foot-holds, Herford was able to struggle to the top of the flake of rock and complete the climb. Herford enlisted with the Royal Fusiliers in 1915, but a few months later was killed in action.

THE OLD MAN AND ME

by Bob Duncan

THE TRAIN JOURNEY NORTH seemed to go on for ever, but eventually we found ourselves in Thurso. It was the school October break in 1985, and Val and I were on our way to Hoy to stay with her friends Neil and Isobel. Spending time with them and exploring Hoy and the Orkney mainland were the main reasons for the trip; but to go to Hoy and not be in a position to try the Old Man if the opportunity arose (and I felt up to it) seemed daft, so I'd brought a rucksack full of ropes and gear and had spent an hour or two practising backrope technique in the house a few days before. I had my doubts about the enterprise: apart from the weather, which was cold and unpromising with autumn well advanced so far north, I'd never used a backrope before and I was very aware of the undoubted seriousness of the undertaking, with no climbing back-up at all.

And so, after we had earlier in the week visited Rackwick Bay, lain in the Dwarfie Stane en route, and walked over to look at the Old Man – an experience that did little to quell my trepidation – Isobel drove me and Val over to Rackwick again, and the three of us walked once more past the battered warning sign and over the rough track to the clifftop overlooking the Old Man. It was a dry and sunny day, though with a chill in the air, and I was feeling more positive, although the second pitch looked very steep and in my head I kept seeing pictures of an overhanging crack stuffed with old wooden wedges.

Leaving the girls to their picnic I descended rough ground to the foot of the climb. By then my curiosity as to how the route negotiated the very obvious steep crack of the second pitch at a reasonable grade was beginning to win out over nerves, so it was almost with eagerness that I got everything ready and climbed the first pitch. This was covered in big holds, and the rock was dry and sounder than the appearance of the Old Man might suggest. Tied to the rock at the top were the many ropes left by previous parties for the diagonal abseil from the top of the second pitch – many more than I had expected, and of widely varying antiquity. As advised by the current guidebook I had brought my own and tied in the bottom end with the others, though I could have got by with what was already there.

Next I tied on to my double climbing ropes, then prepared for the first time a skirt of rope loops, each with a knot clipped into a karabiner. The final knots I clipped into one of a couple of beefy screwgate karabiners on my harness, beside the climbing end of the rope. This was about twenty feet from the belay end of the rope, which I tied into the anchors. As I got to the end of each length of rope I would clip the next knot into the unused screwgate and untie the previous one, freeing that karabiner and giving me another length of rope for the next however-many feet. It seemed logical enough, with however the only-too-obvious problem that a fall soon after moving to a new length would be a bit of a monster, with the only dynamic element being the stretch in the rope, so the forces on runners and belays could be substantial. The only solution I could think of was not to fall.

I moved round the edge on my right and into instant exposure as I made the relatively easy but very exciting traverse to the little ledge below the crack of the second pitch. This was overhanging with a couple of substantial bulges, but there were lots of helpful holds and it was possible to bridge much of the way so it went relatively easily, with one awkward

The author atop The Old Man of Hoy after his solo ascent. Photo: Valerie Lyon.

move through one of the bulges. My brother Ali had given me a Friend 4 for Christmas a year or two previously that proved particularly useful as I was able to move it up the crack two or three times and thus protect myself better (and have something to grab if I felt at risk of falling!). I looped slings around one or two of the better-looking wedges to use them as runners, though mostly for psychological reasons as I doubted they would hold a fall.

At the top of the pitch I tied off the top end of the rope I'd brought to guide my later diagonal abseil, and then set up my main ropes to abseil down the crack and remove my protection. This was very airy but went smoothly, and I then organised jumars to climb the rope, which hung out in space above me, back up to the top of the pitch. When everything was ready I took a deep breath, untied from the anchor at the foot of the crack, and stepped off the ledge into space. This was without doubt the single most scary moment of the climb; although I had taken in as much of the elasticity of the rope as I could while on the ledge, I still dropped a fair way as I spun out over the void. However, the rope held, as I knew it would, and after regaining my composure I set off upwards.

The next two pitches I climbed unprotected, just dragging my ropes behind me. I don't remember much about them; soil and guano-filled grooves and rock I must have found easy enough, though with the constant tension that accompanies soloing, especially in entirely unknown territory. I headed over to the foot of the final corner. This was steep and looked quite hard, so I set up a backrope again, but on starting I found that holds kept coming, and it turned out to be quite straightforward.

And then I was on top. I untied from the ropes, waved to Val and Isobel and briefly explored the summit. There's a photo of me there, a tiny figure alone, though it could be anyone. But it is me.

Years later the film *Rock Queen*, about Catherine Destivelle, was released. This includes great footage of her climb of the Old Man (while four months pregnant – not an option for me). At some point the claim was made that hers was the first solo ascent. Until then I'd always assumed someone had done it before me, and I don't remember thoughts of being the first ever entering my head. I just climbed the Old Man because I wanted to, and circumstances obliged me to do it alone. Whether I was the first or not I don't know. Other than recording it on UK Climbs a few years ago I made no record, though many of my older climbing friends know about it. (Given time I can usually find a way of bringing it up). However, with absolutely no disrespect to Catherine Destivelle, to whom I would not dare to compare myself, nor with any intention of invoking the reactionary tendencies of national chauvinism, just for the record a Scotsman did it thirteen years before her.

THE MOUNTAIN ETCHINGS AND DRAWINGS OF D. Y. CAMERON

by Donald Orr

THE TERM 'SPIRIT OF PLACE' has recently become a well-used phrase within the sphere of landscape writing, and with that there has arisen a degree of confusion as to what exactly it may mean. Many indigenous peoples around the world display cultures that are profoundly affected by spirits of place within their landscape, some being specifically related to landforms and wilderness areas. In Europe, in ancient times, this was often associated with some supernatural entity or guardian animal. In the development of Romanticism there can be seen attempts to re-energise the land as a place of fascination and wonder. The promotion and growth of mountain painting within the Romantic Movement added to this and facilitated a re-establishment of the notion of spirit of place.

The urban environment, through architecture and street design, may be seen as an attempt to afford a sense of place, whereas the idea of spirit is mainly associated with the rural and 'natural' landscape. There are those places linked to human activity where meetings have been held, battles fought, and historical encounters celebrated. These may have been recorded in poetry, song, folktales, and art, and may still be distinguished by festivals and commemorations but there are also the locations where a tangible physical aspect is recognised and recorded. Some corries, woodlands, rivers and mountains – individually and collectively – have established unique and distinctive aspects of place whose status is cherished and revered. Perhaps an example of this maybe seen in the view, when emerging from the woods, of Corrie Fee in Glen Clova – a unique and exceptional landscape feature that has that capacity to stop us in our tracks. This may be described as 'the inter-animating relationship of mind and matter' which is charmed and 'exhilarated by evidence of the earth's vast indifference to human consciousness.'[1] Our awareness of these subtle qualities may only be enhanced when we, like Norman MacCaig who 'persistently explores the act of noticing, and nature of being in the world',[2] respond to, and examine, the emotional significance of what we enter in the mountain environment.

I would suggest that the one Scottish artist who strove, more than any other, to convey the spirit of place was Sir David Young Cameron (1865–1945), who declared in an address of 1928 that what he sought to achieve was 'that spell of mystic beauty, haunted by a strangeness of form and colour, remote from the facts and feelings of common life', enhanced by

---

[1] Nan Shepherd, *In the Cairngorms*; foreword by R. Macfarlane (Cambridge: Galileo, 2014), p. xii.

[2] R. Watson (ed.), *The Many Days – Selected Poems of Norman MacCaig* (Edinburgh: Polygon, 2010), p. xii.

his 'austere shapes, veiled perhaps by distance or muted by the fading light and gathering darkness.'[3] A previous article[4] surveyed Cameron's mountain paintings, but there also exist hundreds of etchings and drawings by him – many being of mountains, or landscapes in which mountains are prominent – where he endeavoured to achieve those ethereal qualities and thereby indicate to the public what lay immediately beyond their vision. The three selected here are a mere indication of the atmospheric variety and graphic styles he produced on his journeys through Scotland.

Ben Ledi

At 879m Ben Ledi is the highest of the hills in the Trossachs area. Clearly seen from Callander, Stirling and other places in the central belt, its prominent position has attracted artists from successive generations, and it still commands attention from contemporary painters as its height and situation create a natural focus and allow it to signal clear evidence of seasonal changes. There has been some debate about the derivation of the name of the mountain. One theory advocated 'the mountain of God', as the original name could have been Beinn Lidi or Lididh, but this would have translated as the 'mountain with God' which apart from being clumsy is also unintelligible. Fortunately, Drummond[5] tells us that the 'more probable meaning is from *leitir* or *leathad*, a slope, from the way its long southern ridge climbs continuously from the valley floor.'

The striking appearance of the mountain first made it a favourite of artists in Victorian times, when access to the area became easier. William Wordsworth and his sister Dorothy visited the Trossachs in 1803 and recorded their impressions in *Recollections of a Tour Made in Scotland* while Sir Walter Scott promoted the area in *The Lady of the Lake* (1810) and further enhanced it in the public mind with *Rob Roy* (1817). The arrival of members of the Pre-Raphaelite Brotherhood in 1851, when Millais recorded Ruskin in Glenfinglas, again added to awareness of the district. Callander railway station opened in 1870, significantly incorporating five platforms. Part of the Callander & Oban Railway, the line continued north through Strathyre and Glen Ogle before turning west at Killin Junction and travelling down Glen Dochart to Crianlarich Lower station and hence to Oban.

Occupying as it does 'a very prominent position on the southern edge of the Highlands',[6] this hill has proved to be an inspirational subject for many who journeyed through the Trossachs, imparting a dramatic first

---

[3] B. Smith, *A Vision of the Hills*, (Edinburgh: Atelier Books, 1992), p. 71.

[4] D.M. Orr, 'The Scottish Mountain Paintings of D.Y. Cameron', *SMCJ*, 49/212 (2021), 57–64.

[5] P. Drummond, *Scottish Hill and Mountain Names* (Scottish Mountaineering Trust, 1992), p. 120.

[6] D.J. Bennet, *The Southern Highlands*, (Scottish Mountaineering Trust, 1991), p. 47.

D.Y. Cameron: 'Ben Ledi'; 1911; etching & drypoint on paper, 38×30cm. Yale Center for British Art.
'So darkly glooms yon thunder-cloud / That swathes, as with a purple shroud / Benledi's distant hill.' – Sir Walter Scott, The Lady of the Lake, Canto VI.

impression of the nature of the Highlands. It was an obvious magnet for Cameron's attention, as it could be seen from his studio window, and was painted, drawn, and sketched many times by the artist. This example 'is regarded as one of his finest prints, the etching and drypoint' being 'rich and full-toned, with dramatic contrast of light and shade.'[7] Copies of this print sold quickly and are held in several major public collections. 'A

---

[7] B. Smith, *op. cit.*, p. 71

prominent landmark from the low country to the south',[8] there is in this image an immediate sense of isolation in the view of this distant mountain, creating 'a noble vision of wide-stretching country'.[9] Remoteness and seclusion are the keynotes, yet the eye is instantly drawn to the horizon where the hill becomes the centre of concern, drawing attention and interest to this unique feature. The flat expanse of water enhances the illusionistic depth and leads the viewer over the tundra-like vastness of moorland to the detached peak. For all its apparent simplicity, this print holds a magnetic appeal that borders on the mesmeric. Viewing this we are lured into thinking of the journey to it, enticed into questioning the ascent of it, and captivated by its separation and remoteness. It has that capacity, inherent in Tennyson's *Ulysses*, to encourage us to travel and to believe that 'some work of noble note may yet be done.'

The Scuir of Eigg

Lesser known than Ben Ledi but still in the collections of numerous national galleries, this austere and desolate, brooding print is a powerful, atmospheric image – perhaps one of the most dramatic of Cameron's printed landscapes – 'rising ethereal on the horizon.'[10] Recorded from the

D.Y. Cameron: 'The Scuir of Eigg'; 1931, drypoint on paper, 12.4×17.6cm. Museum of New Zealand.

---

[8] Seton Gordon, *Highways & Byways in the Central Highlands,* (London: Macmillan, 1948), p. 73.

[9] F. Wedmore, 'The Etchings of D. Y. Cameron', *Art Journal*, October 1901, p. 293.

[10] Seton Gordon, *Highways & Byways in the West Highlands*, p. 174.

south The Scuir (or An Sgùrr) is seen in a dark profile while the eastern cliff, The Nose, still holds the fading light. This would suggest an evening depiction with gathering darkness, perhaps a storm, growing in the west and framing this remarkable rock-feature. There is enough light to reveal aspects of the moorland rising from the foreground to the base of the cliffs anchoring the feature in the landscape. A pale area, the lower part of Grulin Uachdrach, links the halo of light above The Scuir to form a circular movement into which darkness and the wilds of the weather pour. Despite the onset of blackness, or perhaps because of it, this is not an image of doom but one of strength, of solidity, and of promise in the enduring nature of the land. This has the quality of imaging the edge of the world beset by storm and darkness. Challenge dominates the scene; confrontation and encounter are the promises made. Boldness and courage are required to be here and to contend with this landscape as it asks us whether we are regarding the gathering downpour or perhaps a storm inside us.

Ben A'an

The full title of this etching being 'Ben A'an and Loch Katrine', it forms the frontispiece of Seton Gordon's *Highways & Byways in the Central Highlands*, which was first published in 1948. The summit 'commands a view out of all proportion to the modest height of the hill'[11] (454m). This 'lesser summit, dark and rocky'[12] is seen across the loch where a stark tree by the shore and shaded mid-ground throw the delicate, limpid simplicity of the miniature mountain into a delineation of a series of folds and ridges forming this Trossachs classic. Recorded from the south side of the loch (I would suggest from the bay at the foot of the Bealach nam Bo ridge), this etching has a modest effortlessness that is timeless. This magical quality is cited by Seton Gordon in reference to Coire nan Uruisgean as a meeting place for goblins and Loch Ceiteirein (Katrine) as the loch of the furies. Whatever the history of these names it is the setting of the topography across the loch, and its rendition in print, that creates an essay in linear elegance and refinement. In the line drawing of the mountain, it is the total lack of tone and shaded structure that creates an indeterminate height that dignifies the scene and lends a serious charm to the image

Cameron's outstanding skill in line and tone drawing and his exceptional compositional capacity created etchings of an apparent simplicity that are sure signs of mature proficiency and masterful observation. In him we had 'a personality strong and persistent, a strenuous craftsman, an undeterred artist.'[13] His unique and distinctive style attracted Seton Gordon's attention. This led to collaboration with

---

[11] D.J. Bennet, *op. cit.*, p. 46.

[12] Seton Gordon, *Highways & Byways in the Central Highlands*, p. 10.

[13] F. Wedmore, *op. cit.*, p. 290.

*D.Y. Cameron: 'Ben A'an, Loch Katrine'; frontispiece of Seton Gordon's 'Highways &
Byways in the Central Highlands' (Macmillan, 1948).*

Gordon in providing two of his guidebooks with quite a remarkable
amount of illustration. First published in April 1935, and reprinted in June
of that year, Gordon's *Highways & Byways in the West Highlands*

contains 100 examples of Cameron's graphic work. In 1948, three years after Cameron's death, Gordon published his companion guide *Highways & Byways in the Central Highlands* containing 82 plates by Cameron. Gordon acknowledged his debt to Cameron when he wrote in the introduction that he believed that both volumes 'had their values heightened by his genius.'[14] The sheer volume of graphic work produced is amazing. While some 182 illustrations were used, many more would have been completed, considered, and rejected. Overall, Cameron's etchings and drawings project an atmosphere of timelessness and serenity to these volumes and created the most accessible collection of his work immediately available to the public.

Cameron ceased etching in 1932. This may have been partly to do with the loss of his wife in 1931, and many of his paintings from this point reflect a sense of loneliness or solitude. Alongside this, the amount of time necessary to complete even a small edition of prints is considerable, and it can be seen from his many Highland paintings that he still was anxious to record many mountain images. It was in 1932 that he started 'a large series of sepia drawings for Seton Gordon's books.'[15] The technique of sepia drawing was one Cameron used throughout his life, allowing him to detail scenes that could later be used in etchings and engravings. The collection is full of light and shade and reflects the immediacy of this method of drawing while displaying his draughtsmanship and his awareness of style.

A short comparison of style and content may reveal further the qualities of Cameron's work. '*The Pass of Glen Coe*' by James McIntosh Patrick (1907–1998), a Dundee artist who by his mid-twenties had achieved a national reputation as a printmaker and painter of highly detailed landscapes, offers a comprehensive, tonally atmospheric image of Aonach Dubh, with Ossian's Cave prominent on the north face. This print of 1928, while creating a strong, polished, and meticulous rendering of the area, does not exhibit the lyrical qualities displayed by Cameron. 'Glen Coe', as the artist has titled the print in the bottom left-hand corner, relies heavily on tone for its depth and utilises line in all its forms. Broken lines, dotted lines, marks, smooth curves, and ragged hatching render this striking image boldly, but a degree of artistic licence has been applied. From his vantage point, somewhere on Creag nan Gobhar overlooking the bridge that lets the River Coe drain from Loch Achtriochtan, the famous western 'painted wall' of Aonach Dubh should be clearly visible. Similarly, the enhancement of the summit cone, while adding to the drama of the print, creates a division between foreground accuracy and background fantasy. Patrick presents us with a rugged spectacle of the glen, a place of wildness and excitement. This dramatization of a scene was never an aspect of the work of Cameron, whose gift was a gentle

---

[14] Seton Gordon, *Highways & Byways in the Central Highlands*, p. vi.

[15] B. Smith, *op. cit.*, p. 107.

J. McIntosh Patrick: 'Glen Coe'; 1928, etching on paper, 17×25cm.
National Gallery of Scotland.

simplification of the view that led the spectator deeper, and perhaps more reflectively, into the landscape.

The co-existence of landscape elements, the merging of rock and ice, the flow of water over stone alongside the history of mountaineering activities and the people who recorded them comprise the spirit of place. We should not plan to dominate hills but rather lose ourselves in them. Travelling with the land, instead of merely marching across it to the summit of the day, is more rewarding and memorable. The distillation of these elements in Cameron's etchings and engravings are not merely images of the line and tone of the country. They are encounters with the land. A land that is never inanimate, that is known by us and that was close to the people who were once there. His painted landscapes and graphic illustrations are examples of the way it is remembered and understood. They are contemplative pieces, just as 'against landscape pretension properly fades'[16] whenever you sit in a Highland corrie and consider the view and its history, and reflect on the insignificance of your own time's passage.

For Cameron, as for Nan Shepherd, spirit of place was dependent on a 'sustained contemplation of the outer landscape' that led 'to a subtler understanding of the "spirit".'[17] The vast amount of mountain landscape work produced by Cameron in paint, print and drawings is adequate proof

---

[16] J. Perrin, *Spirits of Place*, (Llandysul, Ceredigion: Gower Press, 1997), p. 13.

[17] Nan Shepherd, *op cit.*, p. xii.

of his many journeys through and into the Highlands – journeys that were an inextricable part, and untiring aspect, of learning and appreciation.

What Cameron celebrates is not merely a representation of the land but a subtle delineation of its awe and wonder. His drawings and etchings are commemorations of landforms, but beyond this they celebrate a quality of spirit. These are places accorded reverence because of the nature of their structure, their atmosphere, and the fact that they trigger in us a notion of beauty – a word many would shy away from using, and yet 'in our specific outdoor world … it is surely the prime and common factor in all our activities.'[18]

ON THE BRIDGE AT POOLEWE

Submarine, powerful,
The salmon lay
Beneath the bridge,
Feeling the gush
Of inland water
From the upper pool.

Tourists and loafers
Watched the travellers;
Their words skipped
Like small trout
In the shallows.

Far beyond Gairloch
Dark Nautilus submerged.
Deep in the pool
The salmon swirled.

P.J. Biggar

---

[18] J. Perrin, *op. cit.*, p. 132.

ON THE PEUTEREY RIDGE & NORTH FACE OF THE EIGER

by Timothy Elson

In the 2020 lockdown, as many people were doing, I was taking stock of things; I made a shortlist of the Alpine routes I most wanted to climb and ordered it because, well, there wasn't really anything else to do. The two routes at the top of my list were the Peuterey Ridge Integral on Mont Blanc and the Eiger North Wall. Making the list was the easy bit, as both these climbs had been at the top of the 'list' (metaphorical until lockdown) for over a decade, and I recruited my friend Alex Mathie to plan an attempt on both routes. The mantra is that you need at least to put yourself at the bottom of the mountain to have a chance of doing the climb.

Initially we planned to visit the Mont Blanc massif in September 2020 and Grindelwald in the winter of 2021; Covid got in the way, however, so we ended up rescheduling for September 2021 and March 2022. Having a limited amount of holiday and needing to book time off in advance mean that luck plays a major role in whether you can even attempt the routes, let alone get up them – and luck proved to be on our side for both trips.

Peuterey Intégrale

When I started Alpine climbing in the early 2000s, my bible was *Extreme Alpinism* by Mark Twight, which engrained the approach of climbing high, light and fast on my early Alpine routes. Attempting any route as multi-day and planning to bivouac was considered a kind of failure. Attempting every climb in one day or a single push has led to some successes such as the *Emperor Ridge* on Mount Robson, but also several failures and 'memorable' cold nights out with inadequate kit.

Therefore, when I first contemplated the trying Peuterey Ridge Integral in 2006, the idea of planning it with bivouacs didn't enter my head, and I could not work out how to climb it. The Peuterey Ridge is one of the longest routes in the Alps, with about 4500m of total ascent on the climb. The route starts with the South Ridge of the Aiguille Noire de Peuterey, which is a long climb in itself. (Both Alex and I had climbed this separately in 2015.) From the top of the Aiguille Noire there is then 800m of abseils down the North Ridge, followed by the traverse of the Dames Anglaises. This is where you join the classic Peuterey Ridge route and climb over the Aiguille Blanche de Peuterey to reach the Col de Peuterey, before ascending the final 900m to the summit of Mont Blanc.

Over the years my attitude to multi-day routes changed: I began to enjoy spending nights out in wild places, immersed in the mountain environment. The idea of the Peuterey as a multi-day outing was now not only comprehensible but preferable. The south side of Mont Blanc is a

The Peuterey Ridge viewed from the Torino Hut. From left to right: Aiguille Noire, Dames Anglaises pinnacles, Aiguille Blanche, Col de Peuterey, Mont Blanc de Courmayeur & Mont Blanc. Photo: Torran Elson.

special place, being such a vast, complex bit of mountain architecture that climbing any of the routes there is a unique experience.

Alex and I eventually made it to the Alps together in September 2021, my first trip to Alpine mountains for two years owing to the Covid restrictions. The trip started badly, with the hire car falling through at the last minute and our failure to climb the North Face of the Dru, followed by days of rain, although we did manage to fit in a one-and-a-half-day traverse of the Peigne, Pèlerins, Deux Aigles and Plan between storms. Presently a big weather window opened for the end of our trip, so we went to attempt the Peuterey Ridge.

On Tuesday 21 September we took a bus through the Mont Blanc tunnel and walked to the Borelli Hut below the Aiguille Noire. On Wednesday we were up at 5 a.m. and out of the door at 6 a.m. My memory of my previous ascent of the South Ridge of the Aiguille Noire was of great thirst, so I was carrying a lot of water, though this proved unnecessary as snow was covering everything vaguely north-facing on the route. Our previous ascent didn't seem to help us much as we could not remember that much about it, and the day passed in a plethora of nice granite pitches. My main memory of the route this time was that my pack was very heavy and the crux pitches were rather wet. We arrived at the top of the penultimate tower, Pointe Bich, just as it was getting dark, did the abseils from it in the dark and found a ledge almost big enough to fit our Firstlight tent on, although the end of the tent was hanging over the side. We had decided that late September on a long route required us to go 'Himalayan' style, with a tent and sleeping bags.

The second day was mentally trying. We got going fairly early and reached the summit quickly, but now we had the infamous abseils down the north ridge ahead of us. I had heard several horror stories about these, and approached them with trepidation. The abseils are not as bad as they once were, because mysteriously – a few weeks before a certain person set a speed record on the Peuterey Ridge – bolts appeared on the north ridge at 25m intervals. We used these, but many of them were buried under ice and fresh snow and we had some 'fun' on the way down with hung-up ropes that required climbing up to free them, missed abseil points and a few episodes of rockfall. It also took us ages to get down the abseils, and they were the most psychologically draining section of the climb.

We spent the afternoon traversing the pile of choss that is the Dames Anglaises; the rock on this section is not the normal granite found in the Mont Blanc massif, but rather is schist, and it seems to form in layers designed to cut the rope while at the same time being both very loose and compact. This section involved climbing up and down the various pinnacles of the Dames Anglaises to reach the Craveri Bivouac, a two-person metal box. Arriving at about four in the afternoon we decided that that was enough for the day and had a pleasant evening taking in the view and the sunset.

Sunset from the Bivacco Craveri. Photo: Alex Mathie.

Our plan for Day 3 of the route was to make a big push and get all the way to the summit, the rationale being to climb the upper ridge (which is south-facing) in the evening and night to get the best conditions, and there were also now high winds forecast for the Saturday. The first job was to climb the Aiguille Blanche de Peuterey; this involved rock scrambling at first, until we traversed on the north-east flank, which was covered in a foot of unhelpful powder snow, resulting in slow going until we regained the ridge proper once more.

Eventually we arrived at the picturesque demilune snow arête that links the triple summits of the Aiguille Blanche. It consisted of sun-affected snow, so the elegant snow traverse turned into very slow going and we tried to stick to the rocks as much as possible. By 2 p.m. we had ticked the summits and abseiled to the Col de Peuterey, where we stopped until the sun was off the upper south-facing slopes of the route, as there was intermittent stonefall and we wanted the snow to re-freeze. The views from the col are stunning and we enjoyably drank a lot of brews while discussing what a remote place it was – we hadn't seen anyone since leaving the valley. The grandstand view of the Central Pillar of Frêney focused our minds on the epic story of Bonatti and his companions, and we asked ourselves what we would do if a storm came in: how would we escape from here?

By about 5 p.m. the sun was leaving the face, and we started up the Grand Pilier d'Angle, which has a mixed face a few hundred metres high that leads to the upper Peuterey Ridge. With glaciers receding, there is now quite a section of blank rock at the bottom, and it being so late in the year there was only one place we could see to get through the bergschrund and this rock section. We weaved our way around the face following our noses, reaching the top of the Grand Pilier d'Angle just as it was getting dark. So, it was headtorches on for the upper ridge, which was all front-pointing on snow with a few sections of black ice; and, as ice slopes do, it seemed to go on endlessly. I topped out on Mont Blanc de Courmayeur and was immediately almost knocked over by the strong northerly wind from which we had been sheltered on the south side of the mountain. Once Alex had joined me we put on all our layers and walked over to the summit of Mont Blanc, arriving at about midnight. It was too cold to linger, and we arrived half-an-hour later at the Vallot Hut, where we brewed up, had some Super Noodles and then went to bed. Our sleep was interrupted at about 3 a.m. when the first team attempting Mont Blanc that day came into the hut. They were followed by every other summit candidate, and the hut slowly filled as the wind was so bad that no one made it to the top that day.

After a bad night's sleep, we were slow to get moving but had an uneventful descent. We were taken aback at the number of people and slight chaos on the Goûter route, in contrast with our three days of immaculate isolation on the wild south side of Mont Blanc.

Eiger North Face

March 2022 came around, and after a good Scottish winter season I felt that I might be in shape to have a good go at the Eiger, as long as the variables of weather and conditions were favourable to us. Having booked the week off a year in advance, it was very much a roll of the dice whether we would get anything done. Two weeks before the planned trip I heard that some friends of friends (and fellow SMC members) had climbed the face, and this led to a growing nervous anticipation before leaving for the holiday. I obsessively checked the weather forecast each day and found that the stars were magically aligning: there was seven days' high pressure forecast for our arrival in Switzerland. I met Alex in Interlaken on Saturday 19 March at our Airbnb, and we spent Sunday morning sorting our kit before taking the train then cable car to below the Eiger and a lovely camping spot with the North Face looming above. I would like to say we relaxed there, but we both grew more nervous and were keen to get started on the route.

The aim of our first day was to reach Death Bivouac, a ledge about halfway up the face in terms of height but before the main difficulties. It gets its name from the Mehringer and Sedlmayr team, who made the first serious attempt on the face in 1935 and perished after being stuck in a storm for days on their high point at that ledge. We assumed we were going to be slow as we were not acclimatised and it was Alex's first climb of the year, so we planned a leisurely three-day schedule with a second

At the top of the Difficult Crack on the Eiger's North Face. Photo: Tim Elson.

The author setting off on the Hinterstoisser traverse. Photo: Alex Mathie.

intentional bivouac on the summit. Waking at 2 a.m. and leaving our camp at 3 a.m. we reached the Difficult Crack – the first 'proper' pitch – at first light. I led this and didn't find it too bad, which I took as a good sign for the rest of the route.

Alex then did a long pitch to the start of the Hinterstoisser traverse. I found the climbing of the Hinterstoisser traverse very surreal, as I kept needing to pinch myself (metaphorically) that I was actually there on the North Face of the Eiger! I was very glad to find a fraying fixed rope here to ease the difficulties, as the slab is very blank; without either the fixed rope or ice build-up it would be a very difficult pitch, and I can see how in the 1930s it became a trap for Hinterstoisser and his companions.

The climb on the Eiger seemed to impose a much heavier psychological load than anything else I have been on. Having read *The White Spider*[1] multiple times as a teenager as well as stories of other epics, and having heard tales from friends, I felt its foreboding mystique weighing around the neck on every move. That lore also tells the climber what should come next: the Swallow's Nest, the First Icefield, the Ice Hose (which was very thin, fragile, bold and Alex's lead), the Second Icefield, and then the Flatiron. We ticked off those waymarks and arrived at Death Bivouac around midday. Although it is the biggest ledge on the route it was unappealing to spend much time there as there was a profusion of literal

[1] *The White Spider* by Heinrich Harrer is the classic book about the history of the Eiger's North Face.

Looking down on the Ramp Icefield from the Brittle Ledges. Photo: Tim Elson.

shit. We had a brief conversation about whether we should stop and stick to our plan of bivvying there, before deciding against it.

Again following the stories from *The White Spider*, we crossed the Third Icefield and started up the Ramp; I belayed Alex on one of the easier pitches near the bottom of the ramp, idly thinking to myself that everything was going very well, when Alex suddenly hurtled through the air and hit the slab round the corner from the belay. At that moment I thought he must have broken a leg and I heard a lot of swearing, but I could not see him as we were separated by a rib of rock. After half a minute Alex confirmed that he was OK, just very annoyed, and that the front binding on his crampon had pinged off; luckily we had a spare with us. Alex had absent-mindedly pulled upon a bit of gear; it had come out and the next two runners had ripped, leading to quite a long fall. Alex was furious with himself for not checking the gear in an effort to go quickly.

The fall and getting sorted out lost us a chunk of time, and as we came beneath the Waterfall Chimney we were caught by a Swiss pair attempting a fast time on the face (they had started at 8.30 a.m.), so we let them past. I led the Waterfall Chimney, so named because in summer it is either a waterfall or an ice pitch depending on the time of day. For us it was pure rock, and I found it a much tougher pitch than expected. After that, Alex led a hard slab pitch to avoid the snow mushroom where the Ice Bulge is normally found. One more pitch to the Brittle Ledge, and it was starting to get dark. We stamped out a good sitting ledge in some snow and settled down for the night. I had brought a warm sleeping bag for once, so despite the sitting position had quite a good night sleep. An American team on a ledge next to us did not, as they had only one sleeping bag between them, a NeoAir that popped, and they didn't seem to have a stove, which in quasi-winter on the Eiger didn't seem very sensible. They had been trying to make an 'in-a-day' ascent.

On the second day we started to get ready at 6 a.m. (first light) but it was a good hour and a half before I set off up the first pitch of the day, the Brittle Crack. I made a mistake here by climbing a section without gloves, and got very cold hands, eventually developing blisters on my fingers a week later, though with no sign of frostnip or frostbite. The Traverse of the Gods came next: it is a very scary position traversing above the void and looks improbable, but turned out to be straightforward to climb, and it got us to the bottom of the famous White Spider icefield. From a distance the tentacles of ice that spread from the icefield look like a spider's legs; it was a worrying place to be as we encountered our only bits of rockfall on the route, and I climbed past a fairly large patch of red snow in the middle of the icefield. The pitches once more flowed with nothing being too difficult but much of it a bit fall-offable, insecure and often not as well protected as one would wish. We marvelled at the route-finding of the first ascensionists as there are a lot of clever traverses and improbable-looking sections that turn out not as bad as they seem.

As these things do, the face just seemed to keep going and going until we reached the start of the summit icefield. Here we met the sun and then had some calf-burning ice before attaining the summit ridge and meeting with a very strong southerly wind. Putting on down jackets, we made our way along the final knife-edge to the summit – a tenuous passage as rogue gusts kept threatening to knock us off balance and send us back down the north wall. We arrived at the summit at about 2 p.m. and then descended the west flank, which was rather horrible as it carried a mixture of isothermal snow in which we kept sinking to our knees and the odd slab covered in scree.

It was only when back at the Eigergletscher station that we celebrated our success, although by that point we were feeling both tired and very relieved. The Eiger's North Face is one of the most oppressive places I have ever been. It is the weight of history plus the knowledge that the further you climb the more difficult it would be to get back down, with all the traversing and cunning route-finding that the Heckmair route entails.

Together, these two routes have already given me a lot of retrospective satisfaction. The Peuterey I found the more enjoyable experience because of the solitude and wildness of the situation; the Eiger imposed a bigger psychological burden, and I felt a greater sense of relief in climbing it. The problem, however, with writing a shortlist of Alpine climbs I want to do is that the list isn't actually very short …

STORMY WINTER

by Bob Reid

THE NORTH-EASTERLY COMING ASHORE above Findon Moor just south of Aberdeen, on 28 January 2022, was gusting at over 80mph. I'd walked out above Earnsheugh cliff to feel its force. It was terrifying and terrific in equal measure. I was glad to be only a few hundred metres away from home. Appropriately it was the Danes who had named the storm 'Malik', a 'chief' among storms. It hit them first. It coincided with storm Corrie, which arrived the day after from the west. Wise heads knew to avoid the hills. Arranged meets were cancelled and trips wisely rescheduled. It was not a time to be afoot in high places.

The winter of 2021–2 will be remembered as being particularly stormy. Named storms abounded. Barra followed Arwen in early December 2021. Corrie and Malik blazed a trail which will be seen for decades because of the tree loss in January 2022. And Dudley, Eunice and Franklin all arrived in the middle week of February 2022.

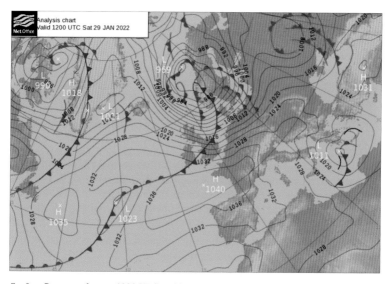

Surface Pressure chart at 1200 UTC on 29 January 2022 showing storm Malik to the NE of the UK with an associated cold front sweeping SE across the country. The tightly packed isobars indicate the strength of the NW winds. By permission of the Met Office.
© Crown Copyright.

It is perhaps inevitable (but shouldn't be) that there would be casualties in the mountains. Six climbers died during those three storms in February 2022 alone. Not for the first time we find ourselves asking 'why?' And reminding ourselves not to condemn.

During the harsh winters of the early 1990s and then again in 2013 we experienced similar levels of tragedy. In *SMCJ*, 42/204 (2013), 464–7, I commented upon the levels of condemnation abroad amongst our Scottish media. There was even talk of banning folk from the hills. I am reminded of a short entreaty I had written for the BBC's *Out of Doors*. It perhaps is worth echoing those sentiments, first written in 1994 and updated and broadcast in 2013.

It would be a very cold heart that didn't miss a beat on hearing about the tragedy in Glen Coe last weekend. There will be funerals and memorial services in the coming weeks. Inquiries will take place and reports will eventually answer the question 'what happened?' But the question 'why?' will be the one that folk repeatedly ask their own inner selves and will struggle to answer. Especially those folk close to the victims.

20 years ago Scotland had a string of very cold winters (in the 1990s). Sad to say, there were many fatalities and the government of the day was asking questions. The winter of 1993–4 was the first time in my memory that the right to climb itself was so frequently drawn into question. I found myself repeatedly having to defend the rights of climbers to go climbing in challenging conditions, to be out on the hills when a blizzard was blowing, or when, heaven forfend, the hills were covered in ice.

Today I'm old enough to reflect that this was just 'selling newspapers', and you can guess the worst culprits. But at the time a response was required. Words from that 1994 response defending mountaineering, attempting to explain, have an eerie resonance this week.

With hindsight I was also far more affected by the death of a friend in the mountains than I cared to admit at the time. When BMC and MCofS met together in those days there was always time for climbing. We worked hard and climbed hard with Bill Wright and Derek Walker and with Andy Fanshawe. Andy's tragic death on Eagle Ridge in 1992 haunted me in a way I couldn't explain but it took ten years before I overcame a nagging, mental block and finally completed Eagle Ridge myself, perhaps, in the process, exorcising a ghost.

The rest of the broadcast repeated what had been said to ministers and media back in 1994 – and is just as relevant in 2022.

It doesn't take long before all the usual, hackneyed reasoning for risking life and limb begins to sound glib in the extreme, especially when it is a climbing pal who has died. Death in sport or recreation can never be justified. All we can do is accept it, and try to prevent it within the constraints that a civilised society puts down. In other words we can educate, train, improve technology, minimise the risk.

But we can't ban, we can't outlaw, nor should we condemn what, in many cases, we simply don't understand. A society that indulges in reactions such as these is not one I would wish to live in.

Most climbers tend to adopt a fatalism toward such incidents.

Regret at the loss of life, tempered with a feeling that those who have died did so doing something that they enjoyed. But that still sounds glib. Perhaps less glib is the recognition that people climb hills because it is a very important and rewarding part of their lives. A death will always be a waste, but it is also true that the experienced climber's life was much enriched and more fulfilled.

Perhaps most realistic and convincing of all is the 'There, but for the grace of God, go I' approach, which at least betrays a recognition by a climber, that they too could die.

Much has been written and said about why climbers climb, why they adventure, and why they take these risks. But I have struggled to find anything written anywhere that gives a satisfactory rationale for loss of life in the mountains. Indeed, the longer I climb the more I realise there is no rationale – just the fact that so many forget: 'mountaineering' is dangerous. What is more, I continue to believe there is no such thing as 'winter hillwalking' in Scotland. 'Hillwalking' is a summer pursuit. In Scotland, in winter, there is only 'mountaineering'.

On the wall, just inside the door at Plas y Brenin in Wales, the words of Edward Whymper are carved into a tablet of Welsh slate. I recite the passage to myself, almost as a mantra, at times of high risk in the mountains, when descending some misty, cliff-strewn, icy Scottish hillside. It has served me well.

'Climb if you will, but remember that courage and strength are nought without prudence, and that a momentary negligence may destroy the happiness of a lifetime. Do nothing in haste; look well to each step; and from the beginning think what may be the end.'

WEATHER RHYME

Weather's truth is often hid
In murk and driving rain,
Yet still we head off north or west
And risk the hills again.

Hamish Brown

A STANCE ON PARNASSUS

by Gavin Anderson

OUR FIRST STOP WAS THE KINGSHOUSE. Bearing in mind the nature of our excursion we opted for the lounge bar, *terra incognita* for us, and were surprised to see so many gentlemen in tweeds sipping their malts. Gentlemen they may have been, but we had to elbow our way to the bar. Feudal privileges die hard. Bonnie Prince Charlie had not fought in vain.

That first night we camped at the head of Glen Etive, optimistically laying out our sleeping bags on the spot where W.H. Murray had laid his before lighting a pipe. Following protocol we breakfasted on kippers. Neither of us had sampled them for years so the taste and texture came as a surprise. Thus fortified we headed out, skipping the pantomime of one of us forgetting our boots, so there was no annoying double-back to the city.

Rod and I were retired, and in need of something to do. Some climbers spice the basic plot by adding a little bit extra, such as climbing the Grand Capucin then parapenting off its summit or ascending Everest in a wheelbarrow, and so on, and so on. With all these extras came possible damage to health and limb, or a rapid termination of the experiment.

Our scheme offered no such unpleasantness. We would follow in the footsteps of the first ascenders of three classic climbs and investigate how far the nature of the climb reflected the personality of the climber, rather like the art historian identifying an artistic masterpiece by the brush strokes or how the hands are painted.

We parked near the foot of Clachaig Gully, listening to the musical tinklings of the waterfall. It was a fabulous spring morning, and we were engulfed by the perfume and colours of the plant life decorating the gully's walls. As I never normally write such giddy prose, I assume we were under the spell of the maestro, and could sense the tread of the fearless MacAlpine, the mysterious Marskell, and the forgetful Dunn following us. The climbing was enjoyable without being necky. We clunked our way up on the unaccustomed big holds. The landmark pitches were interesting but held no terrors. The Great Cave pitch? Modern protection made it safe. The famed Jericho Wall was rock solid. Had WHM oversold the product? I think not. The unknown always holds nameless terrors, and moreover he had had no harness or rock slippers, nor any Camalots – better than Valium for stopping the shakes.

The climb went on and on. Clouds masked the sun, and the rock formerly glowing was now as brick-red as Bolton. Without warning, without any anticipatory slackening, the climb stopped and we found ourselves hard by the starting point of the Aonach Eagach.

It was early in the day, and the sun had reappeared. So far we had stuck to the text, but now broke ranks and skipped over the Aonach Eagach, which I know WHM had done. The first stage in our pilgrimage was over.

Did the climb reflect the man's character? The hanging garden is an instance, echoing Murray's occasional Rococo flourishes, and the finale over the rugged Aonach Eagach speaks to the bold cragsman he really was.

There were no kilts at the bar, but it was even tougher getting served. The words 'Excuse me!' once again failed to elicit any response. They were a rougher crowd, and there was a vague hint of menace in the air. We said *slàinte* to WHM and to the realm of the gentleman climber.

Our next subject lived by the sweat of his brow. I had seen Don Whillans twice in my life: once watering the plants at the Biolay campsite in Chamonix, and once at kicking-out time leaving the Padarn, freighted with a six-pack under each arm to cover any dry spells. Both iconic moments.

We were going to attempt *Centurion* on Ben Nevis in tribute to Whillans. The climb provides a classic example of familiarity breeding contempt. For a long time the route was considered the *ne plus ultra* of hard climbs in my Edinburgh circle. When the Editor of the *Journal* told me it was 'an easy, easy climb,' I put it down to an early example of sandbagging. I had already fallen off the greasy first pitch so I approached with trepidation. First of all it was Impossible; then Desperate; and now an Easy Day Out. After we had done the climb, we were told that was the received opinion.

Whatever!

The rock was perfect, endowed with just enough holds to make it hard, but not too much so. The dreaded second pitch succumbed to aggressive laybacking and jamming. Finding a none-too-desperate crux at either end of pleasant climbing, seemed proof of a benevolent deity smiling on us. Everything was golden. At the top we descended a snowed-up Number 5 Gully. Happily the snow was as soft as Mister Softee ice-cream, and we could churn great buckets in it, with a spot of bum-slithering helping us to the bottom. We exchanged notes and agreed: Centurion is the portrait in stone of a formidable, direct, uncompromising man.

There was an unusual sequel to the day. Rod and I were drinking a pint in a Fort William bar and going over the events of the day. The other customers were discussing the Scotland–England match. As we supped our Double Diamond, one of the punters started singing: 'If you hate the English bastards clap your hands!' Obviously a popular refrain, for soon everyone was joining in, stamping feet and banging beer glasses.

They must have been badly out of tune, for a music-lover stood up and flung his pot at the singers. It smashed on the table, spraying beer and glass in the choirmaster's lap. Pandemonium broke out: glasses soared through the air; punches were traded that rarely met their target, as the punchers spun round in a giddy ballet that would have wrung applause at Covent Garden, falling to the deck, tripping up other combatants and generally adding to the mayhem. Bar stools were used for defence and offence. Heads were nutted. It was a classic Wild West moment.

Someone was blocking the light in the doorway. It was a wee lassie, all of five feet and a bit, dressed in a policewoman's uniform. Like a prim primary-school teacher, she clapped her hands just the once and this amazing lass then said: 'Right lads, time to get hame to the missus.' There was silence; sheepishly without a whisper of protest, glass crunching underfoot, the warriors stumbled home. As we drove north we couldn't help thinking the young policewoman had made us non-combatants contemptible.

We had toasted our farewell to Whillans amongst the shambles of the damaged pub. To every man his own memorial. If Bob Dylan could win the Nobel Literature Prize for his corny not-very-literary lyrics, so Whillans can scrape onto the list by his off-the-cuff comments. In his dismissal of Tolkien's *Lord of the Rings* as 'A load of f***ing fairies,' you are about as far from Murray's German Romanticism as you can get. Don had a way of putting down boasters with an impromptu aphorism that sticks in the mind of those stung, remaining in the folk memory of any Anglophone climber. Hearing them for the hundredth time, I believe them all. Some dullards say they were fabricated in a post-alcoholic haze. I refuse to accept that – but then I believe Marie Antoinette made that mistake about the cakes.

Fionn Loch. If your favourite artist is Landseer and your literary avatar is Sir Walter Scott, then a glorious Heaven upon Earth awaits you here. This was some time ago, and I'll never go back. I suspect like many other Shangri-Las it has been spoilt by the well-intentioned destroying what they came to worship.

We were off to follow the masters, Smith and Haston, on their first ascent. A magnificent route given the crappy name of *Gob*.

After a straightforward first pitch, the climax is reached: a long, sensational traverse under an overhanging roof; technically not desperate, but the exposure is gripping, like climbing the inside of Hagia Sophia, terror creating a maelstrom in your bowels. But holds and runners are plentiful. You finish, gasping with breathless relief, coil the ropes and settle down to enjoy the Pre-Raphaelite colours – Scotland at its best. At the same time you are wondering whether Smith and Haston were speaking to each other when they created this masterpiece. They had a rough friendship, but then they were both prima donnas. And there were plenty of those to go round on the climbing circuit, some too good to make you a cup of tea.

And now the understudy, Dougal Haston. Years ago I saw him at Traprain Law, attempting to solo the overhang clad in winklepickers and drainpipes. His mates were taking no notice. To get their attention, he swarmed boldly onto the overhang. Unfortunately winklepickers are not rock-shoes, and he lost contact with the rock, scrabbled for a second, then off he came. He fell quite a distance, badly injuring his shoulder. What impressed me was his refusal to show any pain, particularly to us bumblies milling around the foot of the crag.

Haston was a puzzle. Beyond the fact that the line is daring, *Gob* tells us nothing about the man. His written output was extensive: a novel, an autobiography, numerous diary entries – enough to allow a judgment. Even a couple of articles in the *SMC Journal*. His frequent whooping into the night, and crampons scarting, suggest borrowings from Smith. His novel, *Calculated Risk*, follows an eerie parallel to his own life, even giving uncanny pointers towards his death. His *pensées* are gloomy, introspective, not exactly beach reading. As for his novel, the critics' reviews span the whole gamut from, 'Well, it's his first try,' to 'Rubbish!' Being thus condemned is unfair. Haston can summon up a sentence or two. But his writing is hollow, without inner warmth, reminiscent of Aleister Crowley.

The most telling revelations about his inner life are contained in his journals. They sign off with the valedictory 'Thus spake DH,' which can be taken as the poor man's Nietzsche, or just plain weird. He became a competent writer, serious and strenuous like his climbs. Searching for humour in his *oeuvre* bears little fruit. There is the occasional nugget: 'Clough was my partner; porridge the breakfast.' If that is your sort of thing.

But is that the whole story? His 'Nightshift in Zero'[1] is as good as anything Smith wrote, without the baroque flourishes. Descriptions of the ups and downs of high-altitude climbing are illuminating, while his portrayal of his colleagues' frailties leaves no room for argument. The rubbishing of his novel might owe more to anger at Haston hogging the lead on Annapurna than detached appraisal.

Friends talk about his love for children, and dandling babies on his knees, and how towards the end of his life he visited the Pentlands, a mellow softening of the arteries. Bob Culp, a Colorado guide, told me he had rarely come across such a pleasant personality. The demons had been chased away.

I studied Carnmore Crag for a long time, searching for any clues to Dougal's character. But there was nothing; both the cliff and the man were totally elusive.

Then I realised I had found the word. The weather had set in, sheets of rain spattered loch and cliff in gathering fury. We were going home. We had had a good week, but now it was shoulder the sacks, hoods up and best foot forward through the rain. I turned to say goodbye to our once-friendly cliff. It was dark, unyielding, moody and morose.

The two foregoing subjects would hardly merit a belay stance on Parnassus. That leaves two contenders for the throne, Smith and Murray. Smith was a philosophy student who according to the legend never

---

[1] Published in *Edinburgh University MC Journal*, 1961–62.

submitted a written piece of work, but was so venerated by his professors that they were prepared to let him slide through on the strength of his other qualities. I don't believe it either. Legends tend to accrue around charismatic figures.

His writing was diverse: at times a student rag mag, or a Yank gangster comic, then suddenly breaking out as the poor man's W.H. Murray, as if he were trying to create a separate persona. The style is very descriptive, and if you believe communication is the chief function of pen and ink he gets ten out of ten. There is a fondness for adjectives you think wildly inappropriate, for example 'vulturous mists'. But finish the sentence – '… wheeled slowly around us.' – and recall your last miserable day on the Grey Corries, and you see he's got it spot-on.

There are plenty more like that. Sometimes contrived, a word-technician playing chess with the language, occasionally sounding like any student straining after the *mot juste*. He was only 23 when he died, an age when many writers are still churning out juvenilia. Glimpses of what might have been shine through the various texts like the sparkling stones embedded in the flanks of the Fiescherwand.

Smith gets the silver award. He was a prodigy, whose talents were not restricted to climbing. Marked down as a climbing yobbo by certain groups; marked up as the favoured son of the university's philosophy department. This wobbling on the Richter scale hints at an unsettled personality, unsure of what he wanted to be, unsure of who he was. The episode of the pontoon school at Jacksonville sounds implausible. I believe he was there, but I see him sitting in the soggy background ruminating over a Wittgenstein Proposition. The unelaborated talk of chasing the birds on Saturday sounds like nerdish hankering to be one of the lads. In the early 1960s recognition of his genius was almost mandatory. A lot of his writing was experimental. His best such as 'Walkering in the Alps' marks him as a serious mountain writer. It is a straightforward account without the fizz of 'The Bat and the Wicked'.

And now we come to the saintly Murray. There is no hint of skulduggery in his make-up. No need to count the spoons when he leaves. At one point he sampled the life of a monk in an immersion course at Buckfast Abbey, which sounded like an SAS boot camp in cowl and robe. It would have been Scotland's loss if he had turned monastic. Fortunately for us he dug in his heels over Papal Infallibility, and returned to secular life as a bank clerk, swapping a hair shirt for the marginally more comfortable stiff collar and business suit.

The one time I met him was at the Club Dinner. I was the JMCS Edinburgh representative and his hand was in the row of hands to be shaken. I always feel this is a little bit like running the gauntlet and was too nervous to speak, so we just stared at each other, he wondering who they had pulled off the street, I kicking myself in furious embarrassment.

Like many of us I hadn't opened my Murray in years, and now

approached it as one would a sermon, bracing myself for spiritual uplift but low expectation of pleasure. I had vague memories of his tales following a pattern, namely the evening before spent boozing and plotting with the lads over foaming tankards. Next, off we go, Dunn forgets his boots, swift return to Glasgow. Off again. The climb: Mackenzie or author heroically leading the slippery slope. 'Good show!' through rime-encrusted lips. The summit a final coda rhapsodising on the scenery; as a bonus a spectacular sunset, with God coming in useful here.

Much to my surprise it was nothing like that. The writing was fresh and alive, the climbing portions easily pictured and dramatic, unlike the modern stuff that reads like a treatise on trigonometry and is about as exciting. You are worried he will fall off *Garrick's Shelf*, your toes tingle in their tricounis, you hold your breath, then feel relief as he clinches the pitch, a hundred-foot runnerless horror above a notional belay.

His adventures make you wish you experienced the golden age of mountaineering – though not its unpleasant sequel, fighting the Africa Korps in the desert, then three chilly years in POW camps, writing your memoirs on toilet paper. Escapism was the only exit; hence the Technicolor sunsets and the baying of stags on autumnal Ladhar Bheinn. The Gestapo destroyed his manuscript, and Murray's comments about the face of soulless evil are bone-chilling. He rewrote it from memory. My guess is that the second version is more polished than the original. We shall never know.

Naturally some of his writing is dated: 'The competitive spirit is happily completely foreign to Scottish mountaineering.' Why was he never on first-name terms with his stout-hearted companions? They may have been awe-inspiring risk-takers, but despite throwing themselves whole-heartedly into the fray they don't get much to say. His writing is rarely static. No pitch is so long the reader yawns; the second man has no time for frostbitten toes. These are climbs, not projects. You can be gripped on the Ben, ravished by Ladhar Bheinn, knackered on Rannoch Moor, but you are always *there*. Whole generations can blame Murray for their obsession, hidden between the pages of wholesome home-readers such as *Ivanhoe* and *The Mill on the Floss*, and off they go in their nailed boots to adventure and unforgettable sunsets. The routes reflect the man. *Clachaig Gully* with its long floral passages is the man to a fault, a mountaineer's mountain-climb landing you on top of the hill with easy access to the finest ridge in Britain. His word paintings put him on a par with Turner and Rossetti. Let the Master take his belay stance on Mount Parnassus.

ODE TO THE GODS

Hallelujah! You can dance on sunbeams. Follow your dreams across unreality. The ravenous beasts that devour their own demons. The sorbet gourmets, the epicures of wafer ice and a pinprick tracery of discovery, named, recorded, measured, graded, here today and gone tomorrow.

Yet, an exquisite moment in time, capturing bravery, power, beauty and love more eloquently than sculptured marble; an authored, named, dated, flawless description in a history that will stand the test of time.

There you go again, turning an elemental struggle into a flowing ripple of beauty out and under virgin rock. The commitment to a life well lived and a swing out into space at the edge of the roof. Yet another pivotal point in climbing, but too soon nothing more than yesterday's impossible grade, a name and more names in the guide, achievement beyond comprehension and more whodunnits than an Iain Rankin, one small step for man and another giant book for the printer! Thirty quid gone and some of us never read beyond 5b.

You are purveyors of the finest white powder, crack connoisseurs, isotonic druggies, recovering addicts, high on amino, out cold on lactic. We have our Mother's Pride, a dollop of own-label raspberry and a cuppa builders' with a spoonful or three of refined white sweetness. Your Y-shaped torsos will cold-turkey without organic proteins while our A-frames are shooting up on chips and prescription routes as you're shooting up on class FAs.

You are fantasy swinging angels that can make snow stick to overhangs, the destroyer of the picture editor's neck, a Merlin waving curved wands at rotting cracks of turf and turning them into cascades of ice. Whilst back on Planet Thawing-Ice we are punching axes elbow-deep, cursing our demons, consumers of hope, collapsing the climate, keeping up with the pioneers of the 'thirties.

We can see you float on icy, dry, scintillating light and we grey-haired from worry, red with bloody, bashed knuckles, staining the dripping ice. You with dry-tool fingertips and us hoping for a better life lying to the spouse the new curvers are for hoicking weeds.

Compleaters going round their own world in 80 days. The Black and the Red in 24 hours of winter whiteness. And those who get high on rarified air will have exclusive invites to the 8000m celebration zone but for us it's all picture and no sound back at the kitchen sink.

You are the connect, a junction of sky and sea, dropping poetic names amongst the 'in' crowd, utterly alive at the very edge of possibility, post-holing seals, creating waves and another tsunami of new routes to end another week in another golden age of climbing. And us? We're stalkers, watching the dangling paparazzi digitally catapulting you to fame.

You're talented gods, hanging on air; even your spit defies gravity, while back on Planet Rock the ordinary Joes will always find a double-handed grab at reality and never, ever risk becoming bedridden with a stack of busted bones.

You are the confounding mortgagees, new true adventurers, turning weekends and holidays into greatness, atomically driven alpinists, painting the Messner message across faces in places unknown and unsown. The multi-tasking jugglers of wages, home life, families and the brave, concerned teenagers that want PLANET SOS tattooed on their foreheads.

And let's not bury the new-age Saga climbers, disgracefully refusing to die young, still scratching about, still sticking their necks out, still dodging the axe and still finding a lot for old cocks and hens to crow about.

Respect, man, show respect for the Peaky Climbers, one step ahead of the game, never taking no, answering with a challenge, the alphas, male and female.

You're the new Smiths, Browns and Allens that will turn your names around while we're the bourgeois Bloggs, Esq, HVS, PAYE, the in-awe readers of blogs, the conquistadors of the easy, who will never visit A&E with anything worse than a chip on our shoulders.

Tim Pettifer

JBEL BOU OURIOL

by Hamish Brown

WHEN I FIRST EXPLORED THIS MOUNTAIN (3578m) that dominates the great Tizi n' Tichka road over the Atlas from Marrakech to the deserty south, it had the resonant name of Jbel bou Ouriol, which was later changed to the far less cheery Adrar Tircht (sounds like a sneeze). The former name is apparently derived from it appearing like a recumbent donkey when seen from afar. With the Tizi n' Tichka summit (2260m) on its flanks, the ascent may appear none too challenging, and it isn't to those acclimatised. Our party was not. But let me sandwich my memory of the ascent between two other encounters here.

Fed by snowmelt in spring, there are clear, cold streams and alpine meadows beside the road just before the *tizi* (pass) is reached. On one crossing I stopped my campervan beside a stream to top up the water carriers. Before I could open the door a boy appeared, to scrounge most likely, but then he stopped dead on hearing the tape of Atlas songs I was playing, stood back with a grin and began to sing along to the music, clapping his hands to the insistent rhythm. Out of nowhere it seemed two other boys materialised, and the trio lined up and performed with marvellous élan. I couldn't but smile and clap along with them. When the tape ended they demanded an encore. They had tousled hair and ragged *djellabas* and were obviously poor, with none of the world's goods, but this was their music, in their mountains, and they sang with obvious pride and enviable joy. I still treasure that tape of Berber music, but it has never quite the magic of hearing it augmented by that Berber trio near the Tizi n' Tichka summit.

One reason we camped there, below the pass, on various occasions was to enjoy the rich alpine flora. In spring the slopes were yellow with thousands of small hoop-petticoat daffodils (*Narcissus bulbicodium*), and when they were over, there were thousands of stately purple orchids, some a metre high. The landscape otherwise was harshly barren, lit here and there by the bold brightness of some alpine flower.

The slopes of bou Ouriol when I first came that way had a cable bucket system crossing right over Tizi n' Tichka, part of a large mining infrastructure that has all but gone. Some activity continues, with dirt roads on the lower slopes of bou Ouriol leading up to the odd adit. We set off at 05.00, first light, and an hour later paused out of sight as a lorry passed, in case anyone tried to prohibit our being there. We noticed two of the bright blue domes of hedgehog brooms were white-flowering. (Botanists debate why this happens – and with various flowers.) The lorry had stopped at an adit, so we kept well left up a valley with a pinnacle ridge above and then had to bypass a formidable headwall. One of our unacclimatised party had had enough by then and turned back.

We traversed upwards for what felt interminable time, passing a cave then a big hollow with the main crest beyond. The sun was stuck stickily to the sky, and we sweated in the muggy conditions. Another member hit his altitude ceiling on this tiring exercise and, with his wife, went down. We picked out a recognisable bit of mine track and agreed to meet there for 'lunch'. They'd be quite happy botanising. Strange how, as soon as the descent starts, the enervating struggle disappears. More than once I've seen people carry on, only to hit the ceiling again. Adrian, who had been sick in the night, was going well, as was John, and I was acclimatised. We made what Peyron[1] called 'a dignified plod'. The world below became more map-like, the twisting road up and the perched villages clear. When the grand view along the Taska n' Zat peaks (nearly 4000m) suddenly showed, we knew we were approaching the end. A snow dome proved a false summit, with a shallow dip beyond and then a rise to the summit trig point, reached at 11.20.

The views were impressive rather than attractive, the sun a mere silver disc through a soupy sky. The desert south beyond Ouarzazate was hazy but we could see the volcanic cone of Jbel Sirwa, which links High Atlas with Anti Atlas. I quoted Shakespeare: 'So foul a sky clears not without a storm,' and we set off without much pause. I have never much liked the idea of being fried in a lightning strike. A hint of sleet and a few drops of rain proved a let-off.

We used uncongenial scree slopes to hasten the descent, and the botanisers, watching from below, guided us to a useful gap in the cliffs. A trickle of water where we snacked was bordered by the miniature daffodils. On the meadows we had collected lots of seed, which would be distributed among the Scottish Rock Garden Club members so there will be Atlas gems brightening Scottish gardens. The miners were knocking off at 13.00. They were a cheery bunch and chatted with us – but, sorry, none of us smoked. We came where a *targa* (water channel) ran off to the north – one I'd seen drop as a waterfall on a previous visit, described next. Over the welcome brew at camp we watched a kestrel failing to catch a thrush and a flycatcher dashing out and back from his perch to snaffle large flies. Someone pointed out that the night before it had been *catchflies*; now it was *flycatcher*.

That night we drove through Telouet to Animiter to stay with a family we knew. Over many years Aït Elyazid Mohammed had arranged mules for our explorations into the ranges to the north-east, and we were always welcomed into his home. Sad to say, he decided to try his luck in the big city, Casablanca, and as a farewell gift he had his wife weave a personalised carpet for me. This had his own name ELYAZID M[OHAMM]ED along the top, then, working downwards, the date it was woven (10.01.97), a central motif, my name MR HMISH M. BRO (the 'WN' being inserted above for lack of space), and along the foot, in the largest figures of all, my date of birth. Fortunately, over the years it has faded somewhat;

---

[1] Dr Michael Peyron, expert on Berber language, literature and culture; author of *Great Atlas Traverse* (West Col, 1989).

natural dyes are a thing of the past. Elyazid Mohammed, I may say, was back in the mountains a couple of years later, declaring he'd 'rather be poor in the mountains than a rich man in the city.'

Clockwise from top left:–
a) The author's guide to the waterfall.
b) The gorge below bou Ouriol (Photo: Richard Cormack).
c) Jbel bou Ouriol.
d) Blue-flowering hedgehog broom.
e) The personalised carpet. (Photo: Adrian Snowball).
Photographs are by H.M. Brown unless otherwise stated.

Those flowery meadows made me pull off the road the following year for a quiet solitary night in my campervan. From the upwards corkscrew of a road, I'd sometimes glimpsed a thread of waterfall descending the cliffs, and I decided to try and reach it. And botanise. A shy child in a blue *gandoura* stood and watched me settle in, as I put on the kettle and opened a last packet of our British chocolate digestives. I sat on a folding chair in the sun to read, and the child edged closer to see what it was that so obviously fascinated me. When offered a biscuit he tucked it in his pocket to take home. As the chocolate would melt, I persuaded him to eat it and put a few more in a poly bag to take away – quickly, before they stuck together. I just wondered where home was as he scampered away.

An hour later he was back with two teenagers and, with a grin, handed me a round of freshly baked bread. We all shook hands with the usual greetings. (Teenagers in the Atlas have gracious manners.) When they arrived I was looking through a large colourful picture-book of Morocco I had just bought, which caught their attention, and what followed was fascinating. I discovered they were from a village down on the northern slopes of the Atlas and had, just the day before, moved up for the season to these grazing grounds with their flocks: transhumants. They went to school in the off-season, and for the rest roamed these uplands. They had enough French that we could communicate, and it is amazing what can be conveyed by gesture and expression – and pictures in a book. For something like two hours I sat on that chair with these two teenagers looking over my shoulders, as I slowly went through the book explaining their country to them. Hard to describe the experience. Every now and again they would point and become excited at something. So that's what a *fantasia* looked like (for they had heard of it at home); so that's the sea; and look at that forest! (The landscapes especially captivated them, comparing and contrasting with their own harsh world.) They were intensely curious. Questions, questions: about their country, about the world; their experience may have been limited, but their imaginations were boundless.

The wee boy had just sat watching, but when I mentioned my wanting to visit the waterfall he was up at once, to take my hand and gesture to its location: I had my guide. We all followed a way through wee hills and down to a path across cliffs to reach the spot. The youngsters managed to explain it was only sometimes a waterfall because, above the cliffs, a *targa* (water channel) took the water round and down to irrigate the terraced fields of the high village they came from. (This was the *targa* we had met coming off bou Ouriol.) We parted at the falls: they went on, and I returned to the campervan. In the morning I found that two tins of sardines had been left at the door – the very cheapest of food possible, but all the more moving as indicating how desperately poor the family were. Tokens. Gestures. Enriching. Humbling. I had been the one learning lessons below the lofty slopes of Jbel bou Ouriol.

A PERFECT LITTLE ADVENTURE

by Noel Williams

MANY NEW ROUTES THESE DAYS are so much harder than anything I could get up, even in my prime, that I sometimes wonder if I'm allowed to call myself a climber any more. Fortunately it is still possible to have much fun in our sport pottering about at a lowly level.

We first spotted the stack on the much-depleted Skye Spring Meet last year. Three of us decided to investigate a stretch of coast on the east side of Trotternish, south of Lealt. It was lowish tide and we managed to progress southwards quite quickly. We soon reached some extensive tidal rock-platforms below steep but vegetated cliffs. It looked the sort of place that might have dinosaur footprints, but we didn't find any. A little further south we reached an enormous fallen block on the shore called Eaglais Bhrèagach (perhaps more properly 'Bhreugach'), meaning false or artificial church. This is hollowed out in the middle, and forms an impressive arch feature, which we walked through.

We noticed what we thought was a stack in the distance, and so continued south. Eventually an impassable cliff, the incoming tide and rain signalled a retreat. We left the shore part-way back and managed to clamber to the top of the sea-cliff, though it was 100m high and some care was required on the wet grass.

Back at base we consulted Mark Hudson's exceptionally thorough and comprehensive guide, *Skye Sea-cliffs & Outcrops*. (Grab yourself a copy before it is replaced by a selective guide to the whole island.) He describes reaching Eaglais Bhrèagach by a more direct route from Upper Tote, though it seemed even less attractive than the route up the cliff we had taken. We also found that the stack we had seen was included in the list at the back of the guide, though recorded as unclimbed. Maybe it was worth investigating.

Willie and I returned to Skye during a good spell at the beginning of September. We found an easy way down from the old road above Leac Tressirnish, and soon found the stack close in by the cliff-top. It consisted of dolerite sill but was capped by a layer of calcareous sandstone with a luxurious coating of grass.

The stack was elongated in a north-south direction and barely 20m high. There appeared to be an eminently climbable chimney-groove on the west face, though the exit looked rather loose. Unfortunately the stack was separated from the cliff-top by a deep water-filled channel some 7m wide – a tantalisingly close distance, but enough to dissuade a casual visitor. There was also a commodious platform to abseil to on the landward side. All told, it looked as if it might offer a bit of fun to a couple of ageing climbers.

We knew Simon Fraser had donned a wetsuit on a number of occasions so that Mick Tighe could get across to virgin sea-stacks. When we

The stack viewed from the south. All photos by the author except where stated.

approached him he seemed game to do the same for us. The autumn flew by, however, without a window of good weather coinciding with Simon's availability. He told me that much of his diary fills up a year in advance with Marilyn-bagging and genealogy.

Over the winter I decided another approach was needed. After a quick hunt on the Internet I managed to purchase a two-man plastic dinghy. When it arrived I was pleased to discover it pumped up quite quickly, but it was also plenty sturdy enough for our planned crossing. It was also reassuring that it had three air chambers. I couldn't wait to try it out.

When an excellent couple of days was forecast in January I suggested to Willie that we head to Skye. We drove up late one night and planned to bivvy by the old road on the upper cliff, but the wind was too fierce and the ground wet, so we eventually drove north to Flodigarry. Willie decided to sleep in the van with the boat, while I opted for a bivvy bag at the roadside. Just as I settled down for the night a full moon appeared through a break in the clouds and lit up our surroundings.

I slept really soundly and when I eventually woke I couldn't believe it was already ten o'clock. Willie had been awake for ages but had been reluctant to wake me because the weather was far from encouraging. It was cold and windy and the ground was soaking wet. We knew that low tide was at 12.45, but we didn't realise it was nearly a Spring tide, nor how significant this was. We decided to take the boat and the abseil gear down to the stack first, and then return for the climbing gear later. Willie placed a substantial metal stake as an anchor opposite the sea-stack. I was about to start pumping up the boat, but Willie told me to hang fire. As the

Willie views the channel on the January visit.

tide fell, boulders had become visible in the channel below. There was also a huge swell running, and it soon became apparent that it was too dangerous to try and use the boat. One mass of water came surging up from the southern end of the channel while a similar mass came surging from the north. The two waves then crashed together in a seething wall of surf before the water receded again. This was a bit of a blow. I was all for giving up and coming back on a better day. Willie thought we should at least investigate the abseil and started organising the rope. At the transition from grass to rock the cliff-edge was rather loose, so I fed the rope out as Willie abbed down. He landed on the big platform we had spotted previously from the north.

When I moved along to see where he was, he beckoned me to follow. It was quite dramatic at the bottom as the sea came crashing in. To our surprise yet more boulders started to appear as we neared low tide.

Willie seemed to be studying the waves carefully, and to my amazement he suggested he might make a dash for the stack. We were perfectly safe where we were on the platform, but the rocks below were soaking wet, and I thought he had to be joking. I happened to be facing away at the other end of the platform when I heard an almighty scream. Willie had decided to use the abseil rope to lower himself quickly down a short drop from the platform. When he swung on the rope a big lump of rock had been dislodged from above. Fortunately it struck the face part-way down and broke up, so that only a piece of it struck him on the forearm. He groaned in pain, but still managed to hold on to the rope. I wondered how I was going to get him back up the cliff if his arm was broken. To my huge relief he eventually announced that he was going to be OK, though his arm turned out to be bleeding under his thick clothing.

Willie makes a dash for it.

I thought that might be the end of his heroics, but as soon as he had composed himself he carried on down to a lower ledge. He then carefully awaited his chance before making a dash for the other side. He leapt across the boulders with remarkable agility and managed to climb quickly to a platform at the base of the stack, just before the next big wave came crashing in. He had a quick look up the chimney and then scrambled round to check the options at the southern end of the stack. He then waited, poised above the water, before making his return dash across the boulders. I wasn't going to follow suit.

Even Willie thought it was now best to call it a day, because we didn't have enough time to retrieve the climbing gear from his van before the incoming tide would make it impossible to cross the channel. I stood well clear when Willie started to jumar out, as my helmet was still up in the van. At first I made a mess of organising my foot-sling, but I eventually got going and followed him up. I then spent quite a while clearing the upper section of loose rock, so that we might avoid a repeat of the earlier scare on our next visit. Willie got impatient and started hauling in the abseil rope once I'd reached the easier-angled grass. We packed up quickly and lugged the unused boat 130m back up to the van.

Back home I had a rethink about using a boat to reach the stack. Not being a sailor I had been unaware there was such a big difference between Spring and Neap low tides. By serendipity our visit had almost coincided with a Spring tide, which explained why the water had been so much lower than on our previous visit. I studied the tide tables for Portree and discovered that one of the lowest tides of the year was predicted for Easter Monday – over a metre lower than the tide we had just witnessed. If it really was that low a boat should not be necessary. I gave Willie plenty of warning to keep Easter Monday clear.

It was delightful to have our daughter, son-in-law Mike and new granddaughter stay with us over Easter. I told Mike about our plans for Easter Monday and wondered if he might be interested in joining us. He was thrilled to be invited, but explained that he had to be back at work on the Tuesday. The weather forecast for the Monday kept changing in the week before Easter – first fine, then wet, then windy as well. We wondered about going on Easter Sunday instead, but then rain was forecast for that day too.

I got my gear together in plenty of time for once, but I was puzzled to discover I had only one jumar. I had emptied my rucksack on my office floor after our previous visit and I thought the missing jumar was maybe hidden under a pile of papers. I turned the house upside-down without success, and ended up packing a Croll to use instead.

Willie drove up from Perth on the Sunday evening and we went to bed unsure of what the next day might bring. To our delight the 6 a.m. forecast was more encouraging than that of the night before. Though the wind would be rising to gale force in the afternoon, there would only be showers in the morning and heavy rain wouldn't come in until 4 p.m. We decided to go for it.

We left Fort William just before 8.30 a.m. and had a leisurely drive to Skye. Low tide was not until 2.50 p.m., so we paid a visit to Leac Tressirnish, a delightful natural mini-harbour a little way to the south of the stack. When a heavy shower blew in we retreated to the ruin of a fishermen's building and sheltered under some corrugated sheeting that we found inside.

Once the shower had passed the sun came out again, and we even had time to extract a fine belemnite fossil from a boulder on the shore. The wind was strengthening as predicted, however, and we got well wrapped up in anticipation of worsening conditions.

By the time we arrived at the stack we were being buffeted by the wind and Willie's face was getting longer. He suggested we come back later in the week when there was a better forecast. I explained that low tide would be almost a metre higher on Thursday, and Mike would have to be back at work. I could see that the channel below us was starting to dry out, so I decided to take the initiative for a change. I told Willie the 'Mad Pole' wouldn't give up so easily, and started arranging the abseil rope. Before he had a chance to argue I set off down. I had only descended about 5m when, lo and behold, I came upon my missing jumar complete with krab and foot-sling just lying on the grass. It had been there since January but still looked in good nick, so I clipped it to my harness and carried on down. My homework had certainly paid off because the sea was lower than I had ever seen it here before. It was a simple matter to walk across

Willie abbs in with the belay stakes.

to the stack. Mike soon joined me and together we fixed a rope across the channel to safeguard our return.

At first I wasn't sure if Willie was going to join us, but he eventually abbed down with a rucksack containing a hammer and the vital stakes we would need to descend from the summit of the stack. The wind was backing to the south and now reaching gale force, but at least there was a little bit of shelter in the chimney that we planned to climb.

Willie leads the chimney. Photo: Mike Bauermeister.

Willie set off leading and made steady progress despite his bulky garments. He gave a yelp when a small chockstone he was standing on came out. It ricocheted off the wall and shot between my legs.

We had thought that the easiest option might be to exit the chimney on the left when it steepened, but he continued straight up instead. We knew full well there was loose rock at the top of the chimney, so Mike was standing well back behind me. Willie threw down a big block, which smashed into the channel below us. When he reached the top he gave out such a triumphant yell we could both still hear it above the roaring wind.

As soon as he took in one rope I started climbing. It was months since I'd done a roped climb and I got cramp in my leg as soon as I started bridging, so I had to step down again until it eased off.

The top of the chimney was steep and I was reluctant to move up on two poor hand-jams. I tried to move out left where it looked easier, but this was an illusion. When I returned to the chimney, however, my left hand dropped onto a hidden finger-jug, and this gave me the confidence to make an awkward move up. I threw more rock down as I exited the chimney.

Willie had somehow found quite a good runner in the crumbly sandstone hidden in the grass. When I joined him on the summit he explained how it had emboldened him enough to tackle the final few metres on wobbly clumps of grass. He had hammered two iron stakes into the grass on the east side of the summit for a belay.

Mike on the summit of his first sea stack.

Mike followed me up the pitch with impressive alacrity though he did admit he wouldn't like to have led it. He was as pleased as punch to bag his first sea-stack.

Clouds were rushing up from the south, and the sea was covered in white horses. There was no time to dally. Willie abbed off first and Mike quickly followed him. I added an extra tape so the rope would pull down more easily, then I followed too. Even then it required a mighty tug to get the rope moving. As Willie jumarred out, Mike and I noticed that the tide was already on the turn. It started to rain while we waited our turn, and by the time we had all packed up our gear at the top it was lashing down. We stomped back up the cliff, and quickly piled into the car. We were all soaked through to our underwear, so were very glad to have a flask of hot soup to share among us.

As arranged, Lucy and baby were waiting to pick up Mike in Invergarry. We said cheerio and they headed home to Nairn.

Willie and I arrived back in Torlundy just after 8 p.m. We had been away for less than twelve hours, but it had been a perfect little adventure.[1]

Anyone want to buy a boat?

---

[1] FA of *Gentle Giant*, 20m Severe. Willie Jeffrey, Mike Bauermeister and Noel Williams, 18 April 2022.

OUR TRUST – 60 YEARS AND COUNTING

by John Fowler and James Hotchkis

Having been founded in 1962 by members of the SMC, the Scottish Mountaineering Trust is now celebrating 60 years of charitable work for the good of the hill-going public. Here two long-serving officers of the SMT describe the Trust's origins and evolution.

THE SCOTTISH MOUNTAINEERING TRUST is now well known to hill-goers as the publisher of the Club's extensive series of guidebooks together with other titles, but promotion of knowledge of the Scottish hills goes back to the origins of the Club itself, where enshrined in Rule 2 of the Constitution are the words

> … to collect information regarding routes and to maintain comprehensive coverage and a historical record of such routes. In addition, to collect information regarding distances, means of access, time occupied in ascents, character of rocks, extent of snow, etc, and in general to promote the interests of mountaineering in Scotland.

The Club pursued these aims, and it is not therefore surprising that *Munro's Tables* was its first publication, produced in 1891. The Great War intervened but the series of seven District Guides published in the 1930s were a landmark, with authors of eminence such as Ling and Macphee. The books had plates by noted photographers such as Lamont-Howie, Sang and Robertson and offered advice appropriate to the changing times.

The fishing hotels and inns are for the most part comfortable and the advent of the motor car, when driven suitably to the condition of the roads, has simplified the approach to the hills, which were formerly inaccessible or at any rate only to be gained by stout walkers who could compass a long day.

And while the descriptions of the hills, their locations and local facilities were excellent, little was said to guide any ascent!

In the aftermath of the Second World War, there had been an explosion of climbing development in the Scottish hills. This was mostly club-based, and routes by the likes of Cunningham, Walsh, Smith, Marshall, Brooker, Patey and O'Hara are still sought-after ticks today.

The SMC took up the challenge and produced climbing guides to the popular areas, commencing with Bill Murray's 1949 guide to Glen Coe; and as the number of new routes grew, it was realised that a proper publishing programme was required. But there was a problem. A viable programme could not be sustained if tax had to be paid on profits from sales of books that appealed to a specialised readership and would never make large returns. Fortunately the Club has never been short of professional advisors, and it was Kenneth Dunn[1] (stalwart of the Murray–

---

[1] J.K.W. Dunn, 1911–2001. For an obituary by Donald McIntyre see *SMCJ*, 38/193 (2002), 256–8.

Mackenzie–McAlpine climbing team) together with George Ritchie[2] (he of *Ritchie's Gully* on Creag Meagaidh) who proposed the formation of a charitable trust. Dunn was well qualified to offer advice, being Chief Solicitor to the Inland Revenue in Scotland, while Ritchie was also a solicitor and County Clerk of Midlothian Council.

Instigators of the Scottish Mountaineering Trust: Kenneth Dunn (left) and George Ritchie (right). Photos: SMCJ 2002 (L) and 1997 (R).

The advantage of such an arrangement was that educational and scientific endeavours, being recognised by the Revenue as charitable aims, are zero-rated, with books falling into the former category. It sounded good, and the whole idea of the formation of a trust was put to the Club at the AGM in 1960.

Proposed Trust – resolutions as previously circulated

1. That the Club approve of the establishment of a Scottish Mountaineering Trust with the objects and powers contained in the revised Trust Deed circulated to members in October 1960 and to that end …

2. That this meeting nominate as the first Trustees the following office-bearers for the time being of the Club, all *ex officio* – the President, the two Vice-Presidents, the Secretary, the Treasurer, the Journal Editor, and the Guide Books General Editor, with power to adopt said Deed of Trust and assume Trustees and generally to act thereunder.

The minutes of the 1960 Meeting record the unexpected result.

---

[2] G.J. Ritchie, 1914–97, served as Treasurer of the SMC from 1955 to 1961. For an obituary by Jimmy Marshall, see *SMCJ*, 36/188 (1997), 426–7.

Proposed Trust

Detailed and lengthy resolutions had been circulated prior to the Meeting. The first of these affirmed in principle the establishment of the trust, and was moved by W.B. Speirs seconded by Dr G.G. Macphee. An amendment for its rejection was proposed by R.R. Elton and seconded by C.G.M. Slesser. After some discussion on by-now familiar lines, the resolution was defeated by 49 votes to 10. With this decision the remaining resolutions ceased to be relevant.

This unfavourable outcome perhaps owed something to the President having to explain that the usual afternoon reception with its tea and cakes had been dropped to allow adequate time for discussion of the issue! It appears that the major stumbling blocks were the proposal to appoint external trustees together with the handing over to the new trust all of the accrued cash!

Debate continued for over a year until a Special General Meeting of the Club was convened in March 1962.

A Special General Meeting of the Club will be held in the Clubroom, 369 High Street, Edinburgh at 7.30pm on Friday 30th March 1962 for the purpose of considering and, if thought fit, passing the following resolutions.

1. That a Trust be established in terms of the draft Constitution and Rules … subject to any amendments, if any, as the meeting may resolve.
2. Subject to Resolution No 1 being passed, that Ian G. Charleson, A.H. Hendry, George G. Ritchie, J. Stanley Stewart, J.C. Donaldson, G. Scott Johnstone and G.J. Dutton … be appointed to be the first Trustees of the said Trust.
3. That the Club transfer and make over to the said Trust (a) all stocks … of Guide Books at present held by the Club and (b) the sum of £1,000.

And furthermore

… further investigation and independent professional advice about the Club's financial position have established that a Trust, with very marked tax advantages, might be created (a) without having Trustees from outwith the Club and (b) without necessarily handing over to the Trust the whole sums at credit of guidebook account. These are important differences from the proposals put to and rejected by the 1960 AGM … .

The draft Constitution and Rule of the proposed Trust have been submitted to and approved by the Inland Revenue.

The minutes of the meeting record a satisfactory result.

The meeting then unanimously approved resolutions to the effect that a Trust be established with the office bearers ex officio as Trustees, that there be transferred to the Trust all guidebook stocks and the sum of £1,000 and that the Committee were empowered to lend further sums to the Trust.

But even at this early stage, the Club was keen to seek some measure of payback, and from the 1962 AGM Minutes we read:

> The Hon. Editor wished to retire after the next issue. He spoke of the need for an arrangement whereby the Scottish Mountaineering Trust meet the cost of the New Climbs in the *Journal*.

But the show was on the road, and the Trust declared in its Constitution its objectives to promote and support health, education and recreation in the mountains of Scotland and elsewhere and to foster knowledge of mountain geography, biology and weather, protect the mountain amenities and access and also promote the skills to walk and climb safely in the hills.

The Trust immediately took over publication of the existing series of climbing guides now identified with the classic red hardback cover. In Glen Coe the guide included for the first time comprehensive descriptions of the mysterious Etive Slabs, and there were attractive fine-line ink drawings of the various crags, many by Jimmy Marshall. In the Cairngorms volumes, there appeared a new and unique system of winter gradings developed by Aberdeen activists, which is still the foundation of the grading method in use today. The Cairngorms guide also recommended that in winter, '... tricounied boots should be worn. Crampons have been used but are not really necessary.'!

By 1964, the Trust was able to declare a profit of £364.

The early 1970s saw a range of comprehensive guides to nearly all of Scotland, in bright plastic-coated covers. Income from these publications was, however, relatively modest during this time and the Trust was able to offer only small awards to applicants. But all was to change in 1985 when the Trust produced *The Munros*. This was the first specific guide to climbing these select hills and, with the huge rise in the numbers of walkers aspiring to them, the book was immediately popular. It became a Scottish best-seller, and the Trust moved from having modest capital reserves to becoming guardians of a tidy sum.

But a further problem emerged. Around this time, the Revenue had started taking greater interest in charitable trusts that were not simply looking after a capital sum but also operating for-profit activities. The Trust was in danger of losing its tax-free status. The solution was for the Trust to form its own trading company, which would take over and administer the publication operation. All profits would be covenanted to the Trust, thus avoiding tax liability. This procedure is used by many charities.

In spring 1990 Bill Wallace, who was then the President of the SMC, wrote to the members about the above issue. He reported that the Trustees had considered two courses of action:

(a) To agree to the loss of charitable status; or

(b) To adopt a course of action which would allow the Trust to retain the profits and retain its charity status and continue to fulfil its charitable objectives.

The Trustees had been advised it was within their power to hive off the publishing business (which was then run by the Trust) to a private limited company. The private limited company would be a separate legal entity that would carry on the publishing business. The company would agree to pay to the Trust a fixed proportion of its profit before tax. As the company would covenant to the Trust, which is a charity, that would mean the company's profits would not be subject to Corporation Tax, as would otherwise be the case. The Trustees had been advised that this formula was legal and acceptable to the Inland Revenue and had been adopted already by several well-known charitable bodies.

A decision was made to proceed with the formation of the company, which was and is known as the Scottish Mountaineering Trust (Publications) Ltd. From that time onwards the publishing business was thus conducted by the company, whose share capital was and is owned by the Trust.

From a practical perspective, the Trust lent funds to the company to allow the company to carry out its trading business. In order to give the Trust some security for that loan from the Trust to the company, the company granted a Bond of Floating Charge in favour of the Trust (a bond that 'floats' over the assets of the company; i.e., the company is free to dispose of or sell these assets at any time). The Bond of Floating Charge would only crystallise (i.e. become a fixed security over the assets of the company) in the unlikely event of the company going into receivership or liquidation.

The Trustees changed by rotation over the years, and the business of the Trust in awarding grants (for which there were many applications) was duly considered at Trust meetings, generally held twice each year. Details of the grants awarded appear each year in the *Journal*.

The Trust was the fortunate recipient of donations from a family trust known as the Hamilton Family Trust (Jim Hamilton). Jim Hamilton was a guest at an annual dinner of the Club in Pitlochry some ten years ago.

With the advent of the internet and the availability to the public of online information, the hardcopy sales of the publications company decreased over a number of years, and thus the covenanted payments from the company to the Trust were falling. In 2014, however, the Trust was the beneficiary of 1/60th of the net residue of the estate of an Evelyn Agnes Griffith who died on 12 May 2014. Despite the Secretary writing to the solicitors acting in the executry of that lady, it was regrettably not possible to identify the connection she had had with Scottish mountaineering.

In the autumn of 2016, the Trustees were told that Mrs Isobel Cram who had recently died had bequeathed £300,000 to the Trust. The bequest was in memory of her late husband, Alastair Lorimer Cram,[3] a lifelong member of the Club who had had a distinguished war record and submitted notes regularly to the *Journal* on his mountaineering abroad. Cram's remarkable wartime escape attempts are the subject of a recent biography, *The 21 Escapes of Lt Alastair Cram*, by David Guss.[4]

The financial position of the Trust has thus been hugely augmented principally by the Hamilton Family Trust, the estate of Evelyn Agnes Griffith and the bequest of Mrs Isobel Cram in memory of her husband. Such had come at a propitious time when the annual income from the company had substantially reduced, and as a result, covenanted payments to the Trust had reduced. Those magnanimous gifts enabled the Trust to carry on with its donations for charitable purposes. Since 1990 the SMT has awarded over £1.6m in grants, with footpath maintenance accounting for almost a third of that total.

Stretcher-bearing participants at a recent SMART (Student Mountaineering and Rescue Training) course supported by the Scottish Mountaineering Trust.

Most recently, with a view to celebrating the sixtieth anniversary of the Trust, the Trustees have conceived a Diamond Grant to be awarded to an appropriate recipient, and that grant is now open for applications. It is hoped to award the grant to a successful recipient in November 2022.

And so the future of the Trust seems bright, and the Trustees look forward to supporting Scottish mountaineering projects for many years to come.

---

[3] A.L. Cram, M.C. (1909–94). For an obituary by Geoff Dutton & Bill Murray see *SMCJ*, 35/186 (1995), 745–8. See also 'A Very Special Munroist' by Hamish Brown in *SMCJ*, 48/211(2020), 237.

[4] Macmillan, 2018. Reviewed in *SMCJ*, 46/209 (2018), 283–5.

ON YOUR BIKE
Freewheeling thoughts and observations
on cycling into the hills

by Dave Broadhead

Some History

In 1839 a Dumfriesshire blacksmith named Kirkpatrick Macmillan built what is now acknowledged to have been the world's first bicycle. Another great Scottish invention, the benefits of this revolution in personal transport quickly caught on and have continued to spread and grow ever since. Half a century later, the early prototype machines had evolved into something we would all recognise today, and the bicycle became an essential accessory for some of the early members of the newly formed Scottish Mountaineering Club, as they set about exploring their native Highland hills. One of the more enthusiastic proponents of two wheels, the Reverend A.E. Robertson, had been a keen member of the CTC (Cycle Touring Club) before taking to the hills, and this experience undoubtedly helped him accomplish his historic first Munro compleation in 1901. In his *SMC Journal* article 'The Munros of Scotland'[1] he observed:

The difficulty in getting at the remote hills and securing a suitable base of operations was often a very serious one. In this case I found my bicycle simply invaluable and many of the more distant expeditions … were brought by the aid of the wheel within the compass of a long day.

Other pioneering climbers who used their bikes to overcome the limitations of the public transport system included the two Williams, Tough and Brown. In May 1895, with the Queen's Birthday holiday at their disposal, they had their eyes set on the *North-East Buttress* of Ben Nevis. Although the new railway to Fort William had improved access, they could not find a suitable train on that line, so instead they travelled by the Friday night mail-train to Kingussie on Speyside, then cycled part way across to Lochaber to climb the route and returned to Edinburgh early on Sunday evening after 45 hours of continuous travel. Oblivious to having been beaten to the first ascent by the Hopkinsons from Manchester three years previously, they recounted their trials and tribulations in the *SMC Journal*[2] (reprinted in *A Century of Scottish Mountaineering*). Their cycling efforts finished abruptly some three miles short of the Loch Laggan Hotel.

We had just topped a stiff brae, when a sudden report, resembling the simultaneous opening of six bottles of 'Bouvier', was followed by Tough's despairing cry, 'Your tyre's punctured.'

To this day, the simple puncture remains the cyclist's most likely

[1] *SMCJ*, 7/37 (January 1902), 10–14.

[2] W. Brown, 'Ascent of Ben Nevis by the North-East Buttress', *SMCJ*, 3/18 (September 1895), 323–31.

Rev. A.E. Robertson and his first wife Kate pictured by Loch Leven with their tandem and the Misses Russell. Photo: SMC Image Archive.

inconvenience. A centenary re-enactment of their remarkable journey by Alec Keith and Matt Shaw puts a modern perspective on their grit and determination.[3]

The twentieth century of course saw the development of the internal combustion engine, but although the private motor car gradually became the favourite means of transport throughout much of the developed world, the humble bicycle continued to play a role. As a teenager, the great J.H.B. Bell began his mountain adventures by bicycle with his sister, culminating in his first ascent of Ben Nevis in 1913, when he cycled across from Newtonmore in the teeth of a gale.

The Dundonian George 'Scottie' Dwyer went on to become one of the first professional UK mountain guides, based in North Wales. In the recently published treasure trove *A' Chreag Dhearg* Grant Farquhar[4] quotes from Dwyer's 1935 diary:

> *27 April*: Left Dundee and cycled to Arrochar where I met the Creag Dhu lads. Slept at the Shelter Stone rock on The Cobbler.
>
> *28 April*: Climbed Cobbler by Jug Handle route and Big Buttress route, also a buttress on the other peak of The Cobbler.

---

[3] A. Keith, 'Ben Nevis the Tough Way', *SMCJ*, 36/188 (1997), 291–5.

[4] G. Farquhar, *A' Creag Dhearg – Climbing Stories of the Angus Glens*, (Scottish Mountaineering Press, 2021), p.63.

29 April: Cycled home by Crianlarich and Loch Earn, met Ernie Blyth at Comrie brew up.

South of the border, Colin Kirkus, a brilliant rock-climber from Liverpool, pioneered significant new routes in North Wales and the Lake District in the 1930s with the help of his bike.

Bicycles were also being used overseas. Better known as an astronomer, Horace Dall from Chelmsford used a 3-speed Raleigh roadster to make the first crossing of the High Atlas in North Africa, following which in 1933 he crossed Iceland's Sprengisandur wilderness, emerging after five days with shoes still polished and wearing a tie. While trying to make a living growing coffee in Kenya, Eric Shipton introduced Bill Tilman to mountaineering on Kilimanjaro and Mount Kenya. Writing in his informative *Who's Who in British Climbing*, Colin Wells explained:

> Tilman, in typically idiosyncratic fashion, had decided to return to Britain by cycling across the neck of Africa. In a hint of what was to come on his and Shipton's notoriously spartan expeditions, he lived mostly off roasted bananas.

Meanwhile, in continental Europe young climbers were developing their skills and techniques on local crags before heading off by bicycle across the Alps, picking off many of the plum lines of the time. Hermann Buhl established his reputation with a number of bold and fast Alpine climbs before his historic solo first ascent of Nanga Parbat in 1953. In his inspirational *Nanga Parbat Pilgrimage* he recounted:

> Later, my way was to lead me over and over again southwards across the Brenner, to my home from home in the Dolomites; for good companions I had my bicycle, my sleeping bag and a cooker.

Cycling also helped introduce his fellow Austrian, Kurt Diemberger, to the mountains. In his wonderful *Summits and Secrets* Diemberger devotes a chapter to 'Grandfather's Bicycle':

> That bicycle certainly opened up undreamed-of possibilities for me. What matter that this 1909 show-piece was one of the first made after the famous 'penny-farthings'? Or that it was still rather taller than normal machines and a little peculiar to ride?

The decade following the end of the Second World War saw the start of what would become an explosion in leisure and recreation, with the ascent of Everest in 1953 raising the profile and popularity of mountaineering in the UK. Ironically, at the same time cycling seemed to be in terminal decline, appealing only to a shrinking band of die-hard enthusiasts and a few doughty commuters prepared to risk life and limb amid the ever-growing road traffic. In 1955 a group of adventurous British riders formed the Rough-Stuff Fellowship, tackling off-road routes following footpaths and rights-of-ways, using conventional touring cycles. As recently as 2014 I met a couple of these hardy characters at Over Phawhope bothy in the Southern Uplands, crossing from the east coast to the west with a

The author in East Greenland in 1976, cycling to Mesters Vig from the Skida Hut.
Photo: Mungo Ross.

minimum of basic food and kit. Their main sustenance seemed to be a large loaf of bread which they were attempting to dry out over the bothy fire, having suffered a soaking during an unplanned bivouac the night before. In the 1960s and 1970s a number of Aberdeen-based climbers used old road bikes to speed their way to and from Derry Lodge and beyond. I only tried this once on my own road bike and vowed never again!

Probably the greatest cycling challenge for any mountaineer was accomplished by the late Lars Olof Göran Kropp, who cycled from his home in Sweden to Everest, made an unsupported solo ascent without oxygen in May 1996 and then pedalled home again. Ten years later, while working as marketing manager for Glenmore Lodge, Pauline Sanderson joined the EverestMax team to cycle 8000km from the lowest point on Earth at the Dead Sea to the mountain. Joined by husband Phil they became the first British couple to summit Everest.

A recent Eastern District Zoom talk recounted two contrasting contemporary experiences of cycling to the hills. Concerned about the reliability of his old car, a youthful Jamie Thin decided to cycle from his Dundee home to the Swiss Alps in February 1990 to rendezvous with his climbing partner, taking in a visit to the Katowice Mountain Film Festival in Poland and some winter climbing in the Tatra mountains on the way. Bill Tilman would have approved of his hardiness. In the summer of 2018, following a carefully planned schedule Oli Warlow cycled from Lundy Island down to Cornwall then pedalled steadily north to Skye, climbing

The late Mike Taylor cycling into the hills with langlauf equipment.
Photo: J.M. Taylor Collection.

all 82 routes described in Ken Wilson's *Classic Rock* on the way. Inspired by his friend the late Jamie Fisher who had once done something similar, Oli used this challenge to catch up with climbing friends and publicise the work of the John Muir Trust.

New Technology

Another cycling revolution started in the late 1970s with the appearance of the first mountain bikes, in Marin County, California. With their thick, knobbly tyres, low gearing and tough, light frames, here in Scotland they were quickly recognised as the ideal way to take the slog out of toiling up and down the estate roads which were gradually creeping up the glens leading to the increasingly popular Munros, Corbetts and Grahams defended behind locked gates. These robust and functional new machines – also known as ATBs (All Terrain Bikes) or VTTs (*Vélos Tout-Terrain*) – also appealed to the wider public, who bought them in large numbers, revitalising the whole cycle industry and bringing prices tumbling down. Recent developments have seen the introduction of '29ers', mountain bikes with 29″ wheels rather than the conventional 26″, and 'cross' or 'gravel' bikes, which look like traditional touring bikes with dropped bars but have a stronger frame and wider tyres. Most recently 'fatties' have appeared, distinguished by big fat balloon tyres, apparently good in soft snow or mud! Electric mountain bikes can give a lot of extra help to those not as fit and strong as they used to be and are quickly catching on. I recently pedalled past Ryvoan bothy near Glen More and noticed an electric machine plus trailer parked outside. Although it was only early afternoon, inside the bothy a large fire was blazing, thanks to a sack of coal carried up in the trailer.

Cycling is now more popular than ever, as the sport attracts large numbers of participants and spectators across a range of different disciplines. The annual stage of the Downhill World Championships held at Nevis Range brings something like 20,000 spectators to Fort William. Unfortunately, there are also more people riding their bikes on paths and tracks not intended for wheeled vehicles, causing damage and erosion that regular hill-goers will no doubt have noticed with disapproval. I have encountered cyclists on the summit of Ben Macdui a few times, and on another occasion, when crossing the Lairig an Laoigh, an approaching cyclist went flying over the handlebars as I stepped to one side. Fortunately, he was none the worse for his mishap though I felt quite shaken. If you choose to use a bike to get to the hills, please be considerate to the environment and other people!

Some Personal Experiences

My father often referred to the bicycle as 'the poor man's horse', but apart from some road touring my own interest in off-road cycling started soon after I compleated my first Munro round in September 1989. I had met Donald and Anne Bennet in the hills south of Achnashellach, singing the praises of their new mountain bikes. Carrying them from home on a makeshift wooden rack on the roof of their car, they had cycled up the Glenuaig Lodge track from Craig, and hidden their bikes in the heather. Soon after, I bought my own machine and started a whole new way of thinking about access to the hills. As a rule, wherever there is an estate road, a bike will usually speed up the approach and will always ease the return, except when snow and ice or darkness intervene! When I started researching my chapters for the *North-West Highlands Hillwalkers' Guide* the bike was invaluable for reaching the many and varied new hills to be covered in the limited time available and opened the opportunity to climb hills on a summer evening after work.

For example, Càrn Bàn has always been considered a very remote Corbett, located at the heart of the Freevater Forest behind Seana Bhràigh. One Saturday morning in March I left home in Muir of Ord just after eight, parked the car at the foot of Strath Vaich beside the road to Ullapool, and following an enjoyable cycle over to Gleann Beag reached the summit about midday. In June the same year I left Inverness after work on a Tuesday afternoon, drove across to Kinlochewe then cycled up past the Heights and up Gleann na Muice before cutting across Gleann Tanagaidh to climb remote Beinn Bheag between the Fisherfield and Fannaich Forests. Unfortunately, in order to get home to bed and into work again next morning, I did not quite have time to include neighbouring Groban, but still felt very pleased with the evening's activity. A carefully hidden bike left at the roadside can also facilitate an easier return to the car after a hill traverse. On another occasion, having parked at Bridge of Grudie to climb Beinn a' Chearcaill, I was able to explore Strath Lungard and the spectacular waterfall on the Talladale river then cycle back to the car from the Loch Maree Hotel.

Once into the habit of looking for opportunities to use the bike to access hills, I started to think about longer cross-country routes through the glens. At the end of a couple of family weekends in the west I cycled home to Muir of Ord, once from Achnashellach through Glen Uig and into Strath Conon, and on another occasion from Kintail through Gleann Lichd, Glen Affric and Strath Glass. Both of these trips involved sections pushing the bike and were done in the middle of winter, when the main problem (apart from shortage of daylight) is crossing swollen burns. In the absence of walking poles a carefully placed bike can give useful support. In summer 2004 I cycled from home and linked these two cross-country routes with a visit to Skye, by continuing from Kintail over the Mam Ratagan to the Glenelg ferry on the outward journey, returning on the boat that sailed from Portree to Gairloch for that summer only, then pedalling over the Coulin Pass from Glen Torridon to Achnashellach. Enjoying four nights out in my lightweight tent, the total budget for this trip was less than £10. Another trip that has been in the back of my mind for a long time is a version of the 'SMC Huts Route' as a circuit starting and finishing from home. Brian Davison had nurtured similar ideas, and his account[5]5 of various trials and tribulations before his eventual triumph prompts me to offer some tips in the light of my own experiences.

Some Tips

Most cycle rides into the hills will put serious stresses and strains on the bike, which should be of reasonable quality and well maintained. Brian sourced his bike from a skip, and while this was a commendable bit of recycling, failure was inevitable. Use an old bike for pottering around town, but get the best machine you can for serious trips. Apart from ex-hire bikes that have been regularly maintained, beware buying second-hand unless you can get some expert advice. New bikes are remarkably good value, and a proper bike shop will give good advice and occasional bargains. My trail bike is a 'hard tail' (i.e. front suspension only) with disc brakes and a very light aluminium frame. For mountain trips, however, I prefer a more old-fashioned machine with no suspension, centre-pull brakes and a steel frame. Fitted with wide tyres with a smooth ridge along the centre, this gives a much smoother ride on metalled roads and tracks, and it can cope with anything but the roughest ground.

A well-maintained machine always gives better service, so clean your bike after every trip and keep the moving parts well lubricated. Always carry a small repair kit. Even the toughest tyres will suffer the indignity of an occasional puncture, so a spare inner tube, tyre levers and a pump are essentials. There are remarkably small versions of pumps, along with

[5] 'Mama Mia' note in *SMCJ*, 38/195 (2004), 679–82.

astonishing multi-tool gadgets that take up little space and will sort most problems. The other essential is a helmet. On that final downhill run it is tempting to go as fast as possible, and accidents do happen. Some years ago, I had enjoyed a short trip from home up to the Orrin Reservoir and across the old hydro-board track to Erchless Castle in Strath Glass. On the home run, pedalling flat out along the smooth footpath beside the level and perfectly straight road between Beauly and Muir of Ord, for no obvious reason I suddenly found myself flying through the air, and was aware of the crack as my head hit the ground. Serious damage to the helmet but fortunately not my skull. Helmets are easily replaced, but without one my skull and the rest of me might never have been the same again. Always wear a helmet!

Hill clothing is ideal for cycling too, though once you start riding some serious trails and browsing in the bike shops you will quickly come to appreciate the benefits of specially made cycle gear: those padded shorts and jerseys with big pockets at the back will soon become indispensable. I usually wear lightweight hill-walking boots even if no hills are planned. Short sections where there is no alternative to getting off and pushing are invariably wet and muddy. On a multi-day summer trip consider carrying a pair of sandals to give your feet a chance to breathe and dry out on any long, hot road stages. Other exponents of such trips favoured lightweight trailers for a while, but the latest innovation described as 'bike-packing' involves very light and compact gear packed into glorified waterproofed stuff-sacks fastened to various parts of the bike. All this new gear is of course very expensive, and I have always managed with a pair of light traditional rear panniers for road and tracks, transferring my gear into a large lightweight rucksack for the roughest terrain.

Apart from following the Highway and Countryside Codes, there are no rules. Just go for it, but please fit a bell to your bike to warn walkers before passing.

BEHIND THE CURTAIN

by Dennis Gray

He paved the Paths of Peace
And helped to bridge the gulf that lay
Between the West and East,
That Climbers all might Brothers be
In the Kingdom of the Snow.
— Tom Patey, 'The Joe Brown Song'.

THE INVASION OF UKRAINE and the thinking behind the actions of Russia have come as a great shock to the present climbing world. In different countries activists are taking action, mainly raising funds and donating vital equipment to help those caught in the conflict. These events are less of a surprise to me, because I have been lucky to visit all the countries involved and know that the freedom climbers have enjoyed was hard won. Authoritarianism is the enemy of such freedom, and both Putin and Xi Jinping have expressed a belief that democracy should not be the modus of political systems.

I first encountered this view in the old Yugoslavia, which in terms of Soviet orthodoxy was relatively liberal but in 1964 was still ruled with an iron fist. My worst experience, however, was in East Germany in 1967, on the way to climb in the Polish Tatra. Britain had no consular relations with the DDR, and a visa to drive across that country had only a 24-hour duration. But I was travelling with Jim McArtney from Aberdeen, and Jim being a member of the British Communist Party wanted to travel around, to meet with 'the people' and to climb in the Elbe Valley. A group of students, whom we met at a campsite near Karl Marx Stadt, soon avowed to us that this was no worker's paradise, but we were surprised how many could speak English; although we were the first westerners they had met, they secretly listened to the BBC World Service. We quickly found that the climbs on the Elbe sandstone were the hardest we had ever tried, and we only managed a couple of the easier routes. When we arrived at the DDR's border with Poland we were in trouble, because it had taken us five days instead of the 24 hours permitted by our visa. We were sent back to Berlin, and the subsequent re-applying for another visa nearly landed us in jail after another meeting, with a Rosa Kleb of the state security police.

The Polish climbers in 1967 had more freedom than the people we had met in the DDR, and the Tatra Mountains were a beautiful range. Here was an ideal training ground in both summer and winter for those who within a few years would make stand-out climbs in the Himalaya – climbers with an incredible ability to turn state sponsorship of sport to their advantage.

We were a party of four in 1967. In addition to Jim and me, the other two were Jimmy McDowell from Glasgow and Tom Morrell, who had travelled in Tom's vehicle and finally met us at Zakopane, where they too had their tale to tell of Iron Curtain bureaucracy that had delayed their journey. After a month of climbing in the Tatra the other three departed to drive back to the UK, leaving me to carry out a national lecture tour in Zakopane, Krakow, Lodz, Warsaw and elsewhere. The leader of the mountain rescue team at Zakopane took me out for a drink of vodka after my talk, and showed me his hands. He had been arrested for some reason and under interrogation had had his fingernails pulled out! I was to find out on my lecture tour that many of the climbing fraternity were in the dissident movement. My interpreter was Tadeusz Jankowski, who had been injured as a boy fighting in the Warsaw uprising against the Nazi occupation, and I stayed in Warsaw with the only Jew in the then government of the country. She had grown up in the city's ghetto, and her family had all died in the uprising. Just a few months later came the Prague Spring movement, which led to the Soviet invasion of that city, and climbers in Poland were put on trial for supporting the insurrection, this becoming known as 'The Dissident Climbers' Trial'. Whilst I was in the south of Poland I visited the ruins of the Auschwitz concentration camp, and it was a signal experience for me; this was before it became a visited site, and nobody was there, but it gave a frightening illustration of how such an ideology could lead people to act.

It became a real cops-and-robbers dealing with any of the Warsaw Pact countries (the Soviet answer to NATO), but somehow relations were maintained. One of the people who managed to bridge this gap was a Russian *bon vivant*, mountaineer and sports physiologist, Eugene (or Yevgeniy) Gippenreiter. He figured big in arrangements such as the British visits to the Caucasus in 1958 and the Pamirs in 1962 (the infamous 'Red Pique' expedition), and I kept meeting him in really unusual situations. I came across him on a visit to the Alpine Club when he was acting as the interpreter to the Bolshoi ballet who were in town, and when I was at Bisham Abbey he was there with a Soviet team. But the most surprising encounter was in the Salzburger Alpen; when Michael Butler and I arrived at one of the huts, who should be there but Eugene?

We were old friends by then, but as we sat drinking a beer two ancient-looking climbers appeared and spoke to Gippenreiter in Russian. At first I thought they too must be Russians, but it transpired they were from Vienna. Their story, which we learned from Eugene who translated for us, was that they had been members of the commune in that city in the 1920s and had fled to the Caucasus. They had gone there because they were mountaineers, and over the next decade they made many first ascents in the range. But in the 1930s they suffered persecution because of their nationality, and eventually retreated to Austria. Now they had come to discuss with Gippenreiter their first ascents of routes in the Caucasus, for in a recently published climbing guide to the range, all of their climbs had been credited to Soviet climbers. 'Is this true?' I asked Eugene. 'I'm afraid so,' was his reply 'but there is nothing that can be done about it!'

Over a period of 20 years I visited Bulgaria and climbed in its Rila mountains; went to the Bükk mountains of Hungary; and visited Romania, which was as regimented as the DDR, and subsequently Ukraine and Siberia. For climbing, my several trips to Czechoslovakia stand out.

On any visit to an Iron Curtain country one needed to be careful. In 1984 I was in Prague attending meetings and staying in the inevitable party hotel, *The Red Star*, where one had to be wary of not being compromised. One night the meetings I was attending were over, and I had time to kill until my flight back to the UK. In the bar were several svelte women, and they were asking that I buy them a drink. But also in the bar was Pietro Segantini, the Swiss doctor, mountaineer, and ice hockey player, and the grandson of a famous painter of the Swiss Alps. 'Whatever you do, do not take any of them up to your room,' he advised. 'Some of our Swiss ice hockey team did so last year, and when they arrived home comprising pictures circulated of them.'

Knowing that there was good rock-climbing just north of Prague in the Bohemian Paradise, I asked the meeting's organiser if there was any chance I could go there to climb. And that is how I left the next morning with Jiří Novák, the photographer and climber, heading in his ancient Lada for a cliff named the Suché Skály. It was March and very cold and snowing. I had been warned that Jiří did not speak English, but once clear of Prague he spoke to me in excellent English, a secret that at that time he kept to himself where the authorities were concerned. I was worried that we would not be able to climb, for I knew that the locals did not do so when it was wet, the rock being sandstone. 'We will be alright, for the cliff we are going to climb on overhangs so much it never gets wet!' He was right, and despite the blizzard conditions we managed two impressive routes on the Suché Skály, which takes the form of a large concave wall. After climbing we drove around the area, which lies about 60 miles north of Prague, and I saw its many towers and pinnacles and learned that the first routes there were climbed as long ago as 1888.

Prague was then a ferment of anti-Soviet reaction. In the evenings I visited a coffee house and jazz club in Wenceslas Square, and after a few visits I gained the trust of a few of the locals. They wanted more freedom, to travel and to make contact with western countries; I could have made a fortune if I had been selling jeans. There were no tourists in Prague in March 1984, and yet one could find plenty to interest one, the Senefelder Museum having a particular attraction for me because Alois Senefelder had discovered the secret of lithography. I returned to Czechoslovakia in 1987, to the Adršpach region which boasts over 1000 sandstone towers. A mountain film festival is held every summer there, and the climbing is amongst the best I have been lucky enough to enjoy. Czech climbers have developed unique methods to climb on these sandstone towers, where the routes are protected by knotted slings, threads and ring-bolts that serve as hanging belays. The most frightening challenge was the leaps from pinnacle to pinnacle: these are graded 1 to 4 and I only ever managed a Grade 1. A Grade 4 leap would be a credit to any Olympic long-jump champion, with the possibility of a serious injury. Footgear was another surprise to me, as the Czechs climbed in carpet slippers with the rubber from car tyres glued to the soles, and it was impressive the routes they had pioneered wearing these so-called *bačkory*.

In 1988, along with the orthopaedic surgeon Steve Bollen, I was invited to a medical conference in Prague. Steve and I were fairly regular climbing partners at that time, and our task was to chair sessions at this event. Inevitably all the overseas delegates were staying once again at *The Red Star*, and the first evening became something of a drink-fest, for there was unlimited wine but little or no food. For some reason the organisers had forgotten to provide this, and my abiding memory of the evening is of a contingent of Soviet space scientists, who were presenting papers at the conference, drinking the red wine as if it were water and complaining about the lack of vodka. Once the meeting was over, Steve and I flew to Bratislava to take up an invitation from Slovakian climbers who had visited the UK the previous year, to come to their country.

In Bratislava we stayed at the flat of Svetozár Poláček's mother, who was a doctor. Svetozár had been a member of a group visiting Britain and had amazed the local Peak District climbers by soloing *Downhill Racer* and *Oedipus* at Frogatt Edge whilst wearing his *bačkory*. With Alan, a climbing companion of Sveto, at the wheel of his mother's car we drove

A Czech climber wearing improvised 'bačkory' on steep sandstone. Photo: Jiří Novák.

the next day the many kilometres across Slovakia to the Zadiel gorge. This valley with limestone cliffs aplenty contains The Sugar Cone, a spectacular pinnacle hundreds of feet high. We climbed this by the original route, and though the easiest line it was still a difficult climb. That night we stayed with a local activist, a woman climber who had a flat in a housing development in nearby Košice. During the evening more and more climbers arrived and a sociable atmosphere developed, until 13 bodies eventually bedded down on the floor of this tiny flat.

The next day we drove nearly to the border with Ukraine and climbed on an escarpment high above the valley. Steve and I had brought a pair of modern rock-boots as a gift for Sveto, and wearing these he led me up routes until I had to tell him I could not manage another climb. At this point he set off and soloed several other routes, all of which looked hard. In the valley below us was a large building, and as we climbed we could hear strains of music, but every so often this was broken by a loud scream. 'What is happening?' I ventured to enquire of Alan, who spoke excellent English. 'It will be someone whom the authorities have arrested and are torturing for a confession!' Alan was obviously a dissident and was more than unhappy about this, so it was no surprise when a few years later he contacted me from Canada to where he had emigrated.

When we returned to Bratislava Steve had to fly back to UK, whilst I stayed on to do some climbing with Sveto and Alan north of the city. We were at a line of limestone cliffs of Peak District dimensions on the border with Austria, which was set about by blockhouses and manned by armed men in uniforms. Laughingly Alan told me about a climbing friend who had dived off the top of one of the crags, tied to a hang-glider, and despite being shot at had made it to freedom in the West. Alan led me up a climb that until recently had been the hardest in the country. I confess to falling off it several times before being successful on the end of a very tight rope, alarmed by Sveto soloing behind me. The final day I was with them in Bratislava we climbed on a 40-foot crag that lay within the city, and on their version of a climbing wall – a bunker from the war in which holds had been fashioned. Next day we said our goodbyes after an evening of celebration at the best restaurant in town; although I was paying I found it very cheap. I was never to see Sveto again. A short while after my visit he was killed in a freak accident whilst repairing the roof on his mother's building. He remains one of the best rock-climbers I have ever tied on to.

The war between Russia and Ukraine cannot have any kind of good outcome, and we are left to wonder at the sanity of the Russians and how the clock is being turned back to the years of the Cold War. What have we climbers to learn from our friends in countries where although political systems intrude on their freedoms they somehow always manage to continue climbing? When young I read with great admiration modern Russian poets, who were writing at a time when their country was ruled with an iron fist and no one was allowed to criticise the system; but somehow despite these threats the poets persisted. I remember Don

Whillans telling me that Yevgeny Yevtushenko turned up at their camp in Patagonia, carrying an ancient ice-axe. Yevtushenko was a modern Russian poet I admired, whose heart-rending *Babi Yar* concerns the Nazi atrocities at a valley near Kyiv where over 100,000 people were shot, 34,000 of them Jews, in two days in 1941. But it brought him nothing but disapproval when it was first published: he was suspended from the Soviet writer's federation, and was berated by Khrushchev, the leader of the country at that time. He was still not in favour when Shostakovich wrote his 13th Symphony, based on this poem. And yet somehow he overcame all this, becoming a revered professor in both the USA and Moscow, so we have to hope that eventually such will happen again in Russia, and that the present terrible situation may be resolved according to the Ukrainian people's wishes.

NEW ROUTES

The simplest way to submit a new route is to use the proforma at <https://www.smcnewroutes.org.uk> . This preferred method will input the route description directly into a holding area of our database. The route will then be checked and verified, and you will receive an email confirming receipt of the description and whether it covers new ground. The proforma can accept multiple route descriptions. (For an overview of the database, see Roger Everett's note on page 285 of this issue.)

Alternatively, send an email to the New Routes Editor at newroutes@smc.org.uk. Please ensure the description includes information in the following order: area, crag, route name, length, grade, suggested stars, first ascensionist(s), date, route description. Please include first names of first ascensionists.

Submission of diagrams and topos is strongly encouraged. These are kept on file for future guidebook authors.

The cost of publishing the New Routes Section in the Journal is supported by the Scottish Mountaineering Trust. Their continuing support is gratefully acknowledged.

The deadline for sending route descriptions for the 2023 Journal is 31 May 2023.

The Editor, the New Routes Editor and the other SMC members involved in collating route descriptions can accept no liability for personal injury or death arising directly or indirectly from use of this publication.

OUTER HEBRIDES

ISLE OF LEWIS
Rubha Sith – Searraich Wall, Recessed Slabs Area
Looking for Lucy   25m   VS 5a.   Dave Porter, Simon White. 4 Sep 2021.
Follow the thin crack-line up the slab between *Close Knit* and *Slippery When Wet*. Finish directly up the centre of the final easy slab.

Geodha an Taroin (Taron Meallach), South-West Wall
Koala Copout   30m   HVS 5a *.   Daniel Moore, Anna Fleming, Zoe Strong. 1 Aug 2020.
From the good pedestal halfway up *Copper Koala* before that route steepens (possible belay) follow the obvious left-trending line up past an obvious dubious protruding block (if it's still there). Climb a short steep wall to the top.

Àird Mhòr, Seal Bay
Iain Thow notes that he climbed *The Great Pretender* on 3 Oct 2003, which predates the first ascent recorded in the 'Outer Hebrides' guidebook. 'I thought was the classic *Sunset Rib* (Diff). It's a good name – maybe the pair who recorded it made the same mistake? I wouldn't mind it being added to the record as it's a cracking route.' Iain later wrote: 'Noel Williams tells me that he and a bunch of others from Lochaber MRT climbed that rib in 1987, also under the impression that it was *Sunset Rib*. The name is definitely appropriate!'

Àird Mhòr Crag
(NB 192 452) Alt 50m East facing
A small crag to the east of Àird Mhòr.
Approach: Park at Na Gearrannan Blackhouse Village and follow the Coastal
Path north. The cliff lies on the eastern flank of Àird Mhòr.
Descent: There is an easy walk off on the northern side.

The Lewis Midge 10m Severe 4a *. Gwilym Lynn, Aled Lynn, Bethan Lynn. 3
Jul 2021.
The obvious line to the right of centre following a line of shallow corners. (Topo
provided.)

Dalbeg – Àird Dalbeg, Small West Wall
Pop and Drop 10m VS 4c *. Jonathan Preston, Sarah Atkinson. 30 Aug 2021.
Climb the hanging corner-crack left of *Ready Salted* and *Pringles*.

Ready Salted 10m VS 4c *. Jonathan Preston, Sarah Atkinson. 30 Aug 2021.
The corner left of *Pringles*. The 'Outer Hebrides' guidebook description for
Pringles says 'the corner at the extreme left end is often wet'. We found it
completely dry and climbed it.
Gain the corner awkwardly from below and climb it to the top. (The only bit of
gear found to protect the initial moves was a DMM 7 offset).

Dalbeg North, Solus Wall
The following route lies on the attractive brown wall slightly north of Solus Wall
at Dalbeg. This wall faces west and is high above the water, useful on a day with
a big swell. When viewed from the Solus Wall side the cliff looks impressive, but
is smaller and lower-angled when viewed from the north.

Capstan Medium 20m VS 4b *. Peter Riley, Jane Gallwey. 15 Jul 2021.
Climb the obvious right-hand crack line, starting from the broken mid-height
ledge. Well-protected and good positions for VS. The starting ledge is a bit
shattered and care should be taken with scree. There are several other nice-looking
lines between HS to E1 on the wall, but the first ascensionists only did the one
due to high winds.

Shawbost (Siabost), Rubha Bratag, The Orpheus Wall
Gary Latter notes (April 2022) that there has been a rockfall on the left side of
the crag affecting the lower section of *Sirens of the Sea*. It looks as if there is still
some loose rock remaining, so it would benefit from a quick abseil clean.

Dùn Othail, Grey Tower
Jane Gallwey notes that *Druid* has suffered a rockfall and may not be now worth
three stars. The main rockfall is to the right of the route but there is still hanging
debris in the corner. Her party abseiled off after one pitch rather than climb
through the blocks. The E1 to the right is unaffected.

The Uig Hills
Griomabhal View Crag
(NB 00616 22649) Alt 180m South facing

This is the crag mentioned on p192 of the The Outer Hebrides guide. It is superbly situated with an outlook to both ocean and Griomabhal. The crag faces south and is at the back of a small amphitheatre. Approximately 40 minutes from the road end. The crag is sheltered and quick-drying with descents either side. The rock varies from perfect rough brown gneiss to a firm but more massive crystalline quartz slab halfway along the face. Routes are described from right to left. (Topo provided.)

Approach: Park at the end of the road as described for the Tealasdail Slabs and either head towards the small Dubh Loch or, quicker, climb up behind the turning area at the end of the road and follow a shallow glen up and right past a small ruin to reach a crest in 30 minutes or so.

Original Route 25m V.Diff *. First ascent unknown.
A full description of the V.Diff. mentioned on p192 of 'Outer Hebrides'. The longest climb here. Start by a crack and shallow left-facing corner and climb this to the top tier which is taken by a good left-facing groove.

Original Route Direct 25m Severe. First ascent unknown.
A full description of the VS mentioned on p192 of 'Outer Hebrides'. With blinkers firmly in place, ignore easier options and climb the brown slab to the right of the normal start and climb a bulge above to finish up the good groove of the parent route.

Perfectly Brown 20m MVS 4c *. John Mackenzie, Eve Mackenzie. 2 Jul 2021.
To the left of the *Original Route* is a lovely brown slab split by a narrow crack. Climb to and up the well-protected crack and go straight up the bulge at the top.

Deception Crack 20m VS 4c *. John Mackenzie, Eve Mackenzie. 2 Jul 2021.
To the left of *Perfectly Brown* is a straight crack that is more tricky than it looks. Climb the crack and the twin-cracked bulge above with some entertaining moves.

Quartz Delight 15m VS 4c *. John Mackenzie, Eve Mackenzie. 2 Jul 2021.
The quartz slab to the left has a pod of moss low in a crack. Start left of this, climb a slab and gain then follow a shallow left-facing corner. Above this make a thin move right to reach the top section of the moss-podded crack and finish up this. Some spaced protection but this makes the best use of the slab.

Suaineabhal, Euscleit Mòr
Holiday Arête 20m V.Diff *. Gwilym Lynn, Aled Lynn, Patrick Urwin. 28 Jun 2021.
Climb the arête to the left of the grassy gully.

Peat Cutter's Crag
(NB 06224 30392) Alt 50m East facing
A convenient, quick-drying east-facing crag of perfect gneiss. The routes are described from left to right. (Topo provided.)
Approach: Park at the water treatment works above Loch Suaineabhal, marked 'works' on the 1:50:000 map, which is a little further on than that for Euscleit Mòr. The crag is a 5-minute walk along the track beyond the 'works'.

Ready   25m   V.Diff. John Mackenzie, Eve Mackenzie. 28 Jun 2021.
The horizontally cracked rib on the left side of the face. Start by a diagonal crack and step right to a short groove and slabs to finish.

Steady   22m   H.Severe 4b **. John Mackenzie, Eve Mackenzie. 28 Jun 2021.
Takes the centre of the face cutting through a scoop and mantelshelf to finish by a thin crack. Sustained and very good.

Go   25m   VS 4c *. John Mackenzie, Eve Mackenzie. 28 Jun 2021.
To the right is an undercut wall with diagonal cracks above. Climb the wall direct to the cracks. Move up left to a bigger diagonal crack to reach a heather-filled one. Move right below this to reach and climb a prominent thin crack to the top. Quite sustained with varied climbing.

HARRIS (NA HEARADH)
Horgabost Slab
(NG 044 965)
Less than 5 minutes from the A859 on South Harris, west of Seilebost, is a clean gneiss slab between 8 and 10m long. There are three lines.

Route 1   10m   H.Severe 4b. Charles White, John Mackenzie. 2017.
On the left via the scoop.

Route 2   10m   VS 4c. Charles White, John Mackenzie. 2017.
Up just left of the scoop.

Route 3   10m   H.Severe 4b. Charles White, John Mackenzie. 2017.
Climb right of the scoop.

BARRA (BARRAIGH)
Beinn Chliaid
(NF 6784 0425) Alt 206m
West Buttress   80m   V.Diff. Mark Hudson. 10 Aug 2021.
Two tiers of slabby ribs high on the west flank of Beinn Chliaid (NF 675 047, west-facing) are easily visible from the road. Steep starts to both tiers are followed by cleaner scrambling. A mantel over a jutting lip 8m up the higher rib provides the main difficulty.

Àird Ghrèin, Creag Eilean Eun Beaga
The taller central wall, between the routes *Linking Corners* and *Gaining the Corner*, has a number of striking features, and the following routes take the central and right-hand weaknesses.

Mucker   20m   E2 5c *. Nicola Bassnett, Mark Hudson. 8 Aug 2021.
Climb cracks in the centre of the wall, finishing through a steeper channel at the top.

Oppo   20m   HVS 5b **. Nicola Bassnett, Mark Hudson. 10 Aug 2021.
A striking crack 3m right, arising from a left-facing scooped corner, followed by a steep wall above. This route lies 2m left of *Gaining the Corner*.

The next routes lie on walls right 50m to the right or east, easily accessed via the descent scramble through that area.

Civvy Street   15m   Severe. Mark Hudson, Nicola Bassnett. 8 Aug 2021.
Start about 5m below a huge boulder jammed across the grassy descent rake, by stepping over the deep sea-slot onto the wall. Climb up and gently left past a break to finish up a pleasant rib above.

The Civilian   25m   VS *. Mark Hudson, Nicola Bassnett. 10 Aug 2021.
A diagonal right-rising traverse, taking a line of huge blocky steps across the steeper wall right again. Step over the sea slot as for *Civvy Street* and traverse right to belay in a wet corner niche – calm seas only. Bridge up and out of the niche on sharp flakes to gain the easier but committing line of blocks that cross the wall on huge holds.

Cottage Slab   20m   V.Diff. Mark Hudson. 10 Aug 2021.
A tall south-facing brown slab (NF 652 049) 200m NW of Greian Head Cottage above a bouldery cove. Scramble down from the south to gain the slab from sea-level (low tide needed), stepping in from the right by a cave. Stay central higher up, or take the better-protected left-hand crest at Diff. A steeper direct start to the crest can be made up walls round to the left of the nose.

Rock Island Area, Hot Wall Continuation
Moonrise   20m   HVS 5a **. Nathan Adam (solo). 25 Jun 2021.
Left of *Sunset* the crag turns to face north. This route takes a black groove in the north wall. Climb the groove on thin jams with poor feet until it blanks out. Make a reach rightwards to another crack and pull out of the groove. Go up and slightly left before finishing direct.

Hot Wall
Black Bara Blues   18m   VS 4c *. Kevin Howett, Martin Forsyth, Gordon Grant. 21 May 2022.
Start between *Sunspot* and *Sundae* and climb a direct line crossing *Sundae* up the blankest section of rock on the wall.

Kevin Howett suggests that *Sunspot* is H.Severe 4a and *Barrahamas* Severe 4a.

Ice Cream Gully Wall
Mr Whippy, Right-Hand   15m   E1 5a **. Nathan Adam, Nicholas Wylie. 25 Jun 2021.
A more consistent finish to the original line and gives a fully independent route at a similar standard, avoiding the almost identical pitch 2 finish to *Hot Fudge Sundae*. Step right from the belay for 2m until below a steep shallow groove. Climb this on good holds and flakes to a corner-crack running back left. Take the steep crack immediately right of this and then trend slightly left to the top.

Cream Shots   30m   HVS 5a ***. Nathan Adam, Nicholas Wylie. 25 Jun 2021.
This lies on the previously unclimbed south-facing black wall to the right of other routes here. The rock is mostly excellent and well-covered in jugs, cracks and pockets. It is sheltered in a big northerly swell, while waves crashing over the island and pushing into the back of the geo makes for exciting situations. Right

of *Hot Fudge Sundae* the wall changes direction and steepens. Start from a small spike belay above a flake ledge some 5m right of the platform at the base of *Hot Fudge Sundae* (this point can be reached by easy climbing from the platform or more conveniently by abseil). Superb and well-protected. Traverse right for 2m and go up to a small left-facing flake corner, climb this and mantel delicately onto a small ledge with a blank wall above. Continue right and up to a good ledge. Climb the bulging wall above direct on excellent holds and finish via a thin crack to the top.

Nathan Adam notes that *Mr Whippy* is nowhere near the E3 6a given in the 'Outer Hebrides' guidebook and he thought it generous at E2 5b. It is steep but with excellent holds and good gear. Worth three stars when combined with the right-hand finish. The route lengths quoted in the 'Outer Hebrides' also seem over-estimated: from the shared belay of *Mr Softee* and *Mr Whippy* it is only around 25 to 30m to the top of the crag.

Feudail, Right-Hand Crag
Sundew Left 20m H.Severe *. Mark Hudson. Nicola Bassnett. 13 Aug 2021.
This gains and climbs the hanging flakes referred to in the guidebook to the left of *Suicidal Sundew*. Start as for that route but climb straight up a wall past two horizontal seams to a sloping shelf, then take the steeper hanging flakes above and left to a rounded finish.

SANDRAY (SANNDRAIGH)
The Rune Stones Cliff, Lifeline Wall
Love Jugs 15m HVS/E1 5a **. Nathan Adam (solo). 17 Jun 2021.
Start 1m right of *Mystic Smeg* at a big juggy hold. Campus off the ground and climb direct through orange streaks to *Border Reiver*. Pull right and go steeply up the bulging wall above on good horizontal breaks leading to an easy finish.

Starboard 60m VS 5a *. Nathan Adam (solo). 22 Jun 2021.
A girdle traverse of the Rune Stone Cliff. Start up *Agent Orange*, traverse rightwards and climb to reach the upper of the two black horizontal bands. Follow this (with hands in it) across the entire wall, belay where appropriate. Either finish up *Lifeline* or step right again and up *The Future Is Now*.

Creag Beag, The Destiny Walls, Ripple Buttress
Seals the Same 40m E1 5b *. Nathan Adam, Nicholas Wylie. 20 Jun 2021.
A right-hand partner to *Seal Surfing In The Swell From Hell,* roughly following the abseil line. Step right from the belay ledge and climb the corner to a small roof. Pull left through this and delicately up the wall rightwards (crux) into another corner. Go up this to a second roof and climb past it via a small crack which leads to the flake crack on *Seal Surfing*. Follow this to a ledge and then take the wide crack above through the hairy wall to the top.

PABBAY
Rubha Chàrnain, Small Buoys Geo
Black Wand 10m E4 6a S1. Crispin Waddy. 21 Jun 2021.
On the steep side of the geo, near the seaward end, is a very striking short steep black arête. A really good climb up a stunning feature, although short. Start on a ledge left of the arête. Traverse right to the very edge of the arête and climb this

(crux) to an easing. 'It's got plenty of water beneath the crux with a decent tide, though there's a rock behind you on the first traverse so jumping wildly backwards wouldn't be clever, so it's worth taking a bit of care there, though to be honest I'm sure a typical fall would be fine with a good tide.'

An Tobha, The Grey Wall Recess
Stag-up   50m   E4 6a/b *. Jamie Skelton, Tim Miller 15 May 2022.
Climb *E-up*'s first pitch up the corner (good climbing and pretty tough at the grade). Rather than following the second pitch around the arête, tackle the well-protected overhanging crack and wall directly above the belay ledge. Continue up easy ground to the terrace below the Pink Wall.

Rubha Greotach, The Banded Geo
Gary Latter notes that *Redemption Ark* is described in the wrong place in the 'Outer Hebrides' guidebook. It lies at the far right end of the wall, (not left), down and right of the South Face. *Parting Shot*, the earlier unfinished line, was climbed by the same team – Steve Crowe and Karin Magog.

The Poop Deck
Distant Gods   12m   HVS 5a S0. Crispin Waddy. 20 Jun 2021.
On the right side there is an obvious groove above the sea with a small ledge at its base (accessible by abseil at high tide). Climb a smaller groove to the left of the main one.

Faded Signs.   12m   E3 6a S0. Crispin Waddy. 20 Jun 2021.
From the base of the main groove right of *Distant Gods*, step right and head diagonally up the wall to a shield of rock. Pull onto this and exit rightwards.

The Great Arch
Gary Latter notes that *The Great Arch* was climbed by Steve McLure with one fall in in 2010 (not 2012).

MINGULAY (MIÙGHLAIGH)
Rubha Liath
The Gèarum Walls
Gary Latter notes that the lines of 9 *Horizontal Hamish* and 10 *Hot Enough for Ya?* have been transposed on the topo. The former starts from the right end of the ledge at one-third height, as does 12 *Little Miss Sunshine*. Only 10 *Hot Enough for Ya?* starts from the lower ledge; also, this is probably closer to 20m than 30m. There is a route *The Singing Seal*, 15m E1 5b ** (FA Janet Horrocks, Claudia Birmelin 13 May 1999) omitted; it lies between 19 *Big Sea in My Trousers* and 20 *Screaming Seal.*

Seal Song Wall, The Corners Area
The Meat Injection   30m   HVS 5b ***. David Wood, Nathan Adam. 15 Jul 2021.
The off-width chimney between *Swell-Time* and *Sun-Dew* gives a classic and well protected struggle. Back-and-foot into the squeeze box and squirm until a big ledge on the left is gained. Step right into a left-facing corner and finish up this to a big platform and easy ground leading to the top.

Dun Mingulay, Sròn an Dùin

Gary Latter considers *The Lobster Man* to be definitely E4 6a and much harder than the other E3s here. As noted by Steve Crowe in the 2010 *SMCJ*, *The Swell* is a longer and improved version of his own route *Oceanside Expedition* – he thought the route to be superb, therefore deserving more than one star.

Arnamul Wall

Arnamul vs Predator 80m E2 5b **. James Milton, Sophie Jacobs. 11 Jul 2021.
An alternative top pitch to *Arnamul Magic* that avoids the birds' nests.
1. 35m 5b As for *Arnamul Magic*.
2. 45m 5b From the *Arnamul Magic* belay traverse right along the ledge to a large but short left-facing corner below the left end of the large roof. Climb the corner and then twin cracks directly to the roof that caps the right-hand side of the wall. Pull through the left side of the roof and finish up easy ground above. (Topo provided.)

Don't Play With Wild Arnamuls 85m E1 5b ***. James Milton, Sophie Jacobs. 15 Jul 2021.
Right of *Kraken's Gullet* is a line of weakness going straight up the crag.
1. 40m 5b Climb directly up to a gap in the roof right of *Kraken's Gullet*. Climb into the niche and exit to the right into cracks and a corner above. Continue up a series of corners trending slightly left to belay on the large ledge.
2. 35m 5a From the belay, traverse the ledge 3m left to reach a right-facing corner directly below the large nose of rock on the wall above. Climb the corner above then a series of jugs to beneath the nose of rock. From here traverse hard left through the overlap onto a ledge. Climb up and left to reach a larger ledge and belay above.
3. 10m Climb easy ground to reach the top of the crag. (Topo provided.)

Guarsay Mòr, The South Pillar

Fisherman's Direct 105m E2 5b **. Nathan Adam, David Wood. 10 Jul 2021.
Good climbing going straight through the steep bulging wall left of the guano belay ledge at the end of the original crux pitch.
1. 35m 4c As for the original line.
2. 40m 5b Climb the regular route past its crux. Where the shallow groove goes rightwards, step up and left to the base of the roof. Undercling leftwards until the roof can be breached. Climb through this with difficulty then continue up slightly right to a good foot ledge.
3. 30m 5a Directly above is a cracked groove. Climb this to a small roof and avoid it on the right and go up to below a steep wall. This would provide a good finish but impending darkness necessitated a long traverse left to finish as per the last section of *The Gangplank*.

INNER HEBRIDES AND ARRAN

CANNA
Cnoc Mòr Crags, The Fortress, Left Wing

Lorcail 20m E3 5c. Jamie Skelton, Morag Eagleson. 7 May 2021.
Follow the twin cracks just right of *The Somme* to a depression, then climb onto

the pinnacle on the left. Continue up the crack and move right around the protruding block to a loose finish.

Carasgor
(NG 2247 0607) Partly tidal north-east to north-west facing
Very well protected 15-20m routes on great rock. Bullet-hard basalt cracks and grooves that require both jamming and bridging skills. The main crag has a non-tidal platform below it made up of hexagonal columns at differing heights. The platform may become wave-washed in really rough sea states. The rock is fast-drying but some routes can suffer from some seepage after heavy bouts of rain.
Approach: The fastest way to approach Carasgor and the other crags on the west side of Canna is to cycle along to the end of the Tarbert road, which takes about 20 minutes. It will take at least double this on foot. From the end of the road pass through some gated fields and across the hillside aiming for a burn leading down to the coast at NG 2269 0570. Follow the burn down, picking up a small path at the bottom that leads up and along the top of the cliffs to the west and the crag. A 40-minute walk from the end of the Tarbert road. When approaching keep an eye out for a nose of rock that points towards the sea and a pointed block at the top of the cliff. From the pointed block a short abseil can be made to reach the non-tidal ledge of the main buttress.

Dino Buttress
About 30m further east from the main crag is an attractive wall with a big boulder at its top. The ledge at the bottom of the buttress is only accessible at low tide. The buttress suffers some seepage; there may be potential for further development after a dry spell.

Dino Strikes Again   20m   HVS 5a **. Morag Eagleson, Jamie Skelton. 13 May 2021.
Start in the middle of the wall a few metres right of a big ledge or platform. Climb cracks and face-holds up the pleasant wall to where the angle eases. Step right and climb the flake crack with difficulty to the top.

Dino Strikes Crack finish   20m   HVS 5a. Morag Eagleson, Jamie Skelton. 13 May 2021.
The obvious direct finish through the steep crack.

Main Crag
Sea Beard   18m   HVS 5b *. Jamie Skelton, Morag Eagleson. 10 May 2021.
The furthest route left (east). Start by climbing a short technical crack (crux) to reach a big ledge. Continue up the more straightforward crack above

Carasgor   18m   E1 5b ***. Jamie Skelton, Morag Eagleson. 10 May 2021.
Excellent sustained climbing. Start up the steep groove just right of *Sea Beard*. This leads to a pod and overhang to pass at two-thirds height and the cracked headwall above.

Supercrack of the Sea   18m   HVS 5a **. Jamie Skelton, Morag Eagleson. 9 Sep 2020.
Just before the ledge at the base of the crag gains its full height is another attractive groove. Climb the slowly widening crack.

A Man and His Crocs   16m   E2 5c *. Jamie Skelton, Morag Eagleson. 9 Sep 2020.
The furthest route left once on the top of the non-tidal platform. Tricky climbing up the thin crack and shallow groove (small gear useful). Once over a small bulge the angle eases slightly and the twin cracks just right of *Supercrack of the Sea* can be enjoyed to the top.

Crocs and Glory   16m   E2 5c *. Jamie Skelton, Morag Eagleson. 9 Sep 2020.
Another good route but very similar to the previous one. Start a metre to the right, in a similar groove that leads to more twin cracks.

Soggy Bottom Boys   15m   VS 4c ***. Jamie Skelton, Morag Eagleson. 9 Sep 2020.
The ledge increases in height here. Climb the twin cracks leading to a bulge and a left-facing corner-crack that leads to the top of the crag.

Seal on Sunday   16m   VS 4c. Jamie Skelton, Morag Eagleson. 13 May 2021.
Start up *Soggy Bottom Boys* but traverse out right once at the top of the twin cracks. Climb the wide overhanging crack to reach easier ground.

Croc'in Out   16m   E3 6a. Jamie Skelton, Morag Eagleson. 13 May 2021.
A tricky step across from the right gains access to the groove just right of *Soggy Bottom Boys*. Follow this to a ledge and continue up the recessed twin cracks.

Eight Gates   17m   E3 5c **. Jamie Skelton, Morag Eagleson. 12 May 2021.
Good punchy climbing up the curving crack leading to the same ledge and recessed twin cracks that lead to the top.

Rocketman   17m   E1 5b *. Jamie Skelton, Morag Eagleson. 9 Sep 2020.
Round the corner is a widening crack line. It's easiest to start the route by traversing in from the right side of the crack.

Switch Buttress
A little further west from the main crag. A 60m abseil rope will just get you to the base of the climbs from a large pointed boulder a very long way back from the cliff edge.

Switching It Up   22m   E4 5c. Jamie Skelton, Morag Eagleson. 12 May 2021.
The furthest route left on this part of the crag. Another attractive groove leads to an overhanging crack near the top, climbed on its right side with blind, hard-to-place gear.

Flipping the Switch   22m   E5 6a **. Jamie Skelton, Morag Eagleson. 10 May 2021.
Just left of the large corner of *The Switch* lies a steep smooth groove split by a hairline crack which offers great climbing. Bridge, smear and contort up the groove until it's possible to swing out left onto good holds on the arête and gain a rest below another steepening. Move right and finish as for *The Switch*.

The Switch   22m   E2 5c ***. Jamie Skelton, Morag Eagleson. 13 May 2021.
The corner crack is brilliant but it does seep after rain. Bouldery sections between good rests.

SANDAY
Sputain

Duck n' Roll 12m VS 4b. Morag Eagleson, Jamie Skelton. 8 May 2021.
This bold climb is tucked out of sight on the far-right side of the main buttress.
Climb easily to ledges below the right-facing corner, which provides the crux and
some small fiddly gear.

The Last Rat 6m HVS 5c *. Morag Eagleson, Jamie Skelton. 8 May 2021.
The crack and groove below and left of the nose-shaped roof.

Canna Cattle 6m Severe 4a. Jamie Skelton, Morag Eagleson. 8 May 2021.
Just right of *The Last Rat* is a shallow corner with twin cracks.

Zwartbles 6m H.Severe 4b. Morag Eagleson, Jamie Skelton. 8 May 2021.
The set of twin cracks in the area of yellow rock.

RÙM
Meall Breac, Coire Dubh, Speckled Wall
(NM 387 980) Alt 350m East facing
A prominent, east-facing buttress on the east side of Meall Breac in the upper
reaches of Coire Dubh, featuring an area of south-facing slabs higher on the left.
The main wall extends right from an obvious roof near the left end towards a more
extensive area and provides a number of worthwhile routes. Routes are described
from left to right.

Finnock 8m Diff. *. Steve Kennedy, Colin Moody. 21 May 2021.
The open groove running up the left side of the large roof.

School Peel 8m H.Severe *. Steve Kennedy, Colin Moody. 21 May 2021.
The right side of the roof. Make moves over the bulge at the right end then up the
slab above.

Herling 14m Severe 3c *. Steve Kennedy, Colin Moody. 21 May 2021.
Moving right from the roof, the crag increases in height towards a ramp line
leading up rightwards. This route follows the ramp. Unprotected.

Whitling 14m VS 4b *. Steve Kennedy, Colin Moody. 21 May 2021.
Climb the basalt fault just right of *Herling*.

Sewin 16m HVS 4c *. Steve Kennedy, Colin Moody. 21 May 2021.
This route climbs the wall right of *Whitling*, roughly in the centre. Start at a short
right-facing corner about 3m left of a right-slanting fault. Climb the corner to a
ledge, step right into a small alcove, then directly up the wall above. Sparsely
protected. A spare rope is useful as the belay is well back.

Ferox 16m HVS 4c **. Steve Kennedy, Colin Moody. 21 May 2021.
Start 4m right of *Sewin* at the foot of a right-trending fault. Climb the fault to a
pedestal on the right. Step left and climb the wall above, passing a small bulge.

Charr 17m VS 4c *. Steve Kennedy, Colin Moody. 21 May 2021.
The quartz fault leading rightwards about 4m right of *Ferox*. Climb the fault to a

ledge below the top wall. From the right end of the fault pull onto the wall and finish up leftwards.

The following routes lie on the slabs above and left of the roof at the left end of the main crag. There are two areas separated by a large grassy bay. The lowest slab contains a number of short cracks and grooves and a variety of nice lines can be taken at about V.Diff. to Severe. The upper slab has an overhung alcove in the centre and offers the following routes, described right to left as per the approach.

Brook   18m   Severe 4a *.   Steve Kennedy, Colin Moody. 21 May 2021.
About 5m right of the alcove is a crack running vertically up the slab just left of a rounded edge. Climb the edge, always right of the crack.

Tiger   18m   Severe 4a *.   Steve Kennedy, Colin Moody. 21 May 2021.
Start just left of *Brook* and climb a small bulge leading to the crack.

Golden   15m   Severe 4a *.   Steve Kennedy, Colin Moody. 21 May 2021.
Start about 5m left of *Tiger* at a large flat boulder below a corner and two small roofs. Climb the corner next to the roofs and the continuation crack above.

Brown   15m   H.Severe 4a *.   Steve Kennedy, Colin Moody. 21 May 2021.
Start below the right side of the alcove. Climb a small overlap to the right side of the stepped overhang. Continue right of the overhang and up the slab above.

Rainbow   15m   Severe 4a *.   Steve Kennedy, Colin Moody. 21 May 2021.
Start about 3m left of *Brown*, just left of a heather-filled groove leading up to the left side of the roof. Climb to the roof, turned on the left, and continue up a groove on the right.

Blue   15m   V.Diff *.
Take a line up the slab 3m left of *Rainbow*.

MULL
Ulva Ferry, Creag an Eòin North
Spring Flake   8m   Severe *.   Colin Moody. 1990s.
In the bay to the right of *Pinnacle Crack*. Clamber up the flake then climb the crack on the left side of the next shallow bay.

Summer Crack   8m   VS 4c *.   Colin Moody. 1990s.
Just right. Start up awkward twin cracks and continue up the left-hand crack.

Winter Solo   8m   H.Severe *.   Colin Moody. 14 Nov 2017.
Start near the top of the bay. Climb the hand-crack and continue up.

Boot Crack   12m   VS 4c.   Colin Moody, Cynthia Grindley. 2010s.
Right of the bay. Start up some blocks then climb the wide crack passing some loose blocks.

Right Nest   12m   H.Severe *.   Colin Moody, Cynthia Grindley. 2010s.
Opposite *Barn Crack* is another crack. Start on a block just right of it, climb the pillar for a metre or two, then step left and climb the crack.

To the right is a north-west facing wall which has a few routes.

Permit Crack   8m   VS 4c. Colin Moody, Cynthia Grindley. 2018.
A corner-crack at the left side of the wall.

Secret   8m   HVS 5a. Colin Moody, Jim Hinds. 28 Aug 2017.
The crack in the wall just to the right.

Silence   8m   HVS 5a. Colin Moody, Jim Hinds. 28 Aug 2017.
The crack 2m further right.

Owl Flake   8m   VS 4c *. Colin Moody, Jim Hinds. 28 Aug 2017.
The flake crack on the right-hand end of the wall.

Àird Dearg
Red Cuillin   8m   VS 4c. Colin Moody, Cynthia Grindley. 6 Jul 2020.
Climb twin cracks on the left side of the 3m high block. *Dearg Ard* is just right of
the 3m high block.

Six Foot Rule   6m   Severe. Colin Moody, Martin Kafka. 31 May 2020.
Twin cracks right of *Eilat*. Another Severe was climbed right of this route.

Follow The Rules   6m   VS 4c. Colin Moody, Martin Kafka. 31 May 2020.
The second of four cracks at the right-hand end of the crag.

Bird's Foot   6m   Severe. Colin Moody, Martin Kafka. 31 May 2020.
The fourth crack.

ULVA
Basalt Columns
Main Face
Blek le Rat   10m   E3 5c **. Pete Whillance, Cynthia Grindley. 28 Jun 2018.
Two metres left of *King Robbo* is a faint thin crack-line with a small overhang
crossing its right wall at half-height. The crack provides good sustained climbing
throughout, with a difficult upper section that is awkward to protect.

The following route starts 5m left of *The Rosetta Stone* at the lowest point of the
overhangs and takes a slim, bottomless left-facing groove in the upper part of the
crag.

Apollo   15m   E2 5c ***. Pete Whillance, Cynthia Grindley, Colin Moody. 18
Jun 2021.
Start at a smooth open yellow groove and climb this on its right until a few metres
below an overhang. Pull across right and up steeply to enter the slim groove.
Follow this with continuous interest to the top.

Acropolis Variation   15m   VS 4b. Pete Whillance, Cynthia Grindley. 17 May
2018.
An easier, less direct alternative to *Acropolis* is to climb the slim brown-coloured
groove on the left to a small overhang, then move up left and back right on big
ledges to reach the final upper groove.

Mink Buttress

Edgehog 16m E1 5b. Pete Whillance, Cynthia Grindley, Colin Moody. 19 Jun 2021.
The right-hand arête of the front face of the buttress. Start below a clean chimney-crack line that leads to broken ledges on the right side of the buttress. Follow the chimney until above the line of some small overhangs on the left. Step left onto the rib and go up to reach a slim groove in the arête. Climb this steeply to a flake at its top and step left onto the slab. Finish up the short groove above (as for *Kill It*).

Stoatally Different 16m E1 5b **. Pete Whillance, Cynthia Grindley, Colin Moody. 27 Jun 2018.
The corner crack in the arête left of *Left Rib*. Climb into the corner and follow it steeply to reach better holds where it meets the arête of *Left Rib*. Keep to the left side of the arête following flakes diagonally leftwards across the wall to finish.

The following routes climb the walls of Deep Zawn, the gully defining the left-hand side of Mink Buttress. The gully wall on the opposite side to *Weasely Identified* has some impressive overhanging crack-lines. Just right of the huge boulder is a slim black groove with a shallow crack-line.

Paint it Black 12m E1 5c **. Pete Whillance, Cynthia Grindley, Colin Moody. 18 Jun 2021.
From the top of the boulder pull up right into the groove then use good holds on the right wall before stepping back into the groove and continuing steeply to gain a large ledge at halfway. Continue more easily up the groove line rightwards to the top. A good pitch.

Men in Black 12m E2 5c ***. Pete Whillance, Cynthia Grindley, Colin Moody. 19 Jun 2021.
Five metres left of *Paint it Black* is an inset square groove line. Start from the bottom left-hand corner of the huge boulder. Climb the black wall to reach the groove and follow it steeply to a crux finish. Outstanding.

Just left of Deep Zawn is a wide rounded buttress traversed by a distinctive ledge system at half-height. The next route takes a stepped corner line at the right-hand end of this ledge system, on the edge of Deep Zawn, some 5m left of *Men in Black*.

Fur Coat 10m VS 5a. Pete Whillance, Cynthia Grindley. 9 Aug 2018.
Scramble up ledges then climb an awkward corner to gain the right-hand end of the halfway ledge system. Ascend the corner above to a grassy ledge on the right. Continue more easily to the top.

No Knickers 10m HVS 5b *. Pete Whillance, Cynthia Grindley. 9 Aug 2018.
Start just left of *Fur Coat* and boulder up a short wall to reach the halfway ledge. Climb twin thin cracks in a slight groove using good holds on the wall on the left. Step right onto a ledge to finish at the top of *Fur Coat*.

Rubbish 10m Severe. Pete Whillance, Cynthia Grindley, Colin Moody. 27 Jun 2018.

The line of weakness up the left side of the buttress, some 7m left of *No Knickers* and left of *Deep Groove*. Move up awkward blocks to gain the halfway ledge. Follow an obvious short inset corner to the top.

Left of the above wide rounded buttress is a steep tidal bay before the final headland of Sphinx Buttress. On the right side of this bay is a tall tower, The Watch Tower. On the front of the tower is a prominent twin crack-line in a shallow square groove. Immediately right of this is an obvious leaning jam crack in a slim corner. Right again is a short chimney crack-line marking the left-hand end of the halfway ledge system. Approach by abseil at high tide.

Three metres left of the slim groove running up the left-hand side of The Watch Tower, left of *Editor's Column* and at the back of the steep tidal bay, and just left of a wet chimney-gully, is an open groove leading to a bottomless V-chimney.

Bay Watch   10m   E1 5b. Pete Whillance, Cynthia Grindley, Colin Moody. 18 Jun 2021.
Climb the steep open groove on the right-hand side to where it ends, then make an awkward move left to gain the bottomless chimney. Climb this to the top.

Sphinx Buttress
This is the final headland of the Basalt Columns, which comes to an end as the crag turns westward and gradually runs down into a wide, easily accessible, grassy bay. The East Face of Sphinx Buttress begins immediately left of the back of the tidal bay containing *Bay Watch*. Much of the lower section is quite broken with a distinct line of ledges running across it at half height. This ledge system ends on the nose of the buttress, which then marks the beginning of the more impressive West Face. The whole buttress is tidal but ledges along the base of all the routes are often accessible by abseil. The first two routes are on the east face.

Giza Job   12m   HVS 5a. Pete Whillance, Cynthia Grindley, Colin Moody. 19 Jun 2021.
Start 7m left of *Bay Watch* where the first stepped corners lead up leftwards to give access to the halfway ledge system. Follow the corners, then go back rightwards to reach the right-hand end of the terrace. Climb a steep 3m corner to another ledge. From the left side of the ledge climb the upper wall leftwards on surprisingly good holds to the top. Alternatively, though less pleasant, move up and right to gain the arête then easily left to the top.

Pyramid Selling   12m   HVS 5a *. Pete Whillance, Cynthia Grindley. 10 Aug 2018.
The slim black corner in the centre of the upper wall. Start below this in the middle of the face and climb stepped pillars to the halfway ledge. Climb the steep slim corner to a ledge on the left and continue on good, widely spaced holds up the wall above.

The West Face is quite different in character from the rest of the crag. Here the basalt is generally smoother and the columns much narrower, often only half a metre wide. The crack-lines are hence much closer together, often very thin and sometimes blind.

Mythical Creatures   12m   E1 5b *. Pete Whillance, Cynthia Grindley, Colin Moody. 27 Jun 2018.
The first continuous crack-groove line on the very nose of the buttress. A quality climb that is unfortunately escapable at the ledge system on the right at half-height. Climb an initial blank-looking groove containing two very thin cracks to reach a big ledge on the right (crux). Step back left and go up the steep cracks on better holds to the top.

Medusa   12m   E2/3 5c **. Pete Whillance, Cynthia Grindley, Colin Moody. 19 Jun 2021.
The twin crack-line just left of the nose containing two small overhangs (the upper one forming a perfect pentagon). Start just left of the lower overhang in a slim black groove. Climb steeply to a good hold and runner at 4m, then make a delicate move right and up to gain a foothold just above the first overhang. Continue up the rib and crack to the second overhang. Climb the groove on the left to the top. Excellent.

Harpy Days   12m   E1 5b **. Pete Whillance, Cynthia Grindley. 10 Aug 2018.
This striking route, 3m left of the nose, takes twin parallel thin cracks in a shallow groove. Start just left of the line in a slight groove and follow good holds for 4m before stepping right to footholds in the main groove. Follow the cracks with continuous interest to the top.

Pheonix Nights   12m   VS 4c *. Pete Whillance, Cynthia Grindley, Colin Moody. 27 Jun 2018.
The clean twin crack-line, 6m left of the nose of the buttress and just left of a very small overhang at two-thirds height. Pleasant and well protected climbing.

Pegasus   12m   VS 4c *. Pete Whillance, Cynthia Grindley, Colin Moody. 27 Jun 2018.
The most prominent feature in the middle of the West Face is a 5m high, dark recessed groove-chimney. *Pegasus* takes a cleaned crack-line 2m right of this. Follow an easy ragged crack to a tiny overhang. Step up right and continue up the engaging thin groove above to the top.

The Sirens Song   12m   E1 5b **. Pete Whillance, Cynthia Grindley, Colin Moody. 18 Jun 2021.
The big flake crack line left of *Pegasus*. Start 2m left of the dark recessed groove at a thin crack. Climb the crack and move up right to a ledge at the top of the recess. Follow the flake crack to a good ledge, then continue more steeply to a projecting prow. Pull up leftwards to good holds and finish up the groove on the left.

Chimera   12m   HVS 5a **. Pete Whillance, Cynthia Grindley. 28 Jun 2018.
Start 4m left of the dark, recessed groove and just right of a small square overhang at two-thirds height. The route follows a twin crack-line in a slight groove. Fine, continuously interesting climbing.

Basilisk   12m   E1 5b **. Pete Whillance, Cynthia Grindley. 9 Aug 2018.
Start 2m left of *Chimera* and follow a thin crack in a slight groove. Follow the groove direct, which gradually eases after a tricky start. Pass the small square overhang at two-thirds height on its left. Good climbing.

Hippogriff 12m HVS 5a *. Pete Whillance, Cynthia Grindley. 9 Aug 2018.
Start just left of *Basilisk*, directly below a small overhang at half-height. Climb thin cracks to the overhang. Step up right and pull over on good holds. Continue up the airy wall and thin crack, stepping right to finish. It is also possible to go left at the overhang, up a thin crack and groove at the same grade, but not as good.

The scooped wall left of *Hippogriff* contains two cracks, the last lines on the west face before the rock becomes more broken and vegetated.

Charybdis 10m VS 5a. Pete Whillance, Cynthia Grindley, Colin Moody. 19 Jun 2021.
Start 2m left of *Hippogriff* and climb up rightwards to gain the top of a pillar at 4m. Climb the steepening square groove and crack above to finish on the left.

Scylla 10m VS 4c. Pete Whillance, Cynthia Grindley, Colin Moody. 19 Jun 2021.
Start just left of *Charybdis* at twin cracks. Climb the pleasant cracks and pull up left to a good ledge at the top.

The Twin Headlands, East Head
Whitechapel 8m HVS 5a *. Pete Whillance, Cynthia Grindley. 31 Aug 2018.
Just right of *Bishopgate*, in an inset square groove, are two jamming cracks about a metre apart. Follow the cracks, finishing on the left.

Traitor's Gate 10m E1 5b *. Pete Whillance, Cynthia Grindley. 31 Aug 2018.
Some 4m right again is a flaky crack-line in another inset square groove. Start up an easy 3m-high pillar to a good ledge. Climb the crack to a small ledge on the right then continue steeply up the flaky crack above with help from the crack on the left to the top.

Around the corner to the right is the impressive South Face of the East Headland. This consists of a long wall of steep, clean crack-lines extending for some 50m.

Rotherhithe Tunnel 10m HVS 5a *. Pete Whillance, Cynthia Grindley. 31 Aug 2018.
Just right of *Blackwell Tunnel* is a very similar line, twin cracks in a deep cut square groove, this time guarded by a smaller, 2m-high pillar. Pull up steeply onto a vegetated ledge. Back and foot the chimney-groove, facing left for most of the way.

Tramlines 10m E2 5c **. Pete Whillance, Cynthia Grindley. 31 Aug 2018.
The wall 2m to the right of *Rotherhithe Tunnel* has two thin parallel cracks that converge a few metres before the top. The right-hand crack provides most of the holds and the left-hand one most of the protection. Superb sustained climbing.

The Tube 10m E1 5b *. Pete Whillance, Cynthia Grindley. 31 Aug 2018.
About 30m further right of *Tramlines*, towards the right-hand end of the South Face, are twin cracks in an inset square groove. Scramble up a 2m-high pillar to a good ledge below the cracks. Climb the groove using mainly the right-hand crack. Strenuous, as it is unfortunately a little too flared for back and footing.

Around the corner to the right is the shorter, more broken East Face of the headland that looks back along the coast to the Basalt Columns.

East of Eden   8m   E1 5b **. Pete Whillance, Cynthia Grindley. 1 Sep 2018.
The first line on the East Face is a hanging, right-facing corner that begins with a short steep wall at its base. Start off some large blocks from a collapsed pillar. Make committing moves up the short wall and crack to gain the corner. Steep jamming leads to the top.

Far East   7m   VS 4c *. Pete Whillance, Cynthia Grindley. 1 Sep 2018.
The last line on the East Face is a big right-facing corner. Follow the corner to a steep finish.

Stac Liath, South Face
Hiding from the Light   12m   6c+ *. Morag Eagleson, Jamie Skelton. 24 Apr 2022.
Fingery climbing up the middle of the main wall.

Sea Dog   10m   7a **. Jamie Skelton, Morag Eagleson. 23 Apr 2022.
Climb the left-facing corner next to *Getting Salty* before swinging right into the steepness, sharing the same lower-off as *Getting Salty*.

Laggan, Grey Cave (Uamh Liath)
The Big Bad Buie   25m   7c ***. Jamie Skelton, Morag Eagleson. 23 Apr 2022.
A brilliant journey through the steepest part of the cave. Start at the left end of the crag and power through some hard moves before a rest under the roof. More power is needed to gain the excellent crack feature which is followed to the same lower-off as *Large Boy Stops for No One*. Topo provided.

ERRAID
Asteroid Chasm, North-North-East Face
Hyperdrive   15m   E2 5b *. Jamie Skelton, Morag Eagleson. 19 Mar 2022.
Start up *Venus* and follow the sharp left-leaning hand-crack that joins the top of *Time Warp*.

Beach Ball Wall
Lateral Flow   15m   E2 5c **. Tom Fullen, Jess Williams. 16 Apr 2022.
A traverse of Beach Ball Wall, following the obvious horizontal crack. Start on a grass ledge at the far right, gain the crack and exit as for *Buckets in Spades*. (Topo provided.)

COLONSAY
Cailleach Uragaig, Grooved Slab
Uragaig Hanging Garden   25m   V.Diff. Barry Watts, Michael McAlistair. 3 May 2010.
Start on the south side of the stack at NR 381 980 just right of the first set of boulders. Climb the obvious slabby groove just right of the waterline to more broken ground and the top of the stack. (Topo provided.)

ISLAY
Rinns of Islay, Bhuideil Wall

(NR 263 727) South-facing
A wide, gloomy, block filled, gash connects Port a' Bhuideil and Port Bhreac-
achaidh. Just seaward of the west end of this gash is Bhuideil Wall, a clean,
south-facing greywacke wall with a sea-washed base. Topo provided.

Knave of Hearts 8m VS 5a *. Graham Little. 12 May 2021.
Start 1m right of the smooth wave undercut. Make a couple of hard moves on
smooth rock (crux) then continue, trending slightly left, to the top.

Knave of Diamonds 8m Severe 4c *. Graham Little. 12 May 2021.
Start 3m right of the smooth wave undercut. Make a couple of moves up on
smooth rock (crux) then, after a move right, climb straight up.

Dùn Bheolain and Saligo Area, Squat Pinnacle
(NR 2019 6595)
An obvious squat pinnacle lies in a deep inlet, well seaward of a small shingle
beach and sinister dark pool. The top of the pinnacle can be gained from the south
over blocks and flakes (Moderate). A very narrow dipping ledge on the west side
of the pinnacle gives access to the seaward face at mid to low tide. The seaward
face offers two routes, with a common start from the rock promontory that the
pinnacle sits upon. Although they finish up an easy slab, the first half of both
routes gives excellent climbing. Topo provided.

Hang Left 14m HVS 5a **. Graham Little. 28 Jun 2021.
Move up for a couple of moves, under a roof, to place a good No.1 Friend runner.
Traverse leftwards to make blind moves left and up to gain a ledge. Move up onto
the main slab and climb it easily to the top of the pinnacle.

Hang Right 14m E1 5a **. Graham Little. 28 Jun 2021.
From the No.1 Friend runner on *Hang Left*, traverse right, climb a short hanging
groove, then the easy slab to the top of the pinnacle.

Machir Bay Area, Banded Wall
(NR 203 617) Tidal South-facing
This clean wall of banded rock forms the flank of a narrow geo on the coast below
the communication masts to the south of Machair Bay. It can be identified by a
large wedged block bridging the geo at the highest point of normal tides. Although
the routes are short the rock is really excellent. Low tide is ideal. Routes are
described from left to right (from seaward to landward). The first three routes start
on a beautiful sculptured boss of rock gained by scrambling down the north-facing
flank of the geo. Topo provided.

Single 6m Diff. Graham Little. 16 May 2021.
Climb just right of the wall edge.

Twin 6m Diff. *. Graham Little. 16 May 2021.
Climb the twin cracks.

Limpet 8m Severe **. Graham Little. 16 May 2021.
Traverse 3m right from the sculptured rock boss, then climb straight up.

The remaining routes can be accessed from the bridging block (an awkward descent) or by descending *Down and Out*.

Barnacle   7m   V.Diff *.   Graham Little. 16 May 2021.
The face just left of the wide crack with a jammed float.

Winkle   6m   Diff.   Graham Little. 16 May 2021.
The slabby face 3m right of the wide crack with a jammed float.

Whelk   7m   Diff.   Graham Little. 16 May 2021.
The face 5m left of the slabby corner. Start at the seaward end of the big block that nearly fills the geo.

Down and Out   6m   Moderate *.   Graham Little. 16 May 2021.
The slabby face immediately left of the corner.

On Edge   5m   4c *.   Graham Little. 16 May 2021.
Climb directly up the obvious edge immediately right of the slabby corner.

Mussel   5m   5a *.   Graham Little. 20 Jun 2021.
Start 2m right of the edge. Gain the big right-facing flake then climb the diagonal crack.

Clam   5m   5b.   Graham Little. 20 Jun 2021.
Start 3m right of the edge below a thin crack. Gain the crack directly (crux), then climb it.

There are also a couple of short routes between *Clam* and the bridging block.

Kilchiaran Bay
Matter of Fact   12m   Diff.   Graham Little. 15 Jun 2015.
The north flank of this little geo is a wide, slabby face. Climb the slabby face by a central line.

ARRAN
Beinn Tarsuinn, Meadow Face
Colin Moody comments that the diagram in 'Inner Hebrides and Arran' guidebook has *Meadow Grooves* as V.Diff. but the text has Severe.

Cìr Mhòr, Rosa Pinnacle, Upper East Face
Colin Moody thinks that *Somnambulist* is between *Minotaur* and *Sleeping Crack*. He notes that the diagram has *Labyrinth* in winter as **, but in the text it is ***, and the diagram has *Labyrinth Direct* as Severe but the text has VS. The diagram has *Sunshine Corner* as HVS but the text has VS.

SKYE – THE CUILLIN

Glen Sligachan, Sligachan Buttress
Andy Moles notes that *Cheek of the Devil* is harder and bolder than HVS.

Sgùrr nan Gillean, Low Crag

Tardigrade 50m E2 5b *. Andy Moles, Mike Lates. 19 Jun 2021.
This attractive groove lies well to the left of existing climbs on Low Crag, 30m right of a very deep and prominent dyke that forms a cleft.
1. 20m 4b Climb loose ground to the base of the groove.
2. 30m 5b Pull steeply into the groove and follow it with good protection. At 15m a white vein on the left wall leads boldly to easy slabs.

Am Basteir – West Face (above the Basteir Nick)

Execution Crack 15m E3 6a **. Andy Moles, Ferdia Earle. 3 Jul 2021.
The striking crack rising out of the Basteir Nick is a brilliant add-on to a route on the Tooth. Pumpy and safe. A wobbly block at 4m seems to be keyed in. From the ledge above, either walk off right to descend, or take a choice of easier continuation pitches to the Mouth.

Basteir Tooth, South Face

The Green Mile 40m E3 5c **. Michael Barnard, Sam Simpson. 24 Jul 2021.
A fine companion to *Captain Planet*, and at a similar standard. The highlight is the excellent upper flake-line left of *Naismith's Route*. Start up the first ascending section of *Naismith's Route* (as per the guidebook topo) and continue up the steep crack above, then trend leftwards on small holds to reach a steep flake-crack. Climb this and continue with interest up the flake-line.

Tony Stone notes that the rock is fairly poor on the Basteir Tooth and the lines a bit nondescript (other than *Naismith's*). *Captain Planet* in his opinion is 2 stars rather than 3. *Inconvenient Tooth* is worth 2 stars but may be E6 6c or perhaps E7 rather than E8 as the gear is good and close-by for the crux.

Michael Barnard notes that *Captain Planet* was thought E3 (not E4), but not as well protected as the guidebook suggests.

Sgùrr a' Mhadaidh, North Face

The following new descriptions and grades for *Thor* and *Megaton* have been received from Tony Stone.

Thor E3 **
A bold route with generally good rock on the lower two pitches. It has a short positive crux with a few microwires. The crux pitch would have been well protected before all the many original pegs rotted away. Start about 12m right of *Slanting Gully* where a short gangway leads left into a corner above its undercut base.
1. 40m 5b Follow the gangway into the corner and go up this then, more boldly, the wall above, finishing slightly rightwards to belay on a wide sloping ledge (defunct pegs but other gear, including a good wire, above on the right).
2. 50m 5c Traverse leftwards to pull onto the clean wall. Move up on good holds to the capping roof (many defunct pegs) then traverse left to cross the steep, slightly loose dyke, then go up into a niche. Continue more easily up a slight corner-groove to gain the loose shelf that cuts across the face (*Shining Cleft* traverses this). Follow a right-facing corner above to a belay at a cramped niche.
3. 30m 5a Continue up the right-facing corner and the wall to its right to gain

easy ground beneath the huge open groove-corner split by a vertical dyke.
4. 50m 5a Follow the vertical dyke until it is possible to piece together weaknesses on the right wall to form a rising traversing line underneath some overhangs. Move up to gain the right edge of the overhangs, then continue traversing right to the blunt rib and follow this to its top on *Foxes' Rake*. (Topo provided.)

Megaton E4 **
A route with good climbing, taking in some amazing positions through unlikely ground but, unfortunately, also a lot of hollow rock and some looseness that requires gentle handling. The crux second pitch is likely harder for the short. Start about 80m right of *Slanting Gully* beneath the widest overhangs in the main face far above.
1. 50m 5b Pick a line up the lower slab to gain its top and a fault leading diagonally rightwards through steep ground. Follow the fault with easing difficulty but sustained looseness to a large ledge. It is possible to continue rightwards along the fault-shelf to escape into easier ground.
2. 55m 5c Gain the upper slab, either directly above the belay or by continuing rightwards along the fault-shelf, then step easily onto the slab above and traverse this back leftwards to its far left edge (numerous defunct pegs). Stretch up for good holds on the steep wall above, being careful with hollow rock, to gain a left-slanting ramp up left. Follow the ramp and continue to a sloping stance at the base of a left-facing corner.
3. 60m 5b Climb the corner to gain much easier, open ground. Continue up and then cross higher slabby ground leftwards to the left edge beneath a steeper wall.
4. 60m 5a Pick a way up the blunt rib and its slightly more solid left wall to its top on *Foxes' Rake*. (Topo provided.)

Tony Stone notes that *Shining Cleft* is given VS 4c, but it's probably HVS 5a or more. It may be that *Thor* follows it from high on *Thor*'s pitch 2, but it also reads like *Shining Cleft* may have continued traversing the loose shelf rightwards, in which case *Megaton*'s pitch 4 is probably in common.

Coire Làgan, Loch Làgan Bluffs
The following routes are on some crags just above Loch Làgan, below the main mass of West Buttress.

Iris 40m E4 5c ***. Tim Miller. 2 Jul 2021.
This brilliant and sustained route climbs the steep wall above Loch Làgan, by linking together corner and crack features. Unfortunately it suffers from seepage, but can still be climbable when mostly dry. Start at a big wobbly block. Climb a technical wall until it is possible to swing left into the right of the two left-facing corners. Climb the corner and wall above then follow a wide crack going up to the left. At the end of this move back right across a wet patch to follow another left-trending crack that leads to the base of the hanging corner at the top centre of the wall. Climb this to easier ground up and right. (Topo provided.)

The following climbs are on a short crag 50m north-east of Loch Làgan above the path to the An Stac screes.

Hard 2 Do 10m VS 4b *. Tim Miller, Beth Hitchcock. 2 Jul 2021.
Climb the right-hand obvious crack in the centre of the wall.

Skippy 7m Diff. Beth Hitchcock. Tim Miller. 2 Jul 2021.
Climb a short stepped corner on the left side of the crag.

Sròn na Cìche – Coire Làgan Face, Western Buttress
The Quiet Zone 170m HVS *. Michael Barnard, Alan Hill. 31 May 2021.
The main pitch climbs a fine slabby wall immediately right of *Parallel Cracks Route* and overlooking a corner-groove on the right. Scramble up to the base of the wall.
1. 35m 4c The slabby wall gives a good pitch.
2 etc. 135m 4a Continue up the buttress above.

Cìoch Buttress, The Cìoch
Tony Stone notes that *The Highlander* is definitely 3 stars, and after a bold start on positive holds it is well protected. The microwires near the top are certainly not poor (they're solid for reasonable sized micros).

Lower Cìoch Buttress
Tony Stone notes that *Bastinado* is hard, E2 6a if done free (probably 5c for those with a big span).

Cìoch Upper Buttress, Final Tier
Midge Dancer's Climax 35m HVS 5a *. Paul Donnithorne and Will Dodson. 28 Jun 2021.
A worthwhile extension to *Trophy Crack*, climbing the dog-leg crack just right of the parallel cracks taken by *Box-King Route*. Climb the crack awkwardly to a ledge, then a short corner leads to the final thin, twin face-cracks. Exit through a notch.

Paul Donnithorne notes that the 'alarmingly loose block' in the upper section of *Ajax* no longer appears to be there.

Eastern Buttress – West Wall
Trick or Treat 20m E1 5b *. Michael Barnard, Alan Hill. 30 May 2021.
Starting from the girdle ledge, this route climbs a steep wall just left of the slabby bay on *Direct Route*, visible on p183 of 'Skye – The Cuillin' guidebook. The wall is seamed with a few intermittent cracks. Climb the central one until a wide crack on the right can be gained; continue up this and the arête above.

Trojan Groove, Variation Start 15m E1 5b *. Michael Barnard, Alan Hill. 30 May 2021.
A shallower groove just left of the main line, which is joined at half-height. Low in the grade.

Babble and Squeak 15m HVS 5a *. Alan Hill, Michael Barnard. 30 May 2021.
A vertical crack just left of the above, passing an obvious slot.

Eastern Buttress, Vulcan Wall Area

Tony Stone notes that *Uhuru* and *Clinging On* seemed much the same grade; whether they're tricky E3 5c or easy-ish E4 6a is splitting hairs. Both three stars.

Sròn na Cìche – South-East Face
South Crag, Lower Buttress

Carte Blanche 75m V.Diff *. Steve Kennedy, Eileen Blair. 4 Sep 2021.
A fairly direct line up clean slab left of *Liberty* starting from a grass ledge about 8m right of the left edge. Climb the centre of the slab passing a slight bulge and ledge to the upper slab. Belay at the top of the slab, close to the base of a gully leading up right (50m). Move rightwards onto the rib just right of the gully. Follow the rib to easy ground (25m). Descend by Stony Rake.

Main Cliff

White Slab Superdirect 150m VS 4c **. Steve Kennedy, Colin Moody. 10 Jul 2021.
A good route which is essentially a more direct version of *White Slab Direct*, following the centre of the slab above the horizontal Ledge between *White Slab Direct* and *White Slab* original route.
1. 50m 4c Start as for *White Slab Direct* and climb the V-shaped groove to where it steepens near the top (*White Slab Direct* moves left up slabs from about 5m up the groove). Step right onto a ledge below a pale-coloured wall. Make steep moves up a crack on the right side of the wall to reach a wide ledge on the right. Belay at the right end of the ledge.
2. 55m 4b Gain the Horizontal Ledge above and belay just left of the chimney and rib of *White Slab*. Move leftwards up a sloping shelf to reach a vague system of left-facing corners (right of *White Slab Direct*). Follow the corners and slab above as directly as possible to reach the base of the *White Slab*.
3. 45m 4b Finish up the exposed right edge of the *White Slab* (as per *White Slab Direct*) to reach Pinnacle Rake.

Steve Kennedy considers the description of the first pitch of *White Slab Direct* in the current Cuillin guidebook a little misleading. The original description in previous guidebooks is easier to follow and seems more accurate, i.e. 'Follow the crack in the V-shaped groove for 5m, then climb a slab on the left past three thin ledges.' *White Slab Superdirect* follows the V-shaped groove directly almost to its end.

Odyssey Wall

The following routes are situated on the buttress containing *Zeus* (*SMCJ* 2012) and *Jupiter* (*SMCJ* 2020). Those routes were previously referred to as being located on North Crag but are in fact on a separate buttress immediately right of the upper part of North Crag Gully (above the upper terrace crossing *Slab Buttress*). Accordingly, to avoid possible confusion, the name Odyssey Wall is suggested.

Plutus 50m VS 4b *. Steve Kennedy, Cynthia Grindley, Colin Moody. 21 Aug 2016.
This route takes the line of a basalt dyke running diagonally right across the lower section of the wall. Start at the foot of the dyke (as for *Zeus*) and follow it

rightwards to the foot of a steep groove on the left (*Apollo*). Continue up the steep continuation of the dyke on the right before moving left to reach the girdle ledge. Belay on the ledge just right of the prominent deep groove (*Apollo*) (30m). Climb the steep cracks above (just right of the deep groove) via a flake and finish up slabs close to a right-facing corner (20m).

Apollo   45m   HVS 5a **.   Steve Kennedy, Eileen Blair, Colin Moody. 1 Jul 2021. The prominent groove right of *Jupiter*, passing the right side of the roof and running the whole length of the crag. Start a few metres right of *Jupiter* directly below the groove. Climb the initial groove and slab to a steepening next to the roof. Continue directly up the steep groove (crux) and the slab above to a belay on the girdle ledge below the continuation of the groove (25m). Finish up the deep corner-groove and slabs above (20m).

Sgùrr Alasdair – South Face
Lavatory Groove   45m   Severe **.   Michael Barnard. 21 Jul 2021. A variation start to *W.C. Route*. Climb the obvious big flake-crack right of *West Gully*; a fine pitch. From the belay below the overhang the description for the rest of the route should read: 'Traverse left and go up into a short groove, then make an exposed move back right to below steep cracks. Climb these to the top.'

Central Route Left-Hand   105m   VS 4c *.   Michael Barnard. 21 Jul 2021. Start up a groove on the left side of the initial rib (the winter start). This leads directly to a steep crack; climb this to a ledge then continue up the steep groove above (the normal route takes the main chimney further right). From here, traverse left to the arête and go up this until possible to gain a crack which comes up from the right. Continue more easily.

Theàrlaich–Dubh Gap Buttress
Prince Regent   45m   V.Diff.   Steve Kennedy, Eileen Blair. 4 Sep 2021. The steep groove on the left flank of the buttress leading to a pedestal, starting about 5m left of *Victoria Buttress*. Climb the groove, passing an overhang on the right, to reach the top of the pedestal. Traverse horizontally right along a narrow ledge onto the front of the buttress and finish directly joining *Victoria Buttress*.

Coireachan Ruadha, Bealach Buttress
Tony Stone notes that *Rainman* was thought 2 stars and perhaps low in the grade, definitely not a 'must-do for any aspiring mountain E5 leader'. There is no need to do the traverse left and then back right as described, just go straight up at the same grade.

Coir'-Uisg Buttress
Wild at Heart   170m   E1.   Guy Robertson and partner. 10 Aug 2021. A brilliant atmospheric route finding a way up the big unclimbed buttress facing south-east below the summit of Sgùrr Dubh Mòr. Access via the *Dubhs Ridge*, breaking right shortly after the abseil descent to where a steep crack falls from the base of the Great Slab.
1. 20m 4c Climb a series of short right-trending corner steps to a sloping ledge below the crack.
2. 40m 5b Climb the excellent sustained crack to a slab, climb this then move right and up a shelf to belay in a recess below the Great Slab.

3. 30m 4c Traverse left to gain a line of weakness in the slab and follow this up and back rightwards to belay in the corner.

4. 50m 5a Traverse left onto the slab again and follow the line of least resistance (bold in places) to eventually regain the corner again which is followed directly for a short way to a belay ledge on its right wall

5. 20m Continue up the corner, then a short V-groove to easier blocky ground which leads to the ridge.

Sgùrr na Strì, Loch nan Leachd Crag
(NG 491 194)
This crag faces east and lies parallel to the path to Camasunary via the Bad Step and finishes above the sea inlet.

Porpoiseful 55m Severe 4a **. Chris Dickinson, Jane Allen. 26 Apr 2022.
The left-bounding arête at the seaward end of the crag. Climb an overhang and then follow the blunt arête in a very fine position through two more bulges to the top.

Seal the Deal 50m VS 4c ***. Chris Dickinson, Jane Allen. 27 Apr 2022.
A beautiful route in the centre of the crag. Climb up to a corner on the left and follow this to a crux at the overhang. Pull over into a single horizontal crack and then stand in it to make an exciting tiptoe rightwards above the lip. Gain a slabby scoop, move up and left until moves right give access to a crack that leads to the top of the crag.

Stepping Stone Buttress
Slab and Tickle 150m V.Diff. Chris Dickinson, Jane Allen. 26 Apr 2022.
Start at a large cairn on the path to the Bad Step. (Topo provided.)
1. 50m Climb to the first steep wall via easy slabs.
2. 50m Take the steep left-slanting crack on the right side of a white wall, then easy slabs to the biggest overlapping wall. Belay beside a steep recess.
3. 50m From the recess, climb up left and pass a large horizontal loose block with care, then pull onto the slab above and continue more easily to the top.

Coruisk View Crag
(NG 492 197)
This slabby crag faces west and can be identified as it is directly above the second beach along the east side of Loch Coruisk. Ascend the hillside for a couple of minutes to reach the steep toe of the formation. (Topo provided.)

Celebration Slab 100m V.Diff **. Chris Dickinson. 27 Apr 2022.
Start just left of the toe of the formation, right of a holly tree, where a small slab allows a traverse onto the arête. Climb a crack on the left and then tiptoe right on a small dyke feature to gain the centre of the slab. Follow cracks to an X-shaped basalt dyke and take the top left fork. Possible stance. A corner on the left leads to a step right to gain a dyke and crack system that leads to the top. Descend to the south by an open gully. A sustained and very enjoyable slab route.

Blàbheinn, South-East Buttress
North Buttress Gully 140m III *. Mike Lates, Tilly Cottrell. 27 Nov 2021.
Above the bowl of Coire Uiginish the upper face of Blàbheinn is split by the *Great*

Gully (Grade I winter) that finishes with the South Top on its left and the Munro, North Top on the right. The buttress to the left has most of the climbing and is known as South-East Buttress. The huge broad north face right of *Great Gully* is known as North Buttress. This was misleadingly called the South-East Buttress in the 2011 'Skye – The Cuillin' guidebook. This route starts on the right side of North Buttress where a stream enters an obvious square basalt recess. (Topo provided.)

1. 30m Climb a mixture of turf and snow-ice easily until the angle kicks back.
2. 20m Short easy steps lead to an obvious steeper section of snow-covered turf and slabs.
3. 15m Climb the steeper turf section for 10m and continue by the short narrow groove above.
4. 20m Easy ground leads to a bifurcation in the fault.
5. 25m Gain the groove in the right-hand branch, which gave ice and mixed climbing with good rock protection, to a large block belay.
6. 30m Easier climbing leads to scree slopes.

SKYE – SEA-CLIFFS AND OUTCROPS

South-East Trotternish Sea-Stacks, Tote Stack
(NG 5246 5817)
This stack is at the top of the list of stacks on page 298 of the current 'Skye – Sea-Cliffs and Outcrops' guide. It is named 'Na Famhairean' (The Giants) in the guide, but the stack is unnamed on OS maps. The name Na Famhairean is more correctly associated with some low-lying rocks immediately to the south.

Gentle Giant 20m Severe *. Willie Jeffrey, Mike Bauermeister, Noel Williams. 18 Apr 2022.
A short, but fun sea-stack on the east coast of the Trotternish peninsula, near Tote (NG 5246 5817). Approach by abseiling from an *in situ* stake to a large platform opposite the stack. The intervening channel can only be crossed without difficulty at very low spring tides. Gain a platform on the south-west side of the stack. Climb the prominent chimney-groove and finish on wobbly clumps of grass. Belay on two stakes that were placed on the east side of the summit.

Kilt Rock Area, Ellishadder Wall
Ian Taylor notes that the topo on page 70 of the 'Skye – Sea-Cliffs and Outcrops' guidebook is incorrect. Line 14 should be *Received with Thanks* (which is described in the wrong order in the text, as it is actually between *Elliscrappe*r and *Drop the Pilot*). The line for *Drop the Pilot* should be further left. (Revised topo provided.)

Staffin Slip North – Sgeir Bhàn
Digger Bees 45m HVS **. Lauren Steele, Ed Griffin, David Steele. 13 Sep 2021.
1. 15m 4b As for the first pitch of *Return of the Stone*.
2. 30m 4c From the ivy ledge climb the wide crack in the main wall, using the pinnacle to the left as well, then gain the lower platform of the pinnacle. It is possible and recommended to abseil from here. Alternatively, climb the final 8m up the main face, which is particularly vegetated and loose.

Flodigarry, The Southern Promontory
Orange You Glad   25m   V.Diff.   Mark Hudson, Flora Hudson, Andrew Holden. 1 Jul 2021.
Gains and climbs the right edge of the face right of *Milk Tray Man*. Start as for *First For Murdo* and climb to a large golden scoop on the right edge. Exit the left end of this and follow the right edge above to a good block belay.

The following four routes are found near the northern end of the southern promontory, where it tapers down to the tidal channel on the south side of the Cheeseblock (right of *A First for Murdo* and separated from it by a chimney-slot). They are likely of most interest to the instructing community, offering short but friendly routes above a mostly non-tidal platform, and with a comfortable ledge and good anchors above (there aren't many easy coastal routes like this on Skye). The only downside from a beginner's perspective is the slightly awkward access, scrambling around from the boulder beach with a couple of tricky steps (these can be spotted by the leader). Escape is possibly best made by leading up the ridge above and left, rather than reversing the tricky steps. The rock is excellent.

Itty   9m   Moderate. Andy Moles, Marek Rudnicki. 4 Jun 2021.
The right-hand corner of the recess is pleasant and well-protected.

Bitty   10m   Severe. Andy Moles, Marek Rudnicki. 4 Jun 2021.
The left rib of the seaward slab, with a slightly thin start.

Teenie   10m   Diff. *. Andy Moles, Marek Rudnicki. 4 Jun 2021.
The obvious groove has perfect protection.

Weenie   10m   VS 4b. Andy Moles, Marek Rudnicki. 4 Jun 2021.
Thin cracks up the slab on the right, with small and fiddly gear.

Northern Promontory, South Tunnel Buttress
Lucy in the Sky, Left-Hand Finish   15m   E1 5b. Joe Barlow, Rosie Rothwell. 31 Aug 2021.
At the base of the pedestal climb up and left into a short roofed corner then make exposed moves out onto the wall on the left and climb a crack to the top. Well protected.

Rubha Hunish
Lùb a' Sgiathain
There are two sea-stacks situated in the bay to the east of Rubha Hunish called Lùb a' Sgiathain (Bay of the Promontory) – one is broad, the other is slender. They can be approached by descending a grassy gully at the eastern end of the bay. The stacks are hidden from view behind a slight prow and can only be reached at low tide by crossing rounded boulders covered in very slippery seaweed.

Fingertip   15m   VS. Mike Mavroleon (unseconded). 8 May 2016.
This climb on Slender Stack is situated at NG 42266 76036. Climb the stepped ridge and make an awkward and very long stretch to touch the top. (Topo provided)

The Headland
Middle Stack
Ragdoll 35m HVS 5a *. Robert Giddy, Marion Prieler. 10 Aug 2021.
Scramble 10m north from the triangular ledge described in 'Skye – Sea-Cliffs and Outcrops' (not possible at high tide). Start just before the chimney of *Blue Men of the Minch* at a right-facing corner. Climb the corner to an excellent vertical cam crack. Place gear here and make a thin traverse right to the arête. Climb the arête and wall above which leads to another corner on the right. Climb this to finish (possibly the direct finish mentioned in *Blue Men of the Minch*).

Non-Stack
Tigerbite 25m E2 5c **. Andy Moles, Tilly Cottrell. 12 Sep 2021.
The 'obvious line' mentioned in 'Skye – Sea Cliffs and Outcrops' between *Workout* and *Delicasse* with a layback crux through the small roof. Low in the grade.

Andy Moles suggests that *Delicasse* should be upgraded to HVS 4c.

Meall Deas
Rendezvous 53m E4 6a ***. Nicola Bassnett. 13 Sep 2021.
Right again of *Whispering Crack* lies another immensely long crack-line, demanding wide jamming and cam shuffling. About 10m right of *Whispering Crack* is a right-facing vegetated cliff-height corner, with a blank wall on its right. 10m right again, the wall is split by a vertical crack on top of a patchwork of overhanging roofs. A sizeable volcanic plug helps locate the base of the route and this untidy cone encompasses a left-sloping grassy ramp, which provides the access. Alternatively, approach by abseil from the cluster of stakes 20m west of the top of *Whispering Crack*. The starting crack is 2m left of a short left-facing crack. Flaky hand-jamming atop the grassy block leads towards the left-hand triangular roof, then take a handrail rightwards to a perch below a capping roof (small wire protection). Step up and move tenuously rightwards to the right-hand flake (technical crux). Funnel up to the apex and the start of the soaring crack. Above the overlap, a cunning jiggle right and back left may assist progress as the crack widens and difficulties commence. Battle on to the relief of a resting ledge and much easier climbing above.

The Black Book (*SMCJ* 2021) was repeated and thought E3 5b, 5c *. The rock is too poor on the last pitch for the route to be ***.

Bornesketaig, Organ Pipes
Bourdon 15m VS 4c *. Steve Kennedy, Cynthia Grindley, Colin Moody. 27 Jun 2021.
Approximately 6m left of *One Green Bottle* (named *Falling Time* in *SMCJ* 2021 and since re-named), at the point where the buttress starts to turn uphill, is a crack above some cleaned ledges and a left-facing corner. Climb via the ledges to the base of the crack and follow this to a ledge and a finish up broken ground above.

Neist Point
Poverty Point, Boulder Cove
Breadline 22m E5 6b **. Andy Moles, Niels Ernst-Williams. 4 Sep 2021.
The overhanging scoop between *Vagrants* and *The Poverty Trap*, making up a good trio of mid-Extremes. Excellent climbing, but it lacks an independent finish.

Climb the thin crack to the band of coarse-grained rock (micro-wires handy). Place high runners, then use a pocket to move right and gain a vertical seam (crux). Span back left to the crack and follow it directly to an enormous jug at 12m. Step right and finish up *The Poverty Trap*. (Topo provided.)

Andy Moles notes a tweak to the description of *Vagrants*. 'I described swinging in from the right at the start, but this only applies to a very specific tide-level, so it should just say "Start at an obvious fault 5m right of *Rhubarb Crumble*, and climb boldly but easily on jugs to the coarse band."'

The Ramps
The following routes lie on the fine steep wall between *No Access* and *Patricia*.

Open All Areas   12m   E2 5b *. Michael Barnard, Alan Hill. 7 Sep 2019.
The right-hand line. Start below the wall and move up until forced right into the *No Access* corner. Step back left and climb just left of the arête.

Golden Ticket   15m   E4 6a **. Michael Barnard (unseconded). 8 May 2022.
The left-hand line. Step off the pedestal and traverse left to gain and climb the sustained crack. Pre-practised.

Little California
The following two routes take lines up the splintery recess between *Gloominous* and *Smeg*.

The Red Dwarf Shuffle   20m   E2 5c *. Michael Barnard, Alan Hill. 7 Sep 2019.
The corner on the left. Good solid rock.

Up Up Up the Ziggurat, Lickety Split   20m   E1 5c **. Michael Barnard, Alan Hill. 7 Sep 2019.
The wide crack is easier than it looks, initially!

Bracadale, Struan, Dùn Mhòr
Andy Moles notes that the two retro-bolted and retro-named lines are decent and worth a star. Although the venue is extremely limited, it is convenient and the setting is excellent. As of September 2021 however, there is a confusing spray of bolts around the top of the routes, no lower-offs in place, a hanger missing from the first bolt of the left line, and all of the nuts are very rusty.

Elgol, Suidhe Biorach
Michael Barnard notes an ascent of the central of the three hanging cracks left of *Fertility Left* at E2 5c *. This is recorded on UKC as *Busty Meringue* with an elaborate description, but the above would suffice. Barnard also notes that *Mother's Pride* was thought E2 5c.

Point of Sleat, Creag Mhòr
Orange Pixel   22m   Severe. Mark Hudson. 6 Apr 2022.
A distinct and continuous line just in from the right-hand edge of the slimmer face to the right of *Blue Wind*. Follow a straight slim crack less than a metre in from the right-hand edge, and then cracks above, before finishing up a short wall. The route can be extended via a decent scramble to the top of the crag.

RAASAY
Creag na Bruaich, An Coinneal
The Left Behind   27m   6c ***.
A steep and juggy route up the broad arête that forms the left edge of the wall to the left of the huge chimney and *The Candle*.

Creag na Bruaich Sport Crag
(NG 583 437)
This is a huge sport crag that is still being developed, with plenty of scope for the adventurous. Creag na Bruaich is easy to spot when looking south from Brochel at the north end of the island – the long sandstone escarpment is huge and shoots up out well above the trees. There are a couple of options for approaching, but the most common and least strenuous is to park at NG 578 461 and follow the forestry tracks down to the coast at Screapadal. From there, follow a path that ascends and contours around the hillside below some small outcrops to reach the base of the crag in 45 to 50 minutes. There is a gully on the right side of the buttress that is used to access the top of the crag or for descent if approaching from the top. There are also some hidden walls that are being bolted by Paul Tattersall and are accessible by heading up the gully. This part of the escarpment is just south of An Coinneal. The following routes are described from right to left, starting from the left edge of the wall to the left of the gully.

Sandstorm   45m   7b ***.   Jamie Skelton, Nicky Brierley. 16 Sep 2021.
The north-facing side of the buttress consists of predominantly darker rock. Unfortunately most of this face is vegetated apart from the soaring left arête, which offers a brilliant varied two-pitch climb.
1. 20m 6c The wall below the arête is a great bit of climbing but can be a little more sandy than the upper pitch. It is found just as the hillside starts to slope down towards the corner of *Something's Burning*. A step in from the right helps to gain the first pocket.
2. 25m 7b Spectacular climbing up the right side of the arête.

Something's Burning   70m   7a.   Paul Tattersall (first pitch); Jamie Skelton, Morag Eagleson (second pitch). 17 Aug 2021.
A long adventure up the middle of the west-facing part of the buttress. The first pitch is perhaps the most obvious feature on this face and is useful to help locate the other routes. The route can be abseiled with a 60m rope by using the first anchor of *Eleven Eleven* as an anchor as there is no abseil point at the end of the first pitch.
1. 45m 6b A quality pitch with a slightly traditional feel, be prepared to take a brush or deal with the slightly sandy nature of the rock. Take plenty of draws; the lightly coloured corner seems to almost go on forever.
2. 25m 6c+/7a In contrast a much more modern-feeling headwall pitch. Brilliant exposure!

Na Tùsairean   7b.   Ali Rob, Callum Johnson. 2017.
The first bolted line on the island. At the left-hand end of the buttress is a wide chimney-crack, to the left of which is a pillar that forms a detached tower higher up. This route takes the left arête of the wall to the left of the chimney-crack. Two pitches 6c and 7b.

Little Diabaig
Near Dome
Alasdair Macinnes's Dyno Workshop   10m   H.Severe 4b. Jack Copland. 6 Jun 2021.
To the left of *Tooth Fairy*. Follow easy terrain up to the widest part of a tiny roof. Gain the overhang with small holds and high feet.

Alasdair Macinnes's Mantel Workshop   12m   H.Severe 4b *. Jack Copland. 6 Jun 2021.
Start left of *Bump Saturday*, moving up into a slabby scoop at half-height. Continue straight up utilising the more friendly left-slanting crack before trending back right to finish up the pale slab. (For a contrived but fun challenge, avoid the left-slanting crack and move directly up using thin shallow cracks at HVS 5a.)

Far Dome
Romantic Bottle Opener   10m   VS 5a *. Jack Copland. 6 Jun 2021.
Left of *Shadern*, starting from a higher platform beneath the main central section. Move up to a small roof with side-pulls in the thin seam above. Pull through the roof on small holds to reach more positive terrain the further right you trend. Finish by traversing up and right of the roof above.

RONA
Extra Slab
One Twenty   15m   Severe. Mark Hudson, Andrew Holden. 23 Aug 2021.
A diagonal line across the slab from bottom right to top left, finishing up a creamy wall with a bulge above.

NORTHERN HIGHLANDS NORTH

Beinn Dearg, Diollaid a' Mhill Bhric – Gleann Sguaib
Tower of Babel, Dudley Direct Start   40m   IV,5. Robin Clothier, Di Gilbert, Stuart McFarlane. 9 Feb 2022.
Instead of traversing in above the lower tier, climb the obvious open turfy groove and steps in the centre of the buttress. This lies to the right of the direct start mentioned in the original summer description.

Ardgay, Struie Hill Crag
Dave Allan has provided a complete re-write of this unusually good-quality conglomerate crag above the B9176 Struie road between Alness and Ardgay. It can be found here: <https://smcnewroutes.org.uk/mini-guides/>.
The following is a new addition.

137 Not Out   25m   Severe 4b *. Dave Allan, Davy Moy. May 2017.
This climb takes the next and last steep corner to the right of *Copernicus Corner*, the short corner above, then the corner system above that, finishing over the blocks as for *Copernicus Corner*. Taking the same start as *Copernicus Corner* reduces the grade to 4a.

Ullapool and Ardmair Crags, Rhue Sea-Cliffs
Main Cliff
Kipper's Knickers   25m   E3 5c **. Tess Fryer, Ian Taylor. 16 May 2022.
Start up *Cat's Whiskers*. Pull over the second roof, then move hard right using an undercut, to gain a thin crack. Follow the crack and flakes to a roof. Move over the roof leftwards and finish up the steep headwall.

Gem Walls
Barry's Wall   8m   E3 6a *. Ian Taylor. 2010.
This route, which was originally done as a highball boulder (Font 6C), takes the middle of the wall right of *Fiddler's Elbow*. A hard start up the crack in the middle of the wall (climbed just left of the crack) leads to breaks. Move slightly right and finish straight up.

Rhuematologist   8m   E4 5c. Rory Brown, Thomas Shaw. 16 Apr 2022.
A right-hand start to *Barry's Wall*. Start at the left end of the roof low on the wall. Climb boldly up edges until a tricky move gains the high rail and junction with *Barry's Wall* (first gear here). Finish straight up.

Ardmair (Creag an Uillt Ghairbh)
Monster Buttress
Liver and Strawberries   30m   E2 5c *. Ian Taylor, Tess Fryer. 4 Jun 2021.
Climb *The Raven* to the second tree (an aspen), then move right over steep blocky ground and up into the apex of the huge V-roof. Escape left, with typically awkward Ardmair moves, to pop out the top.

Beast Buttress
Ian Taylor remarks that Michael Barnard's comment in *SMCJ* 2021 regarding a combination of *On Western Skyline* and *Neart nan Gaidheal* being E2 5c seems strange. 'Having climbed all over those routes too many times to count, I can't understand how any combination would be less than E4.'

Keanchulish Sea-Cliffs, Camas an Lochain Crag
Talking of Barnard   7m   HVS 6a. Tom Shaw, Callum Johnson. 18 Sep 2020.
The steep scalloped roofs to the right of *Skimming* on the face left of *Little Wing*. Climb to place some good gear, slap up into the scalloped roofs, reach left to the arête, then continue to the obvious crack which provides an easier though still strenuous finish.

Blughasary Crags, Geodha Ruadh
(NC 086 015) Partly tidal West-facing
Geodha Ruadh is a big sandstone crag not easily seen from the mainland, but often spotted from the Ullapool-Stornoway ferry. There is a fair amount of chossy rock, but protection is generally good. To the west of the crag the land drops away and a jumble of boulders on a ridge affords an excellent view of the cliff. In the lower section of the cliffs is a prominent jutting slab of hairy sea moss and at the left end of this is a large alcove topped by a curving roof. From the left end of the alcove there is a generally left-trending line that gives the main section of the following route.

Tess Fryer on the FA of Tafoni (E4,5c), Geodha Ruadh, Blughasary Crags.
Photo: Ian Taylor.

Approach via the Postie's path from Blughasary, then abseil from the jumble of boulders (10m of rigging rope needed) down a craggy heathery slope to the foot of the route.

Tafoni 80m E4 5c **. Tess Fryer, Ian Taylor. 21 Jun 2021.
From the cliff base scramble right to a ledge below the right end of the hairy jutting slab.
1. 25m 5b From the ledge, climb cracks and grooves to the right end of the slab. Traverse left along a break to belay at a big block in the roofed alcove.
2. 40m 5c Climb the wall left of the block on big pockets, then move left into a diagonal line. Follow the line over a massive horizontal thread. A tricky move left and a steep bulge lead to a belay in a break.
3. 15m 5c Take the steep corner-crack above to a triangular ledge, then continue up cracks to the top. (Topo provided.)

Beinn Mòr Coigach, Fred's Crag
Flintstone, Direct Start 6m HVS 5a. Iain Young, Grant Urquhart. 28 Jun 2021.
Takes a line of gently overhanging flakes above the right end of the flat rock below the crag to join the parent route. (Topo provided.)

Uncle Tex Hardrock 35m VS 4c. Grant Urquhart, Iain Young. 28 Jun 2021.
Some 5m right of *Boss Bird* there is a small square-cut orange recess. Start up the crack immediately right of this and follow intermittent cracks fairly directly to the top, crossing a small overlap at 5m. (Topo provided.)

Pearl Slaghoople 30m H.Severe 4a. Grant Urquhart, Iain Young. 28 Jun 2021.
Start as for *Wilma*. Climb slabs just left of the heather-topped pillar then continue directly to the top. (Topo provided.)

Stac Pollaidh, West (No 1) Buttress, North Face
Positive Vegetation, Left-Hand Finish 95m III,4. Robin Clothier, Di Gilbert, Stuart McFarlane. 19 Feb 2022.
Start from the large terrace at the top of the first pitch of *Positive Vegetation*.
1. 45m Traverse easy snow leftwards beneath two parallel corners (*Three Day Grooves* takes the bigger left-hand corner).
2. 50m Climb the steep corner and pull onto a massive blob of turf. Easy ground leads to summit. (Topo provided.)

Rubha Dùnan Sea-Cliffs, Wake Wall
Southern Softie 10m Severe 4a. Nic Cosmos, Mark Hazell. 29 May 2021.
To the right of the foot of the obvious arch in *Tumbledown Wall*, climb the short left-facing corner with twin lower crack-lines and a split block at its top.

Short But Perfectly Formed 6m H.Severe 4b. Nic Cosmos, Mark Hazell. 29 May 2021.
A short micro route on the far right-hand end of *Tumbledown Wall* taking the clean diagonal crack-line above the V-shaped recess.

Reiff Sea-Cliffs
An Stiùir, Cnoc Àirigh Giorsail
(NB 96698 15973) Alt 30m West-facing

A small inland crag set back from Pooh Cliff. (Topo provided.)

The Poised Block 11m Moderate. Graham Uney, Sharon J. Kennedy. 4 Aug 2021.
Starting towards the left end of the rippled slab, climb leftwards to the obvious poised block and pull over this and go up the wall above.

Ripple 11m Diff. *. Sharon J. Kennedy, Graham Uney. 4 Aug 2021.
Immediately right of *The Poised Block*. Climb up the centre of the left-hand rippled slab, directly to the highest point of the buttress.

Handful of Heather 11m Diff. Graham Uney, Sharon J. Kennedy. 4 Aug 2021.
To the right of *Ripple* is a vegetated crack. Climb the slab to the right of this directly.

Walk the Line 12m Moderate. Sharon J. Kennedy, Graham Uney. 4 Aug 2021.
Start as for *Handful of Heather*. Climb the obvious diagonal break, trending rightwards to the top.

Between a Wet Patch and a Slimy Place 10m Diff. Graham Uney, Sharon J. Kennedy. 4 Aug 2021.
The slab to the right of *Handful of Heather*, crossing directly over *Walk The Line* at the top.

Hundred Acre Traverse 25m Diff. Sharon J. Kennedy, Graham Uney. 4 Aug 2021.
A right-to-left traverse of the whole crag following the obvious hand-traverse line.

Rubha Coigeach, Golden Walls
Buddhism for Vampires 20m E4 6a **. Ian Taylor, Tess Fryer. 1 Jun 2021.
The wall left of *Blood of Eden*. Start up *Blood of Eden* to a good break, move left, then go up then left to the edge of the wall. Pull round left, then trend up and right to the final ledge. Finish up the steep wall left of a broken flake.

Little Book of Death 25m E4 5c ***. Tess Fryer, Ian Taylor. 1 Jun 2021.
The slim wall left of *Necronomican*. Start 2m left of *Necronomican* at a thin crack. Climb the crack to a good break and continue slightly rightwards to the big roof. Move to the centre of the roof and pull over to good holds. Move left to a good undercut and climb direct to a break. Pull on to the ledge above, then follow the left arête of the wall to the top.

Platform Walls
Uisge Draoidheil 25m Severe **. Rory Harper. 30 Aug 2021.
From the beginning of *Minch Crack* take a low rightwards traverse of the wall to join the right arête at its base. Climb the arête, on its left side at first. A low crux and a significantly easing top half make this an excellent deep-water solo (although it's not very deep water).

Leaning Block Cliffs
Shagadelic 20m VS 4c **. Rory Harper, Ethan Dyer. 29 Aug 2021.

Start at the same point as *Crossover* and climb the straightforward slab to the left of the chimney, then step right to join and traverse right across the prominent horizontal break leading to the eye of *Cyclops*. Take a minute to savour the situation before finishing up *Cyclops* (crux).

Amphitheatre Bay, North Face
Ian Taylor disagrees with Michael Barnard's comment in *SMCJ* 2021 regarding *The Roaring Forties* being overgraded. 'Having climbed it three or four times, the original E4 grade seems fair to me.'

Assynt
Inbhirpollaidh 'Rock Gym'
Journey Across the Gym 40m E2 5b *. Tim Miller, Nicky Brierley. 1 Mar 2021.
A two pitch zigzag across the wall following the two obvious fault lines.
1. 15m Start at *Calum's Rest* and follow the fault rightwards to a hanging belay on *Inertia*.
2. 25m Traverse horizontally left to finish up *When I Were a Lad*. Beware of constant ground fall potential, including for the second.

Suilven, Withered Crag
A beautifully situated and remote cliff directly above the notch at the south-east (Meall Beag) end of the main ridge. It faces west-south-west and is characterised by two soaring grooves. It is best approached by striking out left from the base of the approach gully on the main path, then gaining and following a vague path on the right bank of the last major gully. The best conditions are in the afternoon and evening, once the sun has made an appearance.

The Lonely Mountain 80m E4 **. Guy Robertson, Phil Jack. 17 Aug 2020.
Good rock, climbing and exposure. The line starts at the base of the right-hand groove, then trends leftwards up slabs to a crux on the left edge, before stepping around the edge to follow the obvious stepped ramp leading up leftwards across the right wall of the left-hand groove. Start at the base of the right-hand groove on the lowest rocks.
1. 30m 5c Climb a crack on the right of a block, then step right a follow another corner-crack to a pull out left at its top. Go up slightly left on giant flakes below a smooth slab with a thin left-slanting crack. Step across right to the base of the crack then follow it with difficulty to a reach a treacherous sloping ledge on the left. Follow more cracks upwards, then go back right onto the slab before trending up left, passing an overlap, to reach a good belay ledge just right of the edge.
2. 20m 6a To the left is a bottomless groove. Step delicately into this and follow it (crux) to pull onto another ledge on the right. Climb directly up, then traverse easily round left to belay beneath an overhang at the right edge of the steep smooth wall.
3. 35m 5a Pull over the overhang, then follow the obvious left-trending stepped groove in a superb position, passing a steep section at the top.

Lord of the Isles 40m E7 6b ***. Guy Robertson. 26 Aug 2020.
The awe-inspiring smooth right wall of the left-hand groove provides a soul-searching journey with brilliantly precarious climbing. The afternoon sun is required to dry out some seeps on the lower section. Either climb a short pitch up from below and left, or abseil directly down to a good ledge and belay in the

groove, some ten metres or so up from a giant lodged flake. Make a couple of
moves up the groove, then pull right onto the wall at the top of a black V-groove
(often wet). Step across right again to a good hidden slot in a niche, and then,
using an edge above, gain a standing position on the obvious foot-rail to make a
long reach to a dubious block. Quickly pull past this to good protection and a
ledge and rest above. Make thin moves directly up cracks to beneath an overhang,
then pull up on big booming holds (good micro-cam high up and right) to make
a sustained sequence up thin cracks (crux) to where better layaways gain the
stepped flake on the right. A short groove on the right of this leads to another
ledge and rest. Move up, then go left on big sloping holds to gain the left end of
the overlap, then up and slightly left again to where a hard move on poor crimps
gains better holds (crucial micro-cam out right). Layback the left-hand crack
precariously to reach a horizontal break, then step right and make a final tricky
move diagonally up right to better holds and the exit point.

Lochinver Crags
Achmelvich Campsite Crags, Clean Cut
Make Achmelvich Great Again   10m   E5 6b **.   Andy Moles, Ferdia Earle. 27
Jun 2021.
Thin cracks up the leaning front face of the *Hed Kandi* pillar. Short but excellent.

Mass Destruction   20m   E2 6a.   Andy Moles, Ferdia Earle. 27 Jun 2021.
Start left of the giant fallen block at a crack. Initial fingery crux moves are
protected by an overhead micro-wire cluster. Follow the crack for 6m then traverse
left to a short bottomless corner. Go up this to the roof then move left and finish
up the wall, avoiding some dubious wedged blocks. (Topo provided.)

The Certainty of Tides   18m   E7 6c ***.   Ferdia Earle. 26 Jun 2021.
The beautiful blank corner to the right of *Flawless* has more holds than first
appears, but the gear is mostly poor. Climb the slab left of the corner to a narrow
ledge running across the wall at third-height. Step up into the corner, where bold
stemming leads to a good foothold on the left wall. Get what small and shallow
gear you can, before employing wizardry for the very technical crux finish. (Topo
provided.)

Andy Moles suggests renaming *Calypso* to *Collapso* to reflect the significant
change of line post-rockfall. He found *Faithless* high for the grade at E3 6a,
especially as a good foothold fell off the second crux after he had used it. *Faithless*
does not need low tide – just not high tide. The start can be easily gained by
stepping in from the start of *Flightless*.

Strone Crag
Left Edge   Diff. *.   Dave Allan, John McGavin. 9 Jul 2021.
About 10m left of *Borderline* climb the clean left edge of the crag starting up a
short corner.

Dave Allan suggests the following revised grades: *Choc Flakes* (V.Diff. *), *Strone
Flake* (H.Severe is about right), *Pollan Groove* (Mild VS 4b *), *Crofter's Crack*
(Don't know but harder than H.Severe – failed on it), *Pollan Slab* (on a top rope
it felt like 5a), *Mossman* (Severe 4b **), *Borderline* (H.Severe 4b poorly
protected).

Inchnadamph
Glen Oykel – Black Rock Slabs
(NC 322 137) Alt 250m South-east and south-west facing
Sound, pleasant, granite slabs at an easy angle.
Approach: Park at the track end at NC 296 083 on the A837 4 miles east of
Ledmore junction. Cycle along the track for 4 miles past Benmore Lodge and the
crags are on your left. The south-east facing North Slabs are 500m away at map
ref NC 322137 and the south-west facing Main Crag is 1km away, further south.

The first set of routes are on the Main Crag. To descend, go to the top of the
hill and descend to the left.

The Bulges 80m V.Diff. Dave Allan, John McGavin. 28 Jun 2021.
Start at a small cairn beneath a slab at the right side of the face.
1. 40m Climb directly over three small bulges then a large bulge to belay on its
top.
2. 40m Follow a left-slanting fault then easier ground.

The Rib 85m Severe 4a. Dave Allan, John McGavin. 28 Jun 2021.
Start beneath a rib at a small cairn 75m left of *The Bulges*.
1. 35m Climb the rib direct and pass just left of the left-hand of two large rowans.
Continue by parallel cracks then step left and climb onto the arête and belay on a
juniper ledge.
2. 50m Bear right and climb easier slabs to the top.

The next routes are on the North Slabs, described from right to left. To descend,
either go down a steep, grassy gully to the left or the ridge on the right.

White Spots 130m Diff. Dave Allan, John McGavin. 21 Jun 2021.
Start at a small cairn beneath a slab with big white spots on its right side.
1. 45m Climb the slabs to a belay beneath an overlap at a small rowan.
2. 45m Continue up to a belay at a big block on the right.
3. and 4. 40m Continue to the top in two more pitches.

Orange Slab 125m V.Diff. Dave Allan, John McGavin. 21 Jun 2021.
Start just up and left of *White Spots* at a small cairn. Climb straight up the narrow
orange slab, avoiding the grass ledges where possible.

Red Slab 115m V.Diff *. Dave Allan, John McGavin. 27 Sep 2020.
Further up and left again from the *Orange Slab* start at a small cairn beneath a
tongue of slab some way below a small rowan.
1. 35m Ascend the slabs to a belay just below a clump of junipers.
2. and 3. 80m Climb the overlap on the right and follow the clean slabs to the
top.

Black Bulge 80m V.Diff. Dave Allan, John McGavin. 27 Sep 2020.
Start 35m up and left of the start of *Red Slab* at a small cairn, level with the clump
of junipers. Climb straight up and ascend the black bulge higher up.

Conival
Geologists' Ridge 450m IV,4. Iain Young, John Higham. 5 Jan 2022.

The south-west flank of Conival drops some 475m from the summit to the Bealach Trallgil and the upper 300m of this are a mixture of steep turf and rock. The face is split by two wide depressions that narrow downwards into shallow gullies, the left-hand of which terminates in an icefall at its base. The ridge immediately right of this icefall is *Explorers' Ridge* (*SMCJ* 2013). *Geologists' Ridge* takes the ridge just to the right of the right-hand depression.[1]

Start at the lowest rocks (NC 3012 1963) immediately right of the gully and follow the crest, passing a prominent overhanging block on its right, over moderate ground for 240m to just below the obvious barrier wall. Climb this on the front of the face via a left-slanting ramp and a final short wall in two pitches of 30m and 20m, with a belay taken on a huge block just above a large ledge. From here, follow the crest with occasional interest to a junction with the south-east ridge not far below the summit. See topo below.

John Mackenzie notes that the map reference for *Explorers' Ridge* (*SMCJ* 2013) is incorrect. The route takes the line left of *Geologists' Ridge* and finishes just west of the summit.

Quinag, Spidean Còinich, Bucket Buttress

Di Time   35m   IV,5.   Robin Clothier, Stuart McFarlane. 18 Feb 2022.
Climb the corner to the left of *Beer Time* to an overhang. Traverse right to join *Beer Time* and follow this to the top of the blocky chimney and exit right into a fault. Delicate move. (Topo provided.)

Beyond the Pail   90m   IV,5 *.   Rory Brown, Tom Shaw. 5 Jan 2021.
On the face with *Paily Wally* etc but further left than the existing routes. To the left of a very large roofed area are two fault-lines; follow the right-hand of these from its start to the top, with a couple of awkward sections but generally good gear. Belay on a large ledge. Escape left at around Grade III is possible here, but

---

[1] See Iain Young's account of this route in 'Mountaineering in Hyperborea: Land Beyond the North Wind' earlier in this issue of the Journal. – Hon. Ed.

it is far better to step right into a left-facing corner-chimney that is steep but positive and very well protected. After the chimney follow the ridge up a step or two to the top of the hill. (Topo provided.)

Ben Stack, South-West Face
(NC 271 419) Alt 500m South-west facing
There are four buttresses along the south-west face of the hill at an altitude of 500m which have some climbing on gneiss. These are numbered 1 to 4 from the left (west). In addition there is a smaller crag further north-west called Western Crag.
Approach: Park at the stone shed on the A838 opposite Loch Stack Lodge at NC 265 437. Take the stalker's path from here up the hill. After about a mile and above a loch take the steep track on the left. This becomes the path up the north-west ridge of the hill. Ascend until the ridge becomes steep and rocky at about 450m. Now make a rising traverse rightwards round the shoulder to the first of the crags – Western Crag. 3km, 1.5 hours. You can also park at Achfary and take the track up Strath Stack for 3km and the buttresses are above on your right. The first set of routes are on Western Crag and are described from left to right.

Hatchling's Arête 25m Severe 4a. Dave Allan, Duncan McGavin. 11 Jun 2018.
Climb the right side of the first arête.

Left Gully 20m Diff. Dave Allan, Duncan McGavin. 11 Jun 2018.
Right of *Hatchling's Arête*.

Pipit Slab 25m VS 4c. Dave Allan, Duncan McGavin. 3 Jun 2018.
The crack 3m left of the left-facing corner.

Stonechat Corner 25m VS 4b **. Dave Allan, Duncan McGavin. 3 Jun 2018.
The fine left-facing corner.

Plover 25m V.Diff. Dave Allan, Duncan McGavin. 3 Jun 2018.
The slab just right of the corner then the high left-facing corner.

Cuckoo Wall 20m Severe 4b. Dave Allan, Duncan McGavin. 11 Jun 2018.
Climb a shallow left-facing corner then move right into a niche. Step left and climb a steep wall.

Jug Corner 15m V.Diff. Dave Allan, Duncan McGavin. 3 Jun 2018.
The obvious big corner.

Right Buttress 15m V.Diff. Dave Allan, Duncan McGavin. 11 Jun 2018.
Climb the centre of the last short buttress.

The next routes are on The Buttresses, the first being on Buttress 1.

Eagle Feather Arête 80m V.Diff. Davy Moy, Dave Allan. 10 Jul 2014.
Climb the right side of the arête for 20m, then move to the left side above a big rock spike above an overhang. Climb the arête then slabs on the right side, then go into a grassy gully on the left. Climb blocky rocks to finish.

The following three routes are on Buttress 2, described from the left.

Ring Ousel Rib   50m   V.Diff.   Davy Moy, Dave Allan. 28 Jul 2014.
Climb the buttress starting 35m up and left from the toe.

Merlin Corner   50m   HVS 5a.   Davy Moy, Dave Allan. 10 Jul 2014.
The big right-facing corner at the left toe of the buttress.

The Scoop   45m   HVS 5a *.   Davy Moy, Dave Allan. 7 Aug 2014.
Climb *Merlin Corner* until it is possible to traverse right above the overhang to a
point beneath the fine cracked scoop in the wall above. Climb this to the top.

The final two routes are on Buttress 3.

Cave Buttress Left   55m   HVS 5a.   Davy Moy, Dave Allan. 7 Aug 2014.
Start up left of the toe of the buttress and climb a short, steep, dark-brown wall to
holds. Move up to good holds then right through a notch in the arête. Climb a
short corner on the right then a chimney-crack and grassy cracks to big ledges.
Take the steep corner fault on the left then finish up the short wall on the left.

Cave Buttress Right   57m   Severe.   Davy Moy, Dave Allan. 28 Jul 2014.
Start right of the toe of the buttress and move up left onto a slab. Continue by a
shallow right-facing corner then a narrow chimney with chockstones to finish up
a short wall on the left.

Scourie Crags, Solitude Slab
Ankle Grinder   40m   E1 5a.   Ian Taylor, Tess Fryer. 6 Jun 2021.
This route lies on the steeper right-hand buttress, which is accessed by descending
the rib on the south side of the geo and traversing in. Unfortunately the route
deteriorates with height. Climb a nice groove on the left side of the buttress, pull
left below roofs, then go carefully up loose blocky ground to an easing. Finish
rightwards to belay on a ridge. Scramble to the top.

Ian Taylor notes that *In Too Deep* was considered to be E4 and fairly serious with
snappy rock and spaced protection. It is best climbed in two pitches 35m 5c, 15m
5a. The second pitch may be more direct than the original. The approach time to
the crag was over an hour.

Laxford Bay Slabs
Tick Roulette   8m   V.Diff.   Sharon J. Kennedy, Graham Uney. 2 Aug 2021.
Go up the grassy gully to the right of *Evening Sunset*, then start below a corner.
Climb the arête and wall to the right of the corner, gaining an easier-angled slab
that leads to the top.

Ridgway View Crag
The Diagonal   33m   Severe 4a *.   Dave Allan, John McGavin. 3 Aug 2021.
At the higher left-hand part of the crag. Start 10m right of the right end of the
overhang half-way up the crag, at a steep wall with a left-rising vegetated fault.
Climb up steeply below the end of the fault then traverse up and left below the
fault. Take a short corner-crack to a big ledge then follow the ledge leftwards to

a fine corner-crack and climb it and a further short crack directly above.

Kinsaile Crags, Maiden's Crag
Magic Seaweed 15m E5 6b ***. Jamie Skelton, Morag Eagleson. 7 May 2022.
The middle of the pale wall on the right side of the crag. Start up a short steep groove and crack. Continue up the wall above on positive holds. Place some small wires, charge into more steepness aiming for a small right-facing corner at the top of the crag. Well protected and sustained.

Creag an Fhithich
125West 35m E5 6a ***. Mike Gardner (unseconded). 25 Mar 2022.
The parallel line 3 to 5 metres left of *The Swirl*. A committing lower wall is followed by a glorious and easier headwall. Start 5m left of *The Swirl* at the left arête of the wall. Climb up to the overlap and traverse right to the black vein. Climb the wall left of the black vein to a sloping ledge. Continue to the second large ledge above. Continue up beautiful rock on the headwall, gaining a thin crack leading to ledge with a small tree on it. Head up the blunt arête right of the tree and continue right to the tree belay of *The Swirl*. (Topo provided.)

Sheigra, First Geo, North Side
Drangr 15m Severe. Rory Brown, Robert Cross. 12 Jul 2021.
The left-slanting crack up the buttress between *Aegir* and *Blackjack*. Climb the crack, tricky to start, and then continue up the buttress to join *Aegir* at its top.

Durness to Ben Loyal, Port Vasgo
Manhattan Transfer 35m E1 5a **. Neil Adams, Gordon Lacey. 16 Apr 2022.
The near-horizontal break near the top of the prow gives amenable climbing in a wild position. Climb the first pitch of *Burn Brooklyn Burn* / *Statue of Liberty* to belay near the base of the *California Gurls* corner. Climb *California Gurls* to 5m below the top. Place some gear, take a deep breath and launch out leftwards across the break, moving up to a higher break halfway across, and continue to the top left corner of the prow. Good holds and good gear but steep and sustained. (Topo provided.)

Caithness East Coast
South Head of Wick
I Can't Believe It's Not Butter 30m E1 5b. Liam Ingram, James Milton. 9 Jun 2021.
The corner-line on the far north-east end of the wall facing the castle. Abseil down the corner to the large ledge then through a gap in the roof to a sea-level ledge.
1. 10m 5b Climb a friable slab to a gap in the roof. Pull through the gap on big holds and belay on the ledge above.
2. 20m 4c Climb the corner, initially on friable wafers and passing a tricky overlap, after which the rock quality improves.

Sarclet
First Bay
White Pudding 11m H.Severe 4b. Dave Porter, Ben Sparham. 17 Apr 2011.
Start at a small pool near the bottom of the descent (about 4m right of *Black Pudding*). Climb a right-trending fracture line into an open V-groove at half-height.

Gearty Head

(ND 346 425) Partly tidal South-east facing
These routes lie just south of Gearty Head (and north of Oily Buttress). Scramble in from the lower-angled rocks to the north (tidal), or abseil. There is a damp, black cleft running the full height of the cliff. The routes appear to get affected by birds later in the season.

Socialism in the Mainline   25m   H.Severe 4b ***.   Dave Porter, Ben Sparham. 17 Apr 2011.
The arête with a flake crack on its right-hand side, north of the black cleft.

Lost Friend   20m   VS 5a *.   Dave Porter, Ben Sparham. 17 Apr 2011.
Traverse about 20m left (south) from *Mainline*. Climb the slightly right-trending corner-groove system which skirts to the right of a small overhang near the top.

Old Friend   20m   VS 4c.   Ben Sparham, Dave Porter. 17 Apr 2011.
On the left-hand side of the wall just right (north) of *Lost Friend*. Start up initial cracks which peter out to leave a more thought-provoking finish.

Occam's Buttress

Life Before Insanity   35m   E4 6a **.   Michael Barnard, Alan Hill. 10 Jul 2021.
The central line on the wall. Start up a groove left of *The Ugly Bug Ball*, then move left and up to place good gear at the base of the slabby section. Traverse right and move up to the right end of the hanging slab, then undercling back left and place a Camalot 0.3 blindly (it may be possible to place it from below). Make thin moves up left to good holds and protection (crux), then continue up the sustained upper continuation of the *Another Day* groove and out right on underclings to reach for a good jug (bold). Continue more easily, firstly out right on the lip of the roof, then up the wall just right of the daisy to finish up a short flake-crack. Pre-practised. (Topo provided.)

Big Buttress, North Face

Bitzer Maloney   35m   E1 5b *.   Michael Barnard, Alan Hill. 10 Jul 2021.
Start on a ledge below and slightly left of the 'prominent chimney-fault'. Climb the steep groove until 5m below the main bulge, then gain the left arête and continue as for *Slinky Malinky*. Good climbing but often greasy.

Tilted Ledge

Better   12m   E1 5b *.   Dave Porter, Ben Sparham. 16 Apr 2011.
At the north end of Tilted Ledge, where the ledge finally dips into the sea, is a square arête bounded on its left-hand-side by a 1m-deep overhang at about 6m height. This route follows the general line of the arête. Start up the crack to its left (on the short wall under the overhang), then bypass the overhang by stepping round onto the right-hand side of the arête and pulling up steeply onto the lip. Continue up the arête and its right-hand side to finish.

Gloup Ledge

Sarclet Buoy   20m   VS 4c.   Mick Tighe, Kathy Tighe. 28 Aug 2015.
Climb the fine wall a few metres left of *Sarclet Woman* to finish through the obvious V-cleft in the overhang, which is a little fragile. (Topo provided.)

Sarclet Woman   20m   HVS 5a *. Kathy Tighe, Mick Tighe. 28 Aug 2015.
Start a few metres left of *Molly Cough Cocktail*. Climb up to a hole-recess at 8m, exit left via a flake and climb the wall above to a fine horizontal fault. Take this out right for 5 to 6m, then climb straight up to exit at the right-hand end of the overhang. (Topo provided.)

Ulbster, Whaligoe, Ellens Geo
Fight Fire with Fire   30m   E3 5c ***. Michael Barnard, Alan Hill. 11 Jul 2021.
Takes the obvious upper line of weakness between *Pig's Ear* and *The Fracture Clinic*. Start just right of *Towed in the Hole*. Climb directly up the wall, then go right and up to join *Pig's Ear* up to the break. Traverse right and go up a flake-crack right of the *Pig's Ear* crack to its top. Move right, pull into the conglomerate, continue past the right end of the roof and step left into a groove. Step back right onto the wall and climb a thin crack to finish up a short flake-crack.

Michael Barnard comments that Ellens Geo has a topo on UKC with routes not referred to anywhere else. He notes that *The Yellow Line* is the same as *Breaking the Rules*, climbed the previous year, and the recent route *Gently George* is an easier finish to *Pork Scratchings*.

Mid Clyth, Overhanging Wall Area
Abi   12m   V.Diff *. Simon White, Loz Monckton. 21 May 2022.
Starting 2m left (south) of the descent, follow the short stepped corners to the top.

Gemma   12m   V.Diff *. Loz Monckton, Simon White. 21 May 2022.
Starting just left (south) of the descent, climb into the deep niche then finish via a short layback crack.

Latheronwheel
Pinnacle Area
Maggot Surprise   10m   H.Severe 4b. Dave Porter, Simon White. 13 Jun 2021.
The thin crack-line 1m left of *Forgotten Corner*.

Big Flat Wall Area
Imperial Lather Direct   18m   E2 5b **. Steve Crowe, Karin Magog. 29 Aug 2021.
Start up the crack as for *Imperial Lather* (or, better, the wall immediately left of the crack). Step left at the top of the crack and continue directly to the top.

ORKNEY, Westray, Monivey
Puppies of Diplomacy   20m   Severe. James Thacker, Alison Thacker. 10 Jun 2021.
Start about half-way down the huge tidal platform (about the size of two football pitches). Climb up towards the obvious left-facing corner on huge holds, before breaking out left to climb the short wall and slab. (Named owing to the rock's similarity to Yellow Wall at Gogarth. This line is an upside-down *Dogs of War*.)

James Thacker suggests *Nice One, Angus* (VS 4c) deserves a technical grade of 5a.

SHETLAND
Mainland, Ochran Head
(HU 2423 8443) Non Tidal North-West facing
The following two routes lie near the south end of the main Ockran Head cliffs
(once past the more broken smaller walls). Looking down from the top, they take
the most prominent cracked grooves (with an arête between them) on a narrow
buttress between two sea caves. The narrow buttress is visible from the north (see
topo). Abseil the line of each groove to good high non-tidal ledges. (Topo
provided.)

The Pony Saga 30m E1 5b **. Michael Barnard, Alan Hill. 3 Jul 2021.
The left-hand groove; a fine crack climb. From the starting ledge climb the steep
crack to a bulge; go through this then up the easier upper groove.

Neigh Bother 35m E1 5a. Michael Barnard, Alan Hill. 3 Jul 2021.
The right-hand groove. From the starting ledge climb a steep corner-crack to the
mid-height bulge; go through this (crux) then up the much easier upper groove.

Eshaness Lighthouse
Left Wall 35m E2 5b ***. Michael Barnard, Alan Hill. 30 Jun 2021.
Brilliant wall climbing up the left side of *Foy Corner*. The main wall section
requires faith but is not as bold as it looks; take plenty of small cams. Traverse
right from the starting ledge of *Near Perfect Arête*, go up a groove and move right
to below the wall. Climb the wall, moving left and right as holds and protection
dictate, to finish more easily up the blunt arête.

What's in its Pocketses? 30m E1 5a *. Michael Barnard, Alan Hill. 1 Jul 2021.
From the *Ringil* ledge, traverse left to climb the wall between that route and *Foy
Corner*.

Quest for Adventure 45m E2 5b **. Michael Barnard, Alan Hill, Lucy Spark.
1 Jul 2021.
A spectacular and committing trip which would be one of the best in the area, but
loses a star due to rock quality. Abseil to a small ledge just right of and level with
the *Aisha/Vilya* ledge. Go up a thin crack, cross a groove on the right and continue
across the wall, just above the big roof, to near the right arête. Continue up, always
fairly near the arête, to below the upper roofs, then move back up left to finish up
the obvious crack in the top wall. (Topo provided.)

Lunning Crags, Longa Geo
Near the left end of the crag is an undercut corner, immediately left of which is a
fine fin feature. To reach the first route, scramble down the next corner to the left
again, then belay and make a slabby traverse and step down to the base of the fin
(about V.Diff).

Michael Barnard notes that the three sections of the Lunning Crags are separate
areas and don't really lie next to each other, though you would approach them all
from the same parking.

The Fin 12m E1 5a *. Michael Barnard, Alan Hill. 29 Jun 2021.
The wall of the fin features two thin right-slanting cracks. Move up to place gear

Michael Barnard on FA Headless Wall (E3,5c), Bressay, Shetland.
Photo: Robert Durran.

in the upper one, then make thin moves to a jug (harder for the short). Continue up the easier upper arête.

Michael Barnard notes that *Hibernation* (written up on UKC) climbs the lower slanting crack then handrails along the break to finish as for the above. It was repeated from the same logical starting point as *The Fin* and thought HVS 5a **, the best route on the crag. It is written up on UKC as E2 5c, but starting higher avoids the difficult start from sea level.

Left of *Rolling Arête* (the arête at the left end of the main slabby wall) is an undercut corner; abseil this to reach the following route:

Lunning Free   15m   VS 4c. Michael Barnard, Alan Hill. 29 Jun 2021.
The obvious right-rising traverse above the lower bulge and below the upper roof. Finish up *Rolling Arête*.

Cryptic Crab   15m   V.Diff. Alan Hill, Michael Barnard. 29 Jun 2021.
Starting in *Hidden Corner*, climb a diagonal crack above *Rising Crack* to reach a flake, then continue to the top.

Bressay, Muckle Hell
Black Wall
Porcupine Tree   30m   VS 4c. Michael Barnard, Alan Hill. 28 Jun 2021.
Start up *The Brigdi* crack, moving up and right at first opportunity until it is possible to step down and gain an obvious right-slanting crack. Climb this then go up to gain and climb the corner bounding the wall on the right.

Dark Matter   30m   E2 5b **. Michael Barnard, Alan Hill. 28 Jun 2021.
The wall right of *The Brigdi*. Start as for that route, moving up and right at first opportunity, aiming for a short shallow groove. Climb this with difficulty to a break, traverse left, then climb the next section of wall to the next break. Move back right to climb the top wall, trending left to finish on the left side of the big block.

Mirki Wall
Headless Wall   50m   E3 *. Michael Barnard, Alan Hill. 28 Jun 2021.
An attempt at the fine left wall of *Ghost Town*. An excellent questing main pitch, worth ***, but the route really needs a better finish (there are options but there wasn't time to try them).
1. 30m 5c Start up *Ghost Town* for a few metres, then take the wide slanting break out to the left arête. Move up to climb grooves and cracks, then step right and go up past a wide slanting break to a narrower break above. Hand-traverse back left to the arête and move up into grooves leading to a belay below the big roof.
2. 20m 5a Traverse the big break into the *Ghost Town* corner and finish up this.

NORTHERN HIGHLANDS CENTRAL

Beinn a' Mhùinidh, Bonaid Dhonn, Main Wall
Morning Pass   65m   E3 5c **. Michael Barnard, Doug Bartholomew. 23 Jul 2021.

A line right of *Dream Ticket;* similar but slightly harder.

1. 45m 5c From the large block, move up then go rightwards above the low roof to the base of the fine burnt wall. Move boldly up this (at one point pulling out left then stepping back right) to reach a thin crack right of *Dream Ticket*'s twin cracks. Climb this and continue to the far left end of the long overlap. Pull through here and continue directly to just below the belay ledge. Move left and back right to gain the stance.

2. 20m 5b As for *Dream Ticket.*

Bianasdail Buttress

(NH 03394 67531)

Bianasdail Buttress 150m V,6. Simon Richardson, Mark Robson. 19 Feb 2022. The prominent buttress seen on the skyline when walking up Glen Bianasdail. It is characterised by a prominent perched block at three-quarters height. Start just left of the foot of the buttress at NH 03394 67531 where a right-trending fault cuts through the slabby lower tier.

1. 60m Climb the fault for 20m and continue over vegetated walls to belay on a terrace that runs along the line of crag and where the angle steepens.

2. 25m About 20m left of the buttress crest is a large white triangular block. Climb the groove behind the block for 5m then traverse horizontally right for 5m. Climb the short slabby wall above to reach easier ground and belay below a prominent left-facing corner.

3. 35m Move right around the corner and climb a smaller right-facing corner to gain easier ground level with the prominent perched block seen from below. Belay below a prominent V-groove cutting through the headwall.

4. 30m. Climb the groove for 10m then traverse right along a ledge to its end. Make a difficult move up and right and continue up the exposed edge above to the top.

Creag Tharbh

(NG 9256 7398) Alt 300m South-west facing

A long line of crags referred to as Creag Tharbh on the map lie along the north bank of Loch Maree. This small crag lies above the steepest crags of Creag Tharbh and is best distinguished by the large white quartzite outcrop on its south-east flank which can be seen from the main road on the other side of the loch.

Approach: Kayaking is the best approach, setting off from the Slatterdale carpark (NG 88856 72153) and landing on a rocky shoreline at NG 92196 73733. Head directly up the hillside beside the small stream until the crag appears on your right at a height of approximately 300m. Failing this follow the path from Incheril carpark (NH 03770 62411) past Letterewe and up the hillside to about NG 94065 73454, leave the path here and attempt to contour at this level past numerous cliffs to the start of the route. Walking is not recommended!

Descent: Descend on the right-hand side of the crag.

White Patch Arête 200m Diff. *. John Higham. 6 Sep 2020.

The route was approached by kayak on this occasion landing at NG 922 737 and following a steep wooded valley to the foot of the climb. The location of the route can best be seen from across the loch as it is distinguished by a prominent quartz patch of rock, the arête lying 30m to the left side of this. Follow the arête directly from its base, difficulties easing with height. Descent is best made on the right.

Baosbheinn, Creag an Fhithich – North-West Face

Homeview 200m III,3 **. John Higham, Alison Higham. 1 Feb 2021.
This route follows the curving ridge located in the centre of the north-west triangular face immediately right of the 'open chute line' described in the guidebook. Start at its lowest point (NG 8568 6758). Climb the ridge, initially on the left, then follow the ridge directly for four long (60m) pitches to easier ground. The ridge would blank out significantly in an old-style winter with lots of snow but these seem rare now. It provided an enjoyable line with magnificent views over Loch Gairloch.

Gairloch Crags
An Groban – North-West Face

Mashed Banana 100m Diff. Michael Mckenna, Rachel Drummond. 8 Sep 2021.
The curving rib right of the dark gully-line. Start left of a grassy slab at steep juggy rock.
1. 30m Climb trending right in a steep groove to easier ground.
2. 30m Walk up steep heather above pitch 1 to base of a rib. Climb the rib on moderate rock to a niche and good belay.
3. 15m Step out right on steep rock and climb this for 10m to easier ground. Belay below a blocky chimney.
4. 25m Step right on moderate rock and climb this for 5m to broken ground. Scramble to the top and grassy ground. (Topo provided.)

An Groban – South-West Face

(NG 8384 7497) Alt 380m South-West facing
See 'Highland Scrambles North' pages 142–144.
Descent: Descend from summit to the north-east for a short distance (100m) avoiding cliffs to the north. Turn left down a narrow gully heading west and once on easier ground follow an obvious grassy ridge to the north. Continue to the north descending an awkward rock step on the way to the outlet of the Loch Àirigh a' Phuill. A hydroelectric access road here will take you back to the carpark.

Humpback Buttress 300m II/II **. John Higham, Alison Higham. 5 Jan 2021.
A winter ascent based on the excellent scramble Humpback Buttress (see 'Highland Scrambles North' p144). This takes the more natural winter line, but it is low-lying and south-west facing, so it was climbed in the exceptionally cold conditions of January 2021 with snow, ice and rock-hard turf. It may not often be in such good winter condition. The stars reflect these good conditions. Start 10m up from the base of the right-hand end of the buttress (NG 83585 74762). Ascend a short icy wall and continue up a left-trending ramp to a stand of small trees (45m). Ascend a short ice pitch and steep turf above (20m). Teeter up verglassed slabs and then follow mixed turf and short slabs for 20m. Rather than ascend the steep wall above, take a 10m traverse to the right and follow a shallow iced chimney (25m) then snowy slabs (20m) to the top of the 'Humpback'. Descend easily to the saddle and cross this trending right and then follow snow- or ice-covered slabby walls and turf ramps for 125m (minor ice pitches) to a broad terrace. Above and to the left is a steep red wall (summer crux); ascend this at its lowest point (25m). Easier ground leads to the summit (50m).

Rubha Rèidh, Port Erradale, North Stack

About Face 20m Diff. Graham Stein, John Sanders, Cat Stein, Claire Stein, Al Sanders. 1 May 2022.

Start on the plinth on the landward face of the stack at the same place as *Landward Face*. Instead of trending up left, climb straight up the right side of the face on loose, poor rock. A long abseil sling is required at the top for a safe descent. The route name is a clue – about-face and walk away.

No-one Puts Baby in a Corner 20m V.Diff. Al Sanders. 1 May 2022.

Opposite the landward face of the stack is an arête on a flying buttress with an arch through it. Start approximately 3m left of the big arch and 4m left of *The Watchman* beneath a large hanging flake. Climb to the flake (exposed) and ascend behind it in a right-rising line until a platform is reached beneath a prominent open corner. Step left and climb the wall above direct to the top.

Creag Mhòr Thollaidh – North-West Rib

(NG 8603 7801) Alt 180m North-west facing
See Highland Scrambles North p139.

Approach: Follow the Tollie to Slatterdale path from the car park past a steep craglet (Leth Creag) to the foot of the main cliffs. The lowest crag has a steep orange chimney-crack at the bottom. Start just to right of this.

North-West Rib 165m III,3 *. John Higham, Alison Higham. 7 Apr 2021.

A winter ascent of the scramble *North-West Rib* (see 'Highland Scrambles North' p142).

1. 25m Climb the right-hand edge of the buttress on jugs then steep slabs to the top of the buttress.
2. 30m Make a rising traverse across snow-covered heather (above the scramble's steep wall with reddish bands), then follow a turf-filled groove (right of an exposed rib) to a ledge below steeper ground.
3. 25m Move up right back onto the rib and climb a short tricky corner and the slabs above.
4. 20m Easy scrambling leads to a wide ledge below a line of overhangs (seen prominently on approach to the climb).
5. 15m Climb a turfy groove to below the overhangs, traverse up and right past a birch tree onto an exposed ledge (possible belay), move right a couple of metres to a continuation groove, then follow this to below slabs.
6. 20m Follow slabs up onto a wide terrace that lies below the next steeper rocky tier.
7. 30m Climb this short tier on the left via turf ledges and finish just to the right of a prominent brown band.
8. Easy ground leads to the North Summit.

Rubha Mòr
Mellon Udrigle, Forgotten Crag

There is another crag a short distance east of Forgotten Crag at NG 88942 97617. To approach, from the cairn at the 57m spot height (Meall na Creige Mòire) head west along the path towards a second cairn. From the path marker midway between the two cairns head towards the sea. The top of the cliff is visible as a wide fin of rock extending into the sea with an easy-angled hanging slab at its inland end. The cliff itself faces west and is not immediately visible. Descend under the hanging slab to the base of the cliff and a bright green rock pool. The rock is very solid, steep sandstone with perfect incut holds but little or no protection. It provides good, easy routes for children to combine with a trip to the beach. The routes are described from right to left.

Easy Peasy Squeeze a Lemon 8m Diff. Stuart Buchanan, Isla Buchanan. 16 Jul 2021.
At the right side of the cliff where it abuts the hanging slab are two chimneys. This route takes the left-hand chimney via bridging and back and footing. (Topo provided)

Easy Rider 8m V.Diff. Stuart Buchanan, Isla Buchanan. 16 Jul 2021.
Start steeply just left of a large boulder at the base of the cliff. Climb direct up some small ledges, then continue directly or more easily via a set of steps going right. (Topo provided)

Easy Street 8m Diff. Stuart Buchanan, Fergus Buchanan. 16 Jul 2021.
Halfway along the cliff are a set of ledges with a small chimney at the top. Climb direct, with a tricky finish.

Easy Does It 8m V.Diff. Stuart Buchanan. 16 Jul 2021.
Left of the ledges a set of black cracks run the length of the cliff. Climb direct on perfect holds.

Camas Point
Summer Rib 8m H.Severe 4b. Matt Smith, Vicky Smith. 8 Jun 2021.
The blunt edge between *Winter Break* and *Traction Control*. A hard start eases to ledges. Finish by the short steep wall (as per *Traction Control*?).

Dave Kerr notes that the routes described as being in Deep Geo – Sròn an Dùn-Chàirn (NG 864 984) are actually at Geodh' Fuar (NG 86844 98321). *Icicle Works* and *Baltic* at Camas Point have been affected by a rockfall. The 'stepped roof' described in the guidebook has fallen down. *Baltic* is still climbable at about the same grade but the status of *Icicle Works* is unknown. The two routes at Camas Buidhe Eoghainn are correctly described but the GR is incorrect. It should be something like NG 87928 97811 as they are east of Opinan Slabs. And finally, between the two routes above and the seaward end of the Opinan Slab is some excellent, mostly non-tidal bouldering on a variety of small walls and independent boulders.

Mellon Charles, Mellon Cliffs – Leacan Donna
Streaky Bacon 7m E2 6a *. Jason Currie. 12 Jul 2021.
Start 3m left of *MC's Chicken*. Bouldery moves up the black streak lead to a left-slanting crack that flares at the top.

A' Mhaighdean, South Face, Pillar Buttress
The Great Game 190m VS. Erick Baillot. 22 Sep 2019.
A solo ascent approximating to the winter line.

An Teallach, Glas Tholl
The Reckoning 90m X,9 ***. Greg Boswell, Guy Robertson. 2 Apr 2022.

An uncompromising direct line up the left side of the lower wall and through the centre of the headwall above. Start as for *Wailing Wall*.

1. 40m Climb Wailing Wall to just above its crux, before the traverse left into the shallow corner. From here continue straight up the thin crack, well-protected at first but then culminating in a hard and bold section to reach the belay ledge; a stunningly sustained pitch.

2. 30m Climb a short right-facing corner to step out left (loose blocks) where a line of easier flakes lead up and left towards the big gargoyle feature in the centre of the wall. Gain this from the left with difficulty to a resting ledge, then step right and follow a thin crack (bold at first) direct to the top. Another brilliant hard pitch.

Guy Robertson considers *The Wailing Wall* to be IX,8 ****. (See p.271.)

Loch Broom and Little Loch Broom, Badrallach Crag
Pebble Puller's Paradise 30m E1 5b *. Paul Donnithorne, Geoff Bennett. 2 Jun 2021.
Good climbing up the thin crack-line 2m left of *Hunter's Moon*. Adequate protection.

Glen Cannich, Sgùrr nan Clachan Geala, Creag Toll Tuill Bhearnach
Fox Buttress 120m III,3. Roger Webb, Neil Wilson. 28 Dec 2021.
An entertaining mountaineering route up the buttress immediately bounding *Peat Bog Faeries*. Start 10 to 15m right of *Peat Bog Faeries* at a right-facing turfy corner.

1) 25m Climb the corner to reach a narrow pavement ledge. Traverse the ledge leftwards to reach another corner. Climb this to a ledge overlooking *Peat Bog Faeries.*

2. 25m Move up and then right to pass behind a large rectangular block to gain a ledge. Traverse right to a belay ledge below a chimney-groove in the crest of the buttress.

3) 20m Climb the chimney-groove to easier ground and a belay.

4) 50m Cross easier ground for about 20m to gain a left-slanting gully. Climb this to belay at the crest of the buttress. From here, steadily easier ground leads to the top.

Strathconon
Hidden Crag
The Ant 12m VS 5a. Rory Brown, Thomas Shaw. 15 May 2022.
The crack approximately 2m left of, and parallel with, *The Barker*. Climb the crack to where it meets a thin horizontal crack, then finish straight up.

Meig Crag, Left Section
Flex 20m E5 6a *. Gaz Marshall. 15 May 2021.
The arête left of *Lone Pine Groove*, accessed after the first few metres of that route. A couple of big pulls lead to a jug on the arête from which a crucial small cam can be placed in a hidden pocket on the right wall, then step left and climb the arête on its left side. The route eases after a ledge at two-thirds height, taking the slab to the obvious crack in the headwall. Cleaned on a rope over several sessions before leading and will no-doubt be lost to the vegetation again!

Mark Robson on the first ascent of Princess Cut (VI,6), Glas Leathad Beag, Ben Wyvis.
Photo: Simon Richardson.

Creag Ruadh, North-East Face

Curving Gully 140m III. John Mackenzie, Ian Douglas. 20 Mar 2022.
One of the better defined lines here lying to the left of the lower buttress containing *Snow Dome* where the curving gully entrance is visible. Easy ground leads to a rock belay on the left. The route can bank out in full conditions.
1. 35m The gully straightens and steepens to (on this occasion) a snow overhang. Thread belay above under a large flat rock.
2. 45m Step right and continue up snow to the next steep tier where a turfy break going up shelves leads to a rock belay on the left.
3. 60m Move right and continue up snow to below the small summit cairn of the 740m top.

Bac an Eich – Coire Toll Lochain

Horse Play 80m I. M.W. Holland, D.J.E. Spencer, A.P. Williams. 22 Feb 2022.
From the top of the highest snow bay in the crag containing *Angel's Delight* a turfy ramp leads up left to the ridge. (Topo provided.)

Moy Rock, Left – The Bay

The Flying Pebble 18m 6b+. Jamie Skelton, Morag Eagleson. 26 Feb 2022.
A pumpy route just left of *Vangelis* which attempts to climb the steep pale wall.

Wasted Grit 12m 6a+. Jamie Skelton, Morag Eagleson. 26 Feb 2022.
A short line in the middle of the new gorse-cleared wall at the far left side of the crag. Steep climbing separated by a small ledge at half-height.

Ben Wyvis, Glas Leathad Beag, Diamond Buttress

Bort 95m II. Simon Richardson, Mark Robson. 10 Dec 2021.
Easy climbing up the shallow left-facing turfy groove that defines the leftmost edge of the main crag. Start up and left of *Six Finger Gully* (or, with more interest from the same place). Climb the open groove, before a step right to an easy finish on the summit crest.

Princess Cut 70m VI,6. Mark Robson, Simon Richardson. 10 Dec 2021.
Exciting positions across some steep ground. Start in the same place as *Cycle of Doom*.
1. 25m Gain the right-slanting fault and follow it on ice then turf to a fine eyrie on the arête.
2. 45m Steep moves lead out right onto the front face of the crag. Continue in the same fault-line to finish as for *Winter Skills*.

NORTHERN HIGHLANDS SOUTH

SOUTH GLEN SHIEL
Druim Shionnach, West Face

Cave Gully, Direct Start 20m V,5. Joe Barlow, Rosie Rothwell, Ben Hayes. 25 Feb 2022.
Climb directly up a steep but short icefall before belaying on the right wall of the large cave (20m). Continue up the normal route to the top.

Joe Barlow notes that *Cave Gully* is very tough for Grade IV, with sustained climbing and limited protection when climbing up to the chimney. A good route, but feeling more like V,5.

Aonach air Chrith
Coire na Doire Duibhe
(NH 054 092)
This small corrie has a fine area of slabs that can become heavily iced. In the centre of these is the following route (others possible depending on build up).

Gneiss Ice 60m   III *. Chris Dickinson, William Wilson. 27 Nov 2021.
Climb a short steep wall to a fine stepped slabby corner. Climb this and finish up a short wall of ice to the top.

Druim na Cìche
(NH 054 086)
Druim na Cìche is the north ridge of Aonach air Chrith. It has a sizeable east face. (Topo provided.)

Cave Climb 120m   III. Chris Dickinson, William Wilson. 27 Nov 2021.
Start at foot of a rib some 20m left of a vertical corner. Climb the steep turfy rib going left then right to a large cave. Exit right by traversing under an overhang above the vertical corner, then climb easy snow beside a vertical wall on the left. An easier pitch leads to the crest of Druim na Cìche which can be followed to the summit of Aonach air Chrith. (Topo provided.)

The following route is on a triangular buttress, the lower half of Double Diamond Buttress, which lies low down on the left-hand side of the unnamed corrie.

Tumbling Spike 60m   III/IV. Chris Dickinson, Anna Guy. 4 Dec 2021.
Start right of centre of the buttress and make some tricky moves right and then left, before climbing rightwards and then directly up steeper turf-covered rocks to a niche below a final overhang, where a belay is possible. Pull through the overhang to finish. (Topo provided.)

The Saddle, Coire Caol
The Gallows 245m   III,4 *. Steve Kennedy, Andy MacDonald. 5 Mar 2022.
Situated on the right side of the sprawling buttress immediately right of *Caol Couloir*, taking a left-trending line with fairly complex route-finding. An easy descent was made back into the corrie down snow slopes well to the right.
1. 40m Start about 10m left of the gully bounding the right side of the buttress and climb leftwards into a snow bay below a steepening (below a steep groove on the right).
2. 55m Climb mixed ground on the left followed by a slabby corner above to reach a steep wall. Traverse horizontally left below the wall to gain and follow an open groove up to a bay.
3. 55m Move rightwards into an open groove which leads up and left to below a steep barrel-shaped wall. Traverse hard left under the wall to a perch out on the left. Climb the slabby wall above, making an exposed step right below a wall, to reach easier ground and a belay on the left.
4 and 5. 95m Two straightforward pitches up mixed ground lead to the narrow summit ridge.

NORTH GLEN SHIEL
Creag Lundie Slabs
Eastern Zone, Front Zone East
Viva Ukraine 120m VS 4c *. Chris Dickinson, Anna Guy. 1 May 2022.
This route is in the Front Zone East about 50m to the right of *Bits and Pieces*. It
is the longest route at Creag Lundie. Start just right of a giant boulder.
1. Climb the slab, pass a grass ledge and take a stance after 25m to allow you to
reach the big belay ledge after the next pitch.
2. Continue up the fine slab and then surmount the steep overlap via a break on
the left, then continue to a big grassy ledge. Cam belays.
3. 4c Climb straight up the wall above the belay, then follow the slab to the top.
(Topo provided.)

Mariupol Slab 30m Diff. Chris Dickinson, Anna Guy. 1 May 2022.
This clean slab lies about 100m right of *Viva Ukraine*, roughly level with the
second pitch. Climb slightly leftwards from the base to a crack that leads directly
to the top.

Far Eastern Zone, Far East
Dalian Atkinson 20m V.Diff. Chris Dickinson, John Jones. 5 Sep 2021.
A parallel well-protected line left of *George Floyd*. Climb the left-hand diagonal
crack with occasional handholds in the right-hand diagonal crack. The left
diagonal crack leads into a steeper corner where a big move up and right leads to
the top. (Topo provided.)

Càrn Ghluasaid
Toll Creagach Beag
(NH 143 127) Alt 780m
On the north side of Càrn Ghluasaid is Toll Creagach Beag. Just west of the
summit on the northern rim is an easy gully to descend. On the left of that is a rib
between the corries.

Junior Rib 90m I/II. Chris Dickinson, Jane Allen. 2 Dec 2021.
The rib bounding the corrie on the right. Weave up through a steep buttress to
easier ground and follow this to the rim. (Topo provided.)

Coire na Gaoithe an Ear
(NH 163 123)
Càrn Ghluasaid, also has an eastern corrie, below the eastern top of Creag Dhubh
(835m), called Coire na Gaoithe an Ear. The following three routes lie in this
corrie.

Where Eagles Dare 150m III ***. Chris Dickinson, Jane Allen. 25 Dec 2021.
A beautiful route up a giant corner with turf, some ice and interesting rock moves
and spectacular scenery. Left of a steep buttress in the centre of the face is a huge
slanting slab of rock, often snow-covered, with a steep wall bounding it all the
way up on the left. The route follows the corner throughout in three pitches,
exiting up final gully of steep turf. (Topo provided.)

Stormy Petrel 110m III/IV *. Jonny Hawkins, Chris Dickinson. 10 Feb 2022.

On the left of *Where Eagles Dare* is a well-defined steep snow gully. This route takes the steep rock and turf ground left of the snow gully close to a left wall.
1. Climb with increasing steepness to a steep exit left, where the snow gully bends to the right.
2. Take a fine groove direct to the top of the crag.

Mercury Buttress 80m II/III *. Chris Dickinson, Freddy Hunter. 28 Dec 2021.
The right side of Coire na Gaoithe an Ear has a smaller sub corrie above the level of the floor of the main corrie. This is the buttress on the left side of that corrie which can be reached by descending a gully on its north side at NH 158 127. Climb the buttress from the lowest rocks, finishing with steep rocky moves on a small tower.

Sàil Chaorainn, Càrn na Coire Mheadhoin
(NH 139 160)
The crag on the east face of Càrn na Coire Mheadhoin contains the following route.

Engagement 250m II. Chris Dickinson. 2 Apr 2022.
Takes the left-slanting weakness through the lower tier of rock, then a steep snowfield to the fine finishing corner, left of the prominent summit rock buttress, with some fine moves on frozen turf and ice. (Topo provided.)

Sgùrr nan Saighead, Coire Druim na Staidhre
California 160m IV,4 *. James Milton, Robbie Hearns. 27 Nov 2021.
A bold turfy ice climb following the summer line. The route requires good frozen turf and some ice on the second pitch. A selection of pegs and Terriers are recommended. Start at the apex of the left-hand scree cone at the base of an obvious right-facing corner. (Topo provided.)
1. 25m Climb the corner, breaking out right at the top before moving back left to follow a snow slope to the base of a large corner.
2. 45m Climb the corner with increasing difficulty, with very little gear until after the crux moves. Follow the snow slope above to belay below the narrowing of the gully above.
3. and 4. 90m Climb the gully above, then follow easier ground to the top.

GLEN CARRON
Sgùrr na Feartaig, Coire nan Each
(NH 045 451)
The unnamed top on the west side of Coire nan Each of Sgùrr na Feartaig forms a broken rocky fin or cone.

Sea Horse 100m II. M.W. Holland, D.J.E. Spencer, A.P. Williams. 19 Feb 2022.
The cone is climbable almost anywhere and the route starts right of centre. Start down and right of a wide turf groove forming the right side of a large rocky tower.
1. 40m Climb a stepped turfy wall to gain the groove. Follow this with the odd step to a stacked block thread belay on the right.
2. 50m Short steps trending right gain a groove with a rocky right wall. Follow this to a belay in a wall on the right.
3. 10m Climb the short wall (or bypass it) to easy ground a short walk from the cairn. (Topo provided.)

TORRIDON
Ben Shieldaig, Pass Crag
(NG 844 494)

A very accessible crag with some good single pitch climbing on the cleaner sections.

Approach: Approaching from Shieldaig, drive past Loch Dughaill and continue for another 2km down Glen Shieldaig. The crag comes into view just above the road on the left where the glen narrows. Park on the right about 50m before a small hillock on the left of the road. Walk steeply up to the crag (5 minutes).

Bulging Buttress
The leftmost climbing is on an undercut wall which becomes very steep towards its right-hand side, where there is a prominent roofed niche. This roofed niche is probably the best feature for crag orientation. Approximately 30m left of the roofed niche is a sturdy holly tree on a heather ledge at half-height.

Pie in the Sky 22m E1 5b *. Ben Sparham, Simon Clark. 8 May 2022.
From a boulder below and just right of the holly, pull steeply up the wall on large holds until established beneath a flake in the centre of the wall. Stand on the flake (crux) then gain the heather ledge right of the holly. From the holly, climb more easily rightwards up a line of flakes to the top.

The Beckoning 10m E1 6a *. Simon Clark, Maurice O'Connell. 24 Apr 2022.
Further right the wall steepens up and a roof starts that continues under bulging rock to the left of the niche. Towards the left end of this roof is a deep, clean-cut hanging crack. Climb easily up to its start. A well-protected struggle ensues.

Y-Front Left-Hand 15m E1 5a *. Ben Sparham, Dave Porter, Simon Clark. 1 May 2022.
Start directly under the roofed niche. Move steeply up rightwards to a ledge at one-third height, then move left past a holly bush and make tricky moves up the centre of the slabby left wall of the niche, finishing up a short corner past a final bulge.

Y-Front Right-Hand 15m H.Severe 4a. Dave Porter, Maurice O'Connell. 24 Apr 2022.
Take the same start as the previous route to gain the ledge, then go up the crack in the slab and wall above defining the right side of the niche.

Growl Like You Mean It 12m E2 6a *. Steve Archer. 8 May 2022.
On the right of the niche is a narrow gully with a large chockstone. On the left side of this is a very steep hand crack. Short but powerful!

Little Wall
To the right of Bulging Buttress, and set back a few metres higher, is a smaller clean wall with a deep crack on its right-hand side.

Crumple 10m H.Severe 4a. Dave Porter, Simon Clark. 12 Apr 2022.
The left side of the wall. Move up to a horizontal break (which is the continuation of a heather ledge from the left), then straight up a shallow niche and above to the top left edge of the rib. Poorly protected.

Crinkle 10m VS 4b. Dave Porter, Simon Clark. 12 Apr 2022.
The central line. Pass just left of a dodgy-looking rock flake on an eroded pedestal, to a ledge at half-height, then straight up towards cracks above. Pleasant but poorly protected.

Old Time Raver Craic 10m H.Severe 4a. Simon White, Maurice O'Connell. 16 Apr 2022.
The deep crack on the right.

The Slabby Walls
Approximately 50m to the right of Little Wall is a longer section of slabby walls up to 25m high with vegetated sections.

Tryptick 23m VS 5a *. Dave Porter, Simon Clark, Ben Sparham. 1 May 2022.
This takes the left side of the first full-height section of the Slabby Walls. Start up a set of three parallel cracks which lead to the left side of a wide curving break or overlap at 10m height, and a heather ledge above. Continue up a short, slightly left-facing crack, and finish up the arête.

Uphill Gardener 23m HVS 5a. Dave Porter, Maurice O'Connell. 24 Apr 2022.
This takes a line to the right of *Tryptick*. Start up the cracks leading to the right side of the wide curving break. Surmount this slightly to the left, trend back rightwards through the jutting flakes above, then directly up to finish on the left rib of the face.

Galibier 23m HVS 5a **. Simon Clark, Dave Porter. 12 Apr 2022.
The crack system 2 m to the right, finishing at a shallow notch at the top. Start by moving up rightwards into cracks from a niche at ground level and then continue direct. The crux moves are rightwards and then back left from a shallow niche at half-height.

Stelvio 24m E1 5a *. Simon Clark, Maurice O'Connell, Dave Porter. 24 Apr 2022.
In the middle of the Slabby Walls is a clean slab with a brown streak at the base of the wall, to the left of a vegetated chimney. Climb the thin crack to the right of the brown streak, then move left across it to the right end of a heather ledge. Continue direct to finish up a small right-facing corner (beware loose blocks on the left).

The Shieldaig Pimpernel 20m E1 5a. Simon White, Maurice O'Connell. 16 Apr 2022.
Takes the most well-defined crack in the lower part of the last taller section of the Slabby Walls. Climb the crack, then make bold moves rightwards before the heather ledge. Continue upwards to join the last part of *Tourmalet*.

Tourmalet 18m E3 5c **. Simon Clark, Simon White, Maurice O'Connell. 16 Apr 2022.
On the right side of the last taller section of the Slabby Walls is a short seam or crack that starts above the first break. Climb up to this, then make technical moves up the thin seam and beyond to reach the big break. Continue more easily above.

Pass 13m VS 4b. Dave Porter, Ben Sparham. 1 May 2022.
Climb the centre of the shorter, two-tier buttress just before the Slabby Walls descent. Poorly protected.

Corner Buttress
To the right of the descent at the end of the Slabby Walls is a clean jutting buttress set a few metres lower.

Daisy Mai 20m V.Diff *. Maurice O'Connell, Simon White, Simon Clark. 16 Apr 2022.
Start at the toe of the buttress and climb up right of the crest to reach a ledge and the final wall.

Shieldaig Crags, Camas an Lèim
(NG 8185 5532) Alt 5m Non-tidal North-facing
A small crag on the south end of the beautiful Camas an Lèim, a lovely bay on the peninsular north of Shieldaig with lovely views across Loch Torridon. There is also some good bouldering based around the low roof on the right-hand side of the crag.
Approach: Park considerately in Shieldaig village. A good path heads north from Shieldaig Primary School. After about 1km the path comes out of the trees and Camas an Lèim is hidden beyond boggy ground to the right (east) of the path. Skirt the boggy ground on a rough path on its southern edge and drop down to the beach. The crag is obvious at the southern end.
Descent: Walk off to the east or abseil from trees.

Katie Morag 15m E3 6b **. Gareth Marshall. 8 May 2022.
The obvious roof crack near the left end of the crag, with the crux getting established around the lip.

Grannie Island 10m E3 5c *. Gaz Marshall, Andy Emery. 8 May 2022.
Right of the roof crack are twin grooves. This route climbs the left-hand groove, moving out onto the right arête at the steepest section and stepping back in above. Well protected.

Granma Mainland 10m E2 5b *. Gaz Marshall, Murdoch Jamieson. 7 Aug 2021.
This is the right-hand of the twin grooves, which is easier but a bit bolder than the left. Bold and delicate up the initial groove to a rest on the right, then step back left into the groove and follow this to finish leftwards under the tree.

Loch Domhain Crag
(NG 917 514) North-east facing
The cleaner and leftmost of two small (10m) sandstone crags on the hillside above Lochan Domhain. It is divided into two sections, with a small cave in the middle (tucked into the right-hand side of the left wall). The left-hand section is black across its central third, with a thin full-height crack up the middle.
Approach: Approach via the good path from Annat in approximately 1 hour.

Spit Grilled 10m E2 5c *. Simon Clark, Dave Porter. 2 Jun 2021.

The full-height finger-crack up the centre of the left-hand wall (just left of some shallow bulges). It loses a star for being slightly dirty.

Plan B   10m   HVS 5b *.   Simon Clark, Dave Porter. 2 Jun 2021.
The capped right-facing corner at the right end of the left-hand wall (just left of the cave). Climb the corner to the small roof, move right to the arête and pull over, using the fine finishing crack above.

Move it or Park it   10m   E2 6a *.   Simon Clark. 2 Jun 2021.
On the right-hand section, 15–20m right of the cave there is an overlap at half-height bounded on its right by a corner. Start beneath the centre of the overlap, climb to the niche where a crack splits the overlap, and follow its thin and unaccommodating continuation above.

Torridon Sandstone Crags, Pathlet Crag
(NG 938 571)   South-facing
Follow the same path as for Path Crag. After 20 min, a fence line joins from the left, beneath a waterfall: the crag is just off to the right of the path. It consists of two main buttresses separated by a more broken section. Descent can be via the loose gully uphill of the left-hand buttress, with care.

Solstice Cracks   12m   HVS 5a.   Ben Sparham, Dave Porter. 21 Jun 2021.
The front of the uphill, left-hand buttress is split into three vertical sections by two horizontal ledges. This route starts up cracks to reach the left side of the lower ledge via a short corner. Step up and left from the left edge of this ledge to follow cracks to the second ledge (crux). The final wall is steep but easier. (Topo provided.)

The wider right buttress has a blunt arête near its centre, right of which the ground rises.

Fizzle   15m   H.Severe 4b.   Dave Porter, Ben Sparham. 21 Jun 2021.
A poor route owing to its escapability, this takes the left-hand side of the right-hand buttress. Climb the initial crack to a wide horizontal break, then move left and continue more easily to the top. (Topo provided.)

More!   15m   HVS 5b ***.   Dave Porter, Ben Sparham. 21 Jun 2021.
The crack just left of the blunt arête. Leaves you wanting ... ! (Topo provided.)

Inveralligin to Diabaig, Loch a' Choire Bhig Crag
(NG 829 593) South-facing
This is the rather unusual black and white speckled crag on the hillside to the north-east of the loch which lies about a half km north of the viewpoint parking place on the Diabaig road. The best way of locating the crag is to walk north along the road until just before a small weedy loch where one can see the speckled crag through a gap. Crossing the moor to it can be boggy. One can also approach direct from the viewpoint over various hillocks. The crag faces south, has an easy section on the right, but a more compact steeper section to the left where these routes are located.

Step Up Arête   15m   V.Diff.   Peter Biggar, Lisa Hutchison. 31 Jul 2021.
The slabby area steepens to the left ending in an arête with an awkward start.
Climb the cracked slab above to finish.

Inset Slab and Groove   18m   Severe.   Roger Robb, Peter Biggar. 2 Sep 2021.
Left of *Step-Up Arête* there is a steep inset slab. Climb this on the right, traverse
the top edge to the left and climb the groove above. The boulder on the ledge is
loose but useful.

Inset Slab Direct   Severe.   Roger Robb, Peter Biggar. 2 Sep 2021.
Climb the centre-left side of the inset slab to finish up the groove of the previous
route.

Diabaig, Diabaig Pillar
Diabaig Corner – Direct Start   10m   E1 5c *.   Gary Latter, Karen Latter. 4 Jul
2021.
Start at large block directly beneath the main corner. Climb a short steep corner,
then go direct to a block belay at the base of the main corner. This avoids climbing
the fence or thrashing through the bracken from the gate.

Loch a' Bhealaich Mòr and Lochan Dubh Crags
Dead Tree Crag
Small Black Flowers, Variation Finish   5m   HVS 5a *.   Michael Barnard, Alan
Hill. 18 Oct 2020.
A bold traverse just below the normal finish.

To Baldly Go   20m   Severe **.   Alan Hill, Michael Barnard. 18 Oct 2020.
Start as for *Token V.Diff*, then traverse out right just above the lip of the roof to
finish up the crest of the prow.

Fruit Pastille   5m   E1 5a *.   Michael Barnard, Alan Hill. 18 Oct 2020.
Directly above *Token V.Diff*. Climb a thin crack up a small dome, passing a minute
rowan.

Michael Barnard notes the line of the crag, a thin break traversing out left to the
prow, would give an excellent hard route (E5?).

Windy Crag
Banana   15m   Severe.   Richard Biggar, Keir Biggar, Peter Biggar. 15 Apr 2022.
The obvious curving crack to the right of *Safari Crack*.

Isoceles Direct   15m   Severe.   Richard Biggar, Lauren Biggar, Keir Biggar, Peter
Biggar. 15 Apr 2022.
Start under the triangular recess and climb straight up on small holds trending left
at the top.

Valley of the Slabs
Periwig Slab   18m   Diff.   Peter Biggar, Phil Gribbon. 1 May 2019.
The obviously wrinkled slab with an overlap at half-height; choice of starts, easier
to the left. Protection is scanty.

At the head of the valley on the opposite side to the slabs (east) there is a steep blocky wall.

Cubist   18m   VS 4c.   Richard Biggar, Lauren Biggar, Keir Biggar. 15 Apr 2022. A short distance down the valley. A strenuous overhanging start followed by cracks and small ledges leads to a stretchy crux at mid-height. Lichenous in places, it needs to be dry.

Liathach
Creag Dubh nam Fuaran
South Ridge Gully   I.   Peter Biggar, Barry Hard. 3 Jan 1997.
The obvious long narrow gully left west of *Mullach an Rathain, South Ridge* starting at NG 905 565. An impressive, easy line and a good prologue to the traverse of the mountain.

Note: It is rather a moot point just where the gully begins: there is a shallow depression low down which develops into a very well-defined gully higher up. The line of the gully is the bed of the stream which descends to the Mountain Rescue Post (nowadays a very plush affair). For the sake of argument let's say the gully begins at NG905 565. It is a very obvious feature from the road from Annat to Fasaig (or Torridon village). The South Ridge is actually a recorded scrambling route in 'Highland Scrambles North'.

Am Fasarinen – South Side
Y-Gully, Left Fork   200m   I.   Peter Biggar. 31 Dec 1996.
The gully to the left of *South-West Buttress*. Uncomplicated snow.

Beinn Eighe, Coire Mhic Fhearchair
Far East Wall
Keep 'em Sharp   60m   V,7 *.   Jamie Skelton, Nicky Brierley. 14 Feb 2022.
This route follows the right-trending line of weakness across the short buttress right of *Far East Gully*.
1. 20m Climb *Karaoke Wall*'s first blocky pitch to a short crux section before stepping right onto a large belay platform.
2. 40m follow the rising ramp system that trends right across the entire buttress to its top.

Eastern Ramparts
Take Me Back To The Desert   105m   IX,9.   Greg Boswell, Hamish Frost, Graham McGrath. 5 Dec 2021.
This route goes directly up the wall near the left-hand end of the Eastern Ramparts. Start just right of *The Modern Idiot* and climb up to and through the roof of the arch- or half-moon-shaped feature, then follow the continuation cracks above. Continue through the steepness to eventually reach easier ground above which leads to the top.

Tainted Galahad, Pitch 2 Variation   30m   E3 6a *.   Michael Barnard, Doug Bartholomew. 25 Jul 2021.
Immediately left of the big roofed corner, climb a crack and groove above with difficulty to its top. Make a hard sequence right to gain ledges and move up to join the normal route just before its crux. Continue up the rest of pitch 3 to the belay.

THE CAIRNGORMS

COIRE AN T-SNEACHDA
Mess of Pottage
Kenneth Daykin suggests the following alternative (summer) start to *Pot of Gold* that avoids climbing the first pitch of *The Message*, which is dirty and often wet. Start directly beneath the blocky chimney in the main groove line, as for *Mariella*. Scramble directly up to the blocky chimney, common with *The Message*, and climb it until a short traverse right can be made onto the buttress.

Daykin also suggests that the top of the route, instead of moving right and taking the 'fine crack in a slabby buttress', climb the slabby buttress up slightly overlapping tiers. Very pleasant and well protected. Following the very edge of the slab, overlooking the chimney, makes a fine finish and with the direct start and slab finish, the route is possibly worth three stars.

Fluted Buttress
Snow Bunting Climb 135m Moderate. Dave Allan. 26 Jul 2017.
Start 6m left of the narrows at the start of *The Runnel* and climb a shallow left-facing corner for 30m. Continue up the pleasant grassy buttress over rock steps for 70m. Climb the big, left-hand, V-groove in the tower above over a large jammed slab and finish up a short arête.

Broken Gully 130m Moderate. Dave Allan. 26 Jul 2019.
By the winter line.

Fiacaill Buttress
Polished Up 35m VI/VII,6. Wojciech Polkowski, Sebastian Gidelski. 28 Dec 2021.
The line of cracks on the wall between *Slaterless* and *Seam-stress*, going over three minor roofs. Start as for *Short Circuit*. From its last belay on the snowy ramp climb a diagonal right-slanting crack-line to reach the first roof. Continue straight up over two subsequent roofs to the top. (Topo provided.)

COIRE AN LOCHAIN
Ewen Buttress (No 3 Buttress)
Fear of the Unknown 70m VIII,9 **. Greg Boswell, Jamie Skelton. 9 Apr 2022.
The steep featureless wall between *Migrant Direct* and *Nocando Crack*.
1. 30m Climb a short groove just left of the corner crack of *Nocando Crack* to gain a turfy ramp. Move up the wide crack (as for *The Migrant*) and belay below the steep featureless wall.
2. 40m Traverse right across small ledges and climb the wall direct to the top.

Greg Boswell notes that *Happy Tyroleans* is over-graded in the 'Cairngorms' guidebook and this factor is probably stopping people from trying it. He suggests *Happy Tyroleans* is VIII,9 at the most, maybe even Tech 8.

No 4 Buttress
Savage Slit, Alternative Finish 15m Severe **. Ken Daykin, Anne Daykin. 7 Sep 2021.
A worthwhile and recommended extension to *Savage Slit*, and an alternative to

climbing over the blocks of the normal finish (which are further left). After the short open gully followed by a bit of walking (on pitch 4), a fine-looking 10 to 15m corner can be seen up and right. Climb the corner with a move right at half-height. At the top step across the corner to exit onto the edge of the plateau. There is a very fine belay here by a 'stack of pancakes'. Probably climbed before.

SHELTERSTONE CRAG
Central Slabs
Tony Stone has provided the following revised description and a new topo. An observant reader will notice that the latter departs from convention by depicting some of the newer routes (for which diagrams were previously missing) as the trunk lines, though this is not necessarily how a future guidebook will show them.

Shelter Stone Crag
Central Slabs

ab – belays with abseil points

1	The Harp 100m E3 ★★	
2	Snipers 105m E2 ★	
3	Aphrodite 95m E7 ★★★	
4	Thor 110m E5 ★★★	
5	The Run of the Arrow 90m E6 ★★★	
6	Cupid's Bow 85m E5 ★★★	
7	Cupid's True Bow 80m E6 6b ★★★★	
8	The Missing Link 125m E4 ★★★	
9	Sweet Granite Kiss 100m E7 ★★★	
10	Athene 105m E7 ★★★★	
11	Icon of Lust 115m E8 ★★★	
12	The Pin 70m E2 ★★★	

Icon of Lust   115m   E8 ***.

A monumental voyage up the full height of the Central Slabs, taking a direct line through *Realm of the Senses* and *L'Elisir d'Amore*. Start 20m down and left from the initial crack of *The Pin*.

1. 35m 6a The serious pitch! Climb a cracked groove to a ledge at 10m. Pull onto a bleached slab and climb it veering right into a vague left-facing corner at its top (good gear). Go straight up the steep wall on small positive edges to a pocket over the top. Step left, pull onto the ramp and follow this rightwards to the belay

2. 25m 6c A brilliant pitch, desperate and bold. Follow the *Realm of the Senses* groove to the overlap. step right and pull through the overlap with disbelief, sketch up the slab to a weird pocket (00 cam). Move diagonally leftwards (very thin) to join *Missing Link* amidst its crux. Gain good holds and gear then traverse down and left above the overlap to gain a flake leading to the *Thor* belay.

3. 55m 6b Extremely bold, a cool head required. Climb *Thor* to the crescent crack. Step up into pockets, make thin moves up and left to a jug in the red streak. A precarious stretch left enables a 00 cam (possible Pecker and microwires too) to be placed blind in the right side of the *True Bow* overlap, the only protection in 25m of climbing. Climb the red streak to a pocket, step right and up the right edge of the red streak past a flat hold into a scoop (frightening). Climb a vertical wall past a PR (RP2 one metre above) to gain flakes in a scoop, move diagonally left along flakes and on to the slab above. Continue up the slab to a grassy ledge and possible belay. Continue up the wall above to the apex of the slabs, peg belay.

CNAP COIRE NA SPRÈIDHE
Summit Crags

Diagonal Crack   25m   H.Severe.   Ron Walker, Fi Chappell. Jun 2021.
The wall left of *Dinner Date*. Remarkably grippy granite. (Topo provided.)

Dawn Date   30m   Severe.   Ron Walker, Fi Chappell. Jun 2021.
The wall right of *Dinner Date*. Remarkably grippy granite. (Topo provided.)

Creagan Cha-No
International Rib

Chamney Chimney   40m   III,3.   Martin Holland, Steven Cham. 13 Feb 2022.
Three metres right of *The Chimney Sweeper* an open groove leads to twin chimneys. Climb the groove into the right-hand chimney. Step left and climb the left-hand chimney. A short steep corner leads to a belay above *Continental Chimney*. Finish up *International Rib*.

Citizen of Nowhere   70m   III,4.   Simon Richardson, Sophie Grace Chappell. 12 Dec 2021.
The groove system on the right flank of *International Rib*. More difficult than it looks – its northerly aspect means it stays in condition longer than other routes after a thaw. Possibly climbed before.

1. 30m Start 20m right of *Traveller's Tales* around the toe of the buttress. Climb an inset right-facing groove over a step to reach a jammed flake chockstone. Pull over this and surmount the step above to an easing. Belay below a sharp narrow arête. Junction with *Traveller's Tales*.

2. 40m *Traveller's Tales* takes the wide grove left of the sharp arête. Instead, climb the narrow inset corner on the right to gain the top of the arête and finish up steep snow to the cornice.

Blood Buttress

Crampons, Nuts and Navigation   60m   IV,6. Simon Richardson, Roger Webb. 4 Feb 2022.

An eliminate line between *Blood Thirsty* and *Giant Steps* finishing up *The Sundance Kid*. The line is contrived, but the climbing is good and does not rely on frozen turf.

1. 40m Climb the first 3m of *Giant Steps* up a right-facing groove then pull out onto the wall to the left. Traverse delicately left on a ledge and climb a short crack to a platform. Continue up a series of steep steps left of *Giant Steps* and right of *Blood Thirsty* to below the headwall. Step down and left across *Blood Thirsty* and belay by some large blocks on the left edge of the buttress.

2. 20m Step into a hanging flake crack on the wall on the left and climb it for 5m to a ledge. Step left and continue up the crack and ramp of *The Sundance Kid* to the top.

Crookshanks   60m   III. Simon Richardson, Sophie Grace Chappell. 12 Dec 2021.

A natural right-trending line linking the start of *True Blood* with the finish of *Heart is Highland*. The easiest climb on the buttress – it holds snow well and is Grade II apart from the initial chockstone.

1. 30m Pull over the initial chockstone of *True Blood* and follow the right-trending line to belay on cracks on the left.

2. 30m Continue up and right behind a small tower to exit up the final V-groove of *Heart is Highland*.

Right-Hand Ribs

Omicron Groove   60m   III. Simon Richardson, Sophie Grace Chappell. 12 Dec 2021.

The right-slanting groove 10m left of *Big Boy Made Me*. A steep start up a steep chimney leads into the easier main groove which has a steep exit up a narrow crack on the right. Finish up easy ground to the top.

Duke's Wall

Mike Watson notes that the topo and description exaggerates how far left you go on the final pitch of *Kerplunk*. ('I ended up on the steep turfy upper section of *Wile-e-Coyote* having trended left ... . All good fun.')

LURCHER'S CRAG, from Central Gully to Window Gully

An Ice Surprise   365m   IV,4/5 **. Dave Riley, Andy Harrison. 25 Feb 2022.

A long icy adventure up the face on the highest part of the crag, best done when continuous ice leads through the lower overlaps. Start mid-way between *Central Gully* and *Diamond Gully* about 60m below a huge block and a two-tiered icefall.

1. 60m Climb a rope-stretching pitch of iced slabs and small steps to a rock belay in the huge block.

2. 20m Swing up left onto a steep ice pillar (5) and climb it into a groove behind the huge block. Escape the groove to belay on ice beneath the next overlap. This pitch could be outflanked on the right.

3. 60m Climb an ice groove to beneath the overlap, break out right and climb easier-angled ice trending left to a rock belay.

4. 60m Move back out right and climb easy snow before trending left to a block belay near the base of *Reindeer Ridge*.

5. 55m Traverse back right until beneath a groove with a steep ice bulge, move up this into a bay and a block belay on the right below *St Bernard's Ridge*.

6. 50m Climb the big icy groove above (*Have an Ice Day*) to exit out right with difficulty onto easier ground.

7. 60m Climb easier snow and rock steps to the top. (Topo provided.)

NORTHERN CORRIES OF BRAERIACH
Coire Ruadh
Wolf Moon 80m IV,6. Mark Robson, Simon Richardson. 20 Jan 2022.
Interesting climbing up the corner and wall right of *Hostage to Fortune*.

1. 30m Start just right of *Hostage to Fortune* and climb easy ground up and left to a broad terrace where the angle steepens.

2. 30m Enter a line of grooves 3m right of *Hostage to Fortune* and climb over two steep steps to a V-shaped corner. Climb this to a terrace, then move slightly right and climb a steep vertical wall finishing left under a roof (crux) to gain a ledge.

3. 20m Finish up the blocky groove above that leads through the headwall to the top.

Coire an Lochain
Against All Odds 100m IV,6. Simon Richardson, Mark Robson. 20 Jan 2022.
Good climbing up the right-facing arête between *Skeleton Creek* and *Sinister Dredge*.

1. 60m Start just right of *Skeleton Creek* and exit the top right corner of the initial snow depression via a steep corner-crack. Continue up shallow grooves on the right edge of the central part of the buttress overlooking *Sinister Edge*. Belay 5m below the headwall.

2. 25m Move diagonally right and pull right around the clean-cut arête defining the right side of the headwall (crux). Continue up steep grooves in the line of the arête to a good ledge below a steep tower.

3. 15m Climb the corner right of the steep tower to the top.

Derry Cairngorm, Coire na Saobhaidh
Wily Fox 150m III. Simon Richardson. 11 Jan 2022.
To the right of the area of slabs containing *Power of Balance* there is a low angled crescent-shaped gully. Right of this is a more broken area of slabs with four granite tiers separated by snow terraces. In a good winter this becomes covered in ice. Start on the right side of the slabs (NO 027 956) and climb a short icy corner (10m) then trend up and left and climb an icy break (10m) through the first tier. The second tier is breached by a left-facing slabby corner (10m) and a 5m ice wall leads over the third tier. Climb the fourth and final tier via a right-slanting gully (15m) that leads to the final snow slopes.

Fox on the Rocks 70m III. Simon Richardson. 11 Jan 2022.
The steep buttress high up on the right side of the corrie starting at NO 026 957. Climb a short icy slab right of the buttress toe to gain a grove that leads to a terrace. Continue up a left-tending ramp that leads to the buttress crest and the top.

Sgùrr an Lochain Uaine
(NO 0260 9871)

The large corrie cutting into the east flank of Derry Cairngorm has a series of broken crags on its north side.

Iron Man Ridge   200m   III,4.   Simon Richardson, Forrest Templeton. 5 Jan 2022. The prominent central ridge lying between two wide snow gullies. Climb easily for 100m to a notch behind a small tower. Climb the crux wall above via an undercut chimney and step left onto the crest (35m). Continue up more mixed ground bypassing a short vertical rectangular wall on the right (35m). Finish easily to the top.

Beinn a' Bhùird, Garbh Choire
The Flume
Young Hearts Run Free   75m   E4 **.   Tim Miller, Callum Johnson. 15 Jul 2021. Climbs the upper and wider of the two left-slanting diagonal cracks across a distinctive half dome-shaped buttress on the far left of the Flume Area.
1. 45m Broken ground on the far right side of the lower slabs leads to a large grassy bay at the bottom of the 'half dome' wall.
2. 30m 6a Climb the initial wide crack past some blocks to a good ledge. Technical moves gain the crack passing a big flake on the right at mid-height to finish out and left. Well protected. Scramble up easy ground. (Topo provided.)

Mitre Ridge, West Wall
The Altar   180m   E2 *.   Michael Barnard, Alan Hill. 17 Jul 2021. Variations on *The Chancel/Cumming-Crofton*. Avoiding the crux section by staying on *The Chancel* would give a good E1.
1. 15m As for *Cumming-Crofton* to below the chimney.
2. 45m 5c Take the fine diagonal crack out right to join T*he Chancel* and follow this to the top of the shallow groove. Move up to place a good cam in a slanting crack on the right, then step down rightwards on the wall, move right (crux) and go up to the slanting overlap. Follow this up and left to gain the arête and continue up the groove right of *Cumming-Crofton* to belay on the broad platform as for that route.
3. 40m 5b Climb the wall of the First Tower: start up a crack and climb past an obvious undercut flake, then make tricky moves to gain a short slanting crack and pull out right onto a ledge. Continue up a large right-facing flake-groove (beware dodgy blocks) and climb a vertical crack to reach the crest.
4 and 5. 80m As for *Mitre Ridge*. (Topo provided.)

Stob an t-Sluichd
Right of *M & B Buttress* is a grassy gully. The following routes are on the small buttress immediately right of the gully, featuring a fine corner-crack.

The Ugly Sister   25m   Severe.   Alan Hill, Michael Barnard. 18 Jul 2021. The groove left of the corner-crack.

Rock Empire   20m   VS 4c **.   Michael Barnard, Alan Hill. 18 Jul 2021. The roof-capped corner-crack.

Big Bro   20m   Severe.   Michael Barnard. Aug 2020. The slabby wall right of *Rock Empire*. Climb a left-facing groove, then a crack, then move left to continue via cracks and breaks.

Stob an t-Sluichd Tor

(NJ 115 029) Alt 1000m East and west facing
This tor lies north-east of the summit of Stob an t-Sluichd. Routes are described from right to left starting on the east face.

Skating Away 15m E2 5c. Michael Barnard, Alan Hill. 18 Jul 2021.
A shorter wall on the far right end of the crag. Start up a slanting flake on the left, traverse right to gain a steep crack above the wall's initial section. At the top of the crack, step right to finish up the slab above.

Too Old to Rock 'n' Roll 15m E1 5b **. Michael Barnard, Alan Hill. 18 Jul 2021.
Left of *Skating Away* is an easier chimney-gully. This route climbs the steep crack to its immediate left.

War Child 15m E3 5c **. Michael Barnard, Alan Hill. 18 Jul 2021.
The arête left of *Too Old to Rock 'n' Roll*. Go up to place gear under the small overlap, then make committing moves to gain the thin flake-crack (small wires) and use this to reach out right (large sling). Move up to finish as for the above.

The Big Dipper 20m E3 5c **. Michael Barnard, Alan Hill. 18 Jul 2021.
The west face of the tor is an impressive 'wall for the future'. This route climbs a fine groove just right of the blank wall. From high in the groove, gain a jug up and right, and top-out with difficulty (bold). A direct finish to the groove still awaits.

Ben Avon, Fluted Wall

(NJ 124 017) South and west facing
This crag on the Ben Avon side of the Slochd Mòr is the third one on the left on the walk up the glen (Creag na h-Iolaire being the first). The following routes lie on the far-right end of the buttress, the first one taking a fine slanting flake-groove and lying just right of vegetated cracks (visible on the approach). Around the corner right from this is the fluted wall itself.

Flake-tastic 20m HVS 5b **. Michael Barnard, Alan Hill. 19 Jul 2021.
The layback flake, climbed in its entirety. Continue up flake-cracks above.

Krishna 15m E3 5c *. Michael Barnard, Alan Hill. 19 Jul 2021.
A line up the centre of the fluted wall. Climb a semi-detached (but well keyed-in) pillar to its top, continue directly up to the flutings and pull out right. Finish up leftwards.

For Michael Collins, Jeffrey and Me 15m VS 4c. Michael Barnard, Alan Hill. 19 Jul 2021.
The chimney immediately right of the fluted wall.

Never a Dull Moment 20m HVS 5a **. Michael Barnard, Alan Hill. 19 Jul 2021.
The much better right-hand chimney and crack above.

LOCHNAGAR
North-East Corrie, Red Spout Ribs
Pinocchio 70m I/II. Simon Richardson. 24 Nov 2021.
Climb easily up the front face of the buttress left of the right-facing groove of *Sweet William*.

Black Spout Pinnacle
Simon Richardson notes that pitch 2 of *Route 2* is 35m long (and not 25m as described in the 'Cairngorms' guidebook).

Coire na Saobhaidhe
Blunt Approach 60m III. Adrian Crofton, Forrest Templeton. 11 Apr 2021.
The short icefall 30m left of *The Watercourse*.

Invasion of the Corrie Snatchers 120m IV,4. Forrest Templeton, Simon Richardson. 6 Mar 2022.
The corner line immediately right of *The Watercourse*. Start 10m right of *The Watercourse*.
1. 30m Climb easy-angled snow and ice to the foot of the steep section.
2. 40m Move up and over the right side of a of an overlap via a small icefall. Continue up and left into the gully-line and belay on the right.
3. 50m Continue up the gully until the way is blocked by a steep wall. Traverse delicately right along a steep slabby shelf for 5m (crux) to gain a deep left-facing corner chimney and follow this to easier ground.

Vulpes Gully 150m III,4. Simon Richardson, Forrest Templeton. 6 Mar 2022.
The deep right-facing corner-gully bounding the right side of the section of cliff containing *The Watercourse* is a natural winter line.
1. 40m Start by climbing easy angled snow and ice to the foot of gully.
2. 50m Climb the gully, easy at first, with two ice bulges climbed by ice on the left wall in the upper half of the pitch. Belay on the right.
3. 60m Step left and continue up the well-defined upper gully to easier ground.

The Old Fox 150m III. Forrest Templeton, Simon Richardson. 3 Apr 2022.
An enjoyable route up the V-shaped buttress 50m right of *Vulpes Gully*.
1. 70m Start by climbing easy angled snow and ice to the foot of the buttress.
2. 30m Climb turf steps up and left for 20m before breaking out right in to the crest. Move up to a good belay below a clean-cut left-facing corner.
3. 50m Climb the corner and step right up a slot at its top. Continue up the crest of the buttress to belay on jumble of huge blocks.

Renard 150m III. Simon Richardson. 1 Apr 2022.
Start approximately 50m right of *The Old Fox* and climb a left-slanting ramp past a prominent block at 40m and continue over a couple of steep turfy steps. The difficulties end after 70m, but it is most aesthetic to continue up over gradually easing ground to the summit of Lochnagar in another 80m or so.

Ptarmigan Route 100m III. Forrest Templeton, Simon Richardson. 3 Apr 2022.
Start 30m right of *Renard* and climb icy slabs just left of a shallow left-facing corner. After 25m break right up steep turfy steps to belay on the rounded crest.

Forrest Templeton on the first ascent of True Grit (V,7), The Stuic, Lochnagar.
Photo: Simon Richardson.

Continue up awkward slabby ground with the occasional awkward step to where the terrain eases.

Bunting Corner 100m II. Simon Richardson. 1 Apr 2022.
The prominent corner which forms the junction between the steeper crag on the left and the easier-angled slabs on the right (normally banked out in winter). The corner is noted as an unnamed summer Moderate in the 'Cairngorms' guidebook. Climb the corner on good snow-ice for 50m and continue up the easier ground above to where the angle eases.

Coire Loch nan Eun, The Stuic
True Grit 90m V,7. Simon Richardson, Forrest Templeton. 9 Jan 2022.
A good climb up the centre of the depression between *Bonanza* and *Twilight Groove*. The second pitch is steep, strenuous and well-protected, and the third has a sting in its tail.
1. 45m Start 5m right of *Bonanza* and zigzag up diagonal ledges in the centre of the depression until the way is blocked by a steep wall. Climb this via short chimney on the left and move up to a vertical cracked wall.
2. 20m Climb cracks for 3m them move left into an undercut niche (crux). Continue up the narrow chimney above to a good ledge.
3. 25m Above is the finishing V-corner of *Twilight Groove*. Climb its left wall by a crack to reach a platform and then make a difficult exit moving left below an overhung wall to easier ground and the top.

Martin Holland made an ascent of *The Stooee Chimney* on 6 February with Euan Whittaker and believes they may have climbed it differently from previous ascents. 'Euan led the crux pitch. He preferred the look of the left wall, looking up, and climbed this to gain the through-route. From the photo on www.scottishwinter.com it looks like the previous parties who had gone via the through-route climbed the right wall. The left wall was steep, with not much for feet initially until it was possible to bridge one foot back to the right wall and it eventually passed some old tat. Euan still thought IV,7 but you did need to be strong enough to hang about and place gear, which thankfully he is.'

CREAG AN DUBH LOCH
Broad Terrace Wall
The Vulture 135m E2 *. Michael Barnard, Alan Hill. 6 Jun 2021.
Some good climbing between *The Crow* and *Falkenhorst*. Take plenty of small wires and cams.
1. 35m 5b Follow *Falkenhorst* to the base of the short overhanging groove. Step left slightly and go up a short left-facing groove, then take the obvious handrail left across the slab to below a fine twin crack-line. Climb this to a ledge with a big block.
2. 15m 5c Continue a few metres to another ledge. From here, step down right to climb a right-slanting diagonal handrail which goes across immediately above the big blank slab (bold) to gain a good ledge and big flake. Walk right 3m to belay below a cracked groove.
3. 25m 5c Start up the cracked groove and make tricky bold moves to gain a ledge on the crest (as for *Falkenhorst* pitch 2). Continue up the cracked groove (often wet) to its top. Above is a short bulging groove. Step out right and climb the edge (steep but on good holds) to a ledge and big block.

4 and 5. 60m 5a Stand on the block, go up to climb a steep flake-crack and continue to a ledge. Move right and continue more easily via shorter walls and ledges.

Central Gully Wall

Tony Stone has provided the following revised descriptions:

Hybrid Vigour E6 ***
A revised description after a rockfall. An excellent, varied route. The big overhanging alcove, forming the start, makes a fantastic pitch when dry.
1. 25m 6b Climb the groove past a peg runner (new in 2021) to a rest where the groove starts to impend. Climb this via a hard undercut move (good cam) to better holds in the vertical groove above. Continue up the easing groove to a wide slab beneath another steep groove (the Bluebell Groove). Traverse the slab to the left edge, thread belay and possible abseil point, common with *Perilous Journey*.
2. 25m 6c Traverse back right to the groove (via gear in a flake in the wall above the belay) and climb the wall just left of the groove then the groove itself, old peg, to gain the slab on the right (possible belay on a peg in the overlap and a cam in crack in slab further right). Move left to gain a higher slab under the big overlap. Gain good holds on the lip to the right and make wild moves over the bulge. Step left and go up a delicate groove which rapidly eases to belay as for *Voyage of the Beagle* at the end of its third pitch, good wires on slab up and left.
3. 25m 6b The original line followed the overlap above leftward to perched blocks, this is poorly protected, especially for the second! After placing high runners, follow *Voyage of the Beagle* down from the left side of the belay and across the slab to near the arête. Follow twin cracks (as for *Perilous Journey*) up the wall above to a small ledge (being careful of perched blocks on the right), belay on a peg with good nut and spike up on arête on the left (possible abseil point).
4. 30m 6a Move right past stacked blocks (old peg runner in the break above), then hand-traverse a break rightwards into a niche in the overhanging wall. Pull round rightwards onto a sloping ledge at the bottom left corner of the *Cougar* rockfall scar to join and follow *Cougar*. Climb up on positive edges to a deep slot which accommodates a couple of good microwires. Move up, then make a strange move leftwards into the corner, follow this to a roof (good nut) and traverse back right to pull steeply onto the giant blocky flakes. Follow these leftwards to a belay beneath a short steep corner.
5. As for *Cougar* pitch 4. (Topo overleaf.)

Cougar E6 *
A new description after the rockfall. Pitches 1 and 2 are the same as previously described although the lengths may be 20m and 40m.
3. 35m The 'Toyboy' pitch. Traverse the slab left and go onto the rockfall scar, traverse the lip leftwards to a sloping ledge near the left side of the scar. Climb up on positive edges to a deep slot which accommodates a couple of good microwires (these need to be extended a lot as they are a long way sideways from the belay). Move up, then make a strange move leftwards into the corner, follow this up to a roof (good nut) and traverse back right to pull steeply onto the giant blocky flakes of the original pitch. Follow these leftwards to a belay beneath a short steep corner, as for the original route.

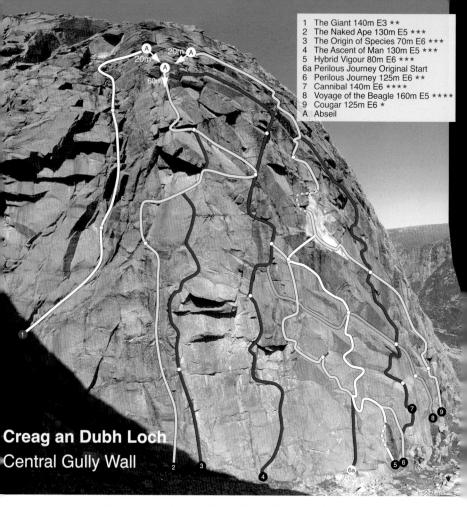

1 The Giant 140m E3 ★★
2 The Naked Ape 130m E5 ★★★
3 The Origin of Species 70m E6 ★★★
4 The Ascent of Man 130m E5 ★★★
5 Hybrid Vigour 80m E6 ★★★
6a Perilous Journey Original Start
6 Perilous Journey 125m E6 ★★
7 Cannibal 140m E6 ★★★★
8 Voyage of the Beagle 160m E5 ★★★★
9 Cougar 125m E6 ★
A Abseil

Creag an Dubh Loch
Central Gully Wall

4. As described in the guidebook but it is possible to make an abseil from a wedged triangular block to the left of the belay at the end of this pitch (anchor *in situ*) to the abseil spike on *Naked Ape/Origin of the Species/Ascent of Man/Voyage of the Beagle* from which a 60m abseil comfortably gains the gully. (Topo provided.)

False Gully Wall
Michael Barnard notes that a combination of *Sans Fer* pitch 1, *Ludwig* pitch 1 (*SMCJ* 2011) and *The Snake* pitch 2 gives an excellent four-pitch E1 (5b, –, 5b, 5b).

Buff Slabs
Stark, Direct Start   15m   5a. Michael Barnard, Alan Hill. 5 Jun 2021.
Climb through the hole. Entertaining!

GLEN CLOVA
Coire Wharral
Heather Left-Hand   120m   II. Gwilym Lynn. 17 Nov 2018.

On the left-hand buttress climbed by *Heather Boulevard*, climb the left edge of the buttress directly up the obvious snowy ramp to finish up the awkward shallow gully of *Heather Boulevard*.

Corlowie
(NO 297 731)
Aurore Buttress 70m II. Simon Richardson. 3 Dec 2021.
The front face of the left-hand buttress. Start below the centre of the lower tier where a stepped ramp leads left to a terrace. Move up and right to the second of two left-tending terraces and follow this diagonally up and left to the top.

Twister Rib 50m II. Simon Richardson. 3 Dec 2021.
Climb the crest of the short buttress in the 'V' formed by the two branches of the dividing gully.

Barra Buttress 70m II/III. Simon Richardson. 3 Dec 2021.
The right-hand buttress. Start on its right side and follow a ramp up and left to a horizontal terrace. Move 5m right below a steep wall and continue up an open discontinuous right-facing corner system to the top.

Coire Farchal
As You Like It 150m II/III. Simon Richardson. 3 Dec 2021.
The left side of two-tiered buttress approximately 50m left of the prominent corner line of *Age Before Beauty*. Follow a left-slanting diagonal line through the lower wall and continue up easy ground to the upper section which is climbed by short walls near the crest.

All The World's a Stage 150m VI,6. Forrest Templeton, Simon Richardson. 6 Feb 2022.
The central line up the two-tiered buttress midway between *As You Like It* and *Age Before Beauty* provides two excellent pitches with easier ground between. The first ascent was made under deep powder and the third pitch would be considerably easier with consolidated snow and ice on the upper slab. Start 20m led of *Age Before Beauty* below a deep chimney.
1. 40m Climb the chimney and step out left below the final roof on to a ledge. Continue up easy ground to a steep wall and traverse 5m right to an undercut niche with a flat pointed block lying at its base.
2. 30m Pull over the steep step on the right and climb discontinuous turf up the slab above to gain a wide terrace below the barrier wall.
3. 40m The barrier wall is cut by a steep groove that finishes below a roof. Climb the groove then traverse horizontally right below the roof on narrow ledges before moving up a dwindling terrace leading under the right side of the roof. Pull over the roof and climb an awkward flake-crack (crux) up the slab above. Move up to a roof below a projecting buttress, traverse left beneath it and climb the icy groove above to a terrace.
4. 40m Easy snow slopes lead to the top.

Age Is Only a Number 60m III,4. Alex Thomson, Jenny Hill. 4 Jan 2015.
A good winter line taking the right flank of the steep buttress high on the right side of the cliff. Climb a ramp and chimney and finish with an exposed traverse and a steep corner.

The Red Craigs, The Doonie, High Crag
Left-Hand Arête   12m   VS 4c.   Gwilym Lynn, Iain Young. 16 Apr 2021.
Climb the arête to the left of *Geotechnician* past a tree at the top.

Dreish, The Scorrie
Storm Arwen Rib   250m   II/III.   Simon Richardson. 28 Nov 2021.
The well-defined rib between *Y Gully Left-Hand Branch* and *Y Gully*. Climb the broad crest over a short steep section to gain a shallow gully in the central part of the rib. Surmount the steeper upper part by following a left-facing corner before exiting up and right over short turfy walls.

NORTH-EAST OUTCROPS

The Coast South from Aberdeen
Girdle Ness Point
These two routes are on the north-facing wall with the existing girdle. Although short, they are accessible on their own via a ramp that descends to tidal ledges at their base about two-thirds of the way along the girdle traverse. They can also be accessed via the *Ness Girdle*.

Greyhope Corner   5m   Moderate.   Rory Brown. 29 Jul 2021.
The obvious short corner approximately two-thirds of the way along the *Ness Girdle*.

Proximity   5m   Diff.   Rory Brown. 29 Jul 2021.
The crack-line up the black wall just to the right of *Greyhope Corner*.

The Coast North of Aberdeen
Collieston, The Graip
Vineyard Direct   15m   HVS 5a.   Simon Richardson, John Ashbridge. 27 May 2003.
Climb up to the roof left of *Knee Trembler*. Pull through on big holds and continue up the arête above to the top. This route supersedes (and pre-dates) *The Vineyard* (*SMCJ* 2014) that accesses the final arête by traversing left above the roof from *Knee Trembler*.

Meikle Partans
Lunatic Fringe for Beginners   10m   VS 4c.   Simon Richardson, Ben Richardson. 26 Jun 2005.
Start as for *Boardman's Crack*. Surmount the overlap rightwards onto slab, then move up left to climb a thin corner-crack to the top.

Harper's Wall
Wilkie's Wall   18m   HVS 5a.   Simon Richardson, John Wilkinson. 14 Jun 1992.
Start between *Renegade* and the Direct Start to *Walkabout*, and climb straight up the slabby wall above to the top.

The Moray Firth Coast
Cummingston, The Stacks Area, Cornflake Walls

I Love to Boogie   12m   Severe. Julie Carter, Mandy Glanvill. 22 Aug 2021.
The arête just left of *Cornflake Wall*. Almost certainly climbed before but not recorded.

Rosehearty Crags, Murcurry, The Sea-Cliffs, East Buttress
Rosemity   10m   Severe 3c *. Dominic Oughton, Helen Oughton. 24 May 2022.
This lies on the west-facing end of East Buttress, between *Fall of Adam* and *Ornithology*. Climb a slab then a shallow chimney to a steep exit on right. There is some poor rock in the chimney but otherwise pleasant climbing.

HIGHLAND OUTCROPS SOUTH

Perthshire and the Southern Highlands
Glen Lednock, Balnacoul Castle, Creag na h-Arairidh, Great Buttress
Wendy's Day Out, Direct Start   10m   E5 6b *. Michael Gardner, Ross Cowie. 26 Aug 2021.
This route follows the line of *Wendy's Day Out* marked on the topos in 'Highland Outcrops South' and Garry Latter's guides. These topos incorrectly mark the line of the original route (*Wendy's Day Out*) which climbs further right. Start up the crack at the right end of the buttress (just left of the start of *No Place for a Wendy*), climb up this for about 3m before a rising traversing left to get under an obvious roof at around 6m, climb over the roof (crux) and continue up the wall above to join the original line up the vague corner system. (Topo provided.)

Cowal
Miracle Wall
Forest Fight   8m   7b *. Jamie Skelton, Morag Eagleson. 17 Mar 2022.
Short intense route just left of *Angles with Dirty Faces*.

Forbidden Fruit   10m   6c ***. Jamie Skelton, Morag Eagleson. 17 Mar 2022.
The old top-rope line in the middle of the crag gives a good challenge linking the obvious huge pockets up the wall to a tricky move gaining the slab. Warning, the route is at the extreme upper limit of the grade! Partly bolted by M.Tweedley. (Topo provided)

On the Seventh Day   8m   6a *. Jamie Skelton, Ed Edwards. 27 Apr 2022.
The furthest route right, a pleasant warm-up.

Jamie Skelton notes that the crag now has a complete set of new stainless bolts and lower-offs. It is no longer scary or minimally bolted. Topo submitted.

Loch Tarsan Crag
(NS 0796 8475) Alt 150m South-West facing
Felling at the start of 2019 meant that Loch Tarsan Crag became visible from the road. Since then seven lines have been bolted with potential for more. The routes are reasonably long and technical on featured schist. (Topo provided.)
Approach: Park at the south-east side of the loch, being careful not to block the gated access. When the water level is low (through most of the summer) the crag can be reached in 20 minutes by walking around the edge of the loch until the

crag comes into view. If the water level gets really high during the winter it can take longer and a kayak or canoe can make for a fun alternative.
Directions: From Dunoon head north on the A815. After a few miles and turn left onto the B836 (just before the petrol station). After 5 miles on this road the loch and the parking will appear on the right-hand side of the road.

Kerchak 20m 6b+ **. Tom Dean-Gately, Jamie Skelton. 2019.
The furthest route left. Climb through a steep bulge passing a seep line (avoidable) and continue up a left-facing corner to the same anchor as *Ape Instinct*.

Ape Instinct 20m 7b *. Jamie Skelton, Morag Eagleson. 21 Jun 2021.
Strenuous climbing just left of the long crack that separates the buttress.

Tarzan's Wall 22m 7a ***. Jamie Skelton, Tom Dean-Gatley. 2019.
A crag classic. Technical punchy climbing just right of the long crack that separates the buttress.

Hold my Loincloth 24m 7a *. Jamie Skelton, Morag Eagleson. 2 Jul 2021.
Climb *Tarzan's Wall* past its crux and join *Zoanthropy* at the top. (Two independent bolts.)

Zoanthropy 24m 6c+ **. Morag Eagleson, Jamie Skelton. 2 Jul 2021.
Climb the middle of the main wall.

Key to the Jungle 24m 6c+ **. Jamie Skelton. 7 Aug 2021.
On the right side of the main wall.

No Pain, No Jane 22m 6c+ *. Jamie Skelton. 21 Sep 2021.
A slightly trickier right-hand finish to *Key to the Jungle*.

Ardgour Crags, Glen Gour, Indian Slab
Mad Cow 90m HVS 4c *. Steve Kennedy, Eileen Blair, Colin Moody, Cynthia Grindley. 3 Jul 2021.
A line right of *Sitting Bull*, starting from a large chockstone in the gully about 15m below the start of that route. Spaced protection.
1. 30m From the chockstone step right and climb a slab to below a bulge at 10m. Follow cracks right then move back left. Continue up a slab (left of a black streak) to reach a grassy alcove below some bulges.
2. 60m Move leftwards before stepping back right above the bulges and continue up clean slabs and ribs to easier ground.

The following routes are scattered across several small outcrops to the left of Indian Slab.

Gneiss 'n' Groovy 15m V.Diff. Tim Miller, Ed Mclaughlin. 13 Jul 2021.
A small wall down and left of *Paleface*. This route climbs the dark crack on the left side of the wall.

Gneiss 'n' Slabby 25m V.Diff. Tim Miller, Ed Mclaughlin. 13 Jul 2021.
The left side of the slab below Paleface and just to the left of *Tonto Say: What You Mean*.

Gneiss 'n' Edgy 30m Severe. Tim Miller, Ed Mclaughlin. 13 Jul 2021.
This climbs the right side of the slab right of *White Wisp*.

Glen Tarbert, Snake Crag
No Sheep 14m Severe. Colin Moody. 1999.
Start up the wall between *Lambleg Slab* and the trees, go left to join and finish up that route.

Trinity 10m V.Diff *. Colin Moody. 27 Jul 2021.
Climb the dark rock right of the trees to a niche then move up right. (Topo provided.)

Pale Slab 12m V.Diff *. Colin Moody. 1999.
The slab up and right. (Topo provided.)

Glen Nevis
Steall Meadows Area, Frontier Crag
(NN 191 686) West-facing
A sprawling west-facing, slabby crag is situated on the south side of the River Nevis, a few hundred metres east of the bridge at the Steall ruins. In dry conditions the river can be easily crossed beyond the bridge. A grass ledge cuts across the crag at about two-thirds height forming an upper tier. Mostly good quality quartzite, often with spaced protection.

The first routes described are located on the clean slabs on the lower far right-hand section beyond the trees. There are three tongues of slab, the rightmost leading to a roof and bulging wall. The routes described are on the left-hand and central areas of slab.

Calamity Jane 30m HVS 5a *. Steve Kennedy, Colin Moody. 25 Jul 2021.
The left-hand slab just right of a grassy gully. Start at the lowest point and climb the initial slab to a grass ledge. Continue up the upper slab via some cracks on the right (gear).

Butch Cassidy 30m HVS 4c *. Steve Kennedy, Colin Moody. 25 Jul 2021.
The central slab, starting 3m right of *Calamity Jane*. Climb the initial slab (between grassy cracks) then directly up the bold top slab.

On the upper tier, just left of centre, is an area of clean slab with left-slanting cracks above a grass ledge. The following routes start from the ledge which is accessed from the left (or by abseil).

Magnum Force 16m Severe *. Colin Moody, Steve Kennedy. 1 Aug 2021.
Takes a line up the clean slab about 8m left of a holly tree (close to the start of *High Noon*). Start up a short slab to below a deep crack. Climb the crack, move left, and finish up the slab above, trending leftwards.

High Noon 22m E2 5b **. Steve Kennedy, Colin Moody. 1 Aug 2021.
A bold undertaking on immaculate rock. Start just right of a holly tree about 8m right of *Magnum Force* and climb a crack to below a bulge. Step left, surmount

the bulge, and climb the slab above for 5m to a crack (reasonable wire). Follow a diagonal line of shallow cracks up leftwards to finish near the far-left edge.

Loch Linnhe to Mallaig
Creag Dhubh na Caillich

The normally dank, seeping outcrop in the forestry about 20 mins from the North Face car park, containing a number of fairly popular dry tooling routes, was almost completely dry during the summer of 2021 and provided some worthwhile bolted sport routes. Several other routes have been reported in UKC.

Main Wall

The first wall at the top of the firebreak.

An Rúnda   15m   D7 **. Jamie Skelton, Morag Eagleson. 20 Oct 2020.
The vertical steep crack on the left side of the main wall. Possibly climbed before.

"Tech" 10   18m   D7 *. Jamie Skelton, Morag Eagleson. 5 Jun 2021.
Follow *"Tech 6"* to the end of its first crack. Instead of trending left, continue up the steep wall above.

Firebreak   18m   D6 *. Jamie Skelton, Morag Eagleson. 20 Oct 2020.
The first route encountered after walking up the firebreak. Climb the obvious and awkward flared groove. Possibly climbed before.

Firebreak   18m   6a. Steve Kennedy, Eileen Blair, Colin Moody. 3 Sep 2021.
A summer ascent of the existing dry tooling route. Reasonable climbing, done after weeks of dry weather when the crag was bone-dry. Probably a rare occurrence.

Barefoot Slab

The upper slab reached by going right from the top of the fire break and back left above. Above the tree line with a fine outlook and drying much quicker than the Main Wall. The following routes use a shared lower-off.

Dancing Queen   14m   5c *. Colin Moody, Eileen Blair, Steve Kennedy. 3 Sep 2021.
The left side of the slab moving slightly right near the top to join *Mamma Mia*.

Mamma Mia   15m   6a *. Steve Kennedy, Eileen Blair, Colin Moody. 3 Sep 2021.
The line right of *Dancing Queen*, the initial moves providing the crux. This route is close to the existing trad route, *No Shoes, No Service* (HVS), and was bolted with the consent of the first ascensionist of that route.

The existing bolted line starting 2 metres to the right, *Barefoot Running* (also used as a dry tooling route), is worthwhile (5a) and deserves a star.

Loch Eil to Mallaig
Gleann Fionn-lighe – Uachan Slab

Booster   20m   Severe. Colin Moody. 19 Mar 2022.
Start left of *The White Streak*. Move up then climb diagonally right crossing *The White Streak*.

Second Dose 10m Severe. Colin Moody. 19 Mar 2022.
Start beside *Phase 3* and climb the vein to finish at a small tree.

Meall a' Choire Chruinn
(NM 8796 7625) Alt 632m
Heading up into Coire Ghiubhsachain the first obvious line of continuous rock
on the north-north-east shoulder of Meall a' Choire Chruinn forms the continuation
of the north-north-east ridge of Sgùrr Ghiubhsachain. Leave the Allt Coire
Ghiubhsachain stream at the first prominent subsidiary stream on its west bank,
heading for an obvious clean slab of rock at the bottom of the following route.

Sgrìodain Spur 150m Moderate **. Daniel Moore. 7 May 2022.
Mostly easy scrambling but the rock is immaculate and provides a great way to
gain the Sgùrr Ghiubhsachain ridge and continue to the summit. Climb the initial
slab by the obvious cracked fault in the middle, then trend slightly left and up
over easy slabs until reaching another even finer clean slab. Continue up this and
more easy broken slabs to the top.

Dome Buttress
Hesperes 8m VS 4b *. Steve Kennedy, Colin Moody. 21 Jun 2021.
Climb the wall about 4m right of *Evening Star* just left of a thin quartz fault and
below a heather-filled alcove. Climb to the alcove and finish up a short groove
above.

Phosphorus 8m V.Diff *. Steve Kennedy, Colin Moody. 21 Jun 2021.
Start up the open corner 5m right of *Hesperes*. Continue up the wall and crack
above.

Eventide 8m V.Diff *. Steve Kennedy, Colin Moody. 12 Jun 2021.
Takes a line directly up the cleanest strip of rock immediately right of *Phosphorus*
(1m left of an embedded boulder).

Daphne 10m Moderate *. Steve Kennedy, Colin Moody. 12 Jun 2021.
The parallel quartz fault about 6m left of *Celeste*. Start up a short slab leading to
the fault and finish up slabs on the right.

There is a small buttress about 15m right of *Celeste*, containing some striking
wavy features, known as Wave Rock.

Air Wave 8m V.Diff *. Steve Kennedy, Colin Moody. 12 Jun 2021.
Start at the lowest point and climb a left-facing corner, finishing up the rib on the
right.

Tidal Wave 8m V.Diff *. Steve Kennedy. 26 Jul 2020.
Navigate through the waves on the front face right of *Air Wave*.

The long featured crag, starting about 15m right of Wave Rock, has been dubbed
Splintered Rock. It gradually tapers and diminishes in height from the left.

Crystal Cascade 13m Severe *. Steve Kennedy, Colin Moody. 12 Jun 2021.
Follows the quartz band on the initial slab at the left end. Start at the toe, move

leftwards across a slab and climb the quartz over the left side of the cracked bulge. Finish up easy slabs.

Hobnailer Wall 13m   VS 4b *. Steve Kennedy, Colin Moody. 12 Jun 2021.
The attractive clean wall 12m right of *Crystal Cascade*. Climb a crack bounding the left side of the wall, step right at about half-height and finish up the wall.

Matrix 10m   Severe *. Steve Kennedy, Cynthia Grindley. 12 Jun 2021.
Up and right of *Hobnailer Wall* is a grassy bay. Climb the right-trending cracks on the cleanest section, starting on the left side of the bay.

Mast Crags
(NM 858 816)
A number of crags are situated on the hillside on the north side of the A830, not far above the large layby below the mast. The following routes are on the closest crag, which contains a prominent corner (*Telegraph Corner*) (5 mins). Several other routes around here have been reported on UKC.

Poles Apart 10m   Diff. *. Cynthia Grindley, Steve Kennedy. 15 May 2021.
The slab on the left side of the crag (left of *Power Line*).

Power Line 8m   Severe *. Steve Kennedy, Cynthia Grindley, Lucy Prins, Phill Thompson. 15 May 2021.
The steep wall left of *Telegraph Corner*, starting up a left-slanting crack. From near the top of the crack move up right and pull onto the slab (joining *Poles Apart*). Finish up the slab.

Squat Buttress
Serena 13m   V.Diff *. Steve Kennedy, Cynthia Grindley. 21 Jun 2021.
Start on the left side below some flakes, just right of a long slanting line of overhangs (about 15m left of *Acadia*). Climb to a flake (left of a small tree) and move rightwards to a further flake. Climb the slabs above, finishing on the right. Block belay well back (spare rope useful).

Voyager 15m   VS 4c *. Steve Kennedy, Cynthia Grindley. 21 Jun 2021.
A bit squeezed in but good climbing. Start at the foot of the cleaned flake on the right as for *Paloma* and climb the wall above for 2m. Move a short distance leftwards along a small ledge then climb the slab above to below the bulging headwall beneath some cracks (right of *Arcadia*). Pull over the headwall via a small rocky ear and finish up the slab.

Lunetta 18m   Severe **. Steve Kennedy, Colin Moody. 12 Jun 2021.
A pleasant line up the left side of the slab (left of *Luna*). Start mid-way along the base and climb the initial short wall to reach the right end of a narrow ledge. Move left along the ledge to reach the left edge of the slab. Follow the edge, keeping to the right. Sparsely protected.

Cat's Eye Crag
Ballard of the Pines 20m   7c **. Jamie Skelton, Morag Eagleson. 3 Aug 2021.
The smooth slab just left of *Layaway to Heaven*. An old Tom Ballard project with a hard fingery crux.

Watchtower Slab
(NM 838 821) Alt 200m South-facing
A south-facing slab on the hillside north of the east end of Loch Eilt. Park in a layby near the end of the loch (NM 841 817) and approach by the side of the track (reseeding work currently ongoing) which leads steeply up left of Cat's Eye Crag. From just above the steepest section of the track, head left across a burn, up the slope above for 50m then head left across the hillside to reach a gully which leads down to the base of the slab (20 mins).

Watchtower 25m H.Severe 4a *. Steve Kennedy, Colin Moody. 26 Jul 2021.
The route generally follows the right side of the slab. Start at the toe, pull over a bulge, step left then move back rightwards. Continue up the rib above and finish up a shallow groove. Poorly protected.

Craiglea
Leftover 10m 5c. Colin Moody, Cynthia Grindley. 12 Apr 2022.
The left-hand line (left of *Alarm*).

Route One 8m 6a+ *. Colin Moody, Cynthia Grindley, Stan Pearson. 22 Jun 2021.
Just left of *Brown Crack*.

Memory Lane 25m 6b **. Steve Kennedy, Colin Moody. 26 May 2021.
Start up *Brown Crack* then foot traverse right onto *Molar.* Move up then traverse right along the break to the lower off of *Fumble*.

The Stripper 10m 6b+ **. Steve Kennedy, Cynthia Grindley, Colin Moody. 16 May 2021.
The route right of *Molar* to the same lower off.

Fly Wall 12m 6c *. Morag Eagleson, Jamie Skelton. 29 Aug 2021.
This route takes the slightly left-trending line up the middle of the slab joining *Great Wall* just before its crux. A long reach is very useful for getting off the ground.

Cry Wolf, Direct Start 4m E1 5c *. Steve Kennedy. 18 May 2021.

Fumble 10m 6a *. Colin Moody, Steve Kennedy, Cynthia Grindley. 20 May 2021.
Start up *April* then move right.

Illegitimate Groove 10m 6a+ *. Colin Moody, Steve Kennedy. 9 Jul 2021.
Round to the right of the other routes.

Box Buttress
(NM 776 832)
The small barrel-shaped buttress located approximately 1km west of Craiglea (*SMCJ* 2021) at about the same altitude. The right side has two prominent crack-lines. A spare rope is useful to reach a block belay above. To avoid a direct approach crossing the railway, use the tunnel access as for Craiglea and traverse west across the hillside above the railway.

Ali Shuffle   12m   E1 5b **. Steve Kennedy, Eileen Blair. 1 Jun 2021.
The left-hand crack, finishing out leftwards on a slab then back right. Quite sustained with good protection.

Rumble in the Jungle   12m   HVS 5a **. Steve Kennedy, Colin Moody. 18 Jul 2021.
The right-hand crack containing a small tree. Awkward initial moves lead to the well-protected crack.

El Paso Crag
(NM 774 823)
On the approach towards the Beinn Bheag Slab, near the end of the flat, boggy area (just beyond the narrow bridge near the last house), a west-facing crag will be seen up on the left. The crag comprises a steep central wall and a south-facing wall, both with sharp left arêtes, above and below.

Schwegler   10m   VS 4c *. Steve Kennedy, Eileen Blair, Cynthia Grindley, Colin Moody. 20 Mar 2022.
Start below the left arête (next to a large block) of the upper wall. Pull strenuously up right onto the edge and continue up wall just right of the edge to a rounded finish from a ledge on the left.

Bird Lounge   12m   VS 4c **. Steve Kennedy, Cynthia Grindley, Colin Moody. 2 Apr 2022.
This route is based on the left arête of the lower wall, starting from a grassy ledge and tree up on the right. From the ledge, pull left onto the wall to gain a crack. Follow the crack just right of the edge to a sloping finish.

Hatchery Slab
(NM 77636 82522) South-west facing
This small slab is obvious on the walk in to Beinn Bheag Slab. It sits left (west) of the main slab and is the upper of two slabs that look out towards the hatchery. The crack routes have protection the others are bold. There are cracks for wired nuts 24m back from the top.

Gyrodactylus   5m   Diff. Colin Moody. 19 Feb 2022.
The crack at the left-hand side.

Fungus   6m   4c. Steve Kennedy, Cynthia Grindley, Colin Moody. 6 Mar 2022.
The line just right finishing up a blind crack.

Costia   6m   4b. Steve Kennedy, Cynthia Grindley, Colin Moody. 6 Mar 2022.
The obvious quartz vein.

White Spot   6m   5a. Steve Kennedy, Cynthia Grindley, Colin Moody. 6 Mar 2022.
Thin veins.

Frunc   6m   Severe. Colin Moody, Steve Kennedy, Cynthia Grindley. 6 Mar 2022.
The crack going up left.

Fin Rot   6m   Severe. Colin Moody, Steve Kennedy, Cynthia Grindley. 6 Mar 2022.
The cracks just right.

Reading Glasses   5m   V.Diff. Colin Moody. 19 Feb 2022.
The scoop.

Microscope   5m   Severe. Colin Moody, Steve Kennedy, Cynthia Grindley. 6 Mar 2022.
The short wall.

There is a low-level traverse starting at *Gyrodactylus* and finishing up a crack at the right-hand end, 15m 4c (Steve Kennedy 6 Mar 2022).

The Gravestones & The White Wall
(NM 778 824)
The hillside below and east of Beinn Bheag Slab has numerous small crags running almost horizontally across the hill. The Upper Tier has the guidebook routes *Spangly Bunnet*, *Stolen Crack*, *Mike's Piece* and *Bonnie Fechter*. The main tier is below (The Graveyard) and is made up of a chaotic collection of flakes, pinnacles and 'tombstone' features. Below The Graveyard is The White Wall. About 10 mins walk beyond El Paso Crag. The first routes described are on The Graveyard and are situated near the left (west) end in a small bay with a pinnacle on the right. A pleasant suntrap.

Mortician   8m   Severe 4a. Steve Kennedy, Eileen Blair, Cynthia Grindley, Colin Moody. 20 Mar 2022.
Climb the left-facing corner on the left side of the bay to a ledge. Finish up the corner on the left using quartz holds on the right wall.

Heidstane   8m   HVS 5a *. Steve Kennedy, Eileen Blair, Cynthia Grindley, Colin Moody. 20 Mar 2022.
The attractive, bold wall right of *Mortician*. Start up a small edge, gain a break and move leftwards to finish.

Ashes to Ashes   8m   Severe 4a. Colin Moody, Eileen Blair, Cynthia Grindley, Steve Kennedy. 20 Mar 2022.
Right of *Heidstane* is an open corner. Start up the right wall to gain and follow the crack above, bridging left into the corner to finish.

Coffin Corner   9m   Severe 4a *. Steve Kennedy, Eileen Blair, Cynthia Grindley, Colin Moody. 20 Mar 2022.
Start up the corner-crack right of *Ashes to Ashes*, formed by the large pinnacle, to gain the ledge. Continue up the corner on the left.

Eulogy   12m   Severe 4a *. Steve Kennedy, Eileen Blair, Cynthia Grindley, Colin Moody. 20 Mar 2022.
A pleasant route following the line of a stepped trough up the clean slab about 5m right of *Coffin Corner*. Start up the slab on the right and step left into the trough.

Necropolis   12m   Severe. Colin Moody, Cynthia Grindley, Steve Kennedy. 2 Apr 2022.
About 12m right of *Eulogy* (and 6m left of a prominent pointed finger) is a left-slanting hand crack passing a small roof. Climb the crack.

Approximately 50m right of *Eulogy* is a holly tree, just right of a large slab with a scooped ramp. To the left of the large slab is a smaller, clean slab containing the following route.

Tombstone   7m   VS 4b *. Colin Moody, Cynthia Grindley, Steve Kennedy, Lucy Prins. 26 Mar 2022.
Pull onto the slab from the undercut toe on the left. Climb the slab initially using the left edge then directly.

Tomb Raider   8m   V.Diff. Phill Thompson, Cynthia Grindley, Steve Kennedy, Colin Moody, Lucy Prins. 26 Mar 2022.
About 5m right of *Tombstone* is a right-slanting corner. Start 2m right of the corner, climb a short slab and move rightwards into a cleaned crack which is followed to the top.

Celebrant   12m   HVS 5a **. Steve Kennedy, Colin Moody. 28 Mar 2022.
The larger area of slab 3m right of *Tomb Raider* contains a scooped ramp running diagonally right (*Cortege*). This good route starts up a short slab (just right of a heather patch) leading to the foot of the ramp. Follow the ramp to the foot of the crack line splitting the centre of the head wall, starting about mid-way up the ramp. Climb the crack. Flake belays well back.

Cortege   14m   HVS 4c **. Steve Kennedy, Cynthia Grindley, Colin Moody, Lucy Prins, Phill Thompson. 26 Mar 2022.
An excellent, fairly bold route following the scooped ramp all the way with sustained interest. Step left at the top. Gear in the cracks on the left wall at half-height.

The lowest band of rocks below The Gravestones (The White Wall) features a small, quartz-studded wall to the right of the leftmost rocks, containing the following routes:

Snatch   6m   HVS 5b *. Steve Kennedy, Cynthia Grindley, Lucy Prins, Phill Thompson. 26 Mar 2022.
The wall has two vertical cracks in the centre. This route follows the left-hand crack.

Grab   6m   VS 5a *. Steve Kennedy, Cynthia Grindley, Colin Moody, Lucy Prins, Phill Thompson. 26 Mar 2022.
The right-hand crack, left of the quartz.

Clasp   6m   Severe 4a *. Colin Moody, Cynthia Grindley, Steve Kennedy, Lucy Prins, Phill Thompson. 26 Mar 2022.
The wall right of *Grab* via the quartz, stepping left to finish.

Lochailort to Arisaig
Church House Crag
(NM 748 833)

Located on the north side of the A830, a few hundred metres south-east of the Penmeanach layby from which the School House Crags are accessed. Park at the first layby just west of Polnish Church on the north side of the A830 (NM 747 830). From the layby, ascend the hill leftwards, keeping to some grassy ridges on the left, and the crag will come into view on the right (15 minutes). The first three routes are situated on the slabby, leftmost buttress with a large flake on the left. The crag extends right, initially becoming more broken and featuring a huge block, beyond which is a steep wall containing a corner (*Basilica*) and parallel cracks near the right end.

Revelation   12m   V.Diff *.   Steve Kennedy, Colin Moody. 27 Dec 2021.
The groove on the left side of the buttress, starting in a slot. Bridge up the slot and climb the groove and wall above. Stake belay in place.

Scruffy Jesus   12m   Severe 4a *.   Steve Kennedy, Colin Moody. 19 Sep 2021.
This route follows the vague system of open grooves in the centre of the buttress, just right of *Revelation*, starting at the lowest point.

Isaiah   12m   H.Severe 4a *.   Steve Kennedy, Colin Moody. 6 Oct 2021.
The bold wall right of *Scruffy Jesus*, starting 1m right of that route. Sparsely protected. Climb rightwards aiming for a thin corner-groove about half-way up which is followed directly (avoid moving right onto easier ground) to a rounded finish. Spoilt by being escapable to the right.

Basilica   12m   Severe 4a *.   Steve Kennedy, Colin Moody. 19 Sep 2021.
The left-facing corner on the right-hand section (left of a vertical mossy groove). Climb the corner to a ledge, step right and finish up the short wall above.

Congregation   10m   Severe 4a *.   Steve Kennedy, Colin Moody. 6 Oct 2021.
The left-hand of the parallel vertical cracks close to where the crag peters out on the right. Belay at a block up and right.

Reformation   10m   Severe 4a *.   Steve Kennedy, Colin Moody. 6 Oct 2021.
The right-hand crack.

Schoolhouse Crags
There are a number of crags which can be seen from the layby. The old schoolhouse to the west of the crags was used as a hospital for accidents during the construction of the railway. The rock, psammite, is very good. Most routes face south-west and dry quickly. Many routes are poorly protected and belays can be hard to find; there are a few stakes. Topo submitted.
Approach: Park in the large layby used for Ardnish peninsular. Cross the road; there are often fast vehicles. Walk down the road for a short distance to a very small burn and duck under the fence, then walk up to the crags, boggy to start.

Lower Crag
(NM 74366 83610)
The nearest crag to the road, down and left of the other crags. There are several trees around the crag. There is a belay about 10m up from *Hidden Rib*.

The White Streak   14m   VS 4c.   Steve Kennedy, Colin Moody. 25 May 2021.
Start left of the main rib which has a white quartz line. Move up and right, then climb the rib.

Hidden Rib   14m   VS 5a *.   Steve Kennedy, Colin Moody. 7 Aug 2021.
The rib on the right, behind the trees. Climb the rib directly and finish up a cracked wall.

Twin Crags
(NM 74437 83578)
Up and right from Lower Crag are two crags at the left-hand side of the craggy hill. The upper crag has a huge square block at the base on the right-hand side. Natural belays for the lower crag; there is a stake above the upper crag.

Twin Crags Lower
Pole Dancer   9m   VS 4b.   Steve Kennedy, Colin Moody. 25 May 2021.
The rib left of the main crag, start at a stunted holly up and right from a large angled block. Follow the line of weakness to the break, then pull out left and continue up.

Polecat   10m   Severe *.   Colin Moody, Cynthia Grindley. 13 May 2021.
On the largest part of the lower crag. Climb a clean rib and finish up right between two flake cracks; the left-hand crack sounds hollow.

Linesman   10m   Severe *.   Colin Moody, Cynthia Grindley. 13 May 2021.
Climb a crack at the right-hand side of the lower crag, then move up rightwards.

Twin Crags Upper
Sideline   10m   VS 4b.   Steve Kennedy, Colin Moody. 25 May 2021.
A line left of *Cayce*.

Cayce   12m   VS 4b *.   Colin Moody, Cynthia Grindley. 19 May 2021.
A few metres left of the huge square block is an open groove slanting up left. Climb the groove, step right and continue up.

Whistle   12m   V.Diff *.   Colin Moody, Cynthia Grindley. 19 May 2021.
Start just right of *Cayce* and follow the ramp up right, then climb the slab left of *Promised Land*.

Promised Land   12m   Severe *.   Colin Moody, Cynthia Grindley. 19 May 2021.
Climb the crack on the left side of the huge square block and continue up.

Pine Slab
Pine Staircase   10m   Diff.   Colin Moody. 5 Dec 2021.
A pleasant juggy slab to the right of the Upper Crag.

White Lines
(NM 74474 83572)
Right of Twin Crags Upper (up and right from Pine Slab) is a prominent slab with thin vertical quartz veins, well seen from the parking.

V-22 Osprey   10m   Severe *. Colin Moody, Cynthia Grindley. 19 May 2021.
The crack a few metres left of the quartz veins has a bulge to finish.

Fly-past   12m   VS 4b *. Colin Moody, Cynthia Grindley. 19 May 2021.
Start between the veins and climb up slightly rightwards. Another route was climbed here but they joined before the top.

Holly Crag
This is the first of a line of small crags right of Twin Crags Lower, overlooking a small burn.

Plop   7m   VS 4b *. Colin Moody. 7 May 2021.
Above the left side of Holly Crag is a fine short dark slab.

Brush Past   8m   V.Diff. Colin Moody. 5 Dec 2021.
Left of the holly tree is a chimney. Start just right of the wide crack which is left of the chimney. Gain then climb the wide crack, step left and finish easily.

Birch Wall
(NM 74491 83524)
A bigger crag right of Holly Crag.

West Pole   8m   Severe. Colin Moody, Pete Whillance. 24 Jul 2021.
Start left of *Poles Apart*. Climb up crossing two cracks and finish up a shallow groove, often wet.

Poles Apart   10m   H.Severe. Colin Moody, Pete Whillance. 24 Jul 2021.
Start left of the birch tree, below and left of a large block. Climb up crossing two cracks and finish leftwards up the shallow corner. Poorly protected.

Polar Explorer   10m   E2 5c. Pete Whillance, Colin Moody. 24 Jul 2021.
The wall right of the birch tree. Start just right of a small overhang and climb the wall to a thin break. Step left and climb the slab leftwards to better holds. Continue more easily to the top.

East Pole   8m   V.Diff. Colin Moody. 7 May 2021.
The crack at the right-hand side, then step right and up.

Grey Buttress
About 50m up and right from Birch Wall is a grey buttress with a large grass patch above the right-hand side.

Grey Day   12m   Severe. Colin Moody. 7 May 2021.
Climb the awkward slim corner at the left-hand side, step right and continue up the rounded rib.

Land of Grey and Pink   12m   V.Diff *. Colin Moody. 7 May 2021.
The shallow corner to the right.

Pink   12m   V.Diff. Colin Moody. 9 Aug 2021.
Start just right and climb a shallow corner to the left end of the grass patch, then
follow the rib.

Quartz Wall
About 15m right is a short steep wall.

Energy Crisis   7m   E1 5b. Pete Whillance, Colin Moody. 24 Jul 2021.
Follow the awkward thin crack (towards the left side of the wall) leftwards.

Central Crack   7m   HVS 5a. Pete Whillance, Colin Moody. 24 Jul 2021.
The crack is quite sustained.

Right Crack   8m   VS 4c. Pete Whillance, Colin Moody. 24 Jul 2021.
The prominent right-hand quartz crack. The tricky bulge is overcome with a high
hold on the right.

Welly Rib   8m   Moderate. Colin Moody. 9 Aug 2021.
The rib 6m to the right.

Anvil Crag
About 20m right is another crag.

Anvil Rib   10m   V.Diff. Steve Kennedy, Colin Moody. 29 Dec 2021.
Climb the rib past the big block, then the cracks above.

Hammer   12m   Severe. Colin Moody. 1 Jul 2021.
Climb a faint groove to easier ground then finish over a slight bulge.

Forge   12m   V.Diff. Colin Moody. 1 Jul 2021.
Climb the easy crack then go over the bulge to finish.

Upper Slab
This slab is above Quartz Wall and can be climbed anywhere.

Central Rib   12m   Diff. Colin Moody. 1 Jul 2021.
The central rib finishing between two niches.

Right Rib   12m   Diff. Colin Moody. 1 Jul 2021.
The rib to the right leads to the right-hand niche, then step right and up.

Primary Crags
(NM 74595 83415)
These overlook an open gully south of the gully of Birch Wall, Grey Buttress etc.
They comprise short steep wall and a longer easier-angled wall to the right. There
is a stake above the right-hand wall.

The Huts   7m   VS 4c *. Steve Kennedy, Colin Moody. 29 Sep 2021.
Start near the left-hand side of the steep wall. Climb the wall between two vertical quartz veins to the horizontal break and good cams, then continue up to the right.

Playground   7m   Severe 4b. Steve Kennedy, Colin Moody. 29 Sep 2021.
Start near the right-hand side of the wall and climb up to the left-hand side of a large flake. Stand on the flake, then step left and continue up the open groove.

Waves   12m   V.Diff *. Colin Moody, Eileen Blair. 18 Aug 2021.
Start up the open corner on the right-hand side of the right-hand wall. Step right, go up waves of rock then finish up an open corner just left.

Electric Crag
(NM 74492 83379)
This is hidden in another shallow glen south of Primary Crags and east of Twin Crags. The power lines run in front of the crag.

Power Cut   12m   Diff. Colin Moody. 20 Aug 2021.
Climb the easy lower left wall to the grass ledge, move left then climb the upper wall.

Power Sharing   12m   V.Diff. Colin Moody, Eileen Blair. 18 Aug 2021.
Left of the next route with an awkward scoop low down.

Power and the Glory   12m   Diff. Colin Moody, Eileen Blair. 18 Aug 2021.
Start left of a small overhang and climb up.

Upper Crags
These are above the main crags beyond a dip and not visible from the road. Approach from Schoolhouse Crags or Church House Crag.

Skyhook Wall
A small buttress on the north side of the grassy trough, containing a right-slanting crack on the left and a steep, smooth central wall. It lies about 50m left of Triangle Slab and at a lower elevation.

Wet Pants   10m   VS 4b *. Steve Kennedy, Cynthia Grindley, Colin Moody. 28 Dec 2021.
Start 5m right of the central wall below a bulge. Climb to a small ledge and over the bulge. Move leftwards up a pale coloured slab to finish. Good but poorly protected. Small block belay above.

Blundering Nurse   15m   Moderate. Colin Moody, Cynthia Grindley, Steve Kennedy. 28 Dec 2021.
Above and right of Skyhook Wall is an area of clean slab with a left-slanting fault. Climb the slab directly, starting at its lowest point.

Triangle Slab
(NM 747 836)
The triangular-shaped slab situated on the upper right of the top tier. Descend on

the left (requires care when damp). Belay well back at some cracks in the upper wall. Can conveniently be combined with some routes on Church House Crag using the approach for that crag.

Trig Point   12m   VS 5a *. Steve Kennedy, Colin Moody. 13 Nov 2021.
On the left is a smooth wall with a hanging crack. Climb a short corner leading to a slim groove. From the foot of the groove, move left into the base of the crack and finish directly.

Hippo   12m   V.Diff *. Colin Moody, Steve Kennedy. 13 Nov 2021.
Climb the cracked wall just right of *Trig Point* and continue as directly as possible moving left below a block to finish.

Squaw   12m   V.Diff *. Steve Kennedy, Colin Moody. 13 Nov 2021.
Right of *Hippo* is a deep crack. Climb the crack and the slabs directly above. Step right near the top onto a hanging slab (just right of some heather) leading to a ledge and short slab.

Hide   18m   V.Diff *. Steve Kennedy, Colin Moody. 13 Nov 2021.
The slabby rib on the far right taking in all three tiers, starting lower than the previous routes. Start up the lowest slab and climb each tier directly, finishing up a prominent vertical crack.

Arnabol Crags
The hillside to the north-west of the Arnabol Viaduct near Polnish (south of the A830), close to the east end of Loch Beag, contains a number of small, south-facing crags. The crags extend across the hill from left to right by a right-rising line above the railway on the north side of the loch. The westmost crag, Burnt Tree Slab, is situated a few hundred metres east of Loch Beag Slab (*SMCJ* 2021). Discreet parking is available on the wide grassy verge on the south side of the A830 before the railway viaduct (NM 734 841) from where the hill is accessed. A vague deer track leads rightwards over the crest of the hill to the top of the crags. Alternatively, park close to the viaduct and walk back up the road.

Burnt Tree Slab
(NM 7315 8387)
The slab has a steep headwall in the centre and the remains of a burnt tree at the foot.

Flashpoint   10m   V.Diff. Colin Moody, Cynthia Grindley, Steve Kennedy, Lucy Prins, Phill Thompson. 12 Sep 2021.
The clean slabs about 5m left of the burnt tree. Climb the initial slab, step left and continue up a groove. Alternatively and better, at the left step climb the thin slab on the left directly (5a).

Conflagration   10m   Severe 4a *. Steve Kennedy, Cynthia Grindley, Colin Moody, Lucy Prins, Phill Thompson. 12 Sep 2021.
Start behind the tree. Climb thin cracks directly to the headwall and finish up the steep left-slanting crack.

Too Hot to Handle   10m   Severe 4a. Steve Kennedy, Cynthia Grindley, Colin Moody, Lucy Prins, Phill Thompson. 12 Sep 2021.
Climb the slab on the right via a succession of cleaned ledges to the right-hand end of the headwall. Finish up the steep cracks above.

Stag Crag
(NM 7322 8386)
Situated a short distance east of and at a slightly lower level than Burnt Tree Slab. Tree belay well back from the top (spare rope useful). The crag overlooks the railway. Descend on the left (west) side.

Train Spotting   15m   VS 4c *. Steve Kennedy, Cynthia Grindley, Colin Moody, Lucy Prins, Phill Thompson. 12 Sep 2021.
The left-facing corner-groove bounding the left side of the clean central wall, starting at a large embedded flake. Climb the corner (formed by a huge flake) and groove above to a ledge and finish up slabs.

Dark Wall
(NM 734 838)
The first of three crags situated a few hundred metres east of Stag Crag above a heather-filled trough. The crag is characterised by a crack leading from a small roof just left of centre and left of a black streak.

Crack of Doom   15m   HVS 5a *. Steve Kennedy, Colin Moody. 16 Sep 2021.
Start directly below the crack and climb the initial wall to the base of the crack. Follow the crack to a ledge and finish up the slabs above.

Owl Crag
(NM 734 838)
The slabby crag about 25m right of Cracked Slab with an oak tree just left of the base, and a prominent left-facing corner (*Hedwig*) which forms the left side of a huge flake.

Hedwig   15m   VS 4b *. Colin Moody, Steve Kennedy. 16 Sep 2021.
Climb the corner (awkward start) to reach the top of the large break on the right. Pull onto the right edge to reach the top of the flake and finish up the slab.

Pigwidgeon   15m   HVS 4c *. Steve Kennedy, Colin Moody. 16 Sep 2021.
The bold quartz studded wall right of *Hedwig*, starting at the lowest point, joining that route near the top.

Paraffin Slab
(NM 735 839)
Situated about 50m right (east) of Owl Crag. It is characterised by an undercut base which provides the cruxes of the routes followed by a pleasant slab.

Kerosene   9m   HVS 5b *. Steve Kennedy, Colin Moody. 14 Aug 2021.
Start at the left end of the undercut base at a left-facing wall. Make strenuous moves up the overhanging wall and finish up the slab (belay in a crack on the left).

Alkane   9m   VS 5a *. Steve Kennedy, Colin Moody. 14 Aug 2021.
The obvious break though the overhang right of centre below some heather. Pull through the break, move left below the heather patch, and finish directly up the slab.

Meths   9m   HVS 5b *. Steve Kennedy, Colin Moody. 14 Aug 2021.
Start on the far right of the undercut base at the base of the right-facing wall. Climb the undercut wall and pull strenuously leftwards onto the slab. Finish up the slab on the left to the highest point.

Borrodale Crags, Fortress Wall
Unarmed Combat   14m   5c *. Colin Moody, Steve Kennedy. 30 Jul 2021.
The right arête. Start directly below the arête on flat holds. One tricky move at the second bolt.

Wire Crag, West Wall
Cutwater   7m   VS 4b *. Steve Kennedy, Colin Moody. 15 Jan 2022.
This route is on the first east-facing buttress reached on the approach from the Fortress, about 20m left of *Flush Cutter*. The buttress has a smooth, cracked lower wall leading to a prow in the centre. Climb the centre of the wall to the base of the prow which provides a steep finish. Gear at half-height.

Vice Grip   8m   V.Diff. Steve Kennedy, Colin Moody. 15 Jan 2022.
This route aims for the short left-facing corner-groove near the upper left edge to the left of *Flush Cutter*. Start 2m left of *Flush Cutter* and climb the left edge of the lower fault line (sometimes damp) slightly leftwards to finish up the left-facing corner-groove above.

Splicer   7m   Severe *. Steve Kennedy, Colin Moody. 15 Jan 2022.
The cracked wall right of *Clipper* (just left of a hanging slab), starting next to a large block. Finish up a short slab close to the right edge.

Druim Fiaclach
Simon Powell notes an ascent of *Arisaig Arête* on 22 June 1988 (second did not follow). This pre-dates the 2011 first ascent in 'Highland Outcrops South'. The route was climbed in two pitches and graded HVS (4c/5a, 4b).

European Union Crag
Project Fear   12m   E1 5a *. Steve Kennedy, Cynthia Grindley. 3 Apr 2022.
A direct line up the *Green Paper* slab. From the foot of *Maastricht Treaty* pull onto the slab, but instead of following *Green Paper* leftwards, continue directly up the slab (about 1m left of *Maastricht Treaty*) aiming for a crack at the top. Finish via the upper slab as for *Green Paper*.

Clach a' Phrionnsa (Prince's Stone)
Culloden   13m   6a+ *. Steve Kennedy, Colin Moody. 10 Aug 2021.
The corner on the left side of the main slab. Climb the steep initial wall just right of *Highland Laddie*, pull onto the ledge and continue up the corner (crossing *Flight to Safety*) to the roof. Step left at the roof into the upper corner and finish up the right wall to gain the lower off (shared with *Heaven's Darling*).

Loch Laggan to Dalwhinnie
Binnein Shuas, Western Sector, The Fortress
The following two routes climb the walls either side of the top pitch of *Genghis*.

Imran 25m E1 5b. Michael Barnard, Alan Hill. 1 Aug 2021.
Start just left of *Genghis* pitch 2 and climb fairly directly via horizontal breaks to 3m below the slanting break of *Xanadu*. Step left and move up to gain a jug on that route, then finish directly up cracks in the top wall.

Alim 25m VS 4c. Michael Barnard, Alan Hill. 1 Aug 2021.
Gain the first ledge as for *Genghis* pitch 2. Step right into a short corner, then right again to climb twin cracks.

Michael Barnard notes that avoiding the crux of *The Rubaiyat* by briefly stepping right to the arête gives a good HVS 4c pitch.

Creag a' Chuir (Ardverikie), Red Slab
Minke 20m Severe 4a *. Daniel Moore. 16 Aug 2022.
Start a few metres right of the crack of *She Likes Eels* and follow a left-leaning crack onto a rib. Climb this to a bulge and a prominent short horizontal crack. Surmount the bulge and continue up the slab and cracks above.

Dalwhinnie Region
Dirc Mhòr, Ship Rock, Starboard Wall
Overboard 20m E7 6b **. Jamie Skelton, Morag Eagleson. 15 Sep 2021.
Extremely steep climbing up the middle of the Starboard Wall. Climb directly up from the grassy ledge to the small right-facing corner in the right-trending overlap (bold). After a knee-bar rest, an undercut in the overlap can be used to place small cams out left. Continue up the overlap to a blocky jug, stretch to good holds and gear above, move slightly left to a lay-away below a crux span and some more arm-melting moves that gain the top.

Shining Wall
Raspberry Rubble 20m VS 4c. Martin Stephens, Daniel Moore. 26 Aug 2021.
From 15m up the gully past the arête of *Windrush*, climb a prominent wide crack which turns into a deep chimney, finishing in a fine position round a large chockstone at the top.

Leaning Buttress
The following route is on the last major buttress at the south end of the Dirc, a little further on and slightly lower than World's End Wall. It leans forward considerably due to a landslip at its back. It has a west face and a south face with fine viewpoints.

Bogarde's Crack 15m E1 5a **. Daniel Moore. 16 Sep 2021.
The obvious left-slanting wide crack on the left side of the west wall. Climb up into a chimney-slot with a large overhang on its left to gain the hand-crack. Climb the excellent widening crack steeply through a couple of bulges to the top.

North-West Flank, Whitecap Wall
The following routes lie left of *Guardsman*. The descent is to the left, down the heathery terrace.) This is up and left of Whitecap Wall. It is suggested that this section of the crag be called 'Sunnyside'.

Sunshine Superman 30m VS 4c. Zoe Anderson, Ken Applegate, Dave Fowler, Steven Andrews. 26 Mar 2022.
Climb the steep right-facing groove just left of *Guardsman*. Trend left towards the upper cracked slab, which is climbed on its right. (Topo provided.)

30m left of *Sunshine Superman*, before the crag is broken by the descent terrace, lies a compact buttress.

Spring Sun 20m HVS 4c. Dave Fowler, Steven Andrews, Ken Applegate, Zoe Anderson. 26 Mar 2022.
Start 15m left of *Sunshine Superman* below a steep compact buttress. Climb the buttress centrally, aiming for the upper crack and arête above. Poorly protected. (Topo provided.)

Above the left end of the descent terrace lies a crag with a prominent prow.

Cracking Day 20m H.Severe 4b. Steven Andrews, Ken Applegate, Zoe Anderson. 26 Mar 2022.
To the left of the prow left of *Spring Sun* a crack splits a small roof. Follow this to the top. (Topo provided.)

The next route begins on the lowest rocks which lie at the far left of the descent terrace in a grassy bay.

Cosmic Dust 30m VS 4c. Ken Applegate, Dave Fowler, Zoe Anderson, Steven Andrews. 26 Mar 2022.
Start on a slab down and left of *Cracking Day*. Climb a pink slab to access the upper cracked wall which leads to the top and trees.

The White Tower
White Tower Variation 45m VS 5a. Daniel Moore. 17 Aug 2021.
On the south side of the White Tower climb an overhanging hand-crack just left of the arête. Continue up the left side of the tower until forced to join *White Tower* and continue up this to the top

Zigzag 10m 4c. Daniel Moore. 17 Aug 2021.
Up and to the right of White Tower is a short, steep compact wall. Climb the cracked zigzag fault bounding the right of this wall, finishing up a short slab. Descend grass to the right (or continue easily up the rock above).

Strathspey
Creag Dubh, Bedtime Buttress
Ian Taylor notes that a right-hand start to *Hands Off* on Bedtime Buttress (from below *Legover*) following the thin diagonal cracks all the way leftwards to join the original, is E4 6a.

Waterfall Wall
Stream 30m E3 5c **. Gary Latter. 6 Oct 2021.
Good climbing up the wall left of *Wet Dreams*. Start by scrambling up *Oui Oui* to belay left of small rowan beneath large roof. Step up rightwards and go up the flake (large cam 5 in the break). Pull out right and round to a good undercut on the front face. Move rightwards to a good break, then go direct past good breaks, then take the short arête to the abseil point on the top aspen.

Creag a' Mhuilinn
The following route is on a separate section of the crag, at NH 84379 09578. It is a nice but esoteric spot with a sunny setting, very much off the beaten track. Park up towards Alvie Quarry and contour around the hillside as best you can. To descend, walk off either side.

Millennial Mop Up 10m E4 6a **. Nathan White, Emma Holgate. 26 Aug 2021.
Climb the obvious vertical crack in the barrel-shaped buttress. A fantastic wee climb demanding all manner of techniques.

BEN NEVIS, THE AONACHS, CREAG MEAGAIDH & THE CENTRAL HIGHLANDS

BEN NEVIS
Coire Leis, North-East Buttress
The Fear Factory 50m VII,7 ***. Greg Boswell, Guy Robertson, Hamish Frost. 6 Mar 2022.
The free-hanging ice dagger left of *The Snotter*. Start about 10m left of and below the main icicle (about 60m of Grade II/III to reach this point). Traverse right below the icicle then climb directly up behind it to gain and follow a tricky left-slanting icy ramp to a sloping ledge below an overhanging wall with the icicle out in space just to the right. Place your last reliable protection in the wall, then gain the icicle with difficulty (and care!) then climb it directly to the top. A sure contender for best ice pitch in the country. Abseil descent (down and left, facing out).

Tower Ridge, Garadh na Ciste
End of Ethics 50m VII,6 *. Tim Miller, Matt Glenn. 9 Feb 2022.
Start 6m right of *Thea*. Climb easy-angled ramps to a short steep corner protected by Terriers and pegs. Follow the ramp leftwards into a second bigger corner, then follow this to the top of the crag.

Central Trident Buttress
Heidbanger, Arête Finish 30m E1 5a *. Michael Barnard, Dan Moore. 3 Sep 2021.
From the belay below the top pitch, step right and climb the blunt arête (micro cams essential) and the crack above to reach keyed-in blocks. Step left around these and go up to make a delicate move into a short groove on the left. Continue as for the normal route.

Dan Moore notes that he thought the crux of *Metamorphosis* was pitch 1 and probably 5c. A superb route that could be three stars but for some suspect loose rock. It deserves more traffic.

Cousins' Buttress

Andy Clarke notes that the account of the FA of *The Shroud* in 'Ben Nevis, Britain's Highest Mountain' is incorrect. The text states that John Main made a bold lead of the free hanging icicle, when in fact this pitch was led by Andy Clarke. John Main led the first pitch to the small ledge right of the icicle.

South-West and South Face, Coire Ghaimhnean

Ghaimhnean Buttress   300m   II/III. Mark Robson, Simon Richardson. 30 Jan 2022.
The prominent buttress between the two main forks of *Five Finger Gully*. Start at the toe of the buttress and climb easy ground weaving between steeper walls for 200m to below the final headwall. There are a variety of lines through this, but the most continuous climbing is on the right. Trend diagonally across snow and follow the right edge of the headwall finishing up a well-defined groove (crux). Easy ground leads to the plateau.

Schrödinger's Cat   150m   IV,5. Simon Richardson, Roger Webb, Mark Robson. 16 Mar 2022.
An enjoyable route taking the crest of *Paradox Buttress*. On this ascent the foot of the route was gained by climbing the lower 150m of *Ghaimhnean Buttress* and traversing down and right across *Five Finger Gully Right Fork* to gain the foot of the buttress. Start 40m right of the original route at the right end of steep lower wall.
1. 40m Climb up and left into a small bay for 10m and exit steeply right via a fist-sized corner-crack. Continue more easily up and left up a groove-line to gain the belay of *Paradox Buttress* where it narrows to a slender neck.
2. 50m Move up and right through the wall above and continue up snow to a terrace that runs right below a steep wall. Move up 10m and belay on the left.
3. 45m Continue up snow to a short gully capped by a roof. Climb this for 10m to the roof and bear left up a steep corner-ramp on the left that leads to a ledge. Surmount the steep crack above and continue up to a wide terrace.
4. 15m Step right and climb the icy wall above to gain the top of buttress. Continue to the plateau in another 50m as for *Paradox Buttress*.

Granito   70m   V.Diff. Will Rowland. 31 Jul 2014.
Climb the rib right of the first large gully to the left (west) of the Waterslide. (Topo provided.)

AONACH BEAG
North Face

Camilla, Left-Hand Finish   125m   V,5. Nathan Adam, Milo Corbus. 5 Mar 2022.
From halfway up pitch 3 of *Camilla*, above the icicles, trend up and left onto the large hanging snowfield and aim for a shallow bay down below its top right-hand side (35m). Climb moderate mixed ground to reach a short, steep left-facing corner. Climb this and then thin ice up the crest of the buttress (50m). Snow slopes to finish (40m).

Huw Scott on the first ascent of Old Yoker (VI,7), West Face, Aonach Beag.
Photo: Nathan Adam.

West Face, Raw Egg Buttress
Old Yoker   60m   VI,7 **. Huw Scott, Tom Fullen, Nathan Adam. 9 Feb 2022.
Good climbing up the obvious, slim, turfy, left-facing corner in the wall right of
Blackbeard. Start at the base of *Ruadh Eigg Chimney*.
1. 40m Climb *Ruadh Eigg Chimney* over the first small bulge, and at the second
larger bulge move out leftwards on turf to the belay ledge of *Blackbeard*. Gain
the slim corner by a difficult move into a thin crack. Follow the corner on turf
and cracks until it is possible to step right into the small quartz bay (avoiding a
lower escape line) and a belay shared with *Youthful Enthusiasm*.
2. 20m Follow the left leaning ramp/groove above on excellent hooks to the top
of the buttress.

Youthful Enthusiasm   60m   V,6 *. Nathan Adam, Huw Scott, Tom Fullen. 9 Feb
2022.
Climbs the crack and offwidth corner right of *Old Yoker*. Start at the base of *Ruadh
Eigg Chimney*.
1. 40m Climb *Ruadh Eigg Chimney* over its first two bulges and go a further 5m
up the chimney then climb the obvious turfy crack on the left wall with a tricky
move to start. Continue up the crack to belay at a prominent quartz intrusion.
2. 20m Climb up and right into the corner, which is bold but has no hard moves.
Good hooks on the inside left wall of the offwidth just below the bulge allow the
turf above to be reached and some welcome protection. Continue more easily to
the top.

East Face, Stob Coire Bhealaich
Diamond Crossing   420m   III *. Steve Kennedy, Stan Pearson. 5 Dec 2021.
A fine mountaineering expedition covering some impressive ground with a remote
feel. *The Ramp* is situated to the right and the routes join around the final pitch.
The route is initially based on the wide fault running diagonally rightwards across
the lower part of the face, starting below *Helter Skelter*. Climb the fault in two
pitches (90m) to reach the crest forming the upper part of the face. Continue up
the crest on the left, keeping as close as possible to the edge (*The Ramp* follows
a line to the right), following ramps and grooves on the left side in a spectacular
position in the upper section. Finish abruptly on the summit ridge via a small
cornice.

CREAG MEAGAIDH
Puist Coire Ardair, Coire Choille-Rais
East Gully   200m   I. Martin W. Holland, Andy Clark. 13 Mar 2022.
The long easy gully immediately right of the East Ridge of Meall Coire Choille-
rais. Probably climbed before.

Càrn Liath, Coire a' Bhèin
About 500m west of the existing routes (see *SMCJ* 2021) there is a curious ravine
between P823m and the main mass of the mountain at NN 498 926. The following
two routes are situated on the south wall of the ravine.

Gulch Rib   100m   III. Simon Richardson, Sophie Grace Chappell. 5 Dec 2021.
The 50m-high sharp rib at the east of the ravine provides a short fun climb on
good turf and helpful rock. Easy ground leads to the top.

Dead Man's Wall 70m II. Simon Richardson, Sophie Grace Chappell. 5 Dec 2021.
Take a central line up the area of steep mixed ground approximately 90m west of *Gulch Rib*.

GLEN COE AND ARDGOUR

GLEN COE
Stob Coire nan Lochan, Pinnacle Buttress
The Jester 10m V,7. Ryan Balharry, Oliver Skeoch. 9 Dec 2021.
A winter ascent of the summer line. One rest point was taken at the top of the overhanging crack.

Bidean nam Bian, Church Door Buttress
East Face
People Pass but Ideas Don't Die 90m E2 5c **. Bede West, James Stops. 25 Jul 2021.
An exciting line with an outrageous third pitch, with the first two pitches avoiding the looser (in summer) blocks of its neighbouring winter routes. Start at the easy crack immediately right of *Crypt Route*.
1. 25m 5b Follow the easy crack to where it joins the crack of *Angels* and follow this to the break. Traverse this leftwards to a thinner hanging crack just right of the arête and follow this until just below a ledge to belay on small wires.
2. 15m 5c Step right past the arête into the crack round the corner. Follow this to its top, then traverse up left to the ledge and belay of *Crypt Route*.
3. 15m 5a Intimidating but easier than the last pitch. Start up the next pitch of *Crypt Route* but step right onto the wall of the huge leaning block, making delicate progress by pulling and overhanging chimneying up the keyed-in blocks to exit into the light at the top of the gap. Large thread belay.
4. 35m 5a From the belay, head up the arête and crack that leads into a left-trending groove (as for *Knights Templar*) until it is possible to head right to a ledge by delicate moves. Traverse this under a triangular overhang, then head up the groove on the right. Follow this line (joining *Critical Mass*) to the top. (Topo provided.)

West Face
The Last Crusade 60m IX,9 ***. Greg Boswell, Guy Robertson. 21 Feb 2022.
A stunning icy mixed route starting up the summer line and gaining the big ice smear of *Gates of Paradise* high up from the left. Start up the overhanging corner just right of the wide crack of the summer line.
1. 25m Climb the corner, then step right and climb iced slabs boldly up into a tapering overhanging groove. Climb this to a big flake on the right, then swing left to a small stance and semi-hanging belay by a good crack.
2. 45m Climb delicately up the crack to left-slanting overlaps, then follow the underside of these up and left to a wide crack. Climb the crack into an overhanging groove which is followed for a short way until it is possible to traverse right (crux) onto the steep ice cascade of *Gates of Paradise*. Follow the ice in a spectacular position to the top.

*Ali Rose making an early repeat of Tuberculosis (VI,6), Stob Coire nan Lochan, Glen Coe.
Photo: Steve Holmes.*

ARDGOUR
Garbh Bheinn, North-East Buttress
Troll Gate was partly described in the 2021 *SMCJ* (p230) but the last two pitches were missed out. The full description is:

Troll Gate   275m   II **.   Steve Kennedy, Andy MacDonald. 6 Feb 2021.
The left-facing curving corner-gully system bounding the right side of the buttress. A fine mountaineering excursion passing through some impressive rock scenery. This is possibly the 'Unnamed Gully', described in the existing guidebook, which was descended in July 1939 by Barber and Lomas.
1. 60m Climb the initial gully, exiting by a through route, and follow the open gully above.
2. and 3. 55m and 50m Climb easily to a terrace and continue up the corner-groove system on the left in two pitches to a fine belay in a large cave.
4. 55m From the cave, traverse left along a ledge to reach a large snow bay.
5. 55m Finish by following a snowy ramp leading rightwards below the upper wall on the left.

Sgùrr Ghiubhsachain, Jacobite Buttress
Raising the Standard   90m   V,7 ***.   Neil Adams, Nathan Adam, Garry Campbell. 7 Jan 2022.
The first route to breach the steep central wall.[2] Belay in an overhung niche about 10m above the toe of the buttress, and start just up and right again. Gain a groove running up a slight rib, and follow this on good turf to a block below the steep wall (20m). Move right to gain a groove, and go up and right into a slimmer V-groove. Climb this and the continuation groove above (steep and sustained but with good hooks and plentiful gear). Exit left to reach a block belay (35m). Climb the easy-angled turfy groove above, from where easier ground leads to the top.

ARROCHAR & THE SOUTHERN HIGHLANDS

Ben Vorlich (Loch Earn), South Face
Central Gully   110m   I/II.   Andreas Höhn, Kevin Woods. 9 Jan 2022.
The obvious south-facing gully splitting the right-hand and left-hand ribs. It is easy in the lower half and becomes steeper and constricted in its upper half with multiple short steps. In a heavy winter it will bank out to Grade I.

Vulcan Rib   130m   III.   Andreas Höhn, Kevin Woods. 9 Jan 2022.
This rib bounds *Central Gully* on the right and joins *I Can See My House from Here* for the final arête, forming an inverted 'V'. The bottom of the route is defined by a steeper wall, altitude 860m.
1. 55m Start at a slabby rock wall defining the foot of the rib. Climb directly to the easing of angle and continuous easier ground with rock steps. Belay at a ledge between an impressive rock wall on the right, and the steep entrance to *Central Gully* on the left.
2. 30m Climb a left-trending ramp in the same line to reach a right-facing corner. Move up the corner and belay on a large ledge under a wall.
3. 45m Climb the wall and join *I Can See My House from Here* for the final ridge spine.

---

[2] See Neil Adams's account of this route in 'Winter out West' on pp. 1–7.

Macauley Wood on the first ascent of Lucky Sunday Arête (III/IV), Ben Lawers.
Photo: Liam Campbell.

Glen Turret, Creag na Gaoith

Willie Jeffrey notes that A.L. Cram and other members of the JMCS were active on this crag in February and March 1930 and climbed and descended several gullies. These may pre-date some of the routes reported in *SMCJ* 2021. The descriptions are not specific, but as Willie observes 'that's how things were done back then.' (Copies of JMCS Meet Reports supplied).

Ben Lawers, Creag Loisgte

Lucky Sunday Arête 60m III/IV ***. Liam Campbell, Macauley Wood, Jamie Whitehead. 5 Dec 2021.

A short technical pitch taking a very enjoyable line up the right-hand side of the most westerly gully on Creag Loisgte with a short arête to finish. The route lies immediately left (west) of *Balcony Rib*. From Beinn Ghlas, going towards Ben Lawers, before the ascent to Ben Lawers starts, head right towards the small crag. Head up the first wide gully in the crag a short way to a turf ledge leading up to a corner with a large vertical block with a diagonal crack.

1. 30m Climb the large block to the left of the corner (there is an easier option to the right of the corner). Above the large block follow a narrow ledge leftwards.
2. 30m Head up the face of the arête on the left. Follow the obvious line up the corner to the top. Take the arête to top out. (Topo provided.)

Creag an Tulabhain

Willie Jeffrey confirms that *V-Gully East* (*SMCJ* 2021) is the unnamed Grade I gully mentioned in *SMCJ* 2013. Jeffrey climbed it with Anne Craig on 1 Mar 2013. Craig walked off and Jeffrey descended *V-Gully West*.

An Caisteal

(NN 3786 1932) Alt 995m

The steep East Face of An Caisteal provides the following climb.

Castle Gully 200m I. Gerhard Mors. 31 Mar 2022.

Follow the River Falloch into Coire Earb and climb the most prominent gap in the band of rocks on the east face, starting at approximately NN 381 194. The narrows of about 100m are similar to *Central Gully* of Ben Lui. The summit slopes are less well defined and there are a number of finishes, meeting the ridge between the summit and the rock feature of The Castle at NN 379 195. (Topo provided.)

LOWLAND OUTCROPS

Ayrshire
Mauchline Gorge

Ayr on a Shoestring 20m Severe *. Max Twomey, Paul Sammons, Stuart Lampard. 8 May 2022.

Approach from the River Ayr way by going under the viaduct, then taking the path which drops down to the water's edge, and walking upstream to below the viaduct. Start below a short right-facing corner with a tree at its base situated 3m up the face. Climb to and ascend the corner, exiting left. Continue slightly left to a crack going through an overhang. Climb this to its top and the natural finish out right.

Glen Afton – Stayamrie

Right Time 65m   III *. Max Twomey, Johnnie Colquhoun. 2 Jan 1997.
The ridge line atop the right-hand wall of the gully, opposite the car park.
1. 50m Take a ramp heading out right to bypass the initial steep section, then regain the ridge and climb slabs staying close to the ridge line to a ledge. Thread belay.
2. 15m Climb the steep crack above the belay to easier ground above. (Topo provided.)

Numbed 60m III. Max Twomey, Johnnie Colquhoun. 2 Jan 1997.
Climb the ice streaks up the centre of the short walls to the right of *Delirium*, then turfy grooves above. Two pitches, 40m and 20m.

Light That Never Goes Out 60m   III. Johnnie Colquhoun, Max Twomey. 2 Jan 1997.
Climb the ice streaks on the right side of the short walls to the right of *Delirium*, then the turf groove above. Parallel to and right of *Numbed*. Two pitches 40m and 20m.

Dazed 50m   III. Max Twomey, David Finnie. 4 Mar 2018.
Start up an icy slab 10m right of *Delirium*, then join a right-slanting groove before moving out right, passing two small trees and finishing directly up.

Knockdolian – Duniewick
(NX 11620 85116)
The presence of old stakes on this crag means that many of these lines will not be new. While it has been impossible to trace any historic details, the most likely suspect is possibly Robin McAllister, who lived nearby. This notwithstanding the crag is a good easier addition to Ayrshire, being quick of access, with good rock (gabbro in part) and a stunning view south-west to the Mull of Kintyre. The crags are on the south and west faces of the fort of Duniewick, which is 0.5km north-east of the prominent Ayrshire hill of Knockdolian, near Ballantrae. The routes are described left to right. The left-hand (west) face is the most continuous, and has stake belays at the top.
Approach: Parking is on the A7044 at a layby just before Finnart Cottage at NX 11995 84804. Walk NE on the A7044 for 150m, to a gate on the left, continue steeply up fields, until, on cresting the hill, the crags will be seen to the left (1km, 15 mins).
Descent: Descent is to the north-west, or right, looking down. The first four routes, plus the top of *Fortress Slabs*, are on this wall.

King of the Castle 12m Severe 4a. Ian Magill, Andrew Fraser. 23 Apr 2021.
This climb takes the wall and slabs left of the central crack in the wall. Start up a steep rib, move right to above the bulge in the central crack, then back left to climb pleasant slabs on the left side of the central, now vegetatious, crack.

Breaching the Ramparts 15m Severe 4a *. Ian Magill, Andrew Fraser. 23 Apr 2021.
Slabs lead to the central crack on the wall. Once over the bulge, climb slabs to the right of the central, now vegetatious, crack.

Corseclays Wall 15m Severe 4a *. Andrew Fraser, Ian Magill. 23 Apr 2021.
The strongest line on the wall. Right of the central crack are slabs leading to a small curving overhang at one-third height. Surmount the overhang into a diamond-shaped niche which is exited directly (crux). Continue more easily up the wall to the top.

Duniewick Wall 15m V.Diff *. Andrew Fraser, Ian Magill. 14 Apr 2021.
Up and right of the diamond-shaped niche on *Corseclays Wall* is a right-facing corner. Climb lower slabs to gain the start of a grassy ramp which bounds the upper right side of the face. Step left into the corner from here and continue directly to the top.

Fortress Slabs 15m V.Diff. Andrew Fraser, Ian Magill. 23 Apr 2021.
Worthwhile, if disjointed. The top of this climb takes the wall above the top of the grassy ramp mentioned in the foregoing route description. It is reached by two ribs, the first directly below the top wall, the second slightly to the right, from the top of which it is a short step across the grassy ramp to the upper wall.

South Rib 15m Moderate. Andrew Fraser, Ian Magill (solo). 14 Apr 2021.
The easy long slabs in the centre of the south face, seen in profile on the approach.

The following two routes are situated on the left side of the south face, to the left of a steep black wall.

The Wicking Man 12m V.Diff. Andrew Fraser, Ian Magill. 14 Apr 2021.
This takes the longest sweep of rock, up lower slabs to a steeper upper wall climbed by a crack.

Dun for Now 10m Diff. Ian Magill, Andrew Fraser. 23 Apr 2021.
Start at the left side of the steep black wall and climb slabs to finish up the right side of a steeper wall, 2m right of *The Wicking Man.*

Galloway Hills
The Merrick, Dungeon Range and Rhinns of Kells
Craigmasheenie
(NX 414 929)
This collection of Galloway east-facing granite outcrops is unusual in as much as many of the cracks are deep enough for hand-jamming and will readily take cams. Several routes have been climbed but there is scope for more. A grassy gully drops northward from near the summit of Craigmasheenie, and most of the climbs can be found on the west side of this. Near the top of the gully is a prominent crack with a boulder perched ominously at the top; this is *Coyote Crack*. Further down is Wacky Racers Wall, and over the back of this lies a line of east-facing crags, that include *The Clanger* 50m further downhill.
Approach: The best approach is from a car park at NX 407952, reached by following the Forest Drive from Stinchar Bridge and taking a right turn, then a second right turn 200m after crossing a small bridge. From the end of the car park head through the woods to find an old path by the burn. This quickly joins the Cornish Loch path; follow this until 100m after a footbridge where a firebreak leads south-east uphill. From the top of this, Craigmasheenie can be seen 1km to

the south, and the grassy gully should be obvious. Follow a faint path, via a knoll, to the base of the gully and ascend it. Approximately 1 hour from the car park. (Topos provided)

Coyote Buttress
Mac the Fork   9m   E1 5b *. Stuart Lampard, Andrew Fraser. 27 Jun 2021.
Takes the crack at the left side of the crag, right of the triangular roof.

Mac the Spoon   9m   HVS 5a. Stuart Lampard, Andrew Fraser, Paul Sammons. 27 Jun 2021.
The crack 2m right of *Mac the Fork*, avoiding stepping into *Dangermouse*.

Dangermouse   9m   VS. Max Twomey, Stuart Lampard. 6 Jun 2021.
The jamming crack right of *Mac the Spoon*, moving slightly right to finish. Hard for the grade.

Penfold   9m   VS *. Max Twomey. 31 May 2021.
The crack immediately right of *Dangermouse*, and just left of the vegetated chimney.

Baron Greenback   9m   Diff. Max Twomey, Stuart Lampard. 19 Jun 2021.
The leaning plinth and right (clean) side of the vegetated chimney, right of *Penfold*.

Coyote Crack   11m   E2 5c **. Stuart Lampard, Max Twomey. 17 Apr 2021.
The obvious crack line with the ominously perched boulder at the top.

Road Runner   11m   E1 5b *. Stuart Lampard, Max Twomey. 1 May 2021.
The cracked wall right of *Coyote*, joining that route above the horizontal break. Gain the sloping ledge, and follow cracks from its left end, trending left to *Coyote Crack*.

Hill Runner   11m   E2 5b *. Stuart Lampard, Max Twomey. 1 May 2021.
The central crack with an overhang at 4m, which is bypassed on the right. Climb up then move left to below parallel cracks, use these and finish up the niche at the top of the left crack.

Yabba Dabba Do   11m   E2 5c. Stuart Lampard. 31 May 2021.
Left of the obvious twin cracks at the right side of the crag. A boulder problem start through an overhang leads to a good ledge, then up and left to join the parallel cracks of *Hill Runner*.

Wacky Racers' Wall
The smaller wall 50m downhill from Coyote Buttress.

Penelope Pitstop   7m   VS *. Max Twomey, Stuart Lampard. 17 Apr 2021.
The left-hand crack, moving slightly right to a thin crack to finish.

Muttley   7m   Severe. Max Twomey. 17 Apr 2021.
Start up *Dastardly* but move left up the curving crack, then finish between it and *Penelope Pitstop*.

Dastardly 7m VS. Max Twomey, Stuart Lampard. 17 Apr 2021.
The right-hand obvious crack, finishing direct.

The Clanger 7m H.Severe. Stuart Lampard, Max Twomey. 6 Jun 2021.
This lies behind (west) of Wacky Racer's Wall and 50m downhill, taking the clean rib with cracks at the top.

Craignairny Crag
(NX 45486 84543) Alt 511m
A small crag about 9m high near the bealach between Dungeon Hill and Craignaw at NX 45486 84543. There look to be plenty more routes to climb, maybe eight or so more, with perfect grippy granite with lots of cracks for gear. The long, boggy unpleasant walk in will put most folk off though. Might be worth a look if you've been climbing on Dungeon of Buchan and can face the bog and slog up the hill.
Approach: The easiest way is via Dungeon Hill. It's probably about 15–20 minutes from the summit.

The Crack So Obvious You Don't Need an Eye Test 9m Diff. *. Fiona Reid. 6 Jul 2020.
Climb the easiest rocky crack-line just to the left of the vegetated gully. (Topo provided.)

Minigaff Hills
Craigdews, Ramp Slabs
The Old Goats 25m H.Severe 3c. Andrew Fraser, Stephen Reid. 7 Jul 2021.
This route climbs the narrow, lichen-free corridor to the right of *Capricorn Relish*. It is technically straightforward but with little protection other than a cam in the central break, though the diligent may locate a sideways wire placement on the upper slab.

The Goat of Christmas Past 25m H.Severe 4a *. Andrew Fraser, Stephen Reid. 7 Jul 2021.
Just right again is another clean narrow streak with a distinctive overlap above the break. There is no gear in the lower half but the climbing is steady; make an unobvious move left just before the break. Much better protected but steeper climbing overcomes the overlap, but then a runout is required to gain the top.

Billy Goat Bluff
Goat's Head Soup 25m E2 5b *. Brian Davison, Andrew Fraser, Stephen Reid. 29 Aug 2021.
Tasty climbing. On the left side of the rib of *Guerdon Hooves* a tapering white ramp will be seen; scramble up to belay under this. The ramp gets harder with each move and poor wires and microcams do little towards attaining the zen-like state required to levitate onto the ledge. Follow a cracking leftwards hand traverse on the wall above before easier climbing gains the top.

Central Section
Tough as Old Goats 48m E2 *. Brian Davison, Andrew Fraser, Stephen Reid. 29 Aug 2021.

A tricky layback, hard fingery climbing, a puzzling mantelshelf – and that's just in the first 5m! A large sloping ledge dominates the middle of the wall right of *Up Perisgoat*; start below the right end of this at a crack formed by a huge triangular block.

1. 23m 5c Climb onto the block and make hard moves with just adequate protection up an open groove to gain the ledge. Traverse left 2m and move up to a turfy break, before traversing back right 2m to a good flake crack. Haul up the flake and flounder onto the large ledge beside a spike belay.
2. 25m 4a Traverse right 2m and follow the cleanest line up slabs to emerge into a grassy bay. Make a tricky move up onto a little rib on the right and belay immediately. Traverse right to descend via the Ramp.

Seen in Tobago at Sunrise   53m   HVS **. Stephen Reid, Chris King. 1 Nov 2016.
A brilliant first pitch – well worth seeking out. Cryptic crossword fans will get the name.

1. 23m 5a Follow *Das Goat* to good spike at 3m and a diagonal crack (gear). Traverse horizontally right and make hard moves rightwards over a bulge into a shallow groove. Climb the groove, exiting right to gain and climb a superb crack in the headwall. Belay at a good wire crack in the highest point of the smooth wall to the left. Variations exist through the headwall.
2. 30m 4c Step right, then climb the wall to a heather ledge. Follow the groove above to a bulge and pull over this on its right, finishing up the arête above. Traverse right to descend via the Ramp.

Cairnsmore of Fleet Range
Big Gairy, Telephoto Buttress
The following climb starts 50m diagonally up and right of the foot of Telephoto Buttress.

Wide-angled and Legless   105m   H.Severe. Andrew Fraser, Ian Magill. 2 Jun 2021.
Decent climbing; much better than appearances suggest.

1. 30m 4a Climb the centre of the blackest slab, easily at first, then past an overlap on its right, then more easily to and over a tricker overlap, to belay where the rock steepens, 3m right of a short chimney.
2. 45m 4b Climb the wall behind the stance, left to right, then step down to slabs on the right. Climb slabs 1m right of a crack, continuing up and left for 8m to a heather ledge. Step right onto a nubbin, then continue up and right for a further 20m, following the line of most rock, to belay under the right edge of the headwall, below cracks higher up.
3. 30m 3b Climb the short wall about 3m left of the stance to a higher ledge which is traversed back right to the start of cracks. Climb these until they ease, then move right to further easy cracks on the edge.

The Cave Area and Cave Buttress
Approximately 200m left of Telephoto Buttress is the Cave, actually a large overhang, to the left of which a grassy ramp leads up left.

Cave Climb   155m   Severe. Stephen Reid, Andrew Fraser. 14 Oct 2016.
A long easy route, with only the second pitch presenting any real difficulty and

the third pitch being almost entirely heather. The rest, however, is on excellent clean granite. Start just down and left of the cave at a clean easy-angled rib.
1. 40m 4a Go easily up the rib to a steepening, overcome this and then pad up the rib above to its end. Belay to the left on the lower of two huge blocks.
2. 25m 4b Climb the two blocks and step right onto heather. Gain a ledge at the foot of a corner and then traverse delicately right across a slab to reach a vertical fault line. Climb this to a heather cornice and belay on a long grass ledge.
3. 40m Overcome a short wall above the belay, then bushwhack leftwards through heather to belay in a small niche at the bottom right corner of a sweep of slabs.
4. 30m 3b Enter the niche from the left and climb straight up to a break. Just left is an open corner, go up this to a terrace.
5. 20m 3c Climb a crack just right of overhanging flakes and the continuation crack to the top.

The Tunnel of Goats   30m   H.Severe 4b *. Andrew Fraser, Ian Magill. 6 Nov 2016.
Some 15m up the grassy ramp, above a gearing up boulder (and about halfway up the first pitch of *Cave Climb*), a deep crack traverses the wall to the right, leaving a detached pinnacle. Follow the crack, then move right through a small oak tree. Climb the arête above, then two further walls. Better than appearances suggest.

Cave Buttress is the small buttress containing the second pitch of *Cave Climb*: it lies further up and left and is easily reached by continuing up the grass ramp.

Smoking Goat   25m   VS 4c. Andrew Fraser, Stephen Reid. 14 Oct 2016.
Testing but well protected climbing up the obvious corner. Start just left at the top of the grass ramp at a huge block belay. Climb the two blocks and step right onto heather. Gain a ledge at the foot of the corner and climb it, initially via its left wall, before moving back right. Step up slightly left then go straight up the wall above.

An Ecumenical Matter   25m   VS 4c *. Andrew Fraser, Ian Magill. 6 Nov 2016.
Start as for *Smoking Goat* but climb twin cracks directly up the wall.

Galloway Sea-Cliffs
Meikle Ross, The Red Slab
Roger Everett notes that the cliff can be conveniently approached by a full 50m abseil from the belay stakes (a 60m rope may be better), avoiding the intimidating steep grass scramble down.

Limehouse Blues Cliff
Roger Everett notes that the whole crag is very overgrown with loose bits of rock on the ledges, much green and yellow lichen obscuring the routes, and far too many very brittle holds for comfort. Not recommended unless it undergoes a very thorough clean.

Garheugh Port, Main Crag, Smuggler's Slab
The Exciseman   10m   Severe 4a *. Andrew Fraser, Ian Magill. 16 Jun 2021.
Worthwhile and well protected. It takes the centre of the pillar at the left side of the crag, left of the existing routes.

The Rhinns
Money Head, The Bear Pit

Hey Big Spender   25m   Severe 4a. Andrew Fraser, Ian Magill. 17 Sep 2020.
Pleasant. Climb the initial steep corner of *Tax Evasion* to a slab. Where that route traverses left, take a corner on the right to another slab. Move up left to climb a rib to gain a further slab which is followed up left to join the easy grassy ground at the top of *Tax Evasion*.

Laggantalluch, Island Walls, South Wall

Galloway Old Hands Gang   12m   VS 4c. Stephen Reid, Linda Biggar, John Biggar, Andrew Fraser. 24 Apr 2022.
Quite a tricky route with a distinct crux that is reasonably protected with microcams. Climb the right side of the big slab just left of *The Fish Ladder* to a ledge where that route goes horizontally left (at half-height it is possible to reach blindly round to a hidden crack on the right and place a Camalot 0.75). Step rightwards off the ledge and make fingery moves up an open groove. Easier climbing leads to the top.

Point of the Cleugh
The following lines all lie to the left of the existing routes and are described left to right.

Shielding   7m   HVS 5a *. Andrew Fraser, Ian Magill. 16 Jul 2020.
Small is beautiful. The left edge of the crag is a shield of rock, situated just left of twin cracks. Climb very thin cracks just right of the edge, then easier cracks above.

Crunchroute Supreme   7m   Severe 4a. Andy Murray, Alasdair Fraser. 9 Aug 2020.
The left of the twin cracks at the left end of the crag.

Covid Crack   7m   V.Diff. Ian Magill, Andrew Fraser. 16 Jul 2020.
The right-hand of the twin cracks.

Ploughing your own Furlough   12m   H.Severe 4b. Ian Magill, Andrew Fraser. 16 Jul 2020.
Nice climbing, if a bit of an eliminate. Right of *Covid Crack* there is an overhang at ground level. Surmount this just right of the widest point, climb slightly left up the smooth slab above, then slightly right to gain and climb the centre of the upper block.

Social Distancing   15m   V.Diff. Ian Magill, Andrew Fraser. 16 Jul 2020.
Start at the right end of the overhang, follow the groove and the wall above. The top wall has the odd loose hold.

Self-Isolation   17m   V.Diff. Ian Magill, Andrew Fraser. 9 Aug 2020.
This takes the groove to the left of the main corner-line of the crag (*Cracked Toes Intolerant*), starting up the wall 4m to its left.

Totally Cleughless   17m   VS 4c *. Andrew Fraser, Ian Magill. 26 Aug 2020.
An excellent route with two contrasting cruxes. About 1m left of the main corner-

line is a bulging crack leading to a large ledge. Climb this, continue up the wall to the right of the groove of *Self-Isolation*, to gain and climb the cracked upper wall which lies between the two grooves of *Self-Isolation* and *Cracked Toes Intolerant*.

Cracked Toes Intolerant 18m E1 5b *. Andy Murray, Alasdair Fraser, Andrew Fraser. 9 Aug 2020.
A fine if unbalanced route up the main corner-line of the crag. The start is considerably harder than the rest. Avoiding the initial section by starting up *Totally Cleughless* and moving into the corner after the large ledge makes the route VS 4c *.

Just Friends Direct Start 20m Severe 4a *. Andrew Fraser, Ian Magill. 16 Jul 2020.
This provides an independent start more in keeping with the remainder of the route. Climb steep ground, above the pool, just left of the lower overhang, to gain an easier groove. Move right above the overhang to gain the original route at a brown streak.

Parallel Cracks 17m Moderate. Andrew Fraser. 16 Jul 2020.
The wall to the right of *Brian Cleugh*.

Crammag Head
Lighthouse Walls
Left of *Reach for the Moon* is an easy gully. The following two routes lie on either end of the wall to the left.

Flying Jib 10m V.Diff. David Henchliffe, Sarah Birkill, Andrew Fraser. 23 Apr 2022.
Climb a rib to reach the bulging left arête of the wall, started from the left.

Befrocked 10m V.Diff. Andrew Fraser, Sarah Birkill, David Henchliffe. 23 Apr 2022.
Climb a steep, easy wall to reach and climb steps at the right edge of the wall.

Infill 15m VS 4b. Roger Everett, Dee Gaffney. 23 Apr 2022.
An unbalanced route but the rock is nice; take care with the protection. Start up a grey pillar just right of *Ascents of Porpoise*. Climb easily towards the left-hand of two triangular niches in the upper wall, then aim steeply to obvious finishing holds above the niche.

Kittiwake Zawn
The South Wall of Kittiwake Zawn is a good venue for low-grade routes. Descent is by a scramble (beware loose rock) or by abseil just left of the routes.

The Great Escape 20m HVD *. Stephen Reid, Sally Reid. 23 Apr 2022.
The buttress immediately left of the obvious chimney of *Dormouse* gives a very pleasant route with a steep wall leading to a finish up a shallow groove. (Topo provided.)

Slim Line Tonic 20m Severe 4b *. Stephen Reid, Sally Reid. 23 Apr 2022.
Just right of *Dormouse*, a thin crack splits the slab; follow it to hard moves where
it bends left through a bulge, and then stick to the crest of the rib to the top. (Topo
provided.)

Stephen Reid notes that *Dormouse* is worth a star but would be better described
as follows. A good climb up the obvious chimney. Step left just below easy ground
to avoid large loose blocks.

Edinburgh Area
Blackford Quarry
Slabomination 35m HVS 4b. Thomas Louth. 17 Jan 2022.
A rising traverse of the entire face. Starting at the base of *Route 1* head up and
left to meet *Route 2*. Step across this and traverse around on steep ground, then
move up slightly to reach *Route 3* at the height of the horizontal break. Continue
up and left above the break, aiming for the small crack near the top of *Route 4*
and *Route 4.5*. From here skirt under the steep headwall and then continue up to
the left of the arête of *Route 5* on easier ground to the top. The rock is best in the
first half, and protection here gives some confidence for the latter half. By linking
up the best opportunities for gear the route avoids the long runouts on *Route 4*
and *Route 5*. (Topo provided.)

Corstorphine Boulders
(NT 204 747) Alt 100m
Twenty-one boulders on Corstorphine Hill have been developed by Loic Galland.
They are described in his excellent mini-guide 'Edinburgh Esoteric Climbing',
which can be found here <https://smcnewroutes.org.uk/mini-guides/>.

Ravelston Quarry
(NT 217 742) Alt 50m North facing
Several dry tool routes have been climbed in the quarry and are described in Loic
Galland's mini-guide 'Edinburgh Esoteric Climbing', which can be found here
<https://smcnewroutes.org.uk/mini-guides/>.

Berwickshire Coast, Souter Area, Blockbuster Buttress
A Plaice in Thyme 20m E5 6b **. Adam Russell, Lia Guest. 23 Jun 2021.
This route tackles the impressive overhanging groove at the back of the bay. Very
good groove climbing in the upper two-thirds that is adequately protected with a
keen eye and a double set of cams, micro to #0.4 Camalot C4. Starting at a short
chimney, climb easily with care to the small roof. Arrange gear and bust a move
up and right into the groove proper. Groove on up until level with the final section.
There is a crucial #2 Camalot C4/s in a perfect but blind diagonal slot-crack out
left, just below the fork in the crack. Continue directly with excitement to the top.
Note: For the belay, as with all things on this buttress, good rock gear is available
approximately 10m back from the edge on the right as you top out, although it is
a good idea to equalise this with either a stake (not *in situ*) or a spare rope (45–
50m) tied off to the fence to fully align things with the route.

MISCELLANEOUS NOTES

THE W.H. MURRAY LITERARY PRIZE

As a tribute to the late Bill Murray, whose mountain and environment writings have been an inspiration to many a budding mountaineer, the SMC have set up a modest writing prize, to be run through the pages of the Journal. The basic rules are set out below, and will be reprinted each year. The prize is run with **a deadline of midnight on the last day of April each year**.

The Rules:

1. There shall be a competition for the best entry on Scottish Mountaineering published in the *Scottish Mountaineering Club Journal*. The competition shall be called the 'W.H. Murray Literary Prize', hereafter called the 'Prize'.
2. The judging panel shall consist of, in the first instance, the following: The current Editor of the *SMC Journal*; The current President of the SMC; and two or three lay members, who may be drawn from the membership of the SMC. The lay members of the panel will sit for three years after which they will be replaced.
3. If, in the view of the panel, there is in any year no entry suitable for the Prize, then there shall be no award that year.
4. Entries shall be writing on the general theme of 'Scottish Mountaineering', and may be prose articles of up to approximately 3000 words in length, or shorter verse. Entries may be fictional.
5. Panel members may not enter for the competition during the period of their membership.
6. Entries must be of original, previously unpublished material. Entries should be submitted to the Editor of the *SMC Journal* by the end of April for consideration that year. Electronic contributions are preferred and should be submitted via e-mail, although double-spaced typewritten hard copies will also be accepted by post. (See Office Bearers page at end of this Journal for address etc.) Any contributor to the *SMC Journal* is entitled to exclude their material from consideration for the Prize and should so notify the Editor of this wish in advance.
7. The Prize will be a cheque for the amount £250.
8. Contributors may make different submissions in different years.
9. The decision of the panel is final.
10. Any winning entry will be announced in the *SMC Journal*, and will be published in the *SMC Journal* and on the SMC Website. Thereafter, authors retain copyright.

THE WH MURRAY LITERARY PRIZE 2022

It has been said that writers live in an ideal world of their own creation from which suffering has disappeared – they view it but are not subject to it. This would store up trouble for a writer if he wanted to get at the truth. If he makes light of the pains he bores by understatement. If he makes too much of the joys he deceives by overstatement. How to get it right?
— W.H. Murray, 'Mountaineering and Writing'.

Our panel of judges, tasked with awarding the Prize in its 25th year, found much to admire among the eligible articles submitted to the *Journal*. As a foil to several retrospective pieces, it was refreshing to read accounts by contemporary climbers pushing the boundaries. As one judge wrote: 'Finlay Wild, Helen Rennard and David Almond are all clearly superb athletes performing at the cutting edge of their sport. I admired their bravery in taking on their mountain challenges and in trying to share their experiences with us lesser performers. Successful on both counts.' Iain Young and Neil Adams also won high praise for recounting with such 'endearing enthusiasm' their exploratory climbing in the Northern and Western Highlands respectively; both these authors write with admirable clarity.

Our judges appreciated the expert insights of Iain Cameron and Bob Reid. 'The former shared his enthusiasm for summer snow patches, and his esoteric but important continuing contribution to "citizen science", while the latter reflected chillingly on the dangers of our hills in winter and some tragic outcomes.' Also highly regarded was Ian Crofton's scholarly 'Night', with its haunting descriptions of nocturnal and crepuscular phenomena in the mountains.

Both Phil Gribbon and Bob Duncan recounted youthful climbs, with Gribbon just gently pulling the reader's leg; but Mike Dixon in 'The Reunion' gave us a 'gripping and disturbing' short story that was 'very well written and held one's attention right to the end.' Another judge deemed this '… a carefully crafted but chilling piece of fiction. As the mystery deepens the tension builds.'

Tim Pettifer's sardonic wit once again delighted more than one of the judges, who in his 'Ode to the Gods' discovered '… a cascade of imagery and word play which held me riveted and sent me straight back to read it all again.' It was 'inventive, interesting, and provocative'.

This year's winning entry is Gavin Anderson's 'A Stance on Parnassus'. A few comments will serve to indicate the character of this piece and why its author was acclaimed. 'Setting himself the novel challenge of comparing four quite different climbing heroes by climbing three of their best routes, he successfully mixed personal reminiscences, climbing history, philosophy and literary criticism to tell an interesting and absorbing story'. It was 'an engaging piece, well-constructed with a good dash of humour'. 'His writing was light, engaging and fluid. Nowhere did it get bogged down with technicalities or historical minutiae.'

Having compared his four climbers, Anderson in the end awarded the laurel wreath to Murray. As one of our judges remarked, 'I trust the conclusion on relative primacy wasn't reached with this Prize in mind!'

Contributions must reach the Editor by 30 April to be considered for the Prize.

– Hon. Ed.

SCOTTISH WINTER NOTES 2021–22

THE 2021–22 SCOTTISH WINTER SEASON started late and the mountains were battered by almost continuous storms from December to February. The only respite from the wind during this period was in December when a deep thaw followed by a high-pressure system meant the hills were bare of snow, and by the time more stable winter weather arrived later in the season, in March, there was insufficient time to allow good conditions to form. Despite the challenging weather there were some exceptional performances. Greg Boswell had an excellent season with five outstanding first ascents, and during the second half of February Tom Livingstone climbed 14 difficult routes up to Grade IX in as many days whilst visiting from Chamonix.

November
Winter made a half-hearted appearance in late October, but climbing opportunities were few and far between and only a handful of snowed-up rock routes in the Northern Corries were completed. November was remarkably mild but all this changed on 26 November when Storm Arwen swept in. Whilst the east of Scotland was battered by hurricane force winds, Mike Lates and Tilly Cottrell took advantage of relative calm in the west with the first ascent of *North Buttress Gully* (III) on Blàbheinn on Skye. The following day, James Milton and Robbie Hearns made an enterprising first winter ascent of *California* (IV,4) in Coire Druim na Staidhre on Sgùrr nan Saighead in Kintail. This Severe is the only summer route in the corrie and was first climbed in 1956, and it had probably not seen a repeat. Nearby, Chris Dickinson and William Wilson had a productive day, adding a couple of routes to Aonach Air Chrith. *Gneiss Ice* (III), which climbs short steep icy walls and corners in Coire na Doire Duibhe was followed by *Cave Climb* (III) on the right side of the east face of Druim na Cìche.

December
The cold weather continued into early December. On 5 December, Liam Campbell, Macauley Wood and Jamie Whitehead visited Creag Loisgte on the south-west ridge of Ben Lawers and made the first ascent of *Lucky Sunday Arête* (III,4). The same day, Steve Kennedy and Stan Pearson climbed the 420m-long *Diamond Crossing* (III) between *Helter Skelter* and *The Ramp* on the east face of Aonach Beag. Further north, Greg Boswell, Hamish Frost, Graham McGrath made the first ascent of *Take Me Back to The Desert* (IX,9) on Beinn Eighe. This route goes directly up the wall near the left-hand end of the Eastern Ramparts, starting just right of *The Modern Idiot*.

Four days later, Oliver Skeoch and Ryan Balharry made the first winter ascent of *The Jester* (V,7) on Stob Coire nan Lochan in Glen Coe. This small but impressive pinnacle lies at the foot of Pinnacle Buttress and is well seen on the approach to the corrie. The following day, Mark Robson and I visited Ben Wyvis and climbed *Princess Cut* (VI,6) on the Diamond Buttress of Glas Leathad Beag. The climb is exceptionally steep for a turf-based route, and Bulldogs were the most effective form of protection.

A major thaw followed by a long period of dry weather removed any possibility of winter climbing until snow began to fall again over the festive period. Christmas Day saw Chris Dickinson and Jane Allen exploring Càrn Ghluasaid on the north side of Glen Shiel with *Where Eagles Dare* (III), an excellent mixed route in Coire na Gaoithe an Ear leading directly to the eastern top of Creag

Oliver Skeoch nearing the top of The Jester (V,7) on Stob Coire nan Lochan.
Photo: Ryan Balharry.

Dhubh. On 28 December Roger Webb and Neil Wilson visited Creag Loch Tuill Bheàrnach on Sgùrr nan Clachan Geala and found *Fox Buttress* (III), the buttress immediately bounding *Peat Bog Faeries*. The same day Wojciech Polkowski and Sebastian Gidelski made a good addition to Fiacaill Buttress in Coire an t-Sneachda with *Polished Up* (VII,7), the prominent line of cracks on the wall between *Slaterless* and *Seam-stress*.

January

Overall, January was another disappointing month with limited snowfall quickly taken away by sudden thaws. The month started off on a cold note, however, and on 5 January, John Higham and Iain Young made the first ascent of *Geologists' Ridge* (IV,4) on the 450m-high south-west face of Conival. This 11-pitch route was one of the mountaineering highlights of the winter and an intelligent choice in the early season snowy conditions. A less optimum venue that day was Sgùrr an Lochan Uaine above Glen Derry in the Cairngorms where Forrest Templeton and I battled through knee deep snow to climb the prominent *Iron Man Ridge* (III,4). Two days later, Neil Adams, Nathan Adam and Garry Campbell visited the newly developed Jacobite Buttress on Sgùrr Ghiubhsachain above Loch Shiel and made the first ascent of the excellent-looking *Raising the Standard* (V,7).

The finest climbing day of the month was 9 January when an east-west split resulted in a wonderful winter day on the Cairngorms, with the hills frozen and white with fresh snow. Four parties visited The Stuic on Lochnagar and Stuart McFarlane and Di Gilbert made an early repeat of *The Stooee Chimney* (IV,6). They confirmed that it is best to pass under the barrier chockstone when conditions are lean, rather than climbing over the top, which was the line followed on the first ascent. Ascents were made of *First Light* and *Daybreak Corners*, and Forrest Templeton and I made the first ascent of *True Grit* (V,7), the steep depression between *Bonanza* and *Twilight Groove*.

The band of cold clear air that day also extended across to the far north-west and three teams were in action on An Teallach. Doug Bartholomew and Graham Wyllie made an early repeat of *Lord Berkeley's Seat* (VI,6). Erick Baillot and Andy Sharpe also had their eye on the route, and as consolation, made the third ascent of *Monumental Chimney* (V,7). The most impressive climb on An Teallach that day, was Guy Robertson and Adam Russell's second ascent of *The Wailing Wall* (IX,9). This outstanding line up the left side of the upper Hayfork Wall was first climbed by Martin Moran and Murdoch Jamieson in December 2010.

February

The month started warm, but the temperatures gradually dropped. On 6 February Forrest Templeton and I visited Corrie Farchal in Glen Clova on a hunch that it had been cold enough to freeze the turf above 700m and the cliff would be white with new snow blown over the plateau. The gamble paid off and we made a bee-line for the two-tiered buttress left of *Seven Ages of Man* on the left side of the cliff. The first tier is cut by a deep chimney and was relatively straightforward, but the second tier, a vertical wall capped by an overlap, only succumbed to a brave and forceful lead by Forrest. In keeping with the Shakespeare theme, we called the route *All the World's a Stage* (VI,6).

Three days later, Huw Scott, Tom Fullen and Nathan Adam added a couple of good new mixed routes to Raw Egg Buttress on Aonach Beag. *Old Yoker* (VI,7) starts at the base of *Ruadh Eigg Chimney* and takes the obvious slim turfy left facing corner in the wall right of *Blackbeard*, and *Youthful Enthusiasm* (V,6)

Guy Robertson making the first ascent of Last Crusade Winter Variation (IX,9) on Church Door Buttress, Bidean nam Bian. Photo: Greg Boswell.

climbs the crack and off-width corner right of *Old Yoker*. The same day, Tim Miller and Matt Glenn climbed the short and bold *End of Ethics* (VII,7) on the wall right of *Thea* on The Garadh on Ben Nevis.

From the middle of February it became colder, conditions gradually improved, and a number of good new routes were climbed. Chris Dickinson revisited Càrn Ghluasaid in Kintail with Johnny Hawkins and made the first ascent of *Stormy Petrel* (III/IV) left of *Where Eagles Dare*, and Jamie Skelton and Nick Brierley climbed *Keep 'em Sharp* (V,7), the right-trending line of weakness across the buttress right of *Far East Gully* on Beinn Eighe. Further north, Robin Clothier and Stuart McFarlane added *Di Time* (IV,5) to Bucket Buttress on Quinag, and John Mackenzie and Ian Douglas visited the North-East Face of Creag Ruadh above Strathconon, where they climbed *Curving Gully* (III) to the left of the lower buttress containing *Snow Dome*.

Greg Boswell returned to Scotland in the middle of the month after two months of high-standard ice and mixed climbing in the Alps. He put his fitness to great effect on 21 February with the first ascent of *Last Crusade Winter Variation* on Church Door Buttress with Guy Robertson. This bold IX,9 is a winter version of the summer E3 and finishes up the impressive ice smear of *Gates of Paradise*.

Dave Riley and Andy Harrison had an excellent day on Lurcher's Crag on 25 February, climbing a continuous run of ice between Central and Diamond gullies resulting in the 365m-long *An Ice Surprise* (IV,4/5). Parts of this route may have been climbed before, but there is no record of approaching the upper cliffs from directly below via the icefalls, so that section is likely to be new. (Unfortunately, detailed knowledge about Lurcher's was lost following Andy Nisbet and Steve Perry's tragic accident on Ben Hope in 2019.) Further north the same day, Mark Robson and I ploughed through deep snow to *Bianasdail Buttress* (V,6) on the west flank of Beinn a' Mhùinidh above Loch Maree. This gave an excellent four-pitch mixed route with success in doubt until the very end.

March & April

On 6 March, Greg Boswell succeeded on one of the most prized objectives on Ben Nevis when he made the first ascent of *The Fear Factory* (V,7), the prominent hanging icicle on the Little Brenva Face, with Guy Robertson and Hamish Frost. The upper part of the ice fang had previously been climbed by Dave MacLeod and Andy Nelson in February 2013, but they had ascended steep rock further right to gain the ice, so the prize of the complete ice feature remained. For Boswell, the main difficulty was dealing with the delicate icicle and the lack of protection – it was too dangerous to place screws in case the ice shattered and detached. In the event, Boswell made a 20m run-out up brittle vertical ice to reach the safety of the easy ground above.

The weather became very warm during the second half of March and most winter climbers hung up their axes and crampons with the apparent early onset of spring, although Forrest Templeton and I made a number of additions to Coire na Saobhaidhe on Lochnagar, which remained helpfully icy. Winter returned at the beginning April, however, and Greg Boswell and Guy Robertson made the first ascent of *The Reckoning* (X,9) on the Hayfork Wall of An Teallach.

Boswell's enthusiasm meant he was climbing until the very end of the season so it was appropriate that his persistence paid off with the final new route of the winter. *Fear of the Unknown* (VIII,9) takes the steep featureless wall between *Migrant Direct* and *Nocando Crack* on Number Three Buttress in Coire an Lochain and was climbed with Jamie Skelton on 9 April.

Simon Richardson

274

100 YEARS AGO — THE CLUB IN 1922

BY 1922 THE BRITISH EMPIRE had gained its apogee, or at least its maximum extent in the world, spanning a quarter of the globe and exercising dominion over one in four people. Health for those with diabetes improved, with the use of insulin being introduced. In Germany, hyperinflation was biting deeply, increasing the misery and discontent of that country. In November 1922 the BBC began radio service in the UK.

Poor recovery from the First World War continued, and in 1922 the first hunger march took place. Over one million people were unemployed, while there existed only a poor relief system. Predictably, the shipbuilding and textile industries were the worst hit, but Scottish coalfields were affected too. Many of the marches would terminate in London, with speeches of course, and would continue for the next 14 years, to be sustained by the Great Depression beginning in the mid-1930s.

Temperance

The use of alcohol in Scotland has a long and perhaps not always praiseworthy history; those who like a 'wee drink' but have little control over its effects can be a serious problem to themselves and others. For mountaineers of course it usually means either a refreshing pint or two in a nearby pub, or maybe a celebratory dram when safely at home. What is perhaps not widely known though is that prohibition has occurred occasionally in Scotland.

In 1913 The Temperance (Scotland) Act was introduced. This was a compromise between the zeal of the temperance movement, and those who wished to continue taking their favourite tipple legally. Local councils could stop allowing a licence to sell alcohol, limit the number of licences given out, or continue as before, with a vote every three years.

As the War began and restrictions were placed on movement, nothing much happened until polls started in 1920. Ironically, Wick in Caithness, home of the fine malt whisky Old Pulteney, voted on 28 May 1922 by a majority of 62% to go dry.[1] The local Methodist Minister, aided (believe it or not) by a vociferous American named W.E. 'Pussyfoot' Johnson, was the main instigator, supported by the usual suspects. It may cause some mirth to mention that the American suffered a black eye during one altercation with locals. (In Victorian times the workforce and residents of Wick and nearby Pulteneytown had consumed over 5000 bottles of whisky every week.)

Incredibly, Wick sustained the ban until May 1947. Other areas had also joined the ban, including Lerwick and Stromness. Further south, it was not much of a surprise when the staid adults of Kilmacolm banned alcohol sales, only allowing a licensed pub in 1998. The Wick distillery of course had suffered under the ban, closing in 1930. It reopened two decades later. Temperance hotels had their days of sunshine, though the thought of SMC Meets and Dinners, with the necessity of toasting, obviously meant that 'dry' hotels saw little demand.

Meteorology

We are now paying for our neglect of the planet with some dramatic effects on the climate: extreme weather, changes in weather patterns and more. As this is being written, Storm Malik is roaring across Scotland, with winds gusting up to

[1] <https://www.scotlandmag.com/the-story-of-prohibition-in-wick-caithness/>. Retrieved 08/09/2022.

128 knots (147mph) on Cairn Gorm summit this morning at 6 a.m. But to hardy mountaineers, and especially keen hillwalkers, a windy day is nothing out of the ordinary, though a high wind is to be avoided, and certainly respected.

The SMC New Year Meet of 1921–22 was held at Brodick, on the lovely island of Arran.[2] There had been strong westerly gales before the end of the year, with the ferry crossing initially in some doubt. It eventually sailed, and it must have been a rough passage, as the passengers were happy to gain the shelter of the Arran hills.

On the Sunday, New Year's Day, the President, Willie Ling, organised a motor party for Glen Sannox, with 15 pilgrims joining up in a 'tempest of wind and rain.' William Inglis Clark and John Rennie presumably did not like the weather and returned by road, while the main party climbed Cìoch na h-Oighe. Several of the nine climbers in this main group were blown over on the ridge. Four younger men in the other group climbed Suidhe Fhearghas, and had to lie down frequently as the '... wind blew with hurricane force.'

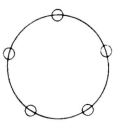

In the 1923 *SMCJ*, William Inglis Clark described a fascinating (and patently dangerous) wind phenomenon from this outing, including a diagram. A light covering of snow made possible the visibility of a series of 'cyclones' sweeping down the slopes, which hit the party on Goatfell. Each cyclone took the form of a large circle, revolving at about 40mph, with five smaller vortices on its circumference, where the wind speed felt more like 100mph. If, unluckily, a climber met one of the latter, he was tossed about.

Clark himself was certainly thrown more than 20 feet in a fraction of a second. Clark was a scientist, among other skills, but he did not report the rotational direction of the vortex, nor the wind direction and where they were on the mountain. I dug deep into some research on wind vortices, and the closest I could find to Clark's observation might be what are known as von Kármán's Vortices, caused by air currents wrapping around tall islands. We could accept that this severe gale certainly met with a tall island!

In a book in my library[3], a chapter titled 'Airflow over Hills' has several diagrams of wind patterns over a hill. An eddy may form in the lee of the crest of a steep windward escarpment. In the diagram provided, the eddy is shown as a vortex. What is most unusual are the mini-vortices spotted by Clark, of which I have as yet found no similar description.

Dr Lüscher & Skye

It is often (though not always!) interesting to read about something familiar, such as our mountains, as seen by someone not of this country. The *SMCJ* of April 1922 had an article that fitted the bill, as it was a description of a summer holiday in Scotland by a Swiss mountaineer, Dr Ery Lüscher. He was a reader in physiology at Berne University, and had been recommended to try Skye by Norman Collie. At the end of July he started his six-week holiday, usually climbing alone.

Lüscher was patently competent, which was just as well, as any rescue in those far-away days relied heavily on local labour: shepherds, farmers, and any other

[2] New Year Meet at Brodick, 1921–2. *SMCJ*, 16/93 (April 1922), 139–142.

[3] C.E. Wallington, *Meteorology for Glider Pilots* (John Murray, 1977).

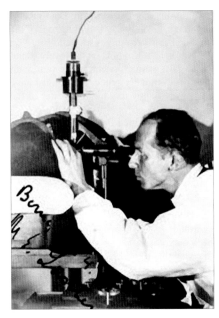

Dr Ery Lüscher in his
Berne laboratory.

hill-goer who could be strong-armed into a rescue party. He wrote an article for the *SMCJ* following his visit, with some fine words for Scottish mountains. Of Skye he wrote as follows.

> It was not quite as I had imagined. I thought that the hills would be higher and nearer, the valleys cut deeper, and I found a wide, lonely island. But I felt the singular charm and I liked it at once.[4]

And of the weather in Scotland, and particularly the rain:

> I was now accustomed to it, and even liked it. I think clouds and mist belong to that country; they make the rocks blacker, the ridges steeper and higher, and give a feeling of extreme loneliness. I heard with pleasure the wind roaring among the rocks.

Routes that he soloed on Skye include the Pinnacle Ridge on Sgùrr nan Gillean and the Inaccessible Pinnacle by the *South Crack*. Lüscher mentions climbing with Bell who was holidaying on Skye with his wife; this would have been the SMC member John Hart Bell (unrelated to the later Jim Bell). Bell has been described as joining the Club in 1894 aged 24, 'a young man of powerful physique and immediately an enthusiastic pioneer of new climbs.' He was President from 1922–24. He died suddenly, aged 68, while playing croquet.

Publications

February 1922 saw the publication of *Ulysses* by James Joyce. As the British Library commented, 'this book may be more talked about than read.' Hands up! Have you started the book and rapidly given up? Many readers would be very happy to own a first edition, however, as the going price would probably be around £100,000 if signed. The centenary of its publication has provoked much interest

---

[4] Lüscher, E. 'A Summer Holiday in Skye', *SMCJ*, 16/93 (April 1922), 99–108.

and a host of explanatory writings, videos and other ways of explaining what Joyce was about. Here is one brief saying from the book, perhaps suitable for our readers:

> I am, a stride at a time. A very short space of time through very short time of space.

Another publication appeared in 1922 which at the time possibly caused more excitement, at least in the outdoor arena. This was a new Ordnance Survey Map to the Cairngorms. It had been suggested to the OS by SMC member James Alexander Parker, a successful civil engineer who lived variously in Glasgow, London and Aberdeen, strewing about grand designs for railway terminals.[5] He was SMC President 1924–6. Lord Mackay, who was an acute observer of human nature, described him thus: '... a teller of times to the mere last second, a repository of all knowledge and one of the great hill lovers.'

The new map was the One-Inch 'Popular' Edition, sheet size ca. 75×93cm. As its review in the *SMCJ* (by Parker himself) remarked, it had many novel features. The overall impression is of brown and green, with two tones of green under 1500ft, and six shades of brown above that height. The appearance quickly shows the overall relief of the land, while the area covered made much more sense than the earlier maps as all the main resorts in the area were included. Through pressure and persuasion, the OS made a special effort to publish the map in time for the Easter Meets of the Cairngorm Club and the SMC at Aviemore. The small portion shown here serves to indicate how pleasing the map was to the eye.

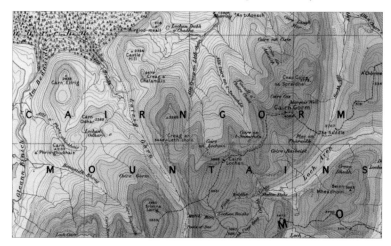

Portion of the innovative 1922 1 Inch to 1 Mile 'Popular' OS map of the Cairngorms.

For this meet, Parker brought three dozen copies of the new map, which were quickly snapped up. As the account of the SMC Meet recorded, the new map was

> ... one of the best pieces of Cartography produced in this country – but, of course, nobody was going to admit this in Parker's presence, and he was rudely asked what commission he was making.

---

[5] See biographical footnote by John Hay in *SMCJ*, 49/212 (2021), 276. – Hon. Ed.

The great interest in climbing on Skye following the War was certainly accelerated by the activities of Everard Wilfred Steeple (1872–1940), Guy Barlow, and Arnold Harry Doughty. In various permutations, they would record numerous routes, opening up new crags. Their various rampages across the Cuillin began in 1912 and continued into the 1920s. Luckily, Steeple was generous with his information, to the extent that a data-starved SMC invited him to produce its first guide to Skye. (See Barlow's separate research[6] into the heights of the island's summits.) Their rock climbs were published in the SMC's *Guide to the Island of Skye* in 1923, which would be the first of a series of District Guides to areas of Scotland, recognisable by their red cloth covers. As W.H. Murray would later remark in a review of the 2nd edition, the covers would readily shed a bloody ooze over damp clothing.

The guides were in any case too large for convenient carrying during a climb, and pocket-sized guides would be published in the future. Perhaps Steeple & Co's best find was the South Crag of Sròn na Cìche in Coire a' Ghrunnda, where they recorded some good routes in the lower standards. Steeple was a bank accountant, while Guy Barlow was an eminent geologist. The obituary[7] of Steeple in the *FRCC Journal* described him as '... one of rock climbing's quietest and most unassuming pioneers.' He joined the SMC in 1921.

Bell & Blisters

One other fruitful event for mountaineering would occur in 1922, with entry to the SMC of James Horst Brunnerman Bell (1896–1975). As might be deduced from his name, he was of mixed parentage, with a Scottish father who was a Presbyterian minister, and a German mother. He was born in the Fife village of Auchtermuchty. His obituary in the *SMC Journal* of 1976 fills an incredible ten pages. *SMCJ* Editor for 24 years and author of *A Progress in Mountaineering*,[8] he was one of the great characters in Scottish mountaineering.

The Easter Meet of 1922 (12–22 April) was based in Aviemore, which posed a quirky question for the Club, as the Cairngorm Club was also holding its meet at Aviemore. How were some SMC members going to be listed, as they were members of both clubs? This gave rise to possibly the only reference to Albert Einstein in the *Journal*. Could a man attend two Meets at the same time? The Reporter for the Meet, Henry Alexander, supposed that you could not be in two places at the same time, but he was told that this was out of date, for 'Einstein says you can.' (In the end, all SMC members were listed.)

A fair amount of heroic walking was performed during the meet, with Braeriach being popular. Scotland was determined to have its winter, and there was a vast amount of snow already on the hills for this time of the year. Several had brought skis, and doubtless had to conceal any smugness as they had an easier time covering the miles. The road up Glen Einich (Gleann Eanaich) was blocked just above the Lower Bothy, to which the village's Ford taxis ferried various members. Guy Barlow gained kudos for walking all the way for Braeriach.

To add further technical interest to this column, we have to include another of William Inglis Clark's interesting notes, this time on one of the frequent problems that the energetic walkers and mountaineers of those days suffered: blisters. Most

[6] G. Barlow, 'The Relative Heights of the Cuillin Peaks', *SMCJ*, 16/95 (April 1923), 244–9.

[7] 'In Memoriam E.W. Steeple, 1872–1940', *FRCCJ*, 13/35 (1941), 76.

[8] J.H.B. Bell, *A Progress in Mountaineering* (Oliver & Boyd, 1950).

An early portrait of J.H.B. Bell,
who joined the SMC in 1922.
Photo: SMC Image Archive.

of us will have experienced these, though it does not appear to be nearly as common an affliction as in the past, presumably owing to the superior design of modern boots and the materials now used to manufacture them.

So appeared the note headed 'Darning of Blisters'.[9] Here is the painful part of the process.

> When one had blisters, the usual proceeding was either to walk with them till they burst, or to prick them with a pin and let out the fluid. Either method had usually disastrous results. I conceived the idea of taking a darning needle and worsted and passing the thread through the blister taking care not to pierce the inner skin. The worsted was then cut off with scissors, leaving about half-an-inch projecting on either side. Drainage immediately took place, the blister collapsed, no air entered, and one could continue to walk with comparative ease. Healing took place in a few hours, and I never knew of bad results. On one occasion, at Uig, in Skye, I darned thirty-one separate blisters.

I have seen modern accounts of how to do this, (complete with diagrams!) and they all state that a sterile condition has to cover any such process. Clark does not mention this, and we have to presume that he at least used alcohol to minimise contamination.

Further Afield

Willie Ling and his best pal George Sang enjoyed a month in the Alps, along with

---

[9] W. Inglis Clark, 'Darning of Blisters', *SMCJ*, 16/93 (April 1922), 204.

Mrs (Dolly) Sang and daughter. Their efforts were often plagued by storms, especially when Sang and Ling raced a storm on the Dom.

> The summit ridge was gained, half an hour from the top, when the storm broke and compelled a hasty and not easy retreat, where experience of what Scottish hills are like in winter proved useful.[10]

Some details from Ling's diary paint the picture. They had left the Dom Hut at 03.10, on a fine starlit morning. The weather began to look poor as they gained the summit ridge at 09.50.

> It then began to blow and snow and we could see nothing, so we turned and hurried down. Our steps were gone and we had to go down by ropes' lengths, often face-in down steep bits till we came to easier ground where we again picked up the tracks, but we had rather a rough time.

With some glacier walking then a route through the séracs they got on to the moraine and so back to the hut at 14.20. After a meal and a rest they left the hut at 16.00 and walked down to Randa, where they caught the train to Zermatt in heavy rain, reaching it at 19.34.[11]

The Dom is a mountain of the Pennine Alps, located between Randa and Saas-Fee in the Swiss canton of Valais. At 4545m, it is the seventh-highest summit in the Alps, overall. Reading several contemporary reports from the Alps, it is understandable why, after a grim number of war years, climbers were keen to enjoy the heights, but the weather appears to be such a fickle entity, that you wonder if the effort was worth it on occasion. From the report above, we must assume they did not quite gain the summit.

In 1919–20, Harold Raeburn had been at the height of his powers, and was appointed mountaineering leader on the initial 1921 British Mount Everest reconnaissance expedition under the leadership of Colonel Charles Howard-Bury. Having worked hard at organising and preparing the party while suffering from influenza, he then caught dysentery, and although he rejoined the expedition after recuperating in Sikkim, he was by then a spent force. Back home, Raeburn was eventually hospitalised in February 1922, and his health continued in a downward spiral, both physically and mentally. He would die in December 1926. His record in Scotland and the Alps remains outstanding.

Ken Crocket.

[10] 'Excursions and Notes', *SMCJ*, 16/94, (October 1922), 206.

[11] Ling Diary, **5**, 15–16 (22 August 1922).

200 YEARS AGO

1822 WAS A YEAR KNOWN PARTICULARLY for a ludicrous but potent event – the visit of George IV to Scotland, the first such visit by a monarch since 1651. Walter Scott was given more-or-less free rein to manipulate the proceedings for the benefit of unionist policy, to celebrate the union of Scotland and England, and encourage amicable relations between Highlands and Lowlands. So George, arriving at Leith in the Royal Yacht, was obliged to appear in over-full Highland dress, which set him back by a huge sum equivalent to £130,000 today. The effect was somewhat spoiled by a too-short mini-kilt and too-fat legs sheathed in pink tights. Lowland bourgeoisie who were accustomed to think of Highland dress as the garb of bandits were also obliged to purchase and wear the full kit if they hoped to be presented at Court. Twenty-one summer days were consumed by pageantry, processions, levées and balls. Four hundred and fifty-seven great and good ladies, decked in their finest rigging, queued at Holyrood to be kissed by the King. Nevertheless, as a result of Scott's florid arrangements, Highland Dress became National Dress, and romantic perceptions of Scotland were strongly reinforced. Forgettable art and poetry were produced in profusion. I offer up some couplets from one of the worst poems, by 'F.W.' of Hampstead.

> He comes! he comes! and Caledonia hails
> The Royal visit through her hills and dales,
> While ev'ry valley, loch, and strath, and glen,
> Again proclaims the tidings and again;
> Lo! at the word, deep Lomond's caves rebound
> And proud Ben Nevis echoes back the sound.
> Her landscapes sketch'd by Nature's plastic hand,
> Mark Scotia's Realm for British Switzerland,
> Where buoyant souls expand with artless ease,
> And all the freedom of the mountain breeze.
> How must such free-born spirits laugh and sing,
> Blest with the cheering presence of their King?

But in that dross there is the nugget that our mountains may be sensibly compared to the Alps. This was also the opinion of Louis-Albert Necker de Saussure (1786–1861), a Swiss geologist whose accounts of earlier visits to Scotland were published in English in 1822. Here is what Necker thought about our mountains.[1]

It may probably be supposed, that the great difference between the height of the mountains of Scotland and those of Switzerland would prevent all comparison as to the aspect of these two countries; however, it is not so. I have already said how much we may be deceived as to the height of mountains, above all, when they are bare, and cut into bold forms. It is also worthy of remark, that the highest mountain seen from its base, does not hold a place in a vertical line, proportionate to its real elevation; consequently, notwithstanding the difference of height, the mountains of Scotland, seen from the valleys open at their feet, produce as much effect as the highest in Switzerland. In fine, although the Scottish mountains are less elevated above the level of the sea than the highest mountains of the Alps, yet as the latter

---

[1] *A Voyage to the Hebrides or Western Isles of Scotland* (Richard Phillips, 1822), p. 8. Online copies may be found on archive.org.

rise above an elevated ground, whilst the former have their bases at the very level of the sea, there is in reality less difference in their height, to the eye of the observer, than might be imagined. Another source of illusion which induces a comparison between the views of the Highlands and those of the Alps of Switzerland, is the relative proportion of the objects composing the landscape, being pretty much the same in both countries. Thus, in the Alps where the mountains are very lofty, the valleys are very wide, and the lakes very extensive. In Scotland the narrow valleys, and the small lakes, are proportionate to the height of the mountains; the enormous forests, seen in Switzerland, commanding at great elevations the inaccessible summits of the rocks, are represented in Scotland by masses of small trees or shrubs, which produce an analogous effect in the landscape. Consequently, if our views in Switzerland present an ensemble more stupendous and striking, in grandeur and majesty nowhere to be equalled, the views of Scotland are, perhaps, more picturesque, taking this word in its true sense; viz. that they offer subjects for a picture more agreeable to the painter, and more varied and graceful in their features. Scotland has not, like Switzerland, those mountains covered with eternal snow; those peaks of bold and light granite, which, by the beauty of their outline, and the contrast which they produce, with the brilliant verdure of the valleys, give to all the distant places so striking an effect; but it has in compensation, lakes abounding with islands of all forms and dimensions; it has the Atlantic Ocean, its isles, and interior gulphs, which give a peculiar beauty to the first ground-work of the landscape.

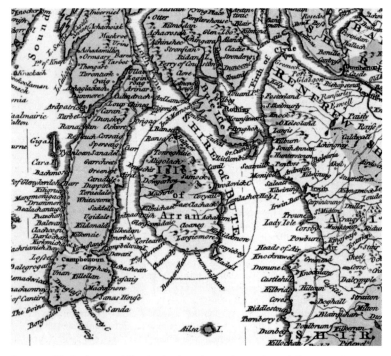

Portion of Necker's map of 'Scotland coloured according to the rock formations'.
Reproduced with the permission of the National Library of Scotland.

Portrait of Louis Albert Necker aged 20,
after a miniature painted shortly before his
first visit to Scotland in 1806.
Source: Trans. Edin. Geol. Soc. 14(2),
Plate VI.

Necker was an extraordinary man, a scion of one of the best-known families in the francophone world. He used his visits in the eighteen-noughties while studying at Edinburgh to produce the first geological map of Scotland.[2] He became so enamoured with the country that he left Switzerland permanently in 1841, and moved to lodgings in Portree, where he remained until his death in 1861. (It is said that this suited his solitary disposition, since no conversation with the inhabitants was possible.) He had befriended the well-known Scottish scientist James D. Forbes earlier, and had travelled with him in Switzerland in 1832; and in 1845 his barometric readings at set times in Portree allowed Forbes, taking his own readings simultaneously aloft on Bruach na Frìthe and Sgùrr nan Gillean, to estimate their heights with good accuracy. He also assisted Forbes in that year in producing the first reasonably accurate map of the Cuillin. He is buried in the kirkyard at Portree beside the Tourist Office, where his grave and headstone are still mysteriously tended.

The final great event of 1822 was the completion of the Caledonian Canal in October, joining the Atlantic and North Seas but also dividing the Jacobite-favouring West Highlands from the Hanoverian-inclined East Highlands with a strategic ditch. Completion was quickly followed by the first boat traverse, which left Inverness on 28 October. The following press release described the journey in colourful terms, and with some patronising socio-political opinions.

> After a labour of nearly twenty years and an expenditure of about £900,000 on this great national undertaking, the country will feel a great degree of satisfaction in hearing of the completion of it. … It has afforded during these eighteen or twenty years employment for the population of those forlorn wastes through which it passes; and not only mitigated the hardships consequent on the late rapid changes of our country, which have chiefly affected the lower classes, but aroused them from a state of inactivity, and, by

---

[2] See <https://lochabergeopark.org.uk/product/neckers-1808-geological-map-of-scotland/> for an opportunity to purchase this map, and to learn more about Necker, by courtesy of our geological expert, Noel Williams.

joining with those skilful workmen who resorted to it from all parts of the kingdom, they have acquired habits of industry and other advantages, which will last while they are a people.

At ten o'clock on Wednesday morning, the Lochness steam-yacht, accompanied by two smacks, departed from the Locks of Muirtown on the first voyage through the Canal, amidst the loud and enthusiastic cheerings of a great concourse of people and the firing of cannon. The morning was peculiarly favourable, although rather calm. There was scarcely a breath of wind to disperse the smoke, which ascended unbroken, after the firing of the guns. The banks of the Canal were crowded with spectators, a great number of whom accompanied the party from the Muirtown Locks to the Bridge of Bught. The band of the Inverness-shire militia went on board at Dochgarroch Lock and immediately played the national air of *God save the King*. As a minute examination of the most remarkable feature of the Canal will be gone into, it was not expected, that the party would arrive at Fort William before Thursday night. They were to be met at Loch Oich by the *Comet* steam-boat … . The Lochness steam-boat passed through Loch Dochfour at ten minutes before one o'clock, on her first voyage through the Caledonian Canal, the band playing, and a salute fired in passing Dochfour, which was answered by Mr Baillie's people on shore by loud cheering, and a salute from a number of small firearms.

Robin N. Campbell

THE SMC CLIMBING DATABASE

A founding aim of the SMC in 1889 was to 'collect information regarding [Scottish] routes and to maintain comprehensive coverage and a historical record'. This note describes, some 130 years later, the history, design and development of a comprehensive new database of Scottish climbs.

Our founding fathers could have had little inkling of how extensive climbing would become in Scotland, encompassing as it does such a vast number and variety of climbs and crags. Of course, the Club has done a sterling job over the past 130 years, publishing guidebooks and recording new climbs in the *Journal*. But it had become an increasingly difficult task to maintain all this information in a comprehensive, up-to-date and readily accessible manner. In 2018, the Club Committee, at Simon Richardson's behest, decided to investigate database systems that could be used for climbing purposes. Much exploratory work was done by John Hutchinson and Mark Atkins, with some input from myself, but to no avail – the existing systems could not be adapted to fit our rather extensive needs. We had come to a dead end.

As so often in life, a series of events, completely unconnected at the time, came together to radically alter the landscape. Simon had become New Routes Editor, adding impetus to the need for a more robust system. Nevil Hewitt, a friend of Simon's from university days, had a vision of a web-based climbing database that would exceed the functionalities of any existing system. Simon discussed the SMC's requirements with Nevil, and lockdown gave Nevil the time to develop his ideas, using the most up-to-date technologies. It should be said that Nevil is rather good at these things. Meanwhile, frustrated with the previous lack of progress and being confined to the house even before lockdown, I set about compiling Word files that included the texts of all the current guides, and incorporating in their appropriate places all the new routes published in successive *Journals*. Altogether, when finished, the files comprised 2,800,000 words.

Shortly after the Word file compilation project was completed, Simon brought Nevil and me together; the database and the content were ready to be married. 20 November 2020 was the day it happened. I sent Nevil my Word files, and later the same day he e-mailed back: 'Thanks for all the data. Everything loads in a couple of minutes.' We had a database. Of course, a great deal of work followed, both in continued development and standardisation of things like first ascent formats by Nevil, and my own curating of the content with help from John Hall. Simon provided continuous input with his clear ideas on what functions were required. It was a happy time: we worked very well as a team, beavering away in the background with the confidence that we were doing something useful. Eventually we were ready to reveal it to the Club, a database which has more than 38,000 routes and 6800 crag headings, and now over 2000 images and topos.

Scope and content

The database defines climbs by type: winter, trad, sport, bouldering, DWS [Deep-Water Soloing] and dry tooling. It embraces all the climbs in SMC publications (both guidebooks and *Journals*), plus some from other sources (e.g. UKC and other web-based resources, although we do not copy any copyrighted material). There are separate entries for summer and winter versions of climbs, and indeed for variations. Another task was to make a separate route entry for all routes that were mentioned only in passing in the linking text paragraphs of the current

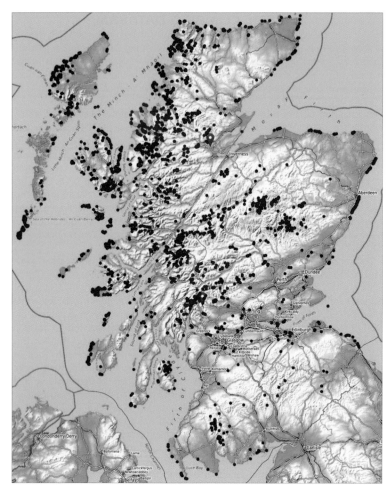

The database depiction of the crags of mainland Scotland & the Hebrides. A dot represents a crag entry in the database. The array of blue dots in the north are those of Northern Highlands Central; those in the south are the Southern Highlands. Purple dots show the crags in other regions. The red flags show Moy Rock and Dumbarton rock (used to generate the whole map as shown).

[Derived from OpenStreetMaps; see <https://www.openstreetmap.org/copyright>]

guidebooks. With the advent of selective guidebooks, these risked being lost from the historical record. Wherever possible, these now also have first ascent details, thereby ensuring that Tom Patey's summer ascents of Cairngorm buttress routes, for example, which are now regarded primarily as winter routes, are retained in a retrievable and searchable manner.

Database design

Compared with other systems, Nevil designed the database with several unique features. Firstly, there is no constraint on heading hierarchy. At the highest level there are the regions (based on the 2002–2018 guidebook series), then any number of chapter, area, mountain, crag, buttress and sub-buttress levels as necessary (although we prefer if there are only five or six levels). Material is easily moved within and between these levels as required. Secondly, crag and climb descriptions are held separately from their heading entries but linked to them. This means that any climb can have more than one description (taken, for example, from a selective as well as a comprehensive guide), and all historical descriptions can be retained when revised versions are produced for a new publication. Thirdly, every entry has a tag that identifies where that text came from (which guidebook or *Journal* issue, for example).

A more recently introduced feature is global 'find and replace', which enables wholesale standardisation of house style (e.g. hyphenation conventions) and application of Gaelic accents (much to some people's relief!). Thus the database can be used to improve the overall textual quality of our information, saving a great deal of time during later stages of guidebook production. The 'search' and 'display' functions are extremely powerful, being possible by crag, climb name, climb type, first ascensionists, and star-rating. For example, one can display all the three-star E1s in the Cairngorms (surprisingly only two, though there is one four-star route), and list the number of climbs having a mention of 'A. Nisbet' or 'Andy Nisbet' in the first ascent information (a total of 2061, as it happens).

Database management

While the database code is owned, maintained and further developed by Nevil, the content is owned by the Club and is stored and backed up on secure Cloud servers via a Club subscription. The content is managed by me, and I am responsible for adding new material (e.g. each batch of *SMCJ* new routes) and for providing output in Word files for authors to begin their task of producing new publications. Importantly, these Word outputs are couched in house style in terms of spacing conventions, grade abbreviations, first ascent formats, pitch description layouts, etc. These output styles can be amended to suit publication type; thus there is a separate style for output destined for the Journal. The final text from any new publication is then entered in the database with its new tag. Authors have read-only access to their relevant sections of the database. At present, we are reluctant to provide editing rights more widely, as experience with other systems highlights the risk of compromising data integrity if editing of existing information is more generally available. In fact, the database functions so quickly and smoothly that it takes but a second or two to download a whole guidebook area, or selection thereof, as a Word file suitable for authors, and it is likely that reloading a complete new guidebook would take no more than a few full days. At present the database is being used for, or has contributed to, the production of eight new guidebooks.

The New Routes Submission module

An adjunct to the main database is a new web-based module for the submission of new routes, crags, topos, images and comments. This is being used to collate all new material, which can be checked and curated before it is loaded into the main database, as well as being the source of the content for the New Routes section of the *Journal*. The system is set up so each entry becomes linked to the

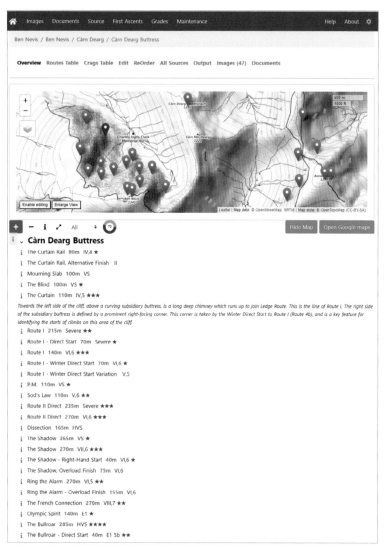

An example Crag page. The red flag on the map shows the location of the crag, the blue flags other crags nearby; one can navigate between crags by clicking on the flags. The descriptions of each item can be revealed by clicking on the 'i' icons. Note the separate descriptions for summer and winter versions of routes.

relevant crag in the main database, thereby ensuring appropriate organisation (not to mention automatic application of Gaelic accents!).

Topos and images

Nevil has also built a 'Topo Editor' which is really a climbing-specific tool for creating topos that would otherwise be made with expensive proprietary software.

The Topo Editor home page, showing one of the draft topos for the forthcoming 'Ben Nevis Winter Climbs' guidebook. Behind the menu buttons is a wealth of drawing, text and editing tools.

It is easy to use (indeed, a cut-down version is available within the new-routes submissions site), and it produces interactive files that can be imported into Illustrator or InDesign for guidebook production. In principle, in the future, the files will be ideal for digital publishing. The interactive element allows lines on the topo to be linked to the database content, thus populating legends automatically and accurately. Author access within the main database allows authors to construct their own topos, thus ensuring that the lines are where they want them to be. The topos are fully editable (to nudge the lines, for example), and the files are catalogued according to region and crag, thus producing a rational organisation. Similarly, action photos, historical topos and other illustrations can be loaded and linked to the crag in question, creating a catalogue that is fully integrated with the text content of the database. In the future, the new SMC archive of digital photographs being developed by Martin McKenna and Rob Lovell will be linked to the database, thereby organising the submitted action photos in a manner consistent with the database crag catalogue.

Other documentation

Although not widely used so far, there is the facility to store other types of documents in a way that links them to particular crags or mountains. This could include miniguides, for example, but also historical or archived material, thereby enhancing the potential use of the database for historical purposes. Indeed, lists of notable climbers' first ascents have already been produced on request; we expect that this facility will be of interest to all those engaged in writing historical texts. Another feature of the database is that the information associated with any route includes a field for notes on additional ascents of significance, and for historical information; all the interesting stories in the first-ascent lists of the current series of guides are now safely stored, permanently linked to the route in question. They would not otherwise have been retained in the new series of guidebooks.

Access and links

As mentioned above, a small team of people have full editing rights, while authors have read-only (text) and topo-editor usage rights. A stand-alone web-based version of the full topo editor is available from Nevil on request (and is already being used by authors from other clubs). The new routes submissions site is accessible to the public via the SMC website or <https://report.smc.org.uk/>.

Future plans and prospects

I actually find it hard to believe that we've come as far as we have since November 2020, when the database was first populated. I think that illustrates what an effective and powerful tool it is. But looking to the future, there are several important questions for the Club to consider. Should read-only access be made more generally available to Club members? What about the wider public, and if we did that, would it compromise the viability of printed guidebook publication? Given that most printed guidebooks in the future will be selective rather than comprehensive, how do we fulfil our remit of making all route descriptions available to all? We could publish PDF supplements, probably at some financial loss; or we could answer most of these questions by developing a mobile app or similar that provides access, perhaps on a subscription model, which is the modern trend. Whatever the answers, we are now perhaps in the fortunate position to be able to pose these tricky questions; we do indeed have a system that comfortably exceeds the functionality and breadth of content of anything else available.

Roger Everett

Appendix: How to submit new route descriptions

The link <https://report.smc.org.uk/> takes you to a page where you can easily submit a new route description. There are fields for your name and e-mail address, then a 'crag search' field. Simply type the name of the crag; after the first few letters a series of suggestions will appear; click on the correct one. If there are named buttresses a secondary list will appear; click on the appropriate one. Then type in the route name and other details in the fields below, it being easiest to use copy–paste from Word for the description, following the format of the example given. First ascent details are added into the fields below. For the date, although the software asks for YYYY-MM-DD format, in practice it will accept and automatically correct most other date formats (but you do need four digits for the year). The rules for first ascent names are only that there are no spaces after a full stop (e.g. middle initial), and a comma after surnames (except the last).

If your new route is on a new crag, you will need to fill in the New Crag page first. Again, this is simply a question of filling in the displayed fields, and as with new routes, only a few of these fields are mandatory (although all information is welcome). When adding the new routes to this crag from the New Route page, use the same crag name in the New Route form and click the 'new crag' box.

If you have done multiple new routes on a crag, the Bulk Load facility is extremely useful. Simply paste in all the route descriptions from a Word file as a single block of text. There are a few formatting rules, as described below the text entry box. The crucial ones are to insert two spaces between route name and length, to place first ascent details on a new line (names first then date, using the conventions above), and then to enter the description. There must be a blank line between different descriptions (but not within a description) and any bits of linking text must start their first line with a #. After pasting text into the submission box, the 'parsed' text appears in the box above. If correct, then the route length will appear in grey bold font, the names will be in italics after 'FA:' (blue text), and the date will be YYYY-MM-DD in bold after 'dated:' (blue text). Linking text will be in italics, and the # will have disappeared. One can edit the text submission box if things are not quite right, and the parsed version will change accordingly in real time. When finished, click on the blue Submit button at the bottom left of the page. Bulk Load is a very powerful function which allows the database manager to load a whole crag's worth of route descriptions in one go when updating the main database.

The new routes submissions page also has tabs for submitting images (e.g. action photos, topos produced in other systems) and comments. These are self-explanatory and should be linked to the relevant crag as above.

The Create Topo tab opens the cut-down version of the topo editor. There is a training video to get you started, then just drag your crag photo jpg into the box and the menu for making a topo will appear. There are a couple of important things to note: firstly, do not exit this page until you have finished the topo and clicked on Submit, because your work will be lost if you leave the page before submitting; secondly, you can use the download icon to download a jpg version of your topo for your records. You can also reload that jpg subsequently if you want to add to it (though you won't be able to edit any existing components). If you've got stuck or into a mess with any of these operations, e-mail Simon or me and we'll sort it out.

The Scottish Mountaineering Club

Committed to maintaining a comprehensive record of Scottish Climbing ⓘ

Please complete all fields marked with *

Your details   Name *   E mail *

Crag *   Search for Crag   ☐ New Crag or can't find crag

Changing tabs will clear tab information, so after completing a form or creating a topo, submit first.

| **New Route** | Image | Create Topo | Comment | Bulk Load | New Crag |

Route Name *		Climb Type *	⇕
Stars	✕ ☆ ☆ ☆ ☆	Grade System	⇕
Length *	m	Grade *	
Pitches		DWS Grade	⇕
No. of Bolts		Aid Grade	⇕

Route Description * ⓘ

e.g. A strenuous but well protected route based on the prominent hanging corner in the centre of the buttress. Start at the lowest tip of the buttress 5m right of Left-Hand Slab.
1. 20m 4a Climb the greasy slab to a large ledge below a hanging corner.
2. 40m 5b Climb the hanging corner to the top.

First Ascent Details

Date *   Names (please include first names) *

YYYY-MM-DD 🗓   e.g. Fred Blogs, John C Grey, Julia Smith

Notes of first ascent (optional)

If possible please also submit a topo using the topo or image tab. Action and crag photos (for possible use in future guidebooks) are also very welcome.

Submit   Give Feedback

This site will not work correctly with old browsers such as Internet Explorer. Please use Chrome, Firefox, Edge or Safari.

© Web application Nevil Hewitt 2021, © Data content Scottish Mountaineering Club 2021.   T&C's, Privacy Policy and Cookies

The New Routes Submissions page <https://report.smc.org.uk/>, as described in the Appendix to this article.

Postscript

This article and its Appendix can provide only the briefest overview of the suite of database functionality. The full Help guides that have been written for authors, editors, and topo creators now total almost 24,000 words, and Nevil's underlying code is massive. Club members may have questions of a technical, functional, organisational, practical or even strategic nature. We shall do our best to answer if asked.

RICK ALLEN, 1954–2021

While last year's Journal was in preparation we had word of Rick Allen's death and were able to include an obituary written by Noel Williams and Sandy Allan. Here Simon Richardson reflects further on a close friend and outstanding climber.

ON 25 JULY 2021 A SERIES OF AVALANCHES swept down the East Flank of K2 taking the life of Rick Allen. In an instant, Britain lost one its finest ever mountaineers.

Rick was born in London on 6 November 1954. His father introduced him to the Scottish hills with ascents of Schiehallion and Ben Nevis, and when Rick joined the University of Birmingham Mountaineering Club his rock climbing took off. Although Rick was a fledgling climber his determination instantly shone through. He quickly became proficient on rock and then developed a strong interest in winter climbing. He made ascents of Castle Ridge and Tower Ridge in 1975 with Robin Walker, and the following winter climbed Point Five Gully with Jim Fotheringham and Chris Duck.

Rick had a strong attraction to wild places and he became a regular visitor to the Alps, completing many of the Chamonix classics. His finest early ascents were in the Bernese Oberland where he climbed the ENE Ridge of the Lauterbrunnen Breithorn and the Welzenbach Route on the North Face of the Gletscherhorn with Chris Duck in 1978 – both big, demanding routes that are now rarely climbed. Further afield, Rick climbed the West Ridge and Diamond Couloir on Mount Kenya with Roy Lindsay in 1980, and later that year he visited Nepal where he made the first ascent of the West Face of Tharpa Chulli (Tent Peak) in the Annapurna Sanctuary.

Wild places also set the theme for his new-routing in Scotland. This often took place in the most inaccessible and serious of locations such as A' Mhaighdean (the remotest Munro), Ladhar Bheinn and Beinn a' Bhùird. Rick's finest contribution was the first winter ascent of Raven's Edge on Buachaille Etive Mòr with Brian Sprunt in 1984, a spectacular route now recognised as one of the finest mixed climbs in Glen Coe.

In 1982 Rick visited the Himalayas for a second time on an expedition organised by Roy Lindsay, where he made the first ascent of Kirti Stambh (6271m) in the Gangotri region of India. He and his long-standing partner Ernie McGlashan backed off owing to dangerous snow conditions, but after the slope avalanched Rick went back up and continued alone to the summit. During the trip Rick met Nick Kekus, and two years later they visited Nepal together and climbed a new route on the 2500m-high South Face of Ganesh II (7111m). They reached the summit on the ninth day in a storm and spent three days descending the face. Their route was a magnificent achievement, and although it was largely ignored by the mainstream climbing press, it made a big impression on the upcoming generation of British alpinists. A benchmark had been set. If your new route was not climbed in pure alpine stye and did not take at least 12 days, then you were not really trying hard enough!

Rick's ability to acclimatise and perform strongly at high altitude was extraordinary. This became apparent on Mal Duff's expedition to the North-East Ridge of Everest in 1985 when, climbing solo, Rick reached the expedition's high point at 8170m. The remainder of the 1980s saw another trip to the NE Ridge of Everest and to Makalu. Neither was successful because of difficult snow conditions, but once again Rick reached over 8000m on both mountains, confirming his strength at altitude.

In 1991 Rick went to the Tien Shan and made the first British ascent of Khan Tegri (7010m), and the following summer he visited Tajikistan and made the first ascent of the difficult East Ridge of Tchimtarga (5482m) with Doug Scott and Russian climber Sergei Efimov. This was a significant turn of events because Sergei invited Rick to join an all-Russian expedition to Dhaulagiri (8176m) in 1993. The seven-man team were successful in forging a difficult new route up the north face. This was Rick's first 8000m peak and an astonishing achievement on a gruelling and technical route. Rick learned to speak Russian before the trip and calmly adapted to their diet – the main sustenance on the seven-day ascent was cabbage soup!

In 2000 Rick climbed Everest with a commercial expedition. His success was well deserved after previous strong performances on the NE Ridge, but Rick soon realised that large, organised expeditions were not where his heart lay. He moved to Tajikistan in 2006 where he climbed extensively, especially in the Fan mountains. Details of his ascents are incomplete (Rick did not leave a comprehensive chronology of his ascents) but in 2006 he made the first British ascent of Pik Karl Marx (6723m) and the first ascent of the North Ridge of Pik Ovalnaya (5935m) with Phil Wickens. In 2008 he made the first British ascent of Pik Korzhenevskaya (7105m).

Rick's pairing with Sandy Allan was the defining climbing partnership of his life. In 1986 they made a brilliant five-day new route on the South Face of Pumori (7161m), a beautiful peak near Everest, and they worked powerfully together the following year on the NE Ridge of Everest. Two years later they climbed the North Face of the Eiger. In 1995 they joined an expedition to attempt the huge and unclimbed Mazeno Ridge on Nanga Parbat (8126m), the longest ridge on any of the 8000m peaks. They were unsuccessful, but in 2009 they returned and climbed the mountain's Diamir Face. This was Rick's third 8000m peak, and two years later he made it four by climbing Hidden Peak (8068m).

By 2012, Rick and Sandy had accumulated a significant amount of high-altitude experience, and they decided to return to Nanga Parbat and try the Mazeno Ridge one last time. The 10km route had been attempted many times since the 1970s and was one of mountaineering's last great problems. To gain the main summit you have to traverse the eight Mazeno peaks – all over 7000m – to reach the Mazeno Gap. An alternative strategy was devised where a team of six – Rick, Sandy, the South African climber Cathy O'Dowd, and Lhakpa Rangdu, Lhakpa Nuru and Lakpa Zarok from Nepal – planned to traverse the ridge together, which would provide more firepower for the summit push.

In the event, it took this strong team nine days to reach the Mazeno Gap, and after a failed summit attempt, only Rick and Sandy had the physical and mental energy to try again. As Cathy and the three Sherpas made a difficult descent of the dangerous Schell Route, Rick and Sandy set off with minimal supplies for their summit bid. Deep snow meant it took two days rather than one to reach the top, but it was on the descent down the Kinshofer Route where their troubles really began. Poor conditions that year meant that all teams had given up the on the Kinshofer so there was no trail in place, and they were unable to light their stove to melt water. The epic three-day descent in extreme avalanche conditions while being exhausted and dehydrated is one of mountaineering's great survival stories.

Rick and Sandy's 18-day traverse of the Mazeno Ridge was widely acclaimed as one of the finest Himalayan climbs this century and hailed as the most important British success in the high Himalayas since Stephen Venables's ascent of Mount Everest's Kangshung Face in 1988. Rick and Sandy were awarded the Piolet d'Or, the highest honour in mountaineering. But Rick was a humble man – rather than putting the trophy on display, he used it to prop up the creaking bookcase in his Chamonix flat.

Rick remained focused on big mountains and was determined to continue climbing them in good style, and in 2017 he attempted a futuristic new route on the NW Face of Annapurna with Felix Berg, Louis Rousseau and Adam Bielecki. They were unsuccessful but came away with an ascent of Tilicho (7134m) as consolation. Later that year Rick climbed the two highest peaks in the Ruwenzori mountains of Uganda with Mike Lean – prized and rarely climbed summits. In 2018 he climbed Broad Peak (8047m), his fifth 8000-er, although success was overshadowed by a 'rescue' aided by a drone.

Rick joined the SMC in 1995 and was very proud to be a member of the Club. On the 1998 Easter Meet he took a boat across Loch Maree and made the first winter ascent of *Ordinary Route* (IV,5) on Beinn Lair's Angel Buttress with Bob Richardson. In February 2017 he hosted a group of French climbers with Dave Broadhead in the Raeburn Hut as part of a joint Alpine Club meet. They had terrible weather but Rick relished the chance to share his experience of the Scottish mountains whatever the conditions. His heart was certainly in the Highlands, and shortly before his death he bought a house on the north side of the Cairngorms near Nethy Bridge.

'Rick was always very good at keeping in touch,' Dave Broadhead recalls. 'He would summarise the highs and lows of his year in a "Christmas letter" that would arrive at some point over the winter. With his wry humour he was always disarmingly honest about his mishaps and modest about his achievements. He enjoyed coming back to the UK for brief visits and we would meet up occasionally at SMC dinners. His expeditions took a physical toll and he invariably looked older than one remembered, but always with the same mischievous grin.'

I've written about Rick the climber and the qualities that made him so successful – drive, skill, experience and an exceptional ability to perform at altitude. This was the Rick I knew best. But there was far more to Rick than mountaineering. He was an outstanding engineer and had a glittering career with Texaco, culminating as safety manager for the huge Gorgon Natural Gas Project in Australia. Rick was also extremely generous. His first marriage to Alison ended in tragedy when she died of cancer in 1999. Rick married Zuhra in Tajikistan in 2006 and gained a stepdaughter Nazira and stepson Farrukh. Sadly, the marriage did not survive, but Rick took on the responsibility for Nazira and Farrukh's education, funding them through their degrees. Rick was proud of their achievements and was delighted to walk Nazira down the aisle at her wedding in 2018.

But most of all, it was Rick's faith that drove him. He recently attended a two-year course at the All Nations Christian College in Hertfordshire and supported Mhoira Leng's work with the Cairdeas Palliative Care Trust in Uganda. On his final expedition to K2 he was raising money for refugees and children in Myanmar.

Jerry Gore, Rick's expedition partner on K2, wrote movingly about the aftermath of the avalanche. 'Pakistani guides Arshad, Shah, Waqar, Rizwan and Ahmed were at Camp 2 when they got the news. They all knew Rick – he was a sort of legendary grandfather in these parts – and they came rushing down the mountain to help. We found Rick late that night and buried him the next morning. We stood together in the shadow of K2 with prayers in different languages and religions filling the air. It was a moment of total unity, and a good way to say

Rick Allen high on the Aiguille du Chardonnet during the first ascent of the East Ridge Integral.

goodbye to a Scotsman who loved these mountains and the people who call them home.'

This tribute has been hard for me to write. Rick was a close friend, and we had been climbing together for nearly 40 years. A few summers ago, we climbed a new route on the Grande Fourche in the Mont Blanc range. We expected to complete the route in a day and were travelling light, but we were caught in darkness near the summit. Despite a good weather forecast it rained through the night and we shivered and cuddled our way to a long-awaited dawn. Rick had survived two open bivouacs high on Nanga Parbat, so I was determined not to be the first to complain. Needless to say, Rick remained infuriatingly cheerful all night and did not comment once about our situation. When we were safely down in Chamonix, the first thing he did was take me to buy a new bivouac sack!

Rick Allen led an extraordinary life. He was one of the world's finest mountaineers and touched the lives of many. His bold alpine-style ascents in the high Himalayas will be remembered for generations. His final resting place, with the mighty K2 as his headstone, could not be more fitting.

Simon Richardson

SCOTTISH MOUNTAINEERING TRUST – 2021

Scottish Charity Number SCO 09117

The Trustees met by Zoom on 16 April and 19 October 2021. During the course of these meetings, support was given to the following: Torridon Mountain Rescue Team – Purchase of thermal scope; Dr James Fenton – Scottish Wild Land Group; John Irving – Glen Brittle Memorial Hut; Lochaber Mountain Rescue Team – Extension of base and fitting out; Scottish Mountaineering Club – Lagangarbh upgrade; Ladies Scottish Climbing Club – Black Rock Cottage; John Muir Trust – Quinag Footpath; Rachel May – Mhor Outdoor; Ben Campbell – Urban Uprising; and Paul Tattersall – Bolting in Wester Ross.

The present Trustees are J.R.R. Fowler (Chairman – *ex officio* immediate Past President of the SMC), D.J Broadhead (*ex officio* President of the SMC), D.N. Williams (*ex officio* Convener of the Publications Sub-Committee), G.D. Morrison (*ex officio* Editor of the SMC Journal), R.D.M. Chalmers, J.R.G. Mackenzie, I.M. Young, G. Cohen and S. Fraser. D. Small is the Trust Treasurer and J.D. Hotchkis is the Trust Secretary.

The following grants & loans have been committed by the Trustees during 2021.

Recipient	Grant	Loan
Torridon MRT – Purchase of thermal scope	£2,000	
Dr James Fenton – Scottish Wild Land Group	£5,000	
John Irving – Glen Brittle Memorial Hut		£5,000
Lochaber MRT – Extension of base and fitting out	£15,000	
Scottish Mountaineering Club – Lagangarbh upgrade	£12,500	£12,500
Ladies Scottish Climbing Club – Black Rock Cottage	£2,125	
John Muir Trust – Quinag Footpath	£10,000	
Rachel May – Mhor Outdoor	£2,000	
Ben Campbell – Urban Uprising	£1,960	
Paul Tattersall – Bolting, Wester Ross	£2,050	

Iain Young has chaired a working group on the Diamond Grant, assisted throughout by John Hutchinson. Each has carried out a huge volume of work, and the Diamond Grant is now live and open for applications. A film on the Trust was commissioned and produced. If you have not seen it, it is well worth viewing at <https://thesmt.org.uk> (only about five minutes long).

The Trustees wish to thank Elsie Riley for her services as Trustee over the last four years, and particularly her input on mountain rescue matters. They also thank Robert Aitken, a valued Trustee since 2018, who has recently stood down.

The Trustees express their appreciation for the valuable input and energy of Simon Richardson over the last five years. Simon's chairmanship over the preceding three years resulted in a number of marketing initiatives, all of which have been followed through by the Trustees.

The Trustees welcome as new Trustees Geoff Cohen and Simon Fraser.

James D. Hotchkis – Trust Secretary

MUNRO MATTERS 2021

by Alison Coull (Clerk of the List)

This report covers 1 January to 31 December 2021. The five columns below give number, name and year of Compleation of Munros, Tops & Furths as appropriate. *SMC member, **LSCC member.

No	Name	M	T	F
6863	Jonathan Collins	2018		
6864	Hugh Montague	2020		
6865	Ruairidh A. Cooper	2020		
6866	David Eaton	2019		
6867	Mark Williams	2020		
6868	Pauline Jones	2020		
6869	David Jones	2020		
6870	Rosslyn Rankin	2017		
6871	Kenneth O'Hara	2002		
6872	Hilary Kerr	2015		
6873	Duncan Wilson	2019		
6874	Tony Cheslett	1997		
6875	Keith Davis	2020		
6876	Callum MacLellan	2007		
6877	Malcolm Hare	2017		
6878	Roger Webb*	1996		
6879	Darryl Wilkinson	1995		
6880	Gary English	2021		
6881	Jonathan J Ladyman	2021		
6882	Edward Tissiman	2021		
6883	Stuart Duncan	2021		
6884	Christine Wilson	2000		
6885	Alec Erskine	2021		
6886	Stephen Cole	2021		
6887	Tim Storer	2021		
6888	Clive Astall	2021		
6889	Sandra Kelly	2021		
6890	Sam Moore	2021		
6891	Paul Gregory	2021		
6892	Alasdair Brooks	2021		
6893	James Lindsay	2021		
6894	David R. McNeill	2021		
6895	Alison Aldred	2021		
6896	Peter Aldred	2021		
6897	Paul Millar	2021		
6898	Charles A Abernethy	2021		
6899	John N. Bennett	2021		
6900	Patrick Frew	2021		
6901	Chris Jones	2021		
6902	Marc Pattullo	2021		
6903	Danny Bacon	2021		
6904	Barry Liddell	2021		
6905	David Uren	2021		
6906	Dawn Waitt	2021		
6907	Charles Kelly	2021		
6908	David Low	2021		
6909	Christian Roberts	2021		
6910	Peter Wallace	2021		
6911	Helen Goode	2021		
6912	Duncan Mckenna	2021		
6913	Jennifer Strachan	2021		
6914	Colin E. Beverly	2021		2021
6915	Iain Paterson	2021		
6916	Pat Richards	2021		
6917	Ross Gilroy	2018		
6918	Jim Hood	2020		
6919	Iain Young	2021		
6920	Gavin Scott	2021		
6921	Jim Wilson	2021		
6922	Robin Sloan	2021		
6923	John Crawford	2021		
6924	Campbell McAulay	2021		
6925	Alan Milne	2021		
6926	Donald Reid	2021		
6927	Andy Stewart	2021		
6928	Mark Jones	2021		
6929	Martin A. Swan	2021		
6930	Jane Gill	2021		
6931	David Simpson	2021		
6932	Kimberley Paris	2021		
6933	Kenny Beaton	2021		
6934	Glyn Harper	2021		
6935	Sally Black	2021		
6936	Catherine Stuart	2012		
6937	Tom Robertson	2012		
6938	Philip R. Garnett	2021		
6939	Fraser Wallace	2021		
6940	John Offord	2021		
6941	Dougie Smeaton	2021		
6942	Olwyn Paxman	2021		
6943	Jim Paxman	2021		
6944	Mike Wardie	2021		
6945	Martin Williams	2021		
6946	Frank Hennessy	2021		
6947	Joyce Skinner	2021		
6948	Doug Cochrane	2021		
6949	Martin Rowe	2021		
6950	Sheena Henderson	2021		
6951	Gregor Henderson	2021		
6952	Rocco Giudice	2021		
6953	Martin Dare	2021		
6954	Jane Walters	2021		
6955	Adrian Walters	2021		
6956	Ian Liddell	2021		
6957	David Clyne	2021		
6958	Helen C. Clark	2021		
6959	Alasdair Anderson	2021		
6960	Carole E Engelman	2021	2021	

6961	John R Martin	2021
6962	Ross Hannah	2021
6963	Gary Lory	2021
6964	Craig Lory	2021
6965	David Qualtrough	2021
6966	Gary Heales	2021
6967	Marie Harrigan (Entwistle)	2021
6968	Jim Bispham	2021
6969	Peter F. Gorecki	2012
6970	Rachel Hartland-Mahon	2021
6971	Marcus Hartland-Mahon	2021
6972	Donald P Ramsay	2018
6973	John Moy	2019
6974	Sarah Clough	2019
6975	Darren Peart	2021
6976	Andrew Hunt	2021
6977	Andy Emms	2021
6978	Charles Kelly	2021
6979	Brian Henderson	2021
6980	Scott Mitchell	2021
6981	Martyn Hutchison	2021
6982	Paul A. Niven	2021
6983	Ian Winterburn	2018
6984	Dave Lockwood	2021
6985	James Brydie	2021
6986	Philip Behan	2021
6987	Barry Veitch	2021
6988	Michael Ward	1995
6989	Kalina Slusarska	2021
6990	Bryan Woolsey	2021
6991	Diane McCombie	2021
6992	Ciaran McDonnell	2021
6993	Gillian Pickering	2021
6994	Peter Wright	2021
6995	David Miller	2021
6996	Gordon A. Laurie	2021
6997	Doreen Campbell	2021
6998	Alleyn Plowright	2021
6999	Iain Watson	2021
7000	Paul Roberts	2021
7001	Audrey Shaw	2021
7002	Catherine Bloomfield	2021
7003	John Findlay	2021
7004	Brian McLeish	2021
7005	Linda B. Allan	2021
7006	Derek Wardlaw	2021
7007	Darren Sutherland	2021
7008	Alan MacBeth	2021
7009	John Wild	2021
7010	David Miller	2020
7011	Jamie Neill	2021
7012	Shona Macpherson	2021
7013	Henning Rische	2021
7014	Elspeth Bleakley	2021
7015	Neil Paterson	2021
7016	John Marjoram	2021
7017	Elspeth Berry	2021
7018	Ian Venables	2021
7019	Lynne Wightman	2021
7020	Pat Stapenhurst	2021

7021	Tim Stapenhurst	2021	
7022	Chris Terrey	2021	
7023	Lesley A Hepburn	2021	
7024	Ian M. Munro	2021	
7025	Neil Mitchell	2021	
7026	Dennis Underwood	2021	
7027	Pete H. Holland	2021	
7028	Alistair Jeffs	2021	
7029	Michael Woodhill	2021	
7030	Angela Honthy	2021	
7031	Dean Shipsey	2021	
7032	Alastair Dunlop	2021	
7033	Gilbert McCurdy	2021	
7034	Karen Macpherson	2021	
7035	Jonathan Hallam	2021	
7036	Will Moran	2021	
7037	Jonathan Mitchell	2021	
7038	Martin Quicke	2021	
7039	Jennifer Stewart	2021	
7040	David Stewart	2021	
7041	Andrew Sudlow	2021	
7042	Marischal Sinclair	1998	
7043	Emma Coutts	2021	
7044	Domenico Caira	2021	
7045	Ross Elder	2021	
7046	Colin Clark	2021	
7047	Karen Bell	2021	
7048	Patrick Neville	2021	
7049	Hannah Evans	2021	
7050	Andy Hague	2021	
7051	Maggie Neilson	2021	
7052	Audrey McFarlane	2021	
7053	Robin Gordon	2021	
7054	John Melvin	2021	
7055	Ronald Dempster	2021	
7056	Phil Trinder	2021	
7057	Chris Burns	2021	
7058	Robert Swinfen	2021	
7059	Peter Loveless	2021	
7060	Valerie Gill	2021	
7061	Cameron McKenzie	2021	
7062	Ed Jones	2021	
7063	Helen Brunton	2021	
7064	Philip Jones	2021	
7065	Moira Webster	2021	
7066	Richard Webster	2021	
7067	Dot M. Primrose	2021	
7068	Willie Primrose	2021	
7069	Timothy A Deakin	2016	
7070	Stephen Montgomery	2021	
7071	Gillian Linnen	2021	
7072	Kay Erskine	2021	
7073	Lee McKnight	2021	
7074	William P. Stephens	2021	2021
7075	Simon A.H. Young	2021	2021
7076	Emma Young	2021	
7077	John D. Kingdom	2021	
7078	Thomas A. Little	2021	
7079	Bob Black	1994	
7080	Colin Richardson	1999	

7081	James Richardson	2021		7090	Audry Dasnoy	2021
7082	Douglas Borthwick	2021		7091	Frank Westerduin	2021
7083	Glynn Dodd	2021		7092	Catriona Webster	2021
7084	James R Jones	2021		7093	James Lamont	2021
7085	Janet Hill	2021		7094	Emma Philip	2021
7086	Dave Hill	2021		7095	Gail Digney	2021
7087	Kay Morgan	2021		7096	John Digney	2021
7088	Elizabeth Barr	2021		7097	Ralph H. Gill	2021
7089	Andy Ravenhill	2021		7098	Patrick Bartlett	2021

The pandemic – Year 2

Munro registration year 2020 finished with optimism that the vaccine programme would provide a way out of the pandemic. There was also a sense, however, that the pandemic was far from over. On 4 January 2021 the Government announced that mainland Scotland would go into lockdown (Level 4) from 5 January, with a new legal requirement preventing anyone from leaving home except for essential purposes (including exercise).

For hillwalkers, 2021 was generally a much less restrictive year than 2020. The most significant restrictions occurred at the start of the year until mid- to late April when Level 4 restrictions prevented travel outside a person's local authority boundary. Not too much of an issue if you lived in Highland (although individual judgments still had to be made about what might or might not be acceptable, and views varied on this). It was a significant restriction on the hillwalking activities of those in local authority areas that did not have an abundance of hills. For example, residents of Edinburgh were restricted to the Pentlands. As it happened Scotland had a remarkable winter of snow, and in Edinburgh these small hills gave an opportunity to imagine being in the Highlands or even an Alpine range, such was the depth of the snow and the length of time that it stayed.

Otherwise, restrictions generally impinged on hillwalkers in relation to socialising and the use of accommodation, with a relatively complex set of rules depending upon which Level (0 to 5) a local authority was in. In addition, international travel was governed by a raft of rules and regulations that were subject to frequent change, often at very short notice. Travel abroad and to Scotland carried some risk of having to quarantine.

The moment all hillwalkers had been waiting for came on Friday 16 April when travel within Scotland was allowed for outdoor socialising, recreation and exercise, and outdoor meetings in groups of up to six adults from up to six households. All of Scotland moved to Level 3 on 26 April, which allowed tourist accommodation to reopen.

On 14 December the new Omicron variant of Covid emerged, so restrictions were reintroduced, although these did not constrain travel or outdoor activity. The end of the Munro registration year coincided with a vaccination programme that gave most adults the opportunity of two vaccine doses and a booster dose.

One of the most impressive Munro achievements of the year was the compleation of all the Munros in a single day by the Carnethy Hill Running Club in August. (Edinburgh University Mountaineering Club had also done this in the 1970s.)

<https://www.bbc.co.uk/news/uk-scotland-edinburgh-east-fife-58305778>
<https://carnethy.com/2021/08/carnethy-munros-in-a-day/>

This feat included some impressively big days, such as Michelle Hetherington doing 50km over the Loch Monar Munros. The final Munro was only bagged at 23.48 after a fair bit of drama.

SMC compleations or connections

Roger Webb (6878) recorded his compleation from 1996, apparently inspired to do so because when doing the housework he came across an ornamental ladder given to him by the Rannoch MC and made by former SMC Treasurer Morton Shaw. This caused him to reflect that three others who were with him that day (Colin Grant, John Dunn and Philip 'Bish' McAra) had now died, and a quarter of a century had gone by. It was time to confess. The last Munro had been an epic of November: dreich, sodden, nil visibility, and a challenging river crossing impressively despatched by one of the party who was six-months pregnant. Roger concluded: 'The living know who they are and I thank them too. Great days made by great company. I must do it again … .'

In a sentiment that is well understood by everyone who lived through this pandemic, Niall Ritchie (6857) described his last Munro as having been 'grabbed between lockdowns'. Seven hours of driving, two-and-a-half hours on the hill and a satisfying Speyside malt waiting on the table when he returned, thanks to his wife.

Elspeth Bleakley (7014) had a huge compleation in August on Stob a' Choire Odhair with 43 people followed by Real Food Café food by the river, brought into Clashgour. Elspeth's dad was particularly pleased to join her because he had been on his own father's final Munro back in the 1960s – SMC member George Chisholm (98). Elspeth's husband Raphael Bleakley (4516) is also a Munroist.

Elspeth Bleakley (7014) and party on Stob a' Choire Odhair, 28 August 2021.
Photo: Chris Sangwin.

An assortment of multiple compleations

Sam Moore (6890) compleated a round of Munros and Corbetts at the same time in May on Beinn na Lap and Leum Uilleim.

John Crawford (6923), Campbell McAulay (6924), Alan Milne (6925), Donald Reid (6926) and Andy Stewart (6927) had a rare five-way compleation on Beinn Sgritheall in June. These five friends had met at Edinburgh University and made a pact to compleat the Munros together on Midsummer's Day 2020. The Glenelg Inn had been block-booked since 2011. Covid restrictions had delayed the compleation.

Marischal Sinclair (7042) also registered rounds of the Donalds, the Corbetts and the Grahams when he registered his Munro compleation on Meall Chuaich in 1998. He is now doing Marilyns between 1500 and 2000 feet, which he has called 'the Marshalls'.

Gillian Linnen (7071) and Kay Sweeney (7072) had a joint compleation on Beinn na Lap, having met at work in an Arbroath GP practice in the early 2000s and joined Friockheim walking club.

James Richardson (7081) compleated on Slioch and took the opportunity to record his father Colin Richardson's (7080) compleation in 1999. Duncan McKenna (6912) joined his compleationist brothers Allister (6614) and Patrick (6783) and father (6782) when he compleated in June. Gary and Craig Lory (6963 & 6964) had a brotherly compleation on Am Basteir.

Frank Westerduin (7091) compleated supported by his eight-year-old dog Alfie, who also compleated. (The Munro Society now provide information about dog compleations. See <https://www.themunrosociety.com/canine-completers.>)

Motivation

Reasons for doing a Munro round are of course many and varied. David Qualtrough (6965) found inspiration for the Munros through the tragic loss of his niece in a car accident. His niece was an outdoor instructor with whom he had done his earliest Munros. Compleation was a way to raise sponsorship for a trust fund founded in her memory to provide opportunities in the outdoors for young people. Again Coronavirus delayed by a year his planned compleation by the age of 50.

Beware the chance remark and what it might lead to. Sandra Kelly (6889) said that a vague comment in the 1990s by her husband, doubting her ability to do the Cuillin ridge, somehow turned out to be highly motivational, and her husband Nick (6146) was very happy to be proved wrong in 2012. Fittingly her last Munro was Sgùrr Dubh Mòr in Skye.

Jennifer Strachan (6913) said that at age 54 she was looking at a lilac rucksack in the sale for £10 in an outdoor shop in Aberfeldy. Her partner laughed, took £10 out of his pocket and said, 'You'll never use it.' A month later she was at the meeting point of Perth Ramblers, lilac rucksack at the ready, later joining Perth Hillwalking Club.

Frank Hennessy told of a typical (for his generation) introduction to the Munros through the school hillwalking club. He remembers wearing jeans and being told that the foil-wrapped pizza his mother had given him was 'not hill food' and that a sandwich was required, along with a checked shirt, gaiters and a headband.

Mistaken identity

Hugh Montague (6864) recounted a couple of incidents of mistaken identity during his round that had caused him to wonder if he had a double or doppelgänger in the mountains. He was greeted warmly by a couple in Glasgow Climbing Centre in late January 2000 who thanked him for sharing a bottle of champagne and a hip-flask full of Macallan in the shelter on Ben Nevis on Hogmanay 1999. This was not Hugh, who had been seeing in the millennium with his future wife. Later, in 2004, when walking into the Monadhliath hills he was chastised by a man who advised him to stay away, because 'I should be ashamed of myself for ruining his talk at Glenmore the previous night.' Again, Hugh says he had been with his then wife, Angela.

Covid again

It was a general feature of this year that many Munroists referred to delays in compleation or changes to Munro celebrations because of Covid restrictions.

Covid disrupted John Findlay's (7003) compleation. He had hoped to finish in 2020. Eventually he planned to compleat in August 2021 with a group of friends. Unfortunately his grandson tested positive on the Friday and he himself did so on the day of compleation! The logistics of arranging another date to suit everyone proved impossible so his subsequent compleation on the Sgùrr na Cìche ridge was a solo walk.

John Marjoram (7016) also compleated on his own owing to Covid, although he did say that at his age most of his friends had retired from climbing Munros or were harbouring injuries. His wife and daughter had provided him with a special T-shirt to put on at the summit. A friendly Scottish lady whom he passed on his descent told him there was no need to celebrate with others today – you can do it tomorrow, next week or next year.

Historical interest

Brian McLeish (7004) compleated on Meall nan Ceapraichean with an interesting twist of history. His great-great-grandfather, Kenneth McLennan, lived in the Grey House on the north side of the bridge over the River Lael 170 years ago, between 1850 and 1860. Describing his Munro journey, Brian recalled signing to join the Lairig Club on bajans' (freshers') day at Aberdeen University in 1970. At some stage (inevitably) he encountered Andy Nisbet (107) and Alf Robertson (116).

Kalina Slusarska (6989) on Ben More (Mull), 29 April 2021.
Photo: Ann Wierzbicka.

Audry Dasnoy (7090) on her final Munro, Beinn Sgulaird, in November 2021.
Photo: Jamie Acutt.

Over his time at Aberdeen they inveigled him into various madcap Munro wheezes, one of which involved getting soaked climbing An Teallach in full kit and overnighting at Shenaval with Ken McLean (115). Ken, Andy and Brian decided to keep their wet kit on and climbed into their sleeping bags warm and wet. This worked well, and they had the added bonus of watching Alf struggle into the freezing-cold and wet long-johns he had taken off the night before.

Donald P. Ramsay (6972) lives in an 1850 former farmworker's cottage. When he first viewed the house there was a plaque presented to the late homeowner from the Rotary Club of Auchterarder acknowledging his achievement of bagging all the Munros twice. Donald hopes to be the second owner of the cottage to do two rounds of the Munros.

Munroists from further afield and abroad

A rare foreign visitor compleating in these Covid times was Henning Rische (7013) of Winterbach in Germany, who finished on 23 August 2021 on Càrn an Fhìdhleir. Of course this was another trip originally planned in 2020. Fast-forward to 2021 and with the help of a Covid test package under international travel regulations he was able to fly to Scotland.

Peter V. Wallace (6910) compleated the Munros from Sussex, assisted by the fact that his work frequently took him to Edinburgh or Glasgow, usually on a Friday, which enabled a Munro extension and often a return from Inverness. He let it be known he would be seriously disgruntled if his Scottish responsibilities were taken off him, but his southern-based colleagues were more than happy to let him keep them.

Challenges

Neil Paterson (7015) described a journey that followed a change of life when at 16 years old he was over 19 stone with asthma. He dedicated his round to his dad, who waited at the car park for him as he came down.

John R. Martin (6961) had a remarkable gap in his Munro journey. After climbing 250 Munros he developed arthritis and was not able to add to his tally for 24 years between 1994 and 2018. Three years ago a new drug régime enabled him to finally compleat.

Lynne Wightman said she didn't really start the Munros in earnest until her first kidney transplant, donated by her dad, Derek. 14 years later she needed another kidney transplant, this time donated by her partner Tom. Within six months she was back climbing Munros with Tom. She said that success really belonged to Derek and Tom for their love, support and generosity.

Special celebrations

Ruairidh Cooper (6865) compleated in October, with the number of friends joining him being limited by the Covid restrictions. He and two friends enjoyed a nip of Chivas Brothers' 21-year-old Royal Salute that his mother had given him ten years previously especially for the occasion.

Alistair Jeffs (7028) compleated in September 2021 on Seana Bràigh with the Moray Mountaineering Club and a party at Magoo's Bothy. This involved clove-hitched fairy lights, homemade cake with risk-assessed 282 safety candles, kegs of craft beer, a selection of whiskies, a Barbados rum, a full cheeseboard with fruit bowl, books, an engraved whisky glass and locally crafted tumbler, and lots of other goodies along with banter, friendliness and kindness.

Alan MacBeth (7008) finished on Creag Mhòr with a piper (Ewan McIntosh) playing in a gorilla suit.

Barry Veitch (6986) compleated on Stùc a' Chroin and said he intended to get his number tattooed on his arm.

Statistics

Comparing this year's data with last year (in parenthesis), we have the following statistics. New Munroists totalled 235 (117), with the 7000 marker passed in the second half of the year. Females comprised 25% (28%), people resident in Scotland 76% (63%), and couples 9% (8%). The average age was 53 (55), the average compleation time was 27 years (25 years), and there were 11 Golden Munroists (6).

Fraser Wallace (6939) was the youngest compleator to register, aged 17, having started the Munros when 12.

This year's Golden Munroists were Chris Jones (6901, taking 62 years), Robin Sloan (6922, 52), Tom Robertson (6937, 53), John R. Martin (6961, 53), Brian McLeish (7004, 50), Gilbert McCurdy (7033, 50), Will Moran (7037, 62), John Melvin (7054, 50), William Stephens (7074, 55), Andy Ravenhill (7089, 50), and John Digney (7096, 52). Ian Ragg registered in 2020 and should also have been mentioned as a Golden Munroist (6793, 50).

The most popular finishing Munros were Ben More on Mull (26), Beinn Sgritheall (14), Beinn na Lap (10), and Ben Lomond (9). The most popular first Munros were Cairn Gorm, Lochnagar, Ben Vorlich (Loch Earn), Ben Lomond, Schiehallion and Ben Nevis.

AMENDMENTS

No	Name	M	T	F	C	G	D
5470	Will Copestake	2014			2017		
5674	Paul Johnston	2014					
		2020					
4274	Graham Lewis	2009			2018		2019
5735	David Sothern	2015					
		2020					
2756	Joy Biggin	2002	2013		2006	2013	
2757	Paul Biggin	2002	2013		2006	2013	
1221	John Wilson	1993	1997		2017		2021
		1999					
		2007					
3814	Richard Kermode	2007	2019		2021		
		2021					
6471	Robert Tully	2017			2019	2021	2019
2672	Alistair Little	2001		2020	2017		
5263	Andy Clifford	2013			2021		
891	Lynn M. Youngs	1990		2017	1997	2005	
		1998			2018		
		2017					
1806	Ross Jervis	1997	2012	2011	2010	2016	2011
		2013					
		2021					
2349	Fiona Wild	2000			2021		
2350	Roger Wild*	2000			2021		
5394	Pavel Hubacek	2013			2021		
		2021					
4108	Charles Kilner	2008	2015	2009	2021		
4734	Sheila Snowden	2011	2011	2009	2021		
4397	Robin Jeffries	2009			2021		
114	Donald Smith	1973	1982	1982	1997	2015	2016
		1988					
		2010					
5110	Bernard Taylor	2012			2021		
1335	James Fish	1994		2007	2021		
2884	Norman Fraser	2002			2007	2019	2021
					2010		
					2013		
1558	Andy Heald	1996	2007	2019	2011		2016
		2014					
		2021					
855	Alan Patrick	1990					2021
4343	Roy R. Smart	2009					2021
600	Hugh Shercliff	1987	2006	1990			
		2021					
573	Tommy Hepburn	1988	1988	2015			
		2014	2014				
5885	Chris Lord	2015			2021		

No.	Name						
4762	Alasdair Cairns	2011 2014 2021			2021		
2871	Peter Hamilton	1992 2002 2008 2013	2017	2002	1997 2011	2019	2021
5568	Derek Hepburn	2014			2019		2021
1260	Brian Cowie	1993 2021					
6255	Janet Reid	2010			2021		
6256	Walter Reid	2010			2021		
3136	Richard Speirs	2004	2004	2002	2019		2021
2393	Dale Allen	2000 2021			2014	2018	
3653	Robert Allan	2006			2014	2018	
5107	Susan Hamilton	2012			2021		
5062	Ruth Mitchell	2012			2021		
5834	Steven Allen	2015 2021					
3366	Anne Butler	2005 2010 2011 2012 2014	2017	2017	2010 2021	2018	2017
3472	Guy Froud	2005 2021			2018		
4288	Donald Forrest	2009			2021		
3217	Ian Ratcliffe	2004 2011 2021			2013		
3865	James Bussey	2007			2021		
359	Alf Barnard	1984 2004 2021	1985 2004 2021	1998	2019		
4615	Julian Fletcher	2010		2021			
4449	Scott Gourlay	2009					2021
4756	Jean Gaskell	2011		2018			
4757	Derek Caborn	2011		2018			
6843	Philip Nelson	2020		2021			
1626	Cameron Johnston	1996 2021	1996				
6275	Sunny He Huang	2017 2020		2021			
6740	Alison Coull *	2000 2021	2018	2019	2008	2015	2018
3000	Michael Urquart	2003			2021	2021	
4381	Simon Sawers	2009 2021	2010	2014	2021	2021	

308   SCOTTISH MOUNTAINEERING CLUB JOURNAL

No.	Name						
3934	Alastair Govan	2007, 2021	2010	2014	2015	2021	
4483	William Forbes*	1986, 2009, 2016	1995	2002	2002, 2015, 2021	2006, 2018	2014
2897	Barry Parker	2003		1995	2021		
3451	Michael Bird	2005			2021		
5883	Chris Abrams	2015			2021		2013
4696	Michael Feliks	1987	1992		2007	2021	
1946	David Brown	1998, 2021			2009		
5874	O. Fraser Clark	2015			2021		2004
4604	Simon Cornelius	2010			2021		
3481	Rick Salter	2005		2007	2013	2016	2021
3523	Jenny Hatfield	2005		2007	2013	2016	2021
2982	George Gallacher	2003			2017	2021	2013
2900	Richard Baker	2003	2011			2021	
6792	Angela Ning	2020					2021
6793	Ian Ragg	2020					2021
4328	Dorothy Stirling	2009, 2011, 2012, 2014, 2018, 2021	2021	2019	2010	2016	2014
6627	David Thompson	2019	2020	2021			
6437	Michelle Haining	2018, 2021					
4234	Elizabeth Stewart	2008				2018	2021
1351	Margaret Beattie	1994, 2000, 2005			2007	2016	2021
5666	John Rosie	2014, 2021			2021		
5759	Mark Willingham	2015	2018				2021
2031	Robert J. Cattanach	2014, 2021					
166	Terry Moore	1978, 2010	1982		2021		
4396	Mark Gibson	2009	2013	2016	2015	2021	2021
5522	Colin Stuart	2014				2021	
5577	Neil A Milloy	2014				2021	2021
3987	Colin Lees	3987, 2007, 2011, 2016	2004	2012	2013	2019	2021
4695	Paul Fitzpatrick	2008			2021		
2649	William S. Maxwell	2001, 2021	2001	2001			

No.	Name						
5089	Neil Kitching	2012	2021				
4883	David Williamson	2011 2021	2011	2011	2017		
3545	Andy Sutton	2006		2005	2012	2018	2021
4949	Duncan Buchanan	2011 2014 2018					2021
4650	Fiona P. Duncan	2010			2021		
2321	Adam J. Turek	2000			2021		
	Simon Glover			1982			
5361	Fiona Clark	2013 2017	2021	2015	2019		
5362	Stuart Clark	2013 2017	2021	2015	2019		
3631	Gordon Roberts	2006			2014	2021	

With last year's figures in parenthesis, in 2021 I heard from 97 (63) people requesting amendments to entries on our Lists, as follows: New Munro Rounds 20 (15), Tops 10 (5), Furths 8 (5), Corbetts 33 (13), Grahams 13 (8), Donalds 21 (16), and Full House 3 (7).

The Donalds continue to be popular, and helpfully most people confirm that they compleated the Donald Tops as well. The total is now 141 summits with the inclusion of Dugland (see *SMCJ*, 48/212 (2020), 296). Alan Patrick (855) noted that the announcement mentioned in *SMCJ*, 47/211 (2019), 252–3 was a bit of a blow. It meant revisiting a few areas of 'less than outstanding interest … just to pick off an obscure lump of heather' although he did say there is perhaps no such thing as a bad hill if the weather is right and the wildlife is abounding. He conceded that his day on Beninner, a subsidiary top of Cairnsmore of Carsphairn, was in fairness a decent day out.

Simon Sawers (4381) and Alastair Govan (3934) had a mega-weekend of compleations in August. On the Friday they compleated a joint second round of the Munros, followed on Saturday by a joint Corbett compleation and a Graham compleation for Alastair.

Dale Allan (2393) recorded a family set of compleations, with his son Robert Allan (3653) registering a second round of Munros, a round of Corbetts and a round of Grahams.

I rather enjoyed Charles Kilner's account of his Corbett journey with his wife Sheila Snowden (4734). He told me that his first Corbett was in 1974 with a round of the Arran Hills of Beinn Nuis, Beinn Tarsuinn, Cìr Mhòr and Goat Fell, walking to and from the ferry. He was aged 10 and said his father always had ambitious holiday plans and dragged him and his mother on the round on a very poor wet-weather August day. They made it to the last ferry in fading evening light, running down the road. His father was very proud of his achievement. Charles just remembers being cold, wet, and at times quite scared as his father had vastly underestimated the arduousness of the difficulties and scrambling to say the least. It did however have a marked effect on him, not putting him off but instilling a desire for the hills that remains just as strong to this day.

In contrast Sheila climbed Meall a' Bhuachaille as her first Corbett. Their last Corbett was Sgùrr a' Choire-bheithe and perhaps in keeping with the spirit of those first Arran Corbetts they went by canoe down Loch Cuaich, also taking in

Alan Patrick (855) compleating the Donalds on Meikle Millyea, 12 June 2021 with his daughter Katie. Photo: Andrew Patrick.

the Graham Slat Bheinn for a wonderful, arduous and rugged day out with heavy snow-showers on the summit.

Will Copestake (5470) registered a 2017 round of the Corbetts, which he did as a continuous round from October 2016 to May 2017. He nicknamed his project 'Coldest Corbett'.

SMC amendments were sparse. Roger Wild (2350) compleated a round of the Corbetts with his wife Fiona (2349). Bill Forbes (4483) compleated a third round of Corbetts. Your Clerk compleated a second round of Munros on An Socach in Glen Affric. This was the same day as the Carnethy Munros-in-a-day challenge, so I can confirm that the weather was not ideal in the North-West.

The total number of Full Housers (by our SMC criteria) is now 69, with 73 Full Houses registered taking account of people who have done more than one Full House. The term Full House was introduced in *SMCJ*, 41/201 (2010) by our previous Clerk, Dave Broadhead, simply to denote compleation of a full line of the compleations of the hills on the SMC register. (The term is used by bingo players when they fill a complete line, although Dave insists that he has never played bingo.) The Full House Table is set out below. New Full Houses this year were Donald Smith (114) – Grahams & Donalds; Peter Hamilton (2871) – Donalds; and Mark Gibson (4386) – Grahams & Donalds.

FULL HOUSE TABLE

FH	No	Name	M	T	F	C	G	D
1=	763	Brian Curle	1990	1991	1991	1992	2000	1994
1=	1298	Graham Illing	1994	1997	1996	1998	2000	2000
1=	319	Ken P. Whyte	1984	1987	1987	2000	2000	2000
1=	816	Rob Woodall	1990	1995	1990	1995	2000	1992
5	1452	Eddie Dealty	1995	1995	1994	2001	2001	1997
6=	452	Ann Bowker	1986	1986	1983	1992	1999	2002
6=	1196	Alan Holmes	1993	1993	1993	1997	2002	1997

6=	1197	George Morl	1993	1993	1993	1997	2002	1997
6=	121	Don Smithies	1973	2001	1998	1996	2000	2002
10	2494	Rhona Fraser**	1984	1995	1997	1990	2003	2000
11	678	Stuart Benn	1989	1989	1990	1996	2000	2004
12=	2606	Colin Crawford	2001	2006	2001	2006	2006	1996
12=	1331	John Mackay	1994	1994	1997	2003	2006	2002
14	5896	Iain Thow*	1984	2004	1994	2004	2007	2004
15=	2009	Alan Dawson	1998	1998	1987	2006	2008	2001
15=	959	Mike Dixon*	1991	2008	2000	1996	2002	2005
17=	387	Richard Fuller	1984	1984	1985	2001	2009	2009
17=	1311	Terry Fuller	1994	1994	1994	2002	2009	2009
17=	276	Gerry Knight	1982	1982	1983	1997	2009	1986
17=	327	Stewart Logan	1981	1981	1981	1984	2009	2000
17=	1432	Karl Nelson	1995	1995	1996	2009	2009	2009
22	539	Diana J. Harkins	1986	2010	1989	2009	2009	2009
23	4691	Frank Baillie	1997	1999	2011	2009	2010	2008
24=	3112	Bert Barnett	2001	2002	2002	1998	2000	2012
24=	1711	Stewart Newman	1997	1998	1998	2006	2011	2012
24=	319	Ken P. Whyte (FH 2)	2010	2011	2011	2012	2012	2012
27=	256	Hugh F. Barron	1981	1997	1988	2002	2013	2010
27=	225	Alan L. Brook	1980	1980	1978	2004	2013	2010
27=	62	Hamish M. Brown*	1965	1965	1967	1976	2013	1982
27=	4305	Michael Earnshaw	2009	2013	2010	2011	2012	2011
27=	3112	Bert Barnett (FH 2)	2001	2009	2007	2007	2009	2013
27=	2291	Neil Sandilands	1999	2013	2004	2006	2009	2008
33=	4483	William A. Forbes*	1986	1995	2002	2002	2006	2014
33=	2269	George Henderson	1999	2014	2005	2004	2010	2010
33=	2268	Susan Henderson	1999	2014	2005	2004	2010	2010
33=	23	Miles Hutchinson*	1955	1955	1970	1992	2009	2014
33=	1933	Dave Irons	1998	2005	2005	2010	2013	2014
33=	1746	James King	1997	1997	2014	2003	2014	2014
39=	1911	Martin J. Almond	1997	1997	2014	2012	2015	2013
39=	3885	David S. Batty	1994	2011	2013	2014	2015	2014
39=	1170	Elaine S. Fenton	1993	2014	1994	2010	2015	2015
39=	1169	Garth Fenton	1993	2014	1994	2010	2015	2013
39=	2003	Bob Macdonald	1998	2006	2006	2006	2015	2014
44=	2346	David Allison	2000	2003	2002	2008	2016	2011
44=	1806	Ross Gervis	1997	2012	2011	2010	2016	2011
44=	1874	Bryan Rynne	1997	1997	1997	2009	2016	2009
44=	114	Donald Smith	1973	1982	1982	1997	2015	2016
48=	5506	Alistair Deering	2014	2015	2017	2015	2017	2016
48=	2991	Ewan J. Lyons	2003	2009	2012	2009	2016	2017
48=	4006	Chris Pine	2007	2017	2015	2012	2013	2014
48=	4151	Norman Wares	2008	2010	2011	2014	2017	2015
52=	3366	Anne Butler	2005	2017	2017	2010	2018	2017
52=	1432	Karl Nelson (FH 2)	2009	2009	2010	2018	2018	2018
52=	3112	Bert Barnett (FH 3)	2009	2015	2015	2013	2018	2017
52=	480	Andrew Finnimore	1986	1986	1986	2003	2013	2018
52=	2795	Maria R. Hybszer	2002	2018	2013	2006	2012	2012
52=	4033	Donald F. Irvine	2002	2002	2008	2015	2018	2016
52=	1279	Nigel P. Morters	1994	2009	2016	1999	2015	2018

52=	6749	Kenny Robb*	1980	1982	2018	1990	2015	2018
52=	5505	Allison Robertson	2014	2018	2017	2015	2017	2017
52=	1635	Eric Young	1996	2018	2006	2001	2005	2010
62=	6740	Alison Coull*	2000	2018	2019	2008	2015	2018
62=	3990	Christine Gordon	1998	2000	2007	2017	2019	2013
62=	798	Margaret Graham	1990	2013	2019	2004	2014	2019
62=	1891	Dave Marshall	1993	2015	2018	2014	2018	2019
62=	5057	Robert Philips	2012	2019	2017	2013	2014	2015
62=	2433	Alan Rowan	2000	2019	2011	2009	2019	2019
62=	2610	Tony Smith	2001	2001	2001	2010	2016	2019
62=	4328	Dorothy Stirling	2009	2019	2019	2010	2016	2014
70=	6755	Peter G.C. Ellis	2005	2017	2015	2018	2020	2020
70=	4120	Frank Johnston	2003	2019	2016	2011	2020	2019
70=	2345	Graham Phillips	2000	2000	2001	2013	2019	2020
70=	455	Laurence Rudkin	1986	1991	1989	1995	2005	2020
70=	1798	Colin P. Watts	1997	2020	2003	2007	2012	2018
70=	2579	Isabel Watts	2001	2020	2003	2007	2012	2018
76=	4396	Mark Gibson	2009	2013	2016	2015	2021	2021
76=	2871	Peter Hamilton	1992	2017	2002	1997	2019	2021

In summary, whilst life in 2021 still felt far from normal for all of us, access to the hills was generally much easier and there was much more of a sense that we were moving into a different phase of the pandemic.

Many thanks to the SMC Webmaster, Martin McKenna, for helping sort out various matters. It remains a long-term objective to move to online registration. Thanks also to Mike Watson, who is responsible for uploading compleation photos, and to Chris Huntley, Keeper of Regalia. Robin Campbell is always on hand for any historical queries.

Registration to our six Lists is done by writing to me, Alison Coull, 258/1 Ferry Road, EDINBURGH, EH5 3AN or e-mailing smcmunroclerk@smc.org.uk. For a Munro or Corbett compleation certificate please enclose an A4 s.a.e. (with correct postage – large letter). Check <www.smc.org.uk> for further details and to view the picture galleries of compleationists celebrating their final summit.

Enjoy your hills.

Alison Coull (Clerk of the List).

SCOTTISH MOUNTAIN ACCIDENTS 2021

Mountain rescue in Scotland is coordinated by Police Scotland. The police receive the initial alert through the 999 system and, if appropriate, contact the local Mountain Rescue Team (MRT). There are 28 voluntary civilian Mountain Rescue Teams in Scotland, 25 of which are members of the representative body, Scottish Mountain Rescue. Each MRT is an independent organisation that submits information annually to the Statistician of SMR, whose Statistical Report for 2021 collates the information received from the 25 civilian teams and three Police Scotland teams. This informative report, covering the calendar year from 1 January to 31 December 2021, can be accessed readily at <https://www.scottishmountainrescue.org/wp-content/uploads/2022/05/SMR-Statistics-Report-2021.pdf>, and owing to space constraints only limited data are presented in this year's *SMCJ*. It should always be borne in mind that three important mountain rescue teams – Cairngorm, Glencoe and Lochaber – are not members of the SMR organisation, so their rescues are not included in its annual reports.

The continuing Covid-19 epidemic and the attendant restrictions on travel made 2021 an abnormal year for Scottish mountain accidents, with a total of 951 'activations', and for several of the teams it was the busiest on record. The authors of the Statistical Report, Tom Adams and Andy Morgan, mention an interesting trend.

> An ongoing theme of discussion has been a possible change in the type and location of call-outs received. This is evident in the numbers of call-outs received in different Police Divisions of Scotland over recent years. The number of call-outs in some, often more remote, regions (Highlands & Islands, Dumfries & Galloway, Ayrshire) has remained fairly stable, while other areas closer to urban centres have seen notable increases (highest ever number of call-outs in Fife, Edinburgh, Lothians & Borders, Forth Valley, and Tayside).

On studying the table below, which summarises accident statistics over the last five years, the reader will see that it was summer 'hillwalking' rather than technical climbing that accounted for last year's increase.

Activity	Annual Number of Incidents				
	2017	**2018**	**2019**	**2020**	**2021**
Hillwalking (summer)	158	151	188	191	248
Hillwalking (winter)	47	75	41	84	82
Rock climbing	5	6	7	8	4
Scrambling	4	2	2	4	10
Snow & ice climbing	1	5	5	2	1
MRT activity	1	0	0	0	0
Total	**216**	**239**	**243**	**289**	**345**

It is worth pointing out that Tayside MRT rejoined SMR in 2021, having been absent from the organisation since 2016, so the year-to-year comparison is very slightly misleading.

Moffat MRT Accident Reports for 2021

I am grateful to Chris Huntley of Moffat MRT for these reports. – HON. ED.

03 Jan Injury to person sledging on slopes on outskirts of Moffat. Team assisted with stretcher-carry to roadside and handover to ambulance service.

21 Jan Team deployed to search for missing walker out on hill after dark. Missing person spotted Team's headtorches and made her way towards them. A very wet, cold night.

Feb–May During this period [owing to the Covid-19 pandemic] Scottish Ambulance Service were concerned that they might be overwhelmed with demand. Moffat MRT did make themselves available for low-clinical-risk casualties in a higher-risk environment needing speedier evacuation. In fact resource not required.

11 Feb Female with lower leg injury whilst walking on Southern Upland Way near Wanlockhead. Casualty evacuated from scene by Coastguard helicopter.

22-Feb Female walker with suspected break in lower leg on Tinto. Team transported casualty to pick up position for transfer to helicopter that landed further down the hill.

27 Mar Assisting Strathclyde Police MRT in search for high-risk missing person. Person found unharmed in Thornhill.

14 Apr Rescue of fallen dog at Grey Mare's Tail, Moffat. Some difficulty in locating dog from above. Dog uninjured despite lengthy fall. Rescue generated more press coverage than any for humans.

09 May Female with suspected lower leg break on slopes of Hart Fell. Team stretchered casualty back to road.

31 May Female with open leg fracture whilst walking on Tinto. Recovery largely handled by Ambulance Service as low on the hill. Helicopter lifted casualty from scene.

22 June Female injured at bottom of ravine under a bridge on outskirts of Moffat. Technical lift of stretcher in confined, awkward location. Very midgy. Ambulance and Fire Service present.

30 Jun Female with suspected broken ankle on Tinto. Team transported casualty by wheeled stretcher to roadside.

06 Jul Male Mountain biker unwell in Mabie forest. After callout to MRT, bystanders managed to transport casualty to roadside and then hospital.

11 Jul Male mountain biker in Forest of Ae with reported head injury. Team called, but less serious than first indicated. Biker extracted by local quad-bike.

20 Jul Male paraglider with broken ankle on summit of Tinto. Helicopter lifted casualty from summit and transported him to lower slopes. Team carried casualty on stretcher to ambulance.

07 Sep Team on standby to assist nearby team to search for missing mountain biker. Found before Team fully deployed.

20 Sep On standby to start search for missing child. Turned up in morning safe.

28 Oct   Team on standby during severe wet weather and rising river levels. Team vehicle deployed to support delivery of medicines to house inaccessible by district nurse's vehicle.

28 Dec   Lost walkers on lower slopes of Criffel at dusk. Team used Phone Find to locate exact position and quickly found the walkers cold but uninjured.

28 Dec   On same evening a runner reported by mobile that they were lost in Dalbeattie Forest. Moffat and Galloway teams called out. A short while later, mobile 'phone text and audio were no longer functioning; but runner found that they could communicate by WhatsApp and actually download What3words. Using What3words, exact position now identified and runner found. Very cold but uninjured. Interesting combination of 'phone Apps to achieve good result.

31 Dec   Small group of visitors to Wanlockhead walking back to accommodation on previous evening but one of party did not arrive. Telephone call indicated he was on bridge at burn through village. No further communication. Initial searches completed by local police and then Team called to support. Just before daylight, missing person found having missed accommodation and kept walking. Walker had overshot the village and only turned after seeing Team torches behind him.

Cairngorm MRT Accident Reports for 2021

I am grateful to Iain Cornfoot of Cairngorm MRT for these reports. – HON. ED.

01 Jan   Search for vulnerable male in Aviemore area. 32.4 man-hours.

06 Feb   Walker fell on ice and fractured his right ankle. 18 man-hours.

29 Apr   Walker with a broken ankle evacuated from Culra bothy by rescue helicopter. 2 man-hours.

30 Apr   Skier in guided group fell, dislocating her shoulder. 21 man-hours.

01 May   Male reported overdue from camping in the Lairig Ghru. Police found him camping near the path. 15 man-hours.

05 Jun   Female with pain in ankle whilst walking out of Lairig Ghru. Companion also exhausted after long day on the hill. Two CMRT members walked to Rothiemurchus path junction to escort the pair back to Land Rover. 6 man-hours.

12 Jun   Reports of injured male requiring assistance in the Shelterstone Crag area. Male had taken a leader fall and was lowered off the climb to the base. Self-rescued to ski area car park. 40 man-hours.

17 Jun   Female suffered head injury on Fiacaill ridge. Evacuated by rescue helicopter. 9 man-hours.

22 Jun   Missing persons were lost over the back of Cairn Gorm. Weather was settled and warm. 2.5 man-hours.

26 Jun   Personal item found at the top of Huntly's Cave; police asked for assistance to search area. Nothing found. 3 man-hours.

29 Jun   Ben Alder area. 18-year-old fell on path, hurting previous back injury, and was unable to continue walking. No aircraft available at start of rescue. 11 team members deployed to meet estate RIB. Helicopter became available and recovered the injured party. 32.2 man-hours.

14 Jul   Party of two on Braeriach, male with ankle injury, feeling cold and dizzy. Helicopter flown direct to location. Two CMRT standing by at base. 5 man-hours.

24 Jul   Unspecified location. 70-year-old could not walk owing to severe back pain, most likely muscular. Very hot weather. 10 man-hours.

02 Aug   Bynack More. Female twisted her knee. She managed to continue to walk off with team members to ATV. 54 man-hours.

09 Aug   Female sustained 2 fractures to ankle, stretchered out of Lairig Ghru to Rothiemurchus lodge. 55 man-hours.

17 Aug   Two persons became lost in the mist on the east side of Cairn Gorm when returning from Loch Avon and Ben Macdui. Directed them via 'phone compass back to Ptarmigan building, where they were met by Team vehicle. 14 man-hours.

18 Aug   Two missing persons lost around Cairn Lochan. Received position from 'phone. Three CMRT groups went to locate and escort off the mountain. 108 man-hours.

24 Aug   Male, mountain biker, fell while descending Càrn Bàn Mòr path, sustaining lower leg injury. Evacuated by rescue helicopter after diverting from another tasking. 22.5 man-hours.

26 Aug   Male fell whilst mountain biking around south side of Loch an Eilein. Rib and wrist fractures, possible upper leg injury. 8 man-hours.

30 Aug   Two males missing overnight in Ben Macdui area. 22.5 man-hours.

30 Aug   Two females became lost and walked out by Strath Nethy after 'phoning police. Met by two members of the team in Land Rover at Bynack Stables. 21 man-hours.

05 Sep   Female slipped in boulder field, dislocating shoulder. 66.5 man-hours.

06 Sep   Party of six. Instructor fell, suffering a head injury whilst descending into Lairig Ghru. Evacuated by rescue helicopter. 36 man-hours.

10 Sep   Female fell when walking dog on Speyside Way, possible fracture or dislocation. SAS in attendance asked for assistance to evacuate casualty. 20 man-hours.

15 Sep   Glen Einich. Male fell whilst mountain biking, injuring chest, neck and shoulder. 7.5 man-hours.

24 Sep   Female with dislocated knee in Strath Nethy. Evacuated by rescue helicopter. 6.8 man-hours.

06 Oct   Party of two reported lost in the Strath Nethy area. No torch when darkness fell. 60 man-hours.

09 Oct   Party of two became separated around Loch nan Cnapan, unable to locate second member. 48 man-hours.

10 Oct   Search carried on from last night, missing person spent two nights out unplanned and was located by helicopter at Corrour bothy. 152 man-hours.

14 Oct   Two males missing overnight. They made sporadic contact with family and were found high up on Mòine Mòr Land Rover track at 11.30 a.m. Unlikely to have been able to make their way off mountain without help. 36 man-hours.

20 Oct   Family of three became lost and very cold after walking through Lairig Ghru from Deeside. They complained of being cold and possibly not being able to continue. 45.5 man-hours.

07 Nov   Lone male in difficulty owing to wintry weather at summit of Ben Macdui, warmed up briefly and walked back to Cairn Gorm car-park. 24 man-hours.

13 Nov   Two walkers without torch or maps became lost on way back from Ben Macdui. 10 man-hours.

21 Nov Party of two struggled to navigate their way from Braeriach and requested assistance. They walked off after getting cold! Full team stood down and a small group escorted them down. 60 man-hours.

04 Dec Party of two avalanched in *Crotched Gully*, Coire an t-Sneachda; fell 7m on to gear, lower leg fracture; stretchered out from rescue box in corrie to car-park. 159.6 man-hours.

05 Dec Two males missing overnight, located by rescue helicopter in Lairig Ghru at 09.30, south of Pools of Dee. 65 man-hours.

05 Dec Two walkers, one sustained knee injury whilst walking in waist-deep snow. Picked up by aircraft, 13 team members standing by at base. 19.5 man-hours.

I am grateful to Lisa Hutchison for collating the MRT reports. – Hon. Ed.

IN MEMORIAM

DERWENT TURNBULL j. 1949

The death of my father, Derwent Turnbull, eight days short of his hundredth birthday, brings to an end a family connection with the SMC going back over 90 years. His father, Professor Herbert Turnbull, joined the Club in 1930 and served as President between 1948 and 1950. His younger cousin Oliver Turnbull, who died in 2002, was the Club's lively Meets Secretary from 1996.

My father served in the Navy during the war, at the naval air station at Crail and in an aircraft carrier in the Pacific. One of his first actions on demobilisation was a visit to the Matterhorn with his father in 1949. They climbed the Hörnli ridge in distinctly iffy conditions, bad enough weather that they had the hill to themselves, which was unusual even in the 1940s. When we watched the TV broadcast of Jamie Andrew's climb there, my dad was disgusted by the amount of fixed cable now defacing the mountain. During the same trip he climbed Monte Rosa along with my mother. They married in 1947 and their honeymoon is still recorded in the visitors' book at the Inveroran Hotel.

During the late 1940s and early 1950s he accompanied his father to various SMC meets, joining the Club in 1949. Continued service in aircraft carriers then limited his attendance until after his father's death in 1961. He was an irregular attender through the 1960s, climbing with John Hartog and W.H. Murray among others. He served on the Committee between 1966 and 1969.

*Derwent Turnbull
on Alpine granite.*

He climbed, at a fairly modest standard, in the Lake District and Scotland in summer and winter. On one occasion he found himself climbing behind Dougal Haston: they were stuck together in the Glen Coe hut in foul weather when their respective partners had failed to show up. His climbing was what was then called 'bold' and nowadays would be 'dangerous and irresponsible'. The style, learned from his father, involved minimal use of protection, the principle that the leader must not fall, and a cultivation of the art of climbing down – this both for its own sake and as an escape from dangerous situations such as when, as leader, he strayed off-route and into VS ground on Esk Buttress on Scafell Pike. As another example, with his cousin Oliver he once short-cutted across Loch Avon in the Cairngorms during a vigorous thaw. (Well, the Garbh Uisge can be troublesome in spate.) In the middle of the loch the ice was groaning under their feet and they were paddling ankle deep in warm water on top of it. Later Oliver told me: 'I knew it would be all right. Derwent was a member of the SMC.' My father's comment was: 'It was no more risky than the normal sort of climbing we did in those days.'

Abroad, he took part enthusiastically in several meets of the *Section Genevois* of the SAC, including one where I believe he was guided up the second ascent of a *Fissure en Z* somewhere above the Aletsch Glacier.

At a meet in the 1960s he was tipped off by Bill Murray about a small wood-lined house, the former youth hostel, up for sale in Alligin village on Loch Torridon. Unfortunately, the closing date was at noon the following day. My father stopped off at a 'phone box and made an offer for it sight unseen. From then on visits to Loch Torridon were frequent, in summer and at New Year, and he climbed on all the nearby hills, often in company with fellow Alligin resident Charlie Rose. Charlie, like others, was astonished by his casual style of protection.

In 1971 he was asked to work on the *Northern Highlands Volume II* (Torridon) guidebook, and invited me to collaborate. We were not especially qualified, not being VS people – I gathered that the original guidebook writer had suffered a mishap on Everest. Our most significant achievement was the upgrading of the *Cioch Nose* from Bonington and Patey's original 'Diff to end all Diffs' to a more realistic Hard V Diff.

Through the 1990s his enthusiasm for the Alps continued, on panoramic paths and hut nights with his second wife Genny and their two children.

Outside climbing he was an aeronautical engineer and weather forecaster in the Royal Navy, a lecturer at Dundee University, and a keen amateur musician. His son Ronald (me) continues the family tradition – ÖAV rather than SMC, I'm afraid – as a fellwalker and guidebook writer.

Ronald Turnbull

NORMAN TODD j. 1964

In his survey of climbs in the Northern Highlands, written in the spring of 1951, Frank Cunningham dismissed Beinn Lair in the Whitbread wilderness as *terra incognita*. By the end of that summer three pioneering groups had explored its 5km of cliffs and discovered a score of routes in 'an amazing burst of rock-climbing activity,' as J.H.B. Bell described it. In the vanguard was a party from Glasgow University MC that included Stewart Orr, Douglas Hutchison, Angela Hood and the 23-year-old Norman Todd, with Todd's new line being *Rose Route* on the Molar Buttress, which he climbed with John Smith. Unlike his carefree

student companions, however, Todd was a house surgeon in Inverness who had to be back at hospital on Monday morning. Having hastened over the bealach to Letterewe on Sunday evening and crossed Loch Maree by boat, Todd would recall in later years how he had despaired of hitching a lift on deserted roads. 'A car stopped. Here my luck changed as the driver was Colonel Whitbread's, driving to Inverness to pick up his employer from the London sleeper next morning. He took me right back to the hospital, and I was able to reward him with a very early breakfast there. Now, 60 years on, it's hard to remember how much sleep I could have had, if any; but after all, sleep deprivation went with that job.'

Norman Alexander Todd was born in 1928 and brought up in Paisley, where his father was headmaster of the ancient Grammar School, and as a pupil he excelled at classics, winning prizes for Greek. After graduating in medicine at Glasgow University he held a National Service commission in the RAMC, serving on troopships and at the military hospital in Münster, Germany. On leaving the Army he spent some time in general practice before specialising in psychiatry, meeting his future wife, Susanne Friedländer, while they were both working at a hospital in Cambridge. After returning to Scotland he was appointed consultant psychiatrist at Leverndale Hospital in Glasgow and later became deputy physician superintendent, eventually retiring in 1990. Although Todd published several papers on forensic psychiatry and was a Fellow of the Royal Colleges of Physicians and of Psychiatrists, he will be remembered above all for his dedication and kindness to his patients, some of whom had very challenging illnesses.

Todd joined the GUMC as a young undergraduate, climbing at Arrochar with Scott Johnstone as early as 1946 and making annual June visits to Glenbrittle in Skye. By the early 1950s he had climbed many of the standard routes in Glen Coe and Ben Nevis, notching up at least four ascents of Stob Ghabhar's *Upper Couloir*, while also enjoying numerous hillwalking expeditions. Stanley Stewart, who would later serve as Secretary of the SMC, was a frequent companion, although it was Len Lovat who proposed him for SMC membership in 1964.

Todd also climbed further afield. In September 1947 he was in Norway with James Hood and Ronald Currie, making a wintry ascent of Store Smørstabbtind in the Jotunheim and attempting the more challenging Skeie peak. On leave while serving in Germany he visited the Wilden Kaiser in 1952, and later that decade climbed in the Julian Alps (with the Maclaurin brothers) and in the Ötztal. Along with his unrelated namesake, John Todd, he enjoyed several Alpine holidays in the 1960s at Grindelwald, Chamonix, and especially Zermatt, where the Hotel Bahnhof provided not only bed and board but the avuncular advice of its owner, the retired guide Bernhard Biner.

In 1973, when John Todd held a lecturing post in Nairobi, Norman Todd flew out to join him in an ascent of Mount Kenya. As they were leaving the Kami Hut at 4400m on the north face, 'a small aeroplane zoomed in between the great peaks and dropped something with a long streamer attached. This turned out to be a small, weighted package with a message. It said: "If you are the overdue German party, sit down. If not, stand up." So we stood up and waved and the plane flew away. … Now we headed off for Point Lenana and climbed it by the north ridge, which was an easy rock and snow scramble.' Later on the same trip he climbed Kilimanjaro.

Although in later years Todd did little technical climbing, he remained a keen hillwalker and spent many weekends in the Highlands with his life-long climbing friends, including Mike Scott and John Todd, and he completed his 52-year round of the Munros in 1997. During his long retirement he and Susanne also enjoyed trekking in Greece, Nepal, India and Iceland, and with a shared interest in music they attended concerts and festivals at home and abroad.

Norman Todd died a few weeks before his 94th birthday, having been predeceased by his wife in 2020. He is survived by his four children, Julie, Allan, Malcolm and Nigel, and ten grandchildren, to whom we offer our sympathy.

DUNCAN TUNSTALL j. 2007

Duncan, a force of nature and a larger-than-life character in climbing and many other walks of life, died in February of the brain tumour that he had been diagnosed with 20 years previously. The world will be a much duller and quieter place for his passing.

He was born in June 1962 and brought up in Chardstock in rural Devon where his great love of the outdoors was evident from an early age, with adventures in the garden and beyond, but invariably outside. His first foray into formal outdoor pursuits was when he joined the Scouts in 1973, having left the Axminster Air Training Corps as it was rather too disciplined. Duncan's lifelong friend, Simon Brooks, gives a flavour of those days:

> The Hawkchurch Scouts were a small and unusual rural Scout group who were very active in outdoor activities such as caving. The caving, mainly in Devon, led on to climbing and Duncan and I would often head off on one of my motorcycles to climb somewhere, me riding and Duncan on the back wearing an unusually large rucksack containing all the outdoor equipment we owned. On one occasion we were heading down to the Dewerstone on my newly acquired 650 BSA Thunderbolt and on our way to Exeter I turned to Duncan and asked if he had ever 'been over a ton'. He somewhat unwisely said no, and I wound the throttle open. Seconds later, Duncan's feet were under my armpits, caused by the fact the heavy rucksack and wind resistance had pulled

him off the back of the bike leaving him hanging upside down with the
rucksack and his head skimming inches off the tarmac. Following this we
travelled at a much more 'large-rucksack-friendly' pace. I can truly say that
most of my more memorable climbing and caving experiences were with
Duncan, who had the ability to dream up some very imaginative climbing
forays and I, like many others, was too trusting to see the inevitable
consequences!

Between 1981 and 1984 Duncan attended Durham University to study geology.
He continued caving and climbing, expanding his horizons to climbing in the
Alps. It was at Durham that I met Duncan, the start of a strong friendship and
climbing partnership of almost 40 years. If you met Duncan, you would never
forget that you had. He was confident, gregarious, intelligent and highly
communicative, with strong opinions on a wide variety of subjects and a great
imagination and appetite for adventure. Spending time him was never a middle-
of-the-road experience, but frequently one of contrasts: he could be highly
infuriating and exasperating or extremely charming; he could be very perceptive

or lacking in any common sense; he loved to start an argument but he was uncomfortable with confrontation; he could be very generous but often quite thoughtless. He was always great company, if at times it was exhausting to keep up with his train of thought and constant conversation. Duncan was a great partner in the mountains: highly motivated, strong, competent, always mindful of his partners' physical and mental state.

Most people, if allowed just one word to describe Duncan, would choose 'loud'. This is one of the reasons you would never forget meeting him. He could be very loud. My favourite example of Duncan's loudness is from a trip to the Roaches with him, my parents and various other family members – oh, and it was the first time my wife-to-be met him. It was the middle of summer and the Roaches was properly packed with climbers. Duncan's first route-choice for the day was *Crack & Corner*, a classic Hard Severe on the Upper Tier, for which the start of the description is 'An exciting expedition up an unlikely line at the grade.' The route was well within Duncan's capability, but he was having a bad day. The first section was accompanied by an expletive-laden running commentary on the difficulty of the climbing. This commentary was loud. Nearby climbers could be seen glancing over in surprise and some in irritation at the disturbance. In the groove to the final overhang, things got worse, progress stopped, and the volume and density of expletives increased significantly. Duncan seemed to have reached an impasse. The gist of the comments, which could now be heard by most people at the Roaches and probably further afield in Staffordshire, was broadly 'I can't do it' and 'It's impossible.' Duncan's failure to make progress lasted for perhaps half an hour. There was now quite a crowd watching and listening with incredulity and embarrassment. In the 30-odd years since that incident, I would occasionally remind him of it and he always looked a bit sheepish, a most un-Duncan expression. It feels slightly mean including this story here, as he is no longer able to defend himself, but I'm sure he would agree that there was really no defence.

Duncan graduated from Durham with an indifferent degree. He often blamed this on his assertion that their geology degree was heavy on fossil identification and that he found this extremely difficult because of his colour blindness. Duncan proclaimed benefits in colour blindness, including that it made military camouflage ineffective – apparently the best snipers are colour blind. He also swore that it enabled him to see the faintest of paths in mountain terrain. Having been lost or drawn into unnecessarily hostile ground on a number of occasions based on his confidence in seeing paths that didn't exist, I would suggest that this power was imagined rather than real.

After university, Duncan got a job as an oil trader with Shell, initially based in London. At that time there was a wheeze to attend interviews with big companies, hitchhike there and back, stay on a local friend's floor and then claim full travel and accommodation expenses. I understand that this was Duncan's primary motivation for his Shell interview, and he was not really expecting them to offer him a job. Shell made a good choice in recruiting him, however, as he turned out to be a dedicated and successful trader for them and for the banks who subsequently employed him in London, Madrid and New York.

On moving to London he met Jacqui, who accompanied him on many adventures, a highlight being an ascent of the Old Man of Hoy, and on the great adventure of marriage. He also fell in with the very active and accomplished crowd at the North London Mountaineering Club, joining them on 1500-mile winter weekends to Scotland, esoteric looseness on North Devon shale cliffs, and chalk climbing at Dover, as well as more sensible climbing around the UK. He continued to climb in the Alps too, and from the late 1980s started to visit the Greater Ranges on expeditions, which continued until his final overseas mountaineering trip in 2009.

His first trip to the Karakoram was in 1987 with Stephen Venables and Phil Bartlett when they made the first ascent of the spectacular Solu Tower (5957m) just south of the Hispar Pass, followed by the first traverse of the Kurdopin Glacier from Snow Lake to Shimshal. Another trip to the Karakoram in 1991 with myself, my sister Wiz and Angus Atkinson explored some sub-6000m peaks around the Nobande Sobande glacier.

In 1988 he was part of the British contingent, led by Mick Fowler, on a BMC-sponsored international meet to the Siberian Altai, hosted by Russian climbers. Ak Ayuk was climbed as a warm-up peak by all of the British contingent, but a lengthy period of appalling weather caused a landslide that engulfed the base camp, after which ascents of Bielukha (4,506m) and 20th October Peak were salvaged in the remaining time and better weather. Duncan's account of the expedition in the *Alpine Journal* (Vol 94) has an equal focus on the base-camp activities of international fraternisation, vodka-drinking and saunas and on the mountaineering activities.

There were two trips to attempt the beautiful peak Nilkanth (6596m) in the Indian Garhwal, the first in 1989 targeting the long and very committing South-East Ridge, and the second in 1993 directed at the South-West Buttress. Neither attained the summit, with the highest altitude being reached on the West Ridge on the later expedition, and retreat frustratingly necessitated by my altitude sickness.

Duncan's most significant mountaineering ascents were both made after his cancer diagnosis. In 2005 he climbed the 1300m-high North Face of the impressive Xiashe (5833m) in Kham in Eastern Tibet with Ed Douglas. Their new route took five days and was the second ascent of the peak by just a few days. And in 2009 with Simon Richardson he made the first ascent of the SW Spur of Punta Baretti on the south side of Mont Blanc. Simon writes:

> Duncan was the perfect partner for this Walker Spur scale adventure that was very much a leap into the unknown. On the second day, Duncan's skill with unstable ground was essential, and he sent tons of rock crashing to the glacier a thousand metres below when we encountered a huge band of rotten schist. We had three bivouacs and Duncan constructed excellent head-to-toe platforms whilst I cooked dinner each night.

Shortly before his 40th birthday Duncan went to the doctor to get a fungal infection in his toenails looked at and came home with a suspected brain tumour. Not long afterwards this was confirmed by scans, with a life expectancy of about two years. The tumour, christened Tommy, turned out to be the slow-burning type, giving him a further 20 years of life and with the symptoms allowing him to continue his activities in the outdoors. Duncan dealt with his diagnosis – the certain prospect of a shortened life, the physical and mental deterioration, and then the reality of the final decline – with a tremendously positive and rational approach and decided to pack as much in as possible, living every year as if it was his last. In 2006 he moved to Aboyne in Aberdeenshire with Jacqui and found adventure and exploration locally with extensive new-routing in Scotland. He carried on climbing and mountaineering as long as he physically could. He focused his remaining energy on skiing, hillwalking, running, sailing and gardening, making new friends in all of these activities.

Despite wanting to carry on working in some capacity, Duncan was very frustrated by discrimination against people with hidden disabilities such as his. He was determined that his illness should not preclude him having a job, but he was unsuccessful in persuading any organisation to employ him once they were aware of his condition. He made up for this by voluntary work, fund-raising and raising awareness for various organisations including The Brain Tumour Charity and Clan Cancer Support charity on Deeside. He also volunteered for The Muir of Dinnet Nature Reserve, where his main achievement was removing lots of old broken barbed wires fences which he worked on for many months.

With no job, Duncan had plenty of time to devote to climbing and other outdoor activities. He was an avid hill-ticker, enjoying the Munros, Corbetts, Donalds, Grahams and Marilyns – he never quite completed any of these lists, but maybe he found things more enjoyable that way with always more to do. He developed a number of local crags that had been previously overlooked, as well as partnering Andy Nisbet, Simon Richardson and others on some summer and winter explorations for a time. Duncan has left a legacy of new routes in the north-east, totalling around 200, which are now gaining popularity, especially those at Burn o' Vat, close to where he lived in Aboyne. These provided endless hours of activity for Duncan, who was obsessed with cleaning areas of crag before climbing the routes or generously pointing his friends at them. I did sometimes wonder if he enjoyed the cleaning more than the climbing – he certainly spent more time on the former! Julian Lines was also very active alongside Duncan at the Vat burn, as well as at Pannanich crag on South Deeside. These routes are described in Jules's guide *Ballater Rock Climbs*. Duncan also developed a sea-cliff at Longhaven on the Aberdeenshire coast.

He thoroughly explored Glen Esk in the Angus glens, an area rarely visited by climbers. He made the 200m high Earn Crag his own with first ascents of *Dschubba* (V,7) and *High Grade Low Grade* (VII,8) with Andy Nisbet and Dave Almond – all big, five-pitch routes on very steep and adventurous terrain. On Craig Maskeldie he added *Snowlake Reunion* (IV,5) with Stephen Venables and the magnificent eight-pitch *Once in a Blue Moon* (VII,7) with Henning Wackerhage and Simon Richardson.

In 2017 Duncan moved to Montrose, and then onwards to Brechin, to live with Kristine, who became his second wife, and Nicholas, his stepson. They enjoyed many travels and adventures during their years together.

Jacqui, Kristine and many dedicated people within the NHS did an amazing job of caring for Duncan during his long illness. Thanks to Kristine, Duncan was able to spend the final months of his life at home, where he died peacefully on 17 February 2022 surrounded by a group of family and friends.

One of the side-effects of Duncan's tumour was making him forget the names of people and places, and he would try to describe them in some roundabout way, so it became a kind of guessing game until you zeroed in on who or where he meant. Some of these descriptions became his regular nicknames for people: Jules Lines – *The Superstar*; Stephen Venables – *Everest Man*; Mel Nicoll – *The Runner*; Andy Nisbet – *The Old Man*; Ed Douglas – *The Journalist*. Nobody who had the good fortune to know Duncan is likely to forget him or his name; and for those who did not get to meet him, he will live on in the legacy of the fine routes he discovered that will be enjoyed by climbers for generations to come.

Chris Pasteur

PROCEEDINGS OF THE CLUB

At the Committee meeting in October 2021 the following were admitted to the Club:

IAIN BALLANTYNE (22), Longforgan
NIEL CRAIG (64), West Kilbride
MICHAEL GARDNER (40), Aberfoyle
ROBERT GIDDY (24), Glasgow
ERIK LANGE (49), Edinburgh
GWILYM LYNN (42), Portlethen
JAMES MILTON (21), Edinburgh
OONAGH THIN (23), Edinburgh
SINEAD THIN (21), Edinburgh

And at the April 2022 meeting:

NATHAN ADAM (29), Fort William
PHILIP AMOS (50), West Linton
MURRAY CUTFORTH (30), Edinburgh
MORAG EAGLESON (30), Roybridge
EWAN FOWLER (31), Hawick
NEVIL HEWITT (62), Reigate
MICHAEL SHORTER (37), Liverpool
GRAHAM WYLLIE (33), Aberdeen.

We warmly welcome these new members.

The 133rd Annual General Meeting & 132nd Annual Dinner 4 December 2021

Ever since the Club's first AGM and first Dinner their ordinal numbers have been synchronised. From now on I expect we'll continue to have our Dinner one number lower than the AGM. Owing to the Coronavirus pandemic no Dinner took place in 2020, and throughout 2021 the prospect of holding a Dinner waxed and waned according to the latest infection rates and the government guidance and restrictions. By October, however, the Committee took the decision in conjunction with the Carrbridge Hotel to plan a Dinner, but with certain restrictions such as limiting the seated number to 80, inviting no speaker or guests from kindred club and unfortunately not allowing members to invite personal guests. It was therefore a low-key affair but nonetheless enjoyable, I believe.

The AGM had a good attendance in the hotel and an additional 30 members connected to the meeting via Zoom. (Thanks to Martin McKenna for arranging that facility.) During the office bearers' reports, the current Treasurer expressed concern that no member had stepped forward to take on this role. An alternative option was likely to be followed, with a member managing the book-keeping and outside help being enlisted for the rest.

During the period of the pandemic, it was reported that hut utilisation had by necessity been low. Hut renovations had however been able to proceed, including the removal of gas fires from Lagangarbh. The AGM supported the Huts Sub-

Committee taking a cautious approach to reopening the huts. The meeting recorded the Club's thanks to Andrew James as he stepped down from the position of Huts Convenor.

As mentioned, the Dinner did proceed but with reduced numbers, and in fact not all the available places were taken. The Carrbridge Hotel welcomed us, fed us well, and with their usual efficiency kept us within the Covid rules. Traditionally Curly Ross has led the Club Song. Illness kept him away on this occasion but thanks to Robin Campbell the song did get sung by all present. The current President, John Fowler, having remained in post for an extra year was now able to hand over the reins to our newly elected President, David Broadhead.

The Dinner closed with the new President declaring that a walk would take place on the following morning from Glenmore car park, with the final destination to be decided on the day. A large group did meet, and with the weather looking OK we headed first to Ryvoan Bothy and then up Meall a' Buachaille. It turned into a grand wintry day rounded off with many of us squeezing into the café back at Glenmore. A truly sociable day with good company. I think all at the Dinner were glad they made the decision to go, and I hope we can all look forward to a more conventional AGM and Dinner next year.

Chris Huntley

On Meall a' Bhuachaille, left to right: Fiona Reid, Graeme Morrison, James Hotchkis, Sarah Atkinson, Mike Watson (at rear), Chris Huntley (at front), Fiona Murray, Gill Irvine (at rear), Alison Coull, David Broadhead (President), Chris Ravey (at front), Brian Shackleton, Donald McLeod, Ian Crofton, Lisa Hutchison, Anthony Walker, Bob Reid, Simon Fraser, Hamish Irvine and John Peden.

Ski Mountaineering Meet, Dalwhinnie
5–6 February 2022

The recently upgraded Raeburn Hut was the venue for the 2022 Ski Mountaineering Meet. The event had been organised by Colwyn Jones, but Stan Pearson stood in as meet secretary when the organiser decided to flee the country in search of reliable snow. The meet had been fully booked, with a reserve list of members, but a combination of a mild winter and a very dire weather forecast for the weekend meant that just five members braved the snowy drive to the hut. Sadly, that snow was superficial, having only fallen during the Friday of the meet, and thus no skiing was possible over the weekend. In fact, no one was optimistic enough to even bring their skis with them.

After overnight storms and rain, most of the fresh snow from Friday had been washed away by Saturday morning. It really wasn't very pleasant outside, but everyone managed to do something. Stan headed north towards Gairloch, David and Niel joined some friends to climb Meall a' Bhuachaille (810m). They enjoyed lunch at Ryvoan bothy, which was like Glasgow Central Station, confirming that most people who were out favoured low-level walks. Mike and Fiona put off going up a hill for as long as possible by visiting the Laggan Coffee Bothy but eventually made their way up Creag Bheag (487m) behind Kingussie after having to find a different route up the hill owing to the fallen trees from the previous weekend's storms. A convivial evening was had in our nice cosy hut.

Sunday dawned slightly better than Saturday, with a fair bit of fresh snow having fallen overnight. A leisurely start was made to give the gritters and ploughs a chance to do their stuff and the participants then departed in different directions towards their respective homes. David and Niel headed for the Sow of Atholl (803m) in a blizzard and Mike and Fiona nipped up Càrn na h-Easgainn (617m), deciding that getting over the high points of the A9 before more snow arrived was a good plan.

Despite the weather and lack of sufficient snow for skiing it was great to meet everyone after the Covid-19 restrictions and to be able to stay in the hut again.

Members present: Nielsen Craig, David Eaton, Stan Pearson, Fiona Reid and Mike Watson.

Fiona Reid

Skye Winter Meet
26–27 February 2022

The magnificent seven had an unusual and memorable two days in Skye, staying at the Glen Brittle Memorial Hut. It was unusual because it was winter, in Skye, people were out on the hills for three days, and they did not get wet (apart from one). This absence of a character-building soaking was offset by the buffeting they got from the severe storm-force wind, particularly on the Saturday. It was strong enough to knock people off their feet, and one member (nameless, to preserve the dignity of their position in the Club) ended up sitting in a river.

The weekend started with great promise, if you did not look at the forecast. Friday was a beautiful day, with snow down to the road, and Stan, John and Geoff managed a brisk day on the mountains above the Cluanie Inn. It started bright and cold so they set off up Am Bàthach. The snow was not too deep and they were passed (going up and going down) by a young runner in trainers and leggings, but

Left to right: David Broadhead (President), John Hutchinson, David Myatt, Geoff Cohen, Steve Kennedy, James Hotchkis. Photo: Stan Pearson.

at least he did have a rucksack. As they sat on the top deciding where to go next, they were surprised to see the runner arrive back at the summit, this time with his mother, who was more sensibly dressed. As the sky was darkening, Sgùrr an Fhuarail was chosen as the next objective, and our party were forced to put on crampons when the snow turned to brick-hard névé. Stan cut steps to impress Geoff, but not for very long.

Friday night in the hut was a convivial affair as the rather depleted party gathered, the poor forecast having put some people off.

On Saturday the promised wind and thaw were well established. David M, James and the President set off south to walk past Coire a' Ghrunnda and watch the waves on the south coast, while Steve, Stan, Geoff and John were slightly more adventurous and drove round to Fiskavaig and walked over the headland looking for the Cave of the Speckled Horses that reputedly has some interesting remains. The wind made for sporting bog-trotting and scrambling. Conditions meant they didn't quite reach the cave, but they did find some spectacular sea-arches, wild breaking waves, and a broch.

Sunday was only slightly less windy, and again the party split. The President went for a walk into Coire Làgan, where he met an impressive Frenchman returning from the top of Sgùrr Alasdair (which he said was stormy). Steve, Stan, Geoff and John walked and scrambled into Coire a' Ghrunnda to see the ice on the lochan, while David M and James headed off to the fleshpots of Kyle.

Members present: D.J. Broadhead (President), G. Cohen, J.D. Hotchkis, J.A.P. Hutchinson, S.D. Kennedy, D. Myatt and S.D. Pearson.

John Hutchinson

Easter Meet, Kinlochewe Hotel
21–24 April 2022

Having long looked forward to this meet, forty members and guests made their various ways from as far as Bristol and Sheffield to north-west Scotland and Kinlochewe. Participants could be found in the hotel, the bunkhouse, under 'canvas' and inevitably also in 'tin tents'. The forecast was excellent for the whole weekend and we were not disappointed: fresh and cool early, blossoming into open blue skies for four days. Everyone was out all day, every day, resulting in an extensive list of climbs, mountaineering and walking being entered in the Easter Meet Book. In these conditions, the giant monoliths of Beinn Eighe and Slioch were stunning in their clarity.

On Friday evening, Noel Williams gave an illustrated talk describing the work of the Boulder Committee, established by the Royal Society of Edinburgh in 1871 to examine large boulders and erratics throughout Scotland. This covered such topics as where they came from, why they occupied their present position, the age and type of rock – all very interesting and well received.

On Saturday, the traditional photograph of everyone outside the hotel was taken meticulously by our Image Custodian, David Stone, then all moved to the dining room for an animated dinner that was also well received and enjoyed.

On Sunday we were all invited to our Honorary Member John Hay's house, East Lodge at Annat, where he was holding an exhibition of his own water-colours of Scottish landscapes, and we were received with generous hospitality.

Among the many hills ascended in the course of the Meet were Slioch (of course), Sgòrr Ruadh, Beinn Liath Mhòr, An Groban, Sìthean Mòr, Beinn Alligin, Cona Mheall, Beinn a' Mhùinidh, Beinn Eighe, Beinn a' Chearcaill, Beinn Àirigh Charr and Meall a' Ghiuthais. Climbing took place at Diabaig, Stone Valley, the

Geoff Cohen and Raymond Simpson enjoying April sunshine at the belay ledge above Pitch 6 of Skyline Highway (HVS,5a) on Slioch, with A'Mhaighdean behind.
Photo: Grahame Nicoll.

Easter Meet 2022 : Kinlochewe

Standing (L to R): Andy James, Graeme Morrison, Kenny Robb, Mungo Ross, Phil Gribbon, Bill McKerrow, Louise James & Faye Brown (guests), Simon Fraser, Hamish Brown, Peter Wilson, John Fowler, Anthony Walker, Grahame Nicoll, Mel Nicoll (guest), Mike P Watson, Eve Mackenzie (guest), Colin Stead, John Mackenzie, Gordon McNair, Jane Naismith, Mike L Watson. Chris Ravey, Raymond Simpson, Roger Robb, Peter Biggar, James Hotchkis, Fiona Reid, Campbell Forrest, Peter Macdonald, Tom Prentice, Gerrie Fellowes (guest), Geoff Cohen.
Front row (L to R): Alison Coull, Noel Williams, John Hay, Dave Broadhead (President), Helen Forde, Lucy (guest), David Stone. *Photo :* D. Stone.

J.Y.L. Hay: 'Slioch from the North-East'; watercolour.

Shieldaig slabs, Raven's Crag and Ardheslaig, and on Slioch. Routes of note were *Boab's Corner* and *Route 2* at Diabaig and *Skyline Highway* on the Atlantic Wall of Slioch – a very good effort by Geoff Cohen, Grahame Nicoll and Raymond Simpson given the three-hour approach! There were numerous ascents of *Open Secret* at Stone Valley!

Many thanks go to John Fowler for spending much time organising such a successful meet. Even the weather was perfect.

Members present: P.J. Biggar, David J. Broadhead (President), H.M. Brown, G. Cohen, Alison Coull, Helen Forde, C. Forrest, J.R.R. Fowler, S. Fraser, P.W.F. Gribbon, J.Y.L. Hay, J.D. Hotchkis, A.M. James, P.F. Macdonald, J.R.G. Mackenzie, W.S. McKerrow, G. MacNair, G.D. Morrison, Jane Naismith, G.S. Nicoll, R.T. Prentice, C.R. Ravey, Fiona Reid, K. Robb, R.J.C. Robb, M. Ross, G.R. Simpson, A.C. Stead, D. Stone, E.A. Walker, M.L. Watson, M.P. Watson, D.N. Williams and P. Wilson.

Guests: Faye Brown, Gerrie Fellowes, Louise James, Eve Mackenzie and Mel Nicoll.

Helen G.S. Forde

Cairngorm Meet, Muir Cottage, Inverey
29 April – 1 May 2022

Covid and the weather forecast cut a swathe through the expected attendance at the Cairngorm Club's well-appointed hut at Muir of Inverey. In all there were seven call-offs, including two due to Omicron. So in the end Bob Reid, the meet secretary, had to content himself with myself, the President, and three guests. As it turned out, this select band made the most of the weekend, the weather, and the far-from-Spartan delights of Muir Cottage, set among Scots pines on the banks of the upper Dee. The weekend was an exchange with the Cairngorm Club, who kindly agreed that we could stay the Sunday night as well.

On the clement Friday, Bob's son Duncan led him up various routes on Ballamore Crag above Pannanich near Ballater (*Vanishing Crack, Right Arête, Fist Fighter, Pillar Crack, North Crack*), plus *Mandrax* at Pass of Ballater. Saturday was wrongly predicted to be the better day of the weekend. The President made his solitary way up Bheinn a' Bhùird, while Bob and Ian opted for Derry Cairngorm, which the latter hadn't been up for forty years, and on that occasion had walked in over Cairn Gorm and Ben Macdui from the ski car park far to the north. The newish path from the south, past Derry Lodge and up over Càrn Crom, is a pleasure, with signs of recovery and new growth among the Scots pines and the montane 'scrub' above. There were only a few patches of snow to kick and slide through, though there were plenty of ptarmigan, and two snow buntings near the summit, by which time the few spots of rain had turned to wind-blown snow. It was a long walk down as the snow turned to rain again. Duncan and his brother Fraser put the oldies to shame by combining Derry Cairngorm with Càrn a' Mhàim and spending less time over their two Munros than we did over our one. That evening we were joined by Andrew Painting, assistant ecologist at the Mar Lodge Estate and author of *Regeneration* (reviewed elsewhere in this issue).

Sunday, as it turned out, was the pleasanter of the weekend days weather-wise, and Duncan and Fraser biked up Glen Ey to climb Càrn Bhac, spotting a number of black grouse, while the President, in the course of his second round of Munro bagging, was shocked to realise that he was climbing Creag Leacach almost fifty years to the day since his first ascent. Bob and Ian had less energy left, and with Bob's wife Izzi followed some faint clues from Andrew Painting and set off up the Dee in search of an old illicit whisky still, rumoured to lurk somewhere up the gorge of the burn coming down off Creag Phadruig. After some bush-whacking and heather-bashing up-and-downing, the site was eventually located – a hidden shelf beneath a rock with just a hint of masonry. Unfortunately, no remaining product was detected, although an imaginary glass was raised. That afternoon, Ian fulfilled a long-standing ambition, and visited the Colonel's Bed hidden in a deep cleft of the Ey Burn, where in 1689 Colonel John Farquharson, a fiery Jacobite, took refuge from Williamite troops while they burnt his castle at Inverey. On inspecting the austere, dank, overhung schist shelf above the dark river, Ian concluded that the comfort on offer at Muir Cottage was a preferable option for the night.

With many thanks to the Cairngorm Club, and to Bob Reid for organising the meet.

Members present: Dave Broadhead (President), Bob Reid (Huts Convenor), Ian Crofton.

Guests: Izzi Davidson, Duncan Reid, Fraser Reid.

Ian Crofton

Sea Kayak Meet
6–8 May 2022

The Club's second Kayak Meet was held over the first weekend of May at Altandhu and the Summer Isles.

Despite some heavy rain on the Friday afternoon a few early arrivals managed some routes at Reiff. It is sad to report that parking remains a problem here.

Saturday offered the rare and welcome experience of a launch direct from the campsite, with no need for shuttles or cars. Surprisingly, given that this was the year's first kayak outing for many and kayaking suffers from more faff than climbing, all were afloat by 9.30 a.m. with the destination of Tannara Beag. This is is one of the Summer Isles, some 4–5km away. Conditions and weather were good, with the previous day's rain and wind clearing to give a fine settled day although some swell remained on the sea. The coasts of Tannara Beag and the adjacent island Eileen Fada Mòr were explored, with calm seas allowing access to the renowned caves and arches. Conditions were sufficiently attractive for a visit to the outlying stacs of Stac Mhic Aonghais to the south-west. Here there was considerably more swell, enough to dissuade even the more adventurous of the party from weaving between the stacs.

After a brief stop for lunch the flotilla headed back towards Isle Ristol, which shelters the campsite. Here the party split, with half going through the sound with Eileen Mullagrach and half going round the outside of the island, where the sea-state was much livelier, killing conversation in contrast to most of the day's paddling. All arrived back on the beach with time to lift the boats out before enjoying a meal at the local pub. Here, after an excellent day on a shared route, individual experiences were exchanged with broad smiles and none of the customary climbers' exaggeration and re-enactment.

By Sunday the weather had deteriorated slightly, offering some showers and a strengthening south-west wind as the day progressed. Horse Island just along the coast offered a suitable objective. This proved to be far more interesting than expected, with a mixture of Lewisian gneiss and sandstone cliffs and caves that sent the group's geologist into raptures, while the rest of the party were treated to

Grant Urquhart & Anthony Walker enjoying calm conditions on the Kayak Meet.
Photo: Stan Pearson.

an extended tutorial made possible by a surprisingly friendly sea-state. Calm conditions allowed a close approach to the cliffs. Experts in the party were also able to identify various bird calls, while all participated in the game of identifying the spectacular skyline from this unusual perspective.

All the cliffs around here have been known about as long as Reiff, but exploration has not been as well documented. Seldom would such calm seas have allowed access to the cliffs, where various potential lines were now identified and photographed.

The return leg, from Horse Island back to the beach at Badentarbat Bay, entailed leaving the shelter of the island and meeting the south-westerly swell that had developed during the day. As expected the wind had picked up, and the canoeists were faced with a lively sea and some breaking white caps in contrast to the flat calm at the start of the day. This provided a little excitement for the party but thankfully there was no surf to negotiate for the boulder-beach landing.

It was an excellent convivial weekend. We were lucky with the weather, had some good and varied kayaking, and got to visit close-up an expanse of cliffs that were new to many. Perhaps the next meet will attempt to access a climbing venue that lends itself to kayaking – good weekends always give birth to great plans.

Thanks to Christine Watkins for organising the meet and planning the routes. This can be tricky when paddling with people for the first time, and the choice relative to the ability of the group and the conditions was excellent, allowing everyone to have a good time.

Members present: J.C. Banks, D. Myatt, S.D. Pearson, C.R. Ravey, B. Reid, G.D. Urquhart, E.A. Walker and C. Watkins.

Stan Pearson

JMCS REPORTS

Edinburgh Section. Club activities in 2021 were still not what they used to be before Covid, but from April onwards there was a sense that the country was moving again. With another hot summer in the offing, *staycation* became the word of the year.

Our membership remains at 96 members. The club members were active, but rather in pairs than in bigger groups. New members therefore had less opportunity to join meets, but we hope soon to be able to socialise in bigger groups again.

As for all clubs, applying the Covid rules and guidelines was a challenge at times, especially in relation to the use of the huts. After taking a cautious approach it became more and more evident that it was down to the clubs how they wanted to manage the risks and, with a thorough risk assessment in place, we were able to rent out the Cabin and the Smiddy from August onwards, albeit to limited numbers. We have also rescheduled many bookings from 2021 by deferring them 12 months down the line.

We witnessed earlier in the year that the huts lying empty over the winter period has not been good for them, as we had to remedy some damp-related damage. The huts being used by members and kindred clubs should ensure that they are being heated for longer periods and any noticeable damage will be reported to the hut custodian as soon as possible.

Although we held our annual slide night via an online Zoom meeting, we were able to hold the Annual Dinner face-to-face, at the Cairngorm Hotel on 20 November. It was great to meet up as a club again and exchange lockdown stories. Also, our guest speaker (and member) Ollie Warlow entertained us with a very captivating presentation about his *Classic Rock*-by-bike adventure. All in all, a successful weekend, even more so as we were able to avoid any Covid-outbreaks afterwards.

Our annual newsletter captured some of the adventures our members have had over the year, both close to home (for example on the Pentland skyline ski traverse) and afar, on trips to Crete and Kalymnos.

Our club activities include regular meets at Alien Rock and EICA Ratho (on Monday and Wednesday evenings respectively), and during the summer months Wednesday evening meets at local and not-so-local crags. We also hold regular weekend meets. (See our website <edinburghjmcs.org.uk> for details.) Once we have reopened, our huts will also be available for booking by kindred clubs by contacting the custodians whose names are below:

Honorary President: John Fowler; President: Thomas Beutenmuller; Vice-President and Smiddy custodian: Helen Forde (helen.forde1@btinternet.com); Treasurer: Bryan Rynne; Cabin Custodian: Ali Borthwick (01383-732-232, before 9 p.m.). The secretary's post is vacant at the moment. Membership Secretary: Nils Krichel; ordinary member: Catrin Thomas.

Thomas Beutenmuller

Glasgow Section. Like everyone else, the JMCS Glasgow Section enjoyed a markedly different year during 2021. Owing to the SARS-CoV-2 pandemic face-to-face club events had been suspended in 2020, and our first, socially distanced, day-meet of the year was on 11 July 2021, when a large group enjoyed a steep and vigorous walk up the north flank of Beinn an Dòthaidh, from Achallader farm.

The 2021 Presidential Dinner and AGM proved to be a most pleasant 'return to normality', and was held at the Isles of Glencoe Hotel, Ballachulish on Saturday 13 November 2021, again with measures in place to combat SARS-CoV-2. Forty-five members and guests enjoyed what had become that rarest of treats, meeting people in the flesh rather than on-line, and were given an entertaining and informative after dinner speech by local climber Kev Shields.

Despite the restrictions the club continued to welcome new members and guests to join, and to attend club meets. The section currently has 88 members with four new members joining during the pandemic year. With much new interest from people looking to join and lots of enthusiastic new members, recruitment and motivation in the club are at an all-time high.

As far as we know no Glasgow JMCS member was fined, or even cautioned, for breaking lockdown restrictions. When the restrictions are fully lifted the club plans to reinstate a full schedule of weekend meets as soon as possible. This will be over 20 meets each year and will include all of the five SMC huts. The meet venues vary each year and cover the whole of Scotland and occasionally further afield. In the late spring and summer there are midweek evening meets to various central-belt rock climbing venues. There are also midweek indoor climbing meets at various climbing or bouldering venues in Glasgow throughout the year, especially through the winter.

One of the meets that is always popular with Glasgow JMCS members is the maintenance meet to the club hut at Coruisk on the Isle of Skye, although this was postponed in 2021. The spectacular boat trip from Elgol to Coruisk (free to workmeet participants) perhaps contributes to that popularity. The hut itself is popular at weekends and we hope that overseas clubs will now restart their regular bookings. To book please contact the hut custodian directly at coruisk@glasgowjmcs.org.uk
or via the Glasgow JMCS website <www.glasgowjmcs.org.uk>
or by Facebook <www.facebook.com/CoruiskMemorialHut>.

The Glasgow JMCS newsletter remains an entertaining read which has continued to thrive under the enthusiastic editorship of Dr Ole Kemi. Four issues are published each year and it can be downloaded from the Glasgow JMCS website. The newsletter publishes contributions from all authors, not restricted to JMCS members, and we welcome all ideas and contributions for future issues.

The winter season 2021 was disrupted everywhere by the SARS-CoV-2 travel restrictions. Nevertheless a few glorious winter days were squeezed in between lockdowns by members on Creag Tharsuinn (*Garrick's Route* and *Eighty Foot Gully*), The Cobbler (*North Wall Traverse*), Ben Nevis (*Glover's Chimney*), and a lucky find of a first ascent on The Brack (*End of the Line*, V,7), as documented in the 2021 *SMC Journal*. Two members out east reported 12 days of fine skiing in The Pentland Hills (admittedly relative to not skiing at all!) and members were also recorded skiing in the Campsie Fells.

At the start of the year the indoor climbing walls were closed, but the Blantyre Towers lie exactly five miles from the Glasgow City Council boundary (apparently) and provided a pleasant training venue in the dry spring weather.

Three members had a great time climbing on the Island of Pabbay in May, with restrictions easing just in time for the trip. After 20 years of no grazing on the island, the spring wildflowers were reported to be magnificent. In August, two past presidents plus two other members enjoyed almost a week of glorious autumn weather and hardly any midges at the Ling Hut, climbing *Sword of Gideon, Kings of Midian, Cioch Corner* and *Cioch Super Direct & Corner* on Sgùrr a'

JMCS Meet to Pabbay: John Hutchinson and Roger Everett on The Priest (E1,5b).
Photo: Jeremy Morris.

Chaorachain; *Pale Rider, Central Buttress, Angel Face*, and *Groovin' High* on
Beinn Eighe; *Dishonour, Ecstasy*, and *Sleeping Beauty* on Càrnan Bàn; and
Salamander on Creag Ghlas, as well as cragging at Sheigra, Ardheslaig and
Diabaig. They also met another Glasgow JMCS party staying in the Torridon
campsite, who unfortunately were less lucky with the midges (but apparently still
enjoyed climbing on Beinn Eighe and Seana Mheallan).

Among other rock climbing achievements, members completed *The Long
Climb* on Ben Nevis; *Via Dolorosa, Satan's Slit, Solitude, Eastern Promise,
Central Grooves, Whortleberry Wall, Engineer's Crack* and *Nirvana Wall* in Glen

Coe; *Jack the Ripper* and *Vlad the Impaler* on Stac Pollaidh; *Horn of Plenty* and *Hamite* on Binnein an Fhìdhleir; *Cardiac Arête* in the Northern Corries; and finally cycling and walking in to Beinn a' Bhùird to climb *Slochd Wall* and *Angel's Edgeway*, which with bikes is an easy ride in but especially out. Am Buachaille was scaled by the landward (VS) route.

Climbs in the Lake District included *Gillercombe Buttress* (with new members), *Praying Mantis* and *DDT* on Goat Crag, and *Gormenghast* on Heron Crag, while in North Wales ascents were made of *The Grooves* (Cyrn Las), *Llithrig* and *Octo* (Clogwyn Du'r Arddu), and *The Groove* (Llech Ddu). The only further addition was two former presidents of the section climbing on Gran Canaria in December, where they report that Roque Nublo was scaled (*Via Alemana*, French 6b+). The Canaries were reported to be nice and warm too.

To break the monotony of not being able to access any significant hills, one member took on a personal 'moon walk' challenge by ascending his local peak (Caldron Hill, 332m) on each night of the full moon for a year. He completed the challenge on 20 September 2021 after 12 months and 13 full moons. One walk he felt was worth recounting, and it should serve to remind people not to become blasé through over-familiarity. The hill is served by a fairly good track throughout. One particularly misty night he was concentrating on a podcast rather than where he was going and suddenly found himself off the track and not quite sure of his whereabouts. Stotting around for a few minutes he eventually saw the lights of home in the distance and headed in that general direction. The ground being quite tussocky he was concentrating on his feet, only looking up occasionally. The lights got no closer and disconcertingly he managed to veer off course considerably. Course correction and repeat gave the same result. Repeat several times until it eventually dawns on him that he had been following sheep, his headtorch reflecting in their eyes as they looked over their shoulders trying to evade their unusually tenacious stalker. Fortunately, they knew where they were going and got him back to the path. He has now climbed the mighty Caldron Hill 92 times, 79 times since Covid started.

President: Douglas McKeith; Vice-President: Alistair MacGregor; Secretary: Iain Young; Treasurer: Andrew Sommerville; New Members Secretary: Mark Gorin; Coruisk Hut Custodian: Neil Wilkie [for bookings, see above].

Colwyn Jones

JMCS (1925–2025) Centenary Anthology. Finally, an appeal to the readers of the *SMC Journal*. In 2025 the Junior Mountaineering Club of Scotland will be 100 years old, and the publication of an anthology of 100 articles is planned to mark the centenary. We are seeking historic material from all JMCS sections that has previously appeared in JMCS newsletters or journals or in the *SMCJ*, as well as new material that brings the JMCS story up to the present. The publication will form a history of the club viewed through character sketches, accounts of significant events, climbing or expedition articles, meet reports, route descriptions, activities, log-books, the club huts, photographs, and so on. If space permits, material relating to non-climbing activities such as sailing or kayaking may also be included if relevant to the club. If you have any suggestions for suitable material, either existing or original, we will be pleased to hear from you. Please contact Niel Craig by e-mail (niel_craig@yahoo.co.uk).

Colwyn Jones

Lochaber Section. No report was received, owing to limited activity in 2021.
Secretary: Iain Macleod, (ia.macleod@btinternet.com).

London Section. The year got off to a slow start owing to Covid restrictions, and our first meet wasn't until May in Edale. The inactivity seemed to have galvanised us into action with a good attendance of 20 despite the cold weather – it doesn't seem right in May wearing more clothing than when skiing! Nevertheless, there was mountain biking (classic Edale round), climbing and hill walking, and lots to catch up on in the Old Nag's Head. In June, we were back in the Lake District camping in Borrowdale. Unlike in 2020 the weather was fantastic – three days of rock climbing and ascents of Scafell Pike and the surrounding fells. Again, there was a good turn-out, the only downside being the midge-infested campsite beside the river, which necessitated a drive to the pub, with a sober driver for the return to the campsite.

The rest of the summer saw us mainly in North Wales at our cottage in Bethesda, with a week in Assynt in August. The incentive for this meet was having missed our traditional one-week Scottish winter meet for the first time in at least 20 years. It's important to our section that we climb in Scotland at least once a year and we hadn't been north of the border since February 2020. It was good to see the Assynt mountains in summer rather than winter, and easier on our ageing bodies. The highlight was belatedly celebrating Ted Wilkins's 80th birthday with a group traverse of Stac Pollaidh, and while the culinary standards were not quite up to the usual standard provided by Nigel Charlesworth at our winter meets we didn't go short of good food, drink or company.

In the autumn there were meets in Pembroke and North Wales and members were active elsewhere including sailing in the Hebrides. We came together for a face-to-face section dinner and AGM in November at the Swallow Falls Hotel near Betws-y-Coed. There were fewer attenders than usual but it was an enjoyable weekend and a good chance to look ahead to better times in 2022. These include investment in our cottage thanks to Covid-related grants (we now have a good local builder lined up) and the prospect of trips abroad again (a return to winter sunshine in Spain). We emerge from the pandemic as enthusiastic as ever and although our numbers have declined (38 ordinary members and four life members) there are a few prospective members in the pipeline.

On a sad note, we lost Hugh Jordan during the year. A former president, honorary vice-president, treasurer and secretary of the section, Hugh had been a member for over 60 years as well as being active in the BMC south-east area forum. A physically strong and powerful rock climber, Hugh was great company on and off the hills. In his later years he joined several trekking groups to Nepal and we remember him arriving at one of our section dinners straight off the plane from Kathmandu!

President: Trevor Burrows;
Secretary: John Firmin (john.firmin3@btinternet.com);
Treasurer: Gordon Burgess Parker;
Hut Custodian: David L Hughes (davidlewishughes@hotmail.com).

John Firmin

Perth Section. Perth Mountaineering Club has made the most of opportunities to organise a wider range of activities and meets since the end of Covid-19 restrictions. Thanks to the efforts of our outgoing meets secretary Craig Gudmundsson and his replacement Stuart McKeggie, the club is now back to offering a full programme of meets with a mix of day and weekend meets as well as midweek climbing. As well as our annual Burns Supper meet in Crianlarich and visits to other favourite haunts including Skye and Glen Coe, this year the club has also had two successful trips to the CIC Hut and a winter backpacking trip. Another camping trip is planned for later in the year as well as a meet at Achnasheen.

Alongside the programme of meets, members continue to make use of our WhatsApp group to organise *ad hoc* activities aimed at taking advantage of the best of the Scottish weather. The club has continued to welcome new faces over the last year, and the membership remains at around 80 with a number of prospective members keen to join the club.

President: Catherine Johnson; Treasurer: Pam Dutton;
Secretary: Tim Storer, (secretary@perthmountaineering-club.co.uk);
Meets Secretary: Stuart McKeggie.

Catherine Johnson

SMC ABROAD

MONT BLANC RANGE

In September 2021, Simon Richardson and Micha Rinn visited Mont Vert de Greuvetta (2810m) on the Italian side of the Mont Blanc range and made several exploratory ascents. Richardson writes: 'Our finest addition was *Bella Vista* (6b+) which follows the east ridge of the peak starting up the prominent pillar situated directly above the Comino Hut. The crux was the second pitch, an overhanging chimney and crack that succumbed to a forceful lead by Micha. Above, cracks, chimneys and a superb 5c crack led up and right of the final pitches of *Gran Diedro Sud*. The rock quality throughout is superb and in the upper half there are outstanding views into the Triolet Basin.

Micha Rinn climbing the superb 5c crack on Bella Vista, Mont Vert de Greuvetta. Photo: Simon Richardson.

'We also found what is probably the easiest route up the mountain. *Way of the Ibex* (AD) bypasses the initial pillar of *Bella Vista* on the left and then takes easy grooves and ramps on the north-east face. Whether it has seen a human ascent before or not, the route is frequently climbed by ibex. During the first ascent of the south-west ridge of the peak with Tom Prentice in 2013 we were greeted by the same ibex at the foot of the climb and on the summit! Micha and I concluded an enjoyable few days by climbing *South Face Route* (AD), a mountaineering line on P2936. This may have been the first time this remote summit had been visited since the first ascent in 1975.'

DAUPHINÉ, AIGUILLES ROUGES & PENNINE ALPS

Adam Kassyk had a rather unsatisfactory visit to the Alps in July 2021. 'The weather was very unsettled, there was too much snow in the northern Alps, and as a result the huts were overcrowded for the limited number of routes in condition.

'The only big peak climbed was the Ailefroide Orientale (3847m) by the normal route, a very pleasant route combing excellent scrambling and snowfields; it is one of the few Alpine peaks that can be climbed without a rope, owing to the absence of glacier terrain. Two rock climbs were also achieved. *Dessin Moi un Katsup* on the Pavé du Chardonnet in the Cerces massif near Briançon; and the South-East Spur of the South Summit of the Aiguilles Crochues in the Aiguilles Rouges at Chamonix. The former was climbed in the rain, the latter was an excellent and very enjoyable rock climb on good rock with nice situations.

'All of these were climbed with Ellen Bruce (AC). Also worthy of note was a very pleasant hike up Mont Thabor (3178m) from the Vallée Etroite, a long but most enjoyable outing, enlivened by fresh snow.'

Kassyk also notes two ski tours in March 2022. These were the Col de Chaudin (2095m) on the Cornettes de Bise in the Chablais Alps, from Miex in the Swiss Valais, and the Fenêtre de Ferret (2695m) from La Fouly in the Swiss Valais, descending via an overnight at the Great St Bernard Hospice. The first tour was done solo, the other with Ellen Bruce.

SENJA ISLAND, NORWAY

Simon Richardson endorses a description of Senja Island in Northern Norway as Scotland on steroids. He writes: 'Steep mountains with fairy-tale summits plunge straight into the sea. The maritime climate combined with Arctic-Circle temperatures provide a host of winter climbing opportunities, and the island attracts a steady stream of adventurous mountaineers. Heavy snowfall makes mountain travel difficult in midwinter, and many enjoy climbing roadside ice.

'I first visited Senja in February 2019 with Micha Rinn and was intrigued by the mountaineering potential in the spring. Rather than focus on easily accessible crags I wanted to attempt longer mountaineering routes leading to summits. Mark Robson was keen to join me, and we arrived in Senja on 11 April 2022. We were hoping for late-season Scottish conditions with fast travel over névé snow-slopes and efficient climbing up gullies filled with snow-ice.

'Local guide Bent Eilertson was intrigued and enthusiastic but a little sceptical about our plans. In truth, our thinking did not quite work out. Our calculations had not allowed for the sun rising higher in the sky than Scotland and the consequent rapid deterioration of snow conditions. Early in the trip we dodged consistent avalanche danger while making first ascents on Steinsethøgda (473m) and Litjebrusen (532m). Both were enjoyable 300m-long Scottish Grade IV mixed

The 500m-high North Ridge of Ulvetanna follows the line between sunshine and shade.
Photo: Simon Richardson.

routes, but they were not quite the objectives we were looking for.

'Our opportunity finally came on 23 April, the last day of our trip. After a week of warm weather the temperature plummeted, bringing the higher mountains back into climbing condition. We opted for the 500m-high North Ridge of Ulvetanna (c800m), an adjacent summit to Stormoa (974m), the second-highest mountain on the island.

'The climbing was straightforward at first and we made rapid progress. But as the ridge narrowed the climbing became more challenging with steep mixed sections between horizontal pitches of narrow and sometimes corniced ridge. The snow was already softening in the early morning sun on the east flank of the ridge, but the shady west side was still deep unconsolidated powder. The only way forward was to follow the exact crest as it reared up to an ever-steepening prow. Silently, we both thought that we would fail on several occasions, but we kept our misgivings private and continued pushing on. The crux was the penultimate pitch, where the crest became a vertical prow of compact rock. It looked impossible from below, but a hidden 15m crack led through the steepest section followed by a scary 20m run out on widely spaced turf.

'When we reached the tiny summit and looked down into the avalanche-ridden Stormoa basin we knew we had no option but to carefully abseil down the way we had come. We graded the route Scottish VI,6 – a grade that captures the uncertainty and insecurity of the terrain.

'That evening Bent told us that Ulvetanna had only been climbed once before, via the east ridge, just three summers before. Our quest for good springtime climbing conditions on Senja had not been completely successful, but if nothing else, it demonstrated the vast possibility for adventurous mountaineering on the island.'

Looking up the North Ridge of Ulvetanna as the angle starts to steepen. The climber is Mark Robson. Photo: Simon Richardson.

AMMASSALIK AREA, SOUTH-EAST GREENLAND

In 2020 an expedition was organised to the island of Ammassalik on the south-east coast of Greenland to celebrate the 50th anniversary of the founding of the Scottish Arctic Club (by a group that included Iain Smart, Phil Gribbon and Hugh Simpson). Unfortunately this had to be postponed twice because of Covid, so it was only at the third attempt that this actually took place this summer.

The original group of over 30 had by then slightly reduced in number and changed in composition so that it was eventually 26 persons of all ages and interests that finally travelled out there via Iceland at the end of July 2022. Nine members of the party were there specifically with mountaineering objectives in mind, and they included SMC Members Simon Fraser and Noel Williams (contributor of this note), the latter being the only one who had visited the area before. The three youngest members were all from St Andrews University.

'The Ridge' viewed from across Ikaasatsivaq Fjord. Photo: Noel Williams.

The unclimbed halfway tower (crux?) viewed from the west.   Photo: Noel Williams.

One of the group's objectives was an unclimbed 24-km long ridge on the north-east side of the island overlooking Ikaasatsivaq Fjord (commonly referred to as 'Grizzly Fjord' by the Anderson family). The ridge is comprised of over 20 summits ranging in height from 650–1100m.

Nîniartivaraq – 'The Big N' (c1160m). This imposing peak can be climbed with ease by the North-West Flank (left-hand skyline). A new climb was added to the broad western flank by Rowland and Tietjen (HVS/VI, 700m). Photo: Noel Williams.

Apart from a couple of dreich days the weather was remarkably good for the duration of our fortnight visit. Unfortunately the poor weather occurred when the trio attempting the ridge (Will Rowland, Simon Tietjen amd Mike Bauermeister) had completed a little less than half of it. The rock on the ridge proved to be very disappointing on the whole, and the dark rock in particular was very slippery when wet. So they escaped while it was still easy to do so on the south-west flank. Meanwhile the support party (Simon Fraser, Fraser Melville and Noel Williams) – who had radio contact with the ridge team – bagged an unclimbed 750m summit on the south-west side of the through valley between Imiilaa and Kuugarmiit

For the remainder of the trip the group transferred by boat to a cirque of peaks on the landward (north-east) side of Ikaasatsivaq Fjord. A number of climbs had been done there in 1975 by Rick Hoare's party, including a conspicuous peak nicknamed 'The Little Dru'.[1]

A major peak called Nîniartivaraq (c1160m), which dominates the view from Ikaasatsivaq Fjord, had also been climbed on three different sides by Hoare's party. On two separate days, seven members of the group managed to reach this summit by a remarkably straightforward Grade 3 scramble up the north-west flank. Later Will Rowland and Simon Tietjen also gained the summit, but by a new route on its unclimbed western flank (HVS/VI, 700m).

The trio from St Andrews (Bethany Carol, Hannah Mortlock and Tom Litchfield ventured further north and, following a high bivvy, managed to bag a 1200m snowy summit. A number of repeat ascents were made of other peaks.

---

[1] R.D. Hoare, 'Greenland Ho Again', *Journal of the Mountain Club of South Africa*, No. 78 (1975), pp. 25–33 and Rick Hoare, 'Blubber and Boats', *Alpine Journal*, No. 89 (1984), pp. 104–07.

REVIEWS

Scottish Winter Climbs West: Neil Adams (Scottish Mountaineering Press, 2022, softback, 424pp, ISBN 978-1-907233-42-5, £30).

Well, can you judge a book by its cover? For this book the cover is artwork. Clear and crisp, if the contents live up to the cover then this should be one of the best guidebooks that the SMC or anyone else has produced.

The good news is that the art, in the form of the writing and the photos, continues long after the book is opened. Niggles are limited and most will concern the few not the many.

It opens with a Murray-like paean to the area, and photos to draw you in. Once over the obligatory acknowledgements, there's a clear and concise summary of the selected crags giving base height, aspect and type of route. This information alone should make choices easier. My only quibble here is that the approach times lean toward the lean, fit, regular winter climber rather than the new, the old or the occasional mountaineer. For us mortals, add a bit. There follows a genuinely interesting summary of the geology and history of the area, then a quick run-through of climbing history followed by a very good summary of the skills required for Scottish winter climbing. This summary reflects the author's vast experience and for those new to winter climbing is probably one of the best bits of succinct advice and warning that they will ever read.

The instructions for using the guidebook are straightforward, with an easy-to-read explanation of symbols used and, even better, the explanation of the grading system is spot on. I do fear that page 27, a list of classics and connoisseur's choices, has created a list of queues but it is hard to argue with the selection.

The whole area is divided into nine subsections, from the Southern Uplands to Glen Shiel. Each subsection has a map of the crags covered, a summary of its characteristics, public transport possibilities, amenities, bad-weather options and, unusually, suggested link-ups.

Within the subsection each crag has the following information: grid reference, rock type, parking, distance, time to crag, whether bikes or boats might help, any convenient bothy, and crucially height of crag-base and aspect. Crags have excellent photo diagrams but for once there is criticism here. For those of advancing years or just poor eyesight the numbers on those diagrams could be a little bigger and, given the work that must have gone into getting them, photo credits would have been appropriate.

Generally route descriptions are clear although very occasionally back-references to other routes can confuse, but a little persistence unravels any problem. The only clear mistake that I have found is that, as far as I am aware the summer route *Central Chimney Direct* on page 171 has not been climbed in winter, an unfortunate choice of name having created another *Central Chimney Direct* on the same crag. Not the author's fault but mine.

The pictures are so good that many will be bitterly disappointed when they realise that the weather is not always so benign. The pictures are so good that I will say that again.

Given the quality of the pictures, the writing and the stunning lifetime's worth of rewarding routes, some might wonder at the format. Why is this not a hardback coffee-table book or a downloadable whatever? I think the answer is that it is a book designed rather to be browsed for inspiration and then taken on that weekend or longer trip and used to check alternatives. A big hardback would be too clumsy, a download less easy to browse. Read the book. Make a general plan. Take the book. Check the conditions. Make some decisions. Photograph the descriptions. Go and have fun. I intend to. It is a book that will draw me south of the Great Glen again.

All in all, to go back to my original question, 'Can you judge a book by its cover?' In this case, Yes.

Roger Webb

Snow and Ice – Winter Mountaineering Routes of Great Britain: Lina Arthur (Oxford Alpine Club, 2021, paperback, 360pp, ISBN 978-1-913167-08-0, £23.99).

This selected winter guide to the UK from the Oxford Alpine press offers full descriptions of over 100 routes across the main winter climbing areas in Wales, the Lake District and Scotland.

The routes selected are all in the lower climbing grades I–III, so appealing to those just starting the sport or who just want a good day out. As with all selected guides there will be the inevitable querying why certain routes were included or not included. I would say that question is more for the connoisseur and those with greater knowledge and experience of the climbing areas, and so not something the target audience of this guide would worry about.

The guide gives a useful introduction to the various types of winter climbing and where, when and what to look out for to ensure the best conditions when you do get a chance to venture out. Information on snow conditions and avalanches and the most suitable clothing and climbing equipment all go to make this a good choice of guide for the beginner, particularly if they don't live close to any of the areas described and so are looking to buy just one guide.

The routes are conveniently divided into geographically accessible sections with an approach description and map extract at the beginning of each section. The selected routes are then described across two pages containing an annotated photo of the route, its description and a useful section of the local map. Helpfully, a selection of other routes in the vicinity is briefly described in case your chosen line is already occupied or not in condition. So perhaps your favourite route may be included in the long list.

With its more reliable conditions and a larger area Scotland gets the lion's share, with 40 of the top 100 routes, followed by the Lake District and then Wales – probably a reflection of the frequency of winter conditions and their duration.

Unlike many modern guidebooks this one is small enough to be pushed in a pocket so it can be carried on the route. The layout places all the relevant information on adjacent pages, allowing it all to be captured in one easy photograph should you choose not to take the guide with you on the climb. (Not a habit I'm in favour of – I'd rather have all of the additional information with me when climbing to aid any necessary change of plan, and would certainly rather drop a guide than an expensive 'phone when fumbling with cold or gloved hands in winter.)

The potted history of the sport and explanation of the grading system and its development and expansion over the years make for good reading and should helpfully occupy a wet, dark evening while waiting for those elusive winter conditions. Some of the history notes at the rear of the guide did seem a bit jumbled, with events out of synch and ending in 2003; surely there has been some activity over the last two decades that was noteworthy?

All in all, a good guide for the occasional climber or those new to winter climbing.

Brian Davison

The Moth and the Mountain: Ed Caesar (Viking, 2020, hardback, 259pp, ISBN 978-0241262313, £18.99).

Maurice Wilson, who died making a hopeless, fatal attempt to climb Everest in 1933, has long been one of the footnotes in the mountain's history. A biography, *I'll Climb Everest Alone* by Dennis Roberts, was published in 1957, but since then he has attracted only intermittent attention. The British writer Ed Caesar has returned to the subject, finding him worthy of a fresh look. Through assiduous searching he has unearthed priceless material, helping to cast Wilson in a new light. He has followed Wade Davis, author of *Into The Silence*, in framing his subject through the prism of his experiences of the First World War. Caesar has placed him in an illuminating personal and cultural context and although we may still be mystified by his apparent act of self-immolation, we have a plentiful source of information to inform our considerations.

Wilson was born in Bradford in 1898, the son of an engineer in the weaving industry who eventually ran his own company. He joined the British army in 1916 and two years later, by then a captain and winner of the Military Cross, he was seriously wounded by German machine-gun fire. Although Wilson was invalided home to recover, Caesar believes he also suffered from undiagnosed shell-shock, the contemporary – and controversial – name for PTSD, or post-traumatic stress disorder. An older brother, Victor, suffered far worse, surviving hideous battles, incurring a near-crippling leg injury, and being effectively disabled by shell-shock or PTSD.

After the war Wilson's life assumed a nomadic quality, as he pursued business ventures and also a spectacular series of relationships. Having married in 1922, he emigrated alone to New Zealand in 1923, working as a travelling salesman. In 1924 he cabled to his wife to join him there. By the time she arrived, he had fallen in love with another woman and his wife sued him for divorce, spending a further 18 months in New Zealand while she saved up for her return fare home. Wilson married for a second time but that marriage ended in 1930. Wilson next headed for South Africa with a new woman by his side but they never married. In 1932 he became involved in an apparent *ménage a trois* with a couple named Len and Enid Evans – and it is Wilson's subsequent letters to Enid that form important new verbatim evidence in this account.

It was in 1932, during a visit to southern Germany, that Wilson was seized with the idea of climbing Everest, triggered by reading an account of the 1924 British expedition that culminated in the disappearance of Mallory and Irvine. Caesar believes that Wilson experienced some kind of epiphany, a religious rebirth that reflected a mixture of fashionable quasi-Christian theories and elements of Indian mysticism. A further contributing factor, Caesar argues, was Wilson's unresolved PTSD after the First World War.

Wilson was undeterred by the grim histories of the three 1920s Everest expeditions, with their accounts of savage weather, illness, frostbite, deprivation, the effects of high altitude, and avalanches. His aspirations achieved another level of implausibility when he resolved to travel to Everest by flying a solo Gypsy Moth from England, even though he had never piloted a plane before.

That part of his ambition he did at least fulfil, doing so wearing boots he intended for both the flight and the subsequent ascent of Everest. After a breath-taking series of adventures and mishaps, he reached Darjeeling in mid-August, just a few days after the defeated British 1933 expedition passed through on its way home. He promptly engaged the services of Karma Paul, the fixer who assisted the British expeditions of the 1920s and 1930s. Running short of money, he sold his Gypsy Moth and solicited a loan from his long-suffering widowed mother; he also wrote copiously to his new love, Enid Evans.

He finally set off on the trek to Everest in March 1934, assisted by three Bhutia porters. Three weeks later he arrived at the Rongbuk Monastery. It is now that his great adventure appears the most preposterous, as he headed alone up the East Rongbuk Glacier with a 45lb pack on his back, planning to reach the summit in five days, his thirty-sixth birthday. When that day arrived he was still floundering, without crampons, on the glacier some way short of the ascent to the North Col. Deciding to retreat, he barely survived a desperate descent to the Rongbuk Glacier.

It was now that by any rational standards Wilson should have renounced his attempt. Caesar argues that what impelled him to continue was an instinctive desire to redeem the gruesome experiences of his brother Victor during the War. Wilson left no evidence to that effect, his diary and his letters to Enid merely recounting how he set off up the glacier again some three weeks later, this time accompanied by two of his Bhutia porters. He felt that the fates were with him when he found both a pair of crampons and a box of food, some of it bearing Fortnum & Mason labels, that had been abandoned by the British expedition the year before. This time he climbed halfway to the North Col before turning back once more. Three days later he made a further attempt to climb to the North Col. He died, most likely from exposure and exhaustion, a day or so later. His body was found the following year by the 1935 Everest reconnaissance expedition led by Eric Shipton.

Caesar admits that his attempt to give meaning to all he learned about Wilson was not entirely successful. He clearly relished his quest, and was rewarded for his persistence and diligence. Some of the records he used are close to home, such as Wilson's diary, which is kept in the Alpine Club library. His best new resource, Wilson's letters to Enid Evans, were harder to come by. They were originally in the keeping of Wilson's previous biographer, Dennis Roberts, who appears to have struck a pact with the Evanses whereby he could use information in the letters without attributing them directly, for fear of revealing their unconventional relationship. Roberts later sold the letters to a German mountaineering author, Peter Meier-Hüsing, who passed them to Caesar in return for a lunch in Berlin.

Such treasures help make a biography rich in researched and descriptive detail, adding to its authenticity. Caesar incorporates his quest into his narrative, although appearing to distance himself by using the second-person 'you' form instead of the first person – perhaps suggesting that said quest is universal in its nature. There is one curious lacuna, however. Caesar adopts a radical approach to chronology in his opening chapters, which works well – apart from the fact that he nowhere provides the precise date or location of Wilson's birth (21 April 1898, according to Wikipedia), leaving us to deduce the year from inferential references. There are just four photographs of Wilson (one is used twice) and because they are incorporated within the text the two that are not portraits are difficult to read. The book has no index.

Those quibbles apart, this is a rewarding read, with a power and clarity to the writing, not quite answering all the questions it poses – and leaving you to ponder them after you have closed the book, a sign of its enduring qualities.

Peter Gillman

The Vanishing Ice – Diaries of a Scottish snow hunter: Iain Cameron (Vertebrate, 2021, hardback, 199pp, ISBN 978-1-83981-108-1, £20).

Many of us will be aware of the small but growing band of enthusiastic chionophiles who annually document and record the extent of old snow accumulations on British hills. As the sub-title to this new book suggests, the author, Iain Cameron, one of the current leading activists in snow-patch observation, recounts his personal experiences of this fascinating labour of love. The bulk of his tale centres around visits (mostly alone and often in winter) to the better known semi-permanent snow patches in shady hollows and gullies on our highest hills, namely Ben Nevis, Ben Macdui, Braeriach and Aonach Mòr. Iain's trips to these out-of-the-way locations are often arduous and sometimes quite gripping. He is clearly a very fit man and rather bold for someone who claims not to have a head for heights. His ascents and descents of loose, wet gullies are definitely mountaineering in my view.

In the first chapter he recalls how, in May 1983, as a nine-year-old living in Port Glasgow, his curiosity was roused by the sight of a single white patch of snow on the south side of Ben Lomond. This early event sparked his interest in the hills, particularly in those with snow accumulations that survived for all or most of the year. Despite his parents and friends not showing any interest in the outdoors, he spent time in his teens studying maps, reading and watching TV programmes like *Weir's Way* and *The Munro Show*. In particular, he remembers an episode of the latter, where Muriel Gray was filmed standing above the Garbh Choire Mòr of Braeriach, looking down dark cliffs to snow patches below. She declared this to be Scotland's most permanent snowfield, only having melted twice in living memory. He wondered how she had acquired this information. His strong desire to visit this and other similar places was further compounded when he read a section of Martin Moran's *Scotland's Winter Mountains* that included information about Scotland's semi-permanent snowfields.

After completing his apprenticeship as an electrician in 1993, Iain did some voluntary work for the NTS in Glen Coe. This gave him an opportunity to observe and take notes on snow patches late in the year, in particular those high on the slopes of Stob Coire Sgreamhach which he believed survived to the start of winter. Twelve years later he read a paper by Adam Watson that stated that snow had never been known to persist from one winter to the next in Glen Coe. With great trepidation he decided to e-mail Adam with his Glen Coe notes, and with much relief received an encouraging reply that ended: 'I am interested to come across a snow enthusiast, as there are so few of us! Best wishes and keep in touch.' Thus commenced regular contact between the two, which later developed into a close friendship. Iain devotes a whole chapter to Adam in this book. It is his tribute to someone he considers to have single-handedly done more on the systematic study of snow patches in Scotland over the last 50 years than virtually all other researchers combined. In 2010 the pair co-authored *Cool Britannia*, a comprehensive historical account of snow patches on British hills.

Other chapters cover the history of snow-patch observation (particularly the work of Gordon Manley, Seton Gordon and Adam Watson), and the nitty-gritty subjects of global warming and climate change. Iain maintains he is only an observer not a scientist or climatologist, and although he has an opinion on climate change, he says he lacks the qualifications to discuss the matter in detail. Nevertheless, the chapter on Scottish snow and climate change includes data showing the number of snow patches visible in north-east Scotland, annually on 1 July, to have dramatically reduced by 50% over the last 50 years.

Probably the best known semi-permanent snowfield in Britain is that which lies below the granite cliffs in the upper Garbh Choire Mòr of Braeriach (the place Muriel Gray visited). Of this high, remote corrie, Iain says: 'For every snow-patch devotee, this is our Mecca. It is the place in Scotland – and indeed the whole of Britain – where snow virtually always lies longest.' My own first visit was inspired by Seton Gordon's *The Charm of the Hills*, which had photographs and a description of the eternal snows in the 'Fuar Garbhchoire'. A school friend and I walked up into this inner sanctum on a hot cloudless day in July 1965. The snowfield was extensive, with long fingers of snow in several of the gullies. Everything was silent except for the sound of dripping water. It really did feel like a special place.

The chapter on Braeriach gives a detailed account and history of the Garbh Choire Mòr snowfield – how it gradually diminishes over the summer and autumn, from a wide expanse to several large areas, then finally to two distinct patches near the top right-hand corner of the talus slope. Over time, these two patches were named after the nearest rock features on the cliff above: *Sphinx*, the largest and most durable patch on the left, and *Pinnacles*, down and farther right. The rock climb above the left-hand patch, *Sphinx Ridge*, was not climbed in 1924 (as stated on page 48), but was actually first climbed in May 1952 by a party led by Kenny Winram. Bill Hendry did name the Sphinx feature after exploring from the plateau ten years earlier in 1942. The Pinnacles patch lies below *Pinnacles Gully*, and this was first climbed in 1924 by James Parker and Henry Alexander. When Seton Gordon wrote about the eternal snows of the Garbh Choire Mòr in 1912, the snowfield had never melted in living memory. Now, in 2021, when Iain wrote this book, it has completely vanished seven times, four of these events being in the last 20 years.

I enjoyed this book; it is well written in a couthie style, and Iain's enthusiasm for his subject is inspiring. There is a good selection of photographs, including spectacular shots taken in snow tunnels. The book could have done with a map or two, and an index would have been helpful. These are very minor points, and I would not hesitate to recommend this book to anyone with an interest in our hills, their snow cover and climate.

Greg Strange

Snow Nomad – an avalanche memoir: Alan Dennis (Friesen Press, 2022, paperback, 228pp, ISBN 978-1-03-910798-4, $20).

Alan Dennis has had so many experiences in 50 years of avalanche reporting, many of which would be worthy of a book to themselves. He consigns them to a series of cryptic paragraphs: no ego, no hyperbole; just a tantalising flickerbook of adventures and lots of self-deprecating humour. Have an atlas handy as you follow this Snow Nomad on multiple seasonal migrations across the globe.

This is Alan's first and only book. The writing style is spare and condensed, punctuated with riddles and quirky allusions that serve to whet the appetite of the reader and keep the libel actions on hold. The lack of a Fatal Accident Inquiry following the Chalamain Gap disaster merits the footnote: 'Stonewalled by the Ministry of Defence (you sign up to die) and a reluctant Sports Scotland (you do not sign up to die)' … could be a Bob Dylan lyric?

His memoir starts with a gypsy childhood as the son of a Royal Navy Officer in Europe and the USA, settling on his father's retirement to Vancouver, Canada where Alan developed a mongrel accent and a school career characterised by a series of perhaps voluntary 'check-outs'. His further education consisted of a gap year or three and was financed by such diverse occupations as jackaroo (Aussie for cowboy), Carnaby Street model, AB negative blood group sales, and tree planting with Maori fellows in New Zealand or ex-shipyard workers at Dalmally, Scotland. Following this he became an Outward Bound instructor and ran a rafting business in the Yukon. From his gap-year experiences he learned that he didn't mind working long hard hours but hated hot climates, so it was only natural that he found winter employment in the developing avalanche control business necessary to keep British Columbia's (BC) mines and highways open throughout the heavy maritime snows of the Canadian north-west.

Over the course of 50 winters, many back-to-back in Northern and Southern Hemispheres, Alan worked long, hard and often dangerous shifts, having a lot of fun with recoil-less rifles (105mm cannon – no recoil, but lethal hot gases blasting out the rear end) and half-hundredweight bags of fertiliser and paraffin primed with temperamental fuses dropped from helicopters. He rose through the ranks to create and lead projects in BC, Argentina and the notorious Milford Road in New Zealand in seven-year cycles, usually 'one year too long'.

His memoirs contain interesting technical discourses on risk. He stresses the importance of AI data, hardware and science but also software and 'intuition, experience and luck' in the prediction of disasters in avalanches, life plans and relationships.

This is the nearest Alan gets to introspection and self-reflection, which is refreshing these days when so many memoirs verge on self-conscious navel-gazing. He aims to amuse and inform the reader and introduce them to a cast of real-life characters (who he implies are far more interesting than himself) with whom he shared a lifetime of work, companionship and adventure.

After reaching the dizzy heights of bureaucracy, heading up what is now Avalanche Canada, his career apparently took a downwardly mobile trajectory. Alan (and Chester, his Border collie) ended up spending his retirement working as a humble fieldworker with Blyth Wright and Mark Diggins in the Scottish Avalanche Information Service (SAIS), 'the most coveted winter job in Scotland'. He describes these episodes as 'saving the best till nearly last'.

For the non-technical reader, there are cameo appearances of the great and the good (and occasionally bad) of the international mountaineering elite in climbing and ski-touring adventures across the world. Alan acknowledges and name-checks, but he does not name-drop. Whenever he stayed with us he would pop over to visit his dad's best man Bill in Blairgowrie; only years later did we learn that old Bill was in fact Sir William Macpherson who coined the phrase 'institutional racism' in his report on the Metropolitan Police and was ostracised by the establishment.

Scottish adventures included the Stack of Handa, winter routes on the Ben – 'kind of mandatory' ascents of *Orion Face* and *Point Five Gully* on an international meet (with the son of KGB apparatchiks) – plus the Alpine Haute

Route and a visit to the Hall of Clestrain, birthplace of his North-West Passage hero, John Rae.

Alan worked, collaborated and cohabited with many members of the SMC over a twenty-year period: Blyth Wright, Allen and Blair Fyffe, Adam Watson, Derek Pyper, Jonathan Preston, Andy Nisbet, and of course the 'Lord of the Flings – not a Tolkien sequel'.

In his youth, Alan spent summers in the Yukon doing exploratory ascents of the Tombstone range – Bugaboo-like peaks of crumbly granite. Perhaps the most interesting climbing stories concern Bill MacLeod, whom Alan employed and climbed with in New Zealand. Bill famously made multiple solo ascents of the Caroline face and other major routes on Mount Cook and Mount Tasman. Alan was 'the first person he did a belay with' when they made winter ascents of Mitre Peak and Mount Christina.

Revelstoke, the powder capital of BC, has been his home for the last 20 years. His 'cosy shack on CPR hill didn't have much of a physical or financial foundation' but has been a welcome refuge for many young Scots discovering themselves on gap years.

When his left knee eventually called a halt to working for the SAIS ('You try following Graham Ettle speed-ballet through a wet boulder-field …') he took to the sea in the 30-foot SV *Griffin*. The boat is named after his dad's WW2 lucky destroyer, and Alan now spends the summers sailing the north-east Pacific with his current companion Fly, another Border collie.

Whether you are an avalanche technician, sailor, climber or ski-tourer or just like cryptic crosswords, I can heartily recommend this good read. It's well worth the postage to have it sent from Canada, or order on Amazon if you must.

Raymond Simpson

A' Chreag Dhearg – Climbing Stories of the Angus Glens: compiled by Grant Farquhar (Scottish Mountaineering Press, 2021, paperback, 375pp, ISBN 978-1-907233-40-1, £20).

In his 1962 guidebook, Mac Smith described the Red Craig of Clova as 'almost Lakeland in atmosphere'. This is undoubtedly true, and, on a fine summer's day the climber is likely to be fried to a crisp owing to the southerly aspect of the crag. Clova aficionados will be aware that the Angus glens embrace a much larger area, and the book covers most of this. The name Red Craig has been Gaelicised to provide the title of the book, and many of the stories are set on and around this crag.

Grant Farquhar has managed to get together an eclectic mix of authors (some of them members of this Club). Most stories are short, covering only a few pages. As well as climbing, there is a mixture of social history, access rights and anecdotal tales. Because of its location Clova was always a favourite stamping ground for Dundonians and other Angus folk. In fact the Carn Dearg Mountaineering Club was formed in Forfar in 1949, and their club hut at Braedownie played an important part in the development of the area.

The book spans the period from the early twentieth century to the more recent winter developments. Many of the articles detail the development of the area, with many covering first ascents and the scary nature of climbing on the Red Craig itself. Of particular interest was the chapter dealing with 'The Men of Steel', a group of Dundonian climbers, and the shenanigans they got up to. This included driving cars off the road on the way back from the pub, falling off the back of tractors and, amazingly, climbing their favourite 'pub routes' on the Lower Doonie in the dark, whilst a wee bit inebriated! It took me all my time to lead *Guinness* in the daylight whilst sober, although we did reward ourselves afterwards with a pint or two of the dark liquid. I particularly enjoyed the writings of Simon Stewart, very well composed and entertaining. The article by Grant Farquhar – 'The Pale Rider' – will interest our ageing membership, and is quite thought-provoking. I won't spoil it by revealing its content. My only criticism of the book is the poor quality of some photographs, which have not reproduced well and in many cases are very dark. Surely in this age of digitisation this should not happen? I did wonder if the author was attempting to replicate the dark nature of the old Kodachrome slides we used to take. That apart, this is an excellent read, covering an area that may be unfamiliar to many climbers but certainly deserves a wider audience.

Brian Findlay

Time on Rock: Anna Fleming (Canongate Books, 2022, 260pp, hardback, ISBN 978-1-83885-176-7, £16.99).

I was a bit worried when I read a comment by Helen Mort (poet and climber) stating that the author Anna Fleming reminds her of a Nan Shepherd one could go out for a pint with. For starters, Nan Shepherd is a supremely tough act to follow. I also think that you could equally have gone out (or stayed in) with Nan Shepherd for a wee jar. Shepherd's many references to alcohol, whether finding its aroma in nature or sampling 'country concoctions' in the homes of people she stayed with, would suggest that you could. But I was relieved and delighted to find that Fleming has her own exquisite voice, though she may well be harnessing and channelling Shepherd's spirit, thus continuing the journey that Shepherd began. This is the journey into the 'heart of the mountain'. In this book Fleming sets out to link two worlds: 'the mountain and the rock climb'. I think that Shepherd would feel hugely happy and honoured to read how Fleming does this.

In my ignorance I also feared that this book might be another 'How I learned to climb' tome. It is certainly not that, although it does contain most helpful elements on climbing development, especially with regard to pacing and psychology, and it shows a particular understanding of the female climbing experience. The author conveys how the process of learning to climb, whatever standard reached, can change how one views the world, the environment and oneself. We are privileged that Fleming shares these insights with us. She manages to put into words feelings that most of us would find difficult to express.

The chapters are arranged in roughly chronological order and are titled and subtitled as place and accompanying rock type. She ends, perhaps deliberately, in the Cairngorms, home and domain of Shepherd to whom she pays great tribute. In this way we are taken full circle. Fleming's progress with self and climbing is charted in parallel and the accompanying comments on geomorphology are cleverly interwoven. Grades are explained but not paraded. Issues such as bolting are presented but not judged. Technical terms are accessible to the non-climber but not laboured for the climber.

It is hard if not impossible in the writing to separate the feel of the rock from the mechanics and adventure of climbing itself. Much stems from the author's childhood, growing up with a builder father and therefore familiar with raw materials and the impact they have on one's endeavours. This brings me to the social content of the book which serves to demonstrate the respect and affection that she has for those who have lived and worked in the regions she explores by climbing. A deep interest in and appreciation of the culture, history and climbing history of an area enriches the climbing experience for her. This is another perspective she shares with Shepherd.

The language is beautifully crafted with generous dollops of alliteration employed to bring the landscape alive and the rock out in relief. If one combines the elements of a fine literary piece, the great sense of discovery and adventure encapsulated in the pages, together with the demystifying of the technical world of climbing, I think this book makes for all-round appeal. There is something for nearly everyone and whilst a natural fit for readers of the *Journal*, I do hope it finds its way into the hands of a readership wider than the mountaineering community.

Ruth Love

The Black Ridge – Amongst the Cuillin of Skye: Simon Ingram (William Collins, 2021, hardback, ISBN 987-0-00-822623-7, £20).

Another book on the Cuillin! 'What more can there be to say?' I asked myself as I embarked on this quite lengthy volume, although I had heard that Ingram adopts a new slant on his subject.

The book opens with a two-page essay on how the mountaineer feels, halfway up the hill, on a miserable day in the clag:

> Your mind tries to reach beyond, scripting visions onto the dead flat before you. Your other senses grasp. They find smells and tastes. The marine sting of salt. The salt of sweat. Rain running over your lips, making them itch and curl. The warm fog of your own body, the heat of hard work. Your neutered sight is like a box around you, and makes even distant sounds feel close and crisp.

I read this several times and, while I acknowledge the writer has expressed himself well, I was concerned that 500 such pages might be a wee bit problematic! I battened down the hatches and continued to the 'Introduction' proper, which continues in like vein:

> More wind roared down the gully, pressing long-soaked, long-warmthless clothing against skin and making me gasp. With cold hands I pulled the map from my pocket. Breathing hard, I looked through rain-beaded eyelashes at contours through the mad lens of wet on the plastic case.

I couldn't put it better! Ingram is a first-rate wordsmith, as one might expect from a former editor of a mountaineering magazine. Yet, while I recognise writers over the centuries have sought to express in words their mountain experiences, and judging by the sales of Robert Macfarlane *et al* such work remains very popular, I have to confess this really isn't my genre!

But then Ingram tells us what he is doing: he is out, on a foul day, in the middle of nowhere; he is on the west flank of Sgùrr Hain, above the path from Sligachan to Camasunary, and has come to visit Captain Maryon's Monument – and he confesses he can't really explain why! Now that struck a chord! Like Ingram, and in addition to getting a buzz from climbing hills, I enjoy the quirky facts I discover along the way. On several occasions I have passed close by this feature on the map but, knackered by the long walk from Slig and dying for a brew at Coruisk, I have postponed the detour. Now Simon Ingram has explained all!

The Black Ridge is a synthesis of its author's feelings for the hill with the story of his own discovery of the Cuillin and tales of the formation of the land, its people and, in particular, those who have contributed to our knowledge of it: the map makers, the geologists and, of course, the mountaineers.

He tells how he found and engaged a guide, and set out with him to 'do' the Ridge 'in a one-er'. Learning all the way from his guide, on whose experience, understanding and local knowledge Ingram showers abundant praise, the pair are forced, in deteriorating weather, to bypass the T–D Gap and spend an uncomfortable night in a dripping cave. Next morning, it doesn't take long for Ingram to accept the guide's suggestion that there are better places to be and, more importantly, to realise that there is more to be learned about the Cuillin than can be gleaned from 'ticking' the Ridge and its individual summits.

Thereafter, he adopts a more gradual approach to his exploration, and intersperses his narrative with diversions to discuss, for example, Ossianic legend, MacCulloch, Henry Chichester Hart (who, had he been less objectionable, might have been granted rather more than a grumbling acknowledgement of his primacy over Collie, on the eponymous Ledge), feminist climbers and Professor Forbes. Foremost among the many climbers, for whom brief sketches are provided, are Sheriff Nicolson, the Pilkingtons, Mackenzie and Collie, Humble, Murray and MacInnes. In each case there is little new, and never a dissertation, but Ingram supplies enough detail to whet the appetite for knowledge. All the while, he is relating how his knowledge of, and love for, these mountains is developing. And, when things go pear-shaped, he is a master of suspense!

The book is attractively presented in an A4 hardback format with a spectacular jacket photograph of the Inaccessible Pinnacle. The text is spacious and clear and the book well indexed. If I have a criticism of the presentation, it is that the illustrations are tableaux of four or five small pictures, apparently designed to portray the gloom of the Cuillin. Sadly, these did nothing for me, either by illustrating or amplifying the text – if only to demonstrate that, at the end of a sunny day on the gabbro, there is no better place to be than on the boiler plate by Lochan Coire Làgan, soaking up the rays!

I can commend this book both for its unique approach to the Cuillin and for its entertaining narrative, giving just the right amount of information on so many side-tracks which are fundamental to the mountaineer gaining a rounded knowledge of Britain's most mountainous mountains.

Simon Fraser

Imaginary Peaks: Katie Ives (Mountaineers Books, 2021, hardback or paperback, 300pp; ISBN (hardback) 978-1-68051-541-1; ISBN (paperback) 978-1-59485-980-9; ISBN (e-book) 978-1-59485-981-6, US$27).

Admirable, widely researched and committed to its theme, Ives's book has as its springboard the Riesenstein Hoax of June 1962, authored by three prominent north-west US mountaineers. A photo of the amazing (and real) Kichatna Spires in Alaska was sneaked into *Summit* Magazine of 1962 and the range stated to be in a remote area of north-west BC. The article had a false account of initial ascents, and a challenge to the next generation was laid down. The caption stated:

> The unclimbed summit of Riensenstein [sic], approximately 8100 feet, near Prince Rupert in British Columbia. It can be reached in two days by bushwhacking up the Klawatti River. Who will be the first to climb it?

All false, apart from the real photo. It was a great wheeze and was substantially believed until the *American Alpine Journal* spoiled the fun in 1966. Some of us perhaps had that picture in our sticky young notebooks.

The Riesenstein Hoax is the springboard for a wider discussion. Ives's childhood experience of nature, nicely encapsulated here, established her sense of mystery and quest for a peak of perfection. Her narrative arc is not about busting myths, fun though this may be; it is about the inevitability and necessity of myth creation in mountain exploration, or indeed, any exploration. It's a productive concept. Essentially all exploration literature is to some degree speculative, tending to exaggeration, justification and outright lies. No matter how beautifully crafted, maps require us to imagine the terrain described and 'map-making is still an act of metaphor'. They contain guesses, hopes, lures, promotions; map-makers were perhaps never altruistic. Our much-loved Ordnance Survey (Jacobite suppression); marine charts, with ghost islands to this day; our GPS a giftie gi'en us to see oursels as ithers allow us! Guidebooks are ... what exactly; or indeed, why? A hoax could and did encapsulate and satirise all of this.

The falsity of accounts provides the fuel for further exploration and self-promotion. There is a breadth of literature on this topic, generously acknowledged: Cabot, Cook, Peary, Marco Polo. The impact cannot be underestimated; no journeys of 'discovery' would be undertaken without curiosity baited by myth; no colonization could proceed without promise of riches (Antilla, El Dorado).

Imagination has produced a wealth of accounts of fantastical sights and locations – in short, 'mythological landscapes' – which are discussed with erudition: Utopia, Shangri La, Xanadu, and Egeria, a fourth-century pilgrim. Philosophy and satire are disguised as travel accounts: Homer, Pope. Or perhaps, unvarnished entertainment: 'Munchhausen', Defoe, and, may I suggest, Douglas Adams and Terry Pratchett? Tolkien is here too, impacting Ives, the Hoaxers, and others of that generation.

Ives lays out the 'pernicious falsehood': the notion that certain long-inhabited lands were ever *terra incognita* where anything might be imagined or drawn. *Terra miscognita* would be a better term, 'evoking the failures of explorers to acknowledge the realities of the traces, paths, and homes of local residents.' Since I live on the unceded lands of the Ktunaxa, this had personal resonance.

The RH appears to be the best prank in a continuum of playfulness instigated by Harvey Manning, Ed LaChapelle and Austin Post. It is amusingly described. Fun was paramount. Ives believes the pranks signify a deeper mystical journey in Manning, and she devotes considerable space to insightful biography of this eminent mountaineer and defender of the Pacific North-west. In SMC terms he was a Salvationist supreme. The pranks were intended to prick the balloons of pedantry and ambition of his contemporaries and remind them of truer values of the mountain experience.

Not surprisingly for an editor of *Alpinist*, Ives has vast experience and deep acquaintance with the core of American alpinism, and this is perhaps over-generously shared. There may be three or four books here for the price of one, and the reader should be prepared for digression. Much of the material is not highly focused on the mystical theme but is fascinating nevertheless. There is much delicious background and narrative of alpine exploration in North America. *Summit* magazine obviously plays its part in the story. There is a delightful account of the birth of the anarchic Vulgarians group; how appropriate it was that they would attempt the Kichatna.

I was pleased to see this: 'Some of the ideas behind the hoax might be even more popular now than they were in the 1960s. Many twenty-first century authors have written nostalgically about "the lost art of getting lost".'

We take the gifts we find from the mountains. What we find depends on who we are, from Wullie to MacSnorrt.[1]

> They sat them doon to rest a bittie:
> Says Wullie, 'Man, isna that pretty?
> Peak upon peak sae fair and grand
> Like elfin towers in fairyland.'
> MacSnorrt said: 'Dinna be sae fulish,
> There's naethin' there but Ballachulish.
> For God's sake dinna get poetic,
> It acts on me like an emetic.'

Ives has wonderfully amplified this spectrum. As our travels become untenable and our horizons diminished, imagination still remains.

Ian Rowe

Extreme Lakeland – a photographic journey through Lake District adventure sports: Nadir Khan & Tom McNally with foreword by Leo Houlding (Vertebrate, 2022, hardback, 192pp, ISBN 978-1-83981-125-8, £20).

I am suspicious of coffee-table books, especially on an urban coffee table. My advice if you are struggling in an ocean of picture-perfect photography celebrating the pleasant ambience of suburbia, is to grip the heaviest by the two bottom corners and whack your forehead before you finally go under.

Coffee-table books of mountain sports are different. I understand their purpose and even their worth, which makes them a good steal, and I have quite a collection hidden on the bottom shelf of my coffee table. Now in front of me is another freebie, *Extreme Lakeland*, that proves great books are not the monopoly of great athletes performing the greatest feats because it is about you and me, enthused by our love of adventure sports, and the vitality that national parks provide for adrenalin junkies.

To open the book, Nadir and Tom have engaged a foreword by the famous mountaineer and adventurer Leo Houlding. But to accompany photography of unique, spontaneous, moment-in-time, stop-you-in-your-tracks, action-packed adventure, and tell a compelling story that illustrates the human psyche at its most potent, they have used a new class of outdoor professionals, blessed with disposable income and the time to spend it, who go out on Friday, swap working miserablism for *joie de vivre* and are away with ropes, axes, skis, chutes or canoes, leaving the conurbations faster than a pine marten after a grey squirrel.

Far from being only another large-format, photographic journey it has interesting narratives from addicts who refuse to be conquistadors of useless living and others who have been dodging the grim reaper for so long the old fella's scythe has gone rusty.

Firstly Tom is obviously in love with the good old days, and he writes of Millican Dalton, the Borrowdale Hermit, who a century ago left his insurance clerk's high stool in London for a simple, sustainable life as a guide. He wrote: 'Use is everything. We dress too much, we eat too much, almost everything we do is too much ... .' How wonderful it would be to be a bat on the wall and to

---

[1] From 'The Conquest of Buachaille Etive or The Orra Lads' Tale' in *SMCJ*, 22/128 (1939), 125; first published in *Cambridge Mountaineering*, 1932. – HON. ED.

eavesdrop on Greta Thunberg and Millican, sitting across a fire at the entrance to his cave.

However, if Millican lived now with access to a car and motorways would he go to all the inconvenience of living in a cave? This is not as cynical as you might think because among all the good writing and great photography in this book about climbers, runners, walkers, mountain bikers, paddlers, base-jumpers, swimmers, skiers, slack-liners, paragliders and hairy men in tweeds, the most significant piece is from Ellis Bland, who puts into perspective the pressures on this small pocket of rare natural beauty that is holding out against the unbridled pressure for more profit, and highlights that open spaces are going to be ever more essential to everyone's well-being.

Anna Taylor's straightforward justification for solo climbing had me as hooked as the *Old Man of the Sea* because of her Hemingway style. She compares the probability of having a nasty climbing fall with being in a pile-up on the motorway. Coincidentally, it was nearly curtains for us when we smashed up a Daihatsu Fourtrack coming back from *The Curtain*, and how I cringed when we soloed *SC Gully* past two novices whose Metro we had run into on our way to Glen Coe just a few hours earlier.

Tom and Nadir have successfully mixed photography with illustration, including paintings by Anna Sharpe. They may have been afraid not to, because Anna can be seen not even using her axes on a winter line of Pinnacle Ridge and Becky Vale can be seen with a nasty-looking lumber axe smashing the ice to swim in a frozen mere in a bikini.

I got confused by Tom's transcendental images of the dancer, Eliza Sandford, spaced out on the Needle in a diaphanous dress, against an inversion. They are superb photos and his mastery of light is also revealed in his ice-skating shots and many others. In collaboration with the highly creative Nadir, the impact can be imagined in his shot at the Coupall Bridge over the River Etive. After seeing it on his website I have not bothered to climb and prefer the thrills of just driving up and down Glen Coe.

Nadir and Tom's superlative technical ability hides superb creativity that sneaks up on you with consummate ease. So it is more than the sum of its parts and I am going to risk calling it a work of art in progress. Threaten to burn me at the stake for heresy but could pulling into focus the playmates of Extreme Wales be even better? And is the folksy nature perfect for Yosemite with its tight vibrancy?

They could be international best-sellers but then would Tom and Nadir still love the Lakes as much? Or would their families demand sunnier climes, with a place on the beach, and we lose two very talented creatives? By then we would surely have a Sir Leo, suitably acknowledged for his heroic deeds, just living as a sodden son of the Lake District.

Tim Pettifer

The Fox of Glencoe – Hamish MacInnes: (Scottish Mountaineering Press, 2021, hardback, 368pp, ISBN 978-1-907233-39-5, £30).

Hamish MacInnes was already a legend when I started hillwalking and climbing as a schoolboy in the mid-1960s. His name rang out with the likes of Dougal Haston, Robin Smith, Jimmy Marshall, Tom Patey *et al* among the heroes and hard men of the Scottish climbing scene. But Hamish was much more than a mere legend of hard climbing, epics and new routes; he was a man of many varied interests and talents, and this book brings together a collection of writings that offer a glimpse into a unique, long and fascinating life lived often right on the edge.

Deziree Wilson has done a remarkable job of editing this selection of prose and photographs from what must be a vast library of Hamish's own material, with contributions from others including Mike Banks, Walter Elliot, John Cleare, Dave Cuthbertson, Chris Bonington and Michael Palin. Hamish was a contemporary of and climbed with many of the famous names of climbing and mountaineering, and the book is liberally peppered with them – Lionel Terray, John Cunningham, Allen Fyffe, Joe Brown, Don Whillans, Mo Antoine, Paul Nunn, Doug Lang, Graeme Hunter and Ian Clough, to mention a few – and amongst his cherished friendships with celebrities that feature in these stories are Clint Eastwood, Sean Connery and Christopher Lambert. With Hamish as the central character and such an illustrious supporting cast, the reader can only expect entertaining and gripping tales of extreme adventure and derring-do, and will not be disappointed.

It is obvious in his writing that Hamish thoroughly enjoyed working and playing with words. I love his own account of having banged out a crime novel in only 16 days supposedly in the spirit of Agatha Christie; a literary critic suggested that it was obvious that he had never actually read any Agatha Christie, while another critic said: 'Dr MacInnes brags about writing this "pile o' shite" in 16 days – just imagine the outcome had he taken an extra day or two' – only for his book to be on the best-seller list for several weeks. His own dry, wry sense of humour, his unsentimental nature and his brevity with embellishment and dramatisation leave the content of his stories naked and exposed. The reader is led directly to the joy, the cold, the hunger, the discomfort, the fear, the companionship – the very essence of what the writer was experiencing at the time. There are stories of his early days in the hills, major first ascents, epic adventures, living in Glen Coe and starting his climbing school there; his pivotal role and involvement in mountain rescue, his innovative development of equipment, the world of movie-making and film stars; motorcycles, fast cars and jets; time spent in hospital, cheating death and disability; friendship and loss.

My only criticism of the publication is that some of the photographs are not quite given the justice they deserve, but that might just be because of my own nit-picky perfectionism when it comes to photography. My own conversations with Hamish over the years included discussing the provision of black and white photographs for his guidebooks in the 1970s, and of 'going digital' in the twenty-first century, so I know how passionate he was about his photography. But other topics of conversation included his 'self-confessed expert knowledge' of the Himalayan Bear, and a telescopic hyperbaric chamber he had installed at the medical post at Pheriche in the Khumbu. For me this sums up the diversity of the man; I suspect everyone who knew him (and that must be a considerable number of people) will have known a slightly, or very, different Hamish MacInnes.

For anyone who has even the slightest interest in the history of Scottish mountaineering this book deserves a place in their library, providing as it does a picture of someone who profoundly influenced Scottish climbing, international mountaineering and mountain rescue. For a wider readership, here is a volume of wonderful stories, well told, of a man unafraid to live his life to the full.

Mungo Ross

The Climbing Bible – Practical Exercises: Martin Morbraten & Stian Christophersen (Vertebrate, 2022, paperback, 189pp, ISBN 978-1-83981-104-3, £20).

This book is intended as a companion piece to the authors' original work, *The Climbing Bible – Technical, Physical & Mental Training for Rock Climbing*, and as such does not explain the underlying theories behind climbing performance and training. Instead it aims to be an adjunct to the mother text, specifically focusing on three areas: movement techniques; strength and power; and children and youths. The authors freely admit that they omitted certain aspects from this book such as endurance, flexibility and mental training exercises, as these areas were well covered previously.

The authors both have over 20 years' experience of competing and coaching with the national team and of performing at the highest levels in Norway. Although the book is translated from Norwegian, the translation is superb and it is well written and easy to understand. Scattered liberally throughout the book are many excellent full-page images show-casing the best of Norwegian rock with an aspirational and inspirational slant; many of the boulder problems and routes featured within are in the upper echelons of climbing standards.

Typically, many books of yore on training for climbing contained five to ten pages of the basic climbing movement techniques, accompanied by some poor black and white photos, which left the reader even more perplexed about how they were supposed to move their bodies on steep rock. Not so here: a whopping one-half of the book (nearly 90 pages) is dedicated to specific techniques, their applications, and exercises to enable the reader to learn them. This section takes a comprehensive look at all aspects of climbing technique, from footwork to balance to body positioning to dynamic methods of climbing, and all clearly illustrated with sequential colour images.

My eyes lit up when I stumbled across a page entitled 'Training for Trad and Alpine' as I imagined learning of revolutionary new training methods that would raise my game on the rock-faces and mountains of Scotland. Alas, my excitement proved to be fleeting, as the section consisted of a short personal account from Norway's top alpinist on her priorities for training for long multi-pitch days (high levels of general fitness and good technique, unsurprisingly). Indeed, scattered throughout the book are many personal accounts from the authors and others about lessons and counter-intuitive principles learned throughout their climbing careers.

Confusingly, the next chapter, 'Strength & Power', starts with several exercises focusing on particular techniques to be carried out on a steep bouldering wall (for example 'compression' and 'gastons') that would, on first glance, appear to belong to the first chapter. However, this illustrates how sports-specific some aspects of training for climbing must be. The chapter then develops into more standard fare covering campus-board, finger-board and pull-up exercises. One criticism I would have of this section is that there are no exercises covering antagonist workouts, an important consideration in injury prevention.

Lastly, Chapter 3, 'Children & Youth', adapts many of the exercises from the first two chapters into fun and child-friendly games: for example, the Quiet Feet exercise from Chapter 1 becomes the Ninja Feet game here. As you would expect, there is a bigger focus on learning techniques rather than strength-training for younger climbers. The authors do, however, advocate a minimal level of strength-conditioning, and the limited number of exercises reflect this.

To summarise, this is an excellent and well-produced tome on training techniques that would suit those who already have the mother text or have a sound understanding of the underlying principles behind training and coaching for climbing. However, the book only illustrates minimal methods for training for longer routes as its focus is on climbing movement technique and strength training with a particular slant towards bouldering and indoor climbing. Nevertheless, for intermediate–expert enthusiasts, instructors, coaches and guides this will provide a useful and informative reference guide to training exercises.

Niall McNair

Walter Parry Haskett Smith [1859–1946], The Climbing Polymath: Francis J. Morgan-Grant (privately published, 2021, paperback, 264pp, ISBN 978-0-9556989-4-1, £20).

Walter Parry Haskett Smith's solo ascent of Napes Needle on Great Gable, in 1886, is considered by many to mark the beginning of the sport of rock climbing in Britain. Because of this he is often referred to as 'the father of British rock climbing', although in fact the activity had started a few years earlier, with Haskett Smith being just one of the four main protagonists. The other three were John Robinson, Cecil Slingsby and Geoffrey Hastings.

WPHS grew up on the family estate, Trowswell in Kent, with three bothers and an older sister. He was educated at Eton and won a scholarship to Trinity College, Oxford, where he studied classics. Although he qualified as a lawyer he never practised, and being independently wealthy never had any form of employment. He was essentially a private man with a range of scholarly interests, who travelled extensively in Europe, North Africa, Mexico, Canada and South America. In later years he was a popular after-dinner speaker with a quick sense of humour. He never married and is buried in an unmarked grave at Parkstone in Dorset.

Morgan-Grant, the author of this biography, has been a diligent researcher, uncovering a considerable amount of new material about this quiet man who left few traces of his life. Amongst the primary sources were descendants of WPHS's younger brother, Edmund, who live in Canada. A trunk belonging to Edmund was found in a loft containing long-forgotten diaries, photographs and other records relating to the family. Edmund climbed regularly with his brother for around twenty years, and the diaries (although the entries are only brief and sporadic) give new insights into activities surrounding the well-known ascents.

The book also draws attention to other facets of WPHS's life that were not previously known about. For example, he edited and updated Murray's *Handbook for Travellers to the English Lakes, including the counties of Cumberland, Westmorland & Lancashire*, which was published in 1889. This was five years prior to the publication of his own two-volume guidebook *Climbing in the British Isles*, which covered England and Wales. There was to be a third volume for Scotland but the manuscript for this has never been found, if indeed it ever existed. (The author concludes that it was either discarded by WPHS himself following mixed reviews and slow sales of the first two volumes or was lost when his London house was bombed during the Second World War.)

There is an explanation of the unusual double-barrelled name, Haskett Smith, which he occasionally hyphened but usually not. The family surname was Smith; Haskett was a deliberate addition by WPHS of his third Christian name for no other reason than he liked it. His parents called him Walter but he disliked that name and preferred his siblings to refer to him as Parry.

Another revelation is that his elder brother, Algernon, who was a talented sportsman and had played cricket for Oxford, was gay and died in a shooting accident, possibly suicide. Furthermore, Algernon's regular companion Montague Druitt was at one time suspected of being Jack the Ripper. Druitt later committed suicide, and when his body was dragged from the Thames WPHS was summoned to give evidence to the police. The family were drawn into further scandal when a gay brothel in London, which Algernon and Druitt along with other prominent society figures had frequented, was raided by the police. The author hints that WPHS shared Algernon's proclivity but was more discrete or celibate.

WPHS inherited the Trowswell estate after his father died in 1895 but did not spend much time there or pay much attention to it. The property gradually fell into a state of disrepair, and this neglect caused tensions with his siblings. He did, however, keep a cellar of fine wines there and, as he was casual about security, some of the locals including his gardener got into the habit of helping themselves to the wine and other *objets d'art*. The property was eventually sold to a local builder in the 1930s. WPHS was closest to Edmund, who eventually emigrated to Nova Scotia, and his older sister, Aletha, with whom he later shared a house in London and finally Dorset.

WPHS stopped serious climbing around 1920 but continued to attend walks organised by the London section of the Fell and Rock Climbing Club. In his later years he became increasingly casual about his appearance and eccentric in manner. After their London home was bombed in 1940 he moved to Parkstone, in Dorset. His final months were spent in a nursing home.

Whilst the author has done some excellent research for this biography, the writing is frequently awkward and repetitive and the content poorly structured. It reads like a first draft with frequent minor errors, particularly with dates and the spelling of names. The book could have been greatly improved with the assistance of a good editor. An index would also have been a useful addition. The book is privately published in a limited signed edition of 100. The production is good and there are some interesting illustrations but, oddly, there are no page numbers. This is an informative and useful reference for the climbing historian but is unlikely to appeal to the general reader.

Michael Cocker

Regeneration – The Rescue of a Wild Land: Andrew Painting (Birlinn; 2021, hardback, 306pp, ISBN 978-1-78027-714-1, £20; 2022, paperback, 304pp, ISBN 978-1-78027-759-2, £9.99).

When I was younger I saw hills differently – as shapes to set off a sunset, as bastions of crags to conquer, as miles to walk, metres to climb, summits to tick. Sometimes I'd spot an orchid lurking amidst long grasses, crush a leaf of bog myrtle to sniff its sweet sharp scent, miss a beat as a dozen deer fled over a distant skyline. But for the most part I noticed little of the detail of the ground on which I trod.

Then towards of the end of the last century I had a quiet sort of epiphany. Late one August we'd walked into the Dubh Loch and pitched our tent by the sands at the far end. The day turned to rain, so we abandoned our climbing plans to make a circuit around the back of the White Mounth. It was while descending from Cairn Bannoch, our last top of the day, that we came across a tiny spring oozing out of a hollow. The spring was surrounded by a garden of mosses – a subtle, living tapestry of reds, yellows and greens, patterns that no one had ordered or designed. It was as though I'd never seen such a thing before. Up to that point, I'd only thought of a bog as a dreary obstacle to squelch through.

The weather recovered the next day, but the rock did not. High on *Black Mamba* a smooth slab streaming with water brought an end to our upward progress. After a nerve-wracking escape sideways through hanging gardens of blaeberries and loose blocks of rock, we eventually returned to the tent, and that evening made our weary way back along the shore of Loch Muick. As dusk turned to dark, my companion, Bob Reid, began to point out to me things I had never noticed before. 'Look at this seedling,' he said. It was a young birch. 'See here, where the tips have all been nibbled. Deer. That birch'll be dead in a year.' It was the same all the way back to the Spittal: wherever birch or rowan or pine had seeded and tried to grow, they had been grazed. There are barely any trees in this landscape, apart from plantations of non-native conifers. 'And this is the Balmoral estate,' Bob continued. 'The royals are meant to care about nature. It's as bad elsewhere. They all love their shooting so much, the lairds turn a blind eye to the consequences. It's become a sort of desert.'

There are glimmers of hope. The Woodland Trust has acquired a few surviving areas of Caledonian Forest, such as Migdale in eastern Sutherland, as well as planting extensive upland areas with native species, notably in Glen Finglas. Creag Meagaidh was purchased by Scottish Natural Heritage in 1985 as a National Nature Reserve, since when, with grazing strictly controlled, there has been a spectacular regrowth of birch, alder, willow, rowan and oak. In 1995 the Mar Lodge Estate, taking in a large area of the high Cairngorms and the extensive Caledonian Forest of upper Deeside, was acquired by the National Trust for Scotland – a process in which my friend Bob had a hand. The NTS managers immediately began a programme of increasing the annual cull of red deer, with a result that within 15 years or so the deer population was more or less halved, and some level of tree regeneration had begun on the more sheltered lower slopes. However, there has been a problem of deer from the neighbouring estates – where there has not been the same level of culling – moving into these regeneration zones. To counter this, the NTS adopted a policy of zero tolerance, and any deer found in a regeneration zone was shot on sight. This policy did not prove popular with the neighbouring estates (including the royal ones), whose deer populations they felt might be threatened, with a consequence that they would not be able to offer paying shooters so many stags to kill. Pressure was apparently applied.

A major review on the future management of the Mar Lodge Estate, commissioned by the NTS and published in 2011, concluded that the best solution would be the erection of many more miles of fencing, although acknowledging that this could have a deleterious effect on rarities such as black grouse and capercaillies (which have a habit of flying straight into such fences and killing themselves). The authors of the review also acknowledged that the appearance of great stretches of new deer fence would detract from the 'wild land' experience that is such a key component of the amenity value of the estate. Critics might argue that this was a case of the sport and income of the toffs becoming the tail that wags the dog of wider common interests.

It is perhaps a promising sign of better things to come that the NTS – long in thrall to Scotland's landed establishment – have allowed Andrew Painting, assistant ecologist at the Mar Lodge Estate since 2016, to discuss very frankly many of the tricky issues involved. Painting – a wonderful writer – is clearly passionate about nature conservation, and is fearless in his discussions of land ownership and land management in the Highlands. These issues are core to his book about the Mar Lodge Estate; and the book's title, *Regeneration: The Rescue of a Wild Land*, is at least partly justified by what has been happening on the ground at Mar Lodge (although it seems that large swathes in the south-west section of the estate have been set aside for 'traditional' methods of grouse shooting and deer stalking, and so remain as treeless wet deserts – in contrast to the more north-easterly glens of Luibeg, Lui, Derry and Quoich, and the even more spectacular regeneration taking place in the neighbouring Glenfeshie estate to the west).

Living landscapes are complicated things, made even more complex by the humans in them, whether acting or merely witnessing. 'We do not come to nature as impartial observers,' writes Painting in his Prologue. 'We all have an emotional and cultural attachment to all the life with which we share the earth, from the smallest weed to the tallest tree.' He describes the Mar Lodge Estate as 'a deeply beautiful place … a place of soaring eagles and roaring stags, a refuge for some of the rarest creatures in Scotland, a place of deadly cold, avalanches and remoteness … But it is also a contested place, which has been damaged by conflicts that blight the nature of Scotland and continue to divide its people.'

The bigger questions and difficulties aside, Painting is an acute and close watcher of nature. He concentrates not just on the poster species – the Scots pine and the Atlantic salmon – but also on the often overlooked, such as green shield-moss and the Kentish glory butterfly – not to mention the humbly named but rare and quite spectacular alpine sow-thistle, which has been reintroduced to Mar Lodge. He explains how all these and many others weave webs and interdepend. The Mar Lodge Estate includes many habitats, from woodland to moorland to the high tops. Painting devotes a section to each, and within each section, each chapter focuses on a key species. But he is also alert to the humans in these landscapes, from his fellow team members (whether ecologists, estate workers or stalkers) to the people who once lived and made a scant living in these high glens, to the city dwellers who arrive in increasing numbers to experience the wild, and sometimes cause great damage to the places where they've come to seek solace by lighting campfires that rage out of control. This damage is perhaps less serious than the continuing and deliberate practice of muirburn across much of Scotland's uplands, intended to maintain red grouse numbers. Painting is clear where he stands on muirburn: not only damaging to environmentally sensitive peatlands, but a significant releaser of carbon into the atmosphere. As for the other key quarry of the 'traditional sportsmen': 'An overabundance of deer may be desirable for deer stalking, and indeed drives up the value of sporting land, but it leads to environmental destruction.' Excessive drainage practices and the planting of dense blocks of non-native conifers have also wrought their damage, both aesthetically and by reducing biodiversity. The results can sadly be seen across much of Scotland's hill country, from the sheep-shorn Southern Uplands to the bare, treeless glens of the Highland deer 'forests'.

What they have been trying to do at Mar Lodge, Painting says, is 'not far off from' that contentious concept: rewilding. The work undertaken includes 'regenerating woodland, allowing natural hydrological processes to shape the land, reprofiling plantations and de-intensifying moorland management' – even reintroducing lost species, such as the alpine sow-thistle (but not yet wolves or boar or lynx). He is aware that rewilding is an emotive and politically charged term, one that the NTS is wary of deploying. Some say rewilding disregards the economic interests of local communities (such as sheep farmers); others claim it is championed only by rich landowners who indulge in such 'vanity projects' to greenwash their wealth; others object that it destroys 'traditional' ways of life in the Highlands, whether deer stalking and grouse shooting or the right to roam over land that has been grazed smooth, the distance views unhindered by growths of juniper and birch and Scots pine. 'F***ing rewilding,' a senior member of the Club was recently overheard to remark, describing the struggles he had just experienced descending from Derry Cairngorm through regenerating woodland. I've heard such regenerating woodland described as 'scrub' by those who dislike it. But the word 'scrub', like the word 'weed', are loaded, disparaging, non-scientific terms employed by those who prefer their landscapes managed to death. It is perhaps a case of not being able to see the future open woodland for the thickets of vigorous young trees. But maybe in time, as attitudes and values change, we will see the hills as places where a rich and complex web of living beauty can thrive again, as places where people can wander at will, and wonder.

Ian Crofton

The Mountain Path: Paul Pritchard (Vertebrate, 2021, hardback, 177pp, ISBN 978-1-839810-92-3, £24).

This is Paul Pritchard's fourth book. His first, the classic *Deep Play*, described ground-breaking climbs and expeditions in the 1980s and 1990s. His second, *The Totem Pole*, described his horrific life-changing accident on The Totem Pole in Tasmania which left him hemiplegic with a brain injury. The third book, *The Longest Climb*, covered the following years of rehabilitation and gradual return to the mountains. *The Mountain Path* takes us on the psychological and spiritual exploration that Paul has made in the two decades since his accident. Accounts of the accident and his eventual redemptive return to the Totem Pole start and finish the book. In between, chapters with titles such as 'Pain', 'Death' and 'Stillness' lead us through episodes in his journey of discovery of mindfulness and meditation to acceptance of the person he has become. Along the way there are flashbacks to entertaining and gripping tales from his earlier life such as a near-death experience at Gogarth alongside later adventures as a disabled person. He becomes interested in Buddhism during a crossing of the Tibetan plateau by tricycle, and this sets him on a voyage via the extremes of Vipassana meditation to his own mindful approach to life. Climbing runs as a thread through the book as a microcosm of this state.

   This is a remarkable book that transcends the climbing genre to become a credo for living through the experiences of a man who has had the privilege (and I think he sees it as that in a sense) to have experienced not only the extreme cutting edge of climbing but also to have had to rebuild his life from the despair of almost losing everything to rediscover the 'mountain path' in his daily struggles and joys. Even if some readers find it difficult to share some of Paul's conclusions, it would be hard not to admire his humility and gratitude for life in the face of so many challenges.

Robert Durran

The Farthest Shore: Alex Roddie (Vertebrate, 2021, paperback, 224pp, ISBN 978-1-839810-20-6, £14.95).

The Farthest Shore recounts Alex's experiences of walking the Cape Wrath Trail in winter. The book evocatively describes the beautiful wild landscapes encountered along the way. Alex does a very good job of transporting the reader to those places, so that you feel almost as if you are there experiencing it for yourself.

I found that the book was more of a slow burn than a page-turning thriller. There are some interesting and unexpected challenges and encounters on the trail, but it never really felt as though the outcome was in question. So I found it to be a book that is better read at a leisurely pace.

There are a couple of particularly strong themes in the book. The first is the impact of climate change on Scottish winters, which Alex's experiences on the trail in February really highlight. The second is Alex's personal experiences of mental health, and the effects of his taking time away from being online. He certainly raises some interesting questions, and by addressing these issues adds a bit of depth to the book.

Overall an enjoyable and interesting read.

Elsie Riley

Kangchenjunga – the Himalayan Giant: Doug Scott (Vertebrate, 2021, hardback, 273pp, ISBN 978-1-912560-19-6, £24.00).

Doug Scott, who died in 2020, is described by Reinhold Messner on the jacket of this book as 'among the greatest climbers of all time'. In addition to his mountaineering achievements Scott was a considerable, though somewhat idiosyncratic, scholar. Thus this posthumously published work, ably edited by Catherine Moorehead, opens with a very brief summary of the topography, climate and peoples of the Kangchenjunga region and then goes on to offer a well-researched history of both early explorations and serious mountaineering attempts.

In a chapter on 'Missionaries, Traders and Politicians' Doug covers briefly the extraordinary travels of the Jesuits in the seventeenth and eighteenth centuries, and (even more briefly) the travels of early British traders and political agents, including the Scots George Bogle, Alexander Hamilton, George Kinloch and David Ochterlony. This is followed by a chapter on the early surveys of the area around Kangchenjunga, and the travels of the famous pundit Sarat Chandra Das and his associates. The botanist J.D. Hooker gets a chapter to himself and then there is a chapter on 'Artists, Writers and Photographers', where the visits of Edward Lear, Marianne North, Mark Twain, Nicholas Roerich, Howard Somervell, Vittorio Sella and others are covered.

Part 3, the largest section of the book, has eight chapters describing the various attempts to explore and climb the mountain prior to the first successful ascent in 1955. The first person to circumnavigate the mountain was the pundit Rinzin Namgyal, who some years later accompanied Freshfield on the great expedition described in his book *Round Kangchenjunga*, published in 1903. The first serious attempt on Kangchenjunga in 1902 was led by our notorious member Aleister Crowley together with the Swiss Dr Guillarmod and ended low-down in disaster. Just under twenty years later Raeburn made two reconnaissances, first to the east (Sikkim) side of the mountain and then to the west (Nepal) side. The latter excursion up to 6100m revealed the route that was later taken in 1955.

Scott devotes a chapter to a detailed examination of the controversy surrounding W.W. Graham's claimed ascent of Kabru. Notwithstanding the arguments presented by Kellas's biographers Mitchell and Rodway in *Prelude to Everest*,

Doug seems inclined to give Graham the benefit of the doubt, but I am not convinced. In 2010 a group of us attempted Jopuno, a peak near Kabru which Graham claimed to have climbed. It was impossible to make any sense of his description of the topography, just as Kenneth Mason had found Graham's description of the peaks he had climbed in Garhwal most obscure.

There were a number of important expeditions to Kangchenjunga between the wars, and rather than deal with them chronologically Doug has chosen to group them by country of origin. Thus he has a chapter covering the explorations of the Greek photographer Tombazi in 1925, the forlorn attempt by the American Edgar Farmer in 1929 and the travels of the British mountaineers Reginald Cooke, John Hunt and Bill Tilman in the later 1930s, all of which added importantly to knowledge of the area. This is followed by a chapter on Dyhrenfurth's international expedition of 1930 (which was fully reported in Smythe's book *The Kangchenjunga Adventure*) and a chapter describing Bauer's three expeditions in 1929, 1931 and 1936 as well as several German-Swiss expeditions in the later 1930s. The final chapter of this section, misleadingly entitled 'War, Partition and Reconnaissance' (there is nothing about Partition), has a short summary of the important political changes in Nepal and Sikkim in the immediate postwar period and goes on to describe a successful 1949 Swiss expedition to the peaks north of Kangchenjunga and several reconnaissance expeditions in the early 1950s that helped to guide the choice of route for the 1955 first ascent.

The last section of the book gives a good account of the first ascent via the south-west face; of the second ascent by an Indian team along the north-east ridge, approaching from the Sikkim side; and finally of the outstanding 1979 ascent of the north ridge, with no oxygen or Sherpa support, by Scott, Tasker, Boardman and Bettembourg (who unfortunately did not quite make the summit).

Although there is much to admire about this book I am afraid that it has several noticeable failings. Doug Scott's writing is occasionally rambling, veering off into sidetracks that are interesting but not germane to the main thread. The photographs, though of good quality, are largely from the 1979 expedition, so do not illustrate the earlier expeditions which form the bulk of the text. Neither are there sufficient maps to help the reader understand the details of topography that take up a great deal of Doug's account. I fail to understand why, in revising Doug's text, more use was not made of the resources of the Alpine Club Library and Royal Geographical Society archives to remedy these defects. It seems incomplete to end the book in 1979. It isn't as if there have not been remarkable achievements and dramatic events on the mountain since that date. Perhaps too much has happened, and only another book could do justice to this more recent history.

Geoff Cohen

The Cairngorms Scene & Unseen: Sydney Scroggie (Scottish Mountaineering Press, 2021, paperback, 199pp, ISBN 978-1-907233-41-8, £12).

Agreeing to review Sydney Scroggie's book, I eagerly awaited its arrival through the post. I was aware of the man and the title, first published in 1989 by the Scottish Mountaineering Trust,[2] but had dismissed it for some reason or other.

---

[2] For reviews of the 1st edition, by W.H. Murray and G.D. Morrison, see *SMCJ*, 34/181 (1990), 557–9. Murray wrote, 'This book is near to a *tour de force* … by reason of his deep insights.' – HON. ED.

Thirty-three years on, and a fresh attractive reprint by our own Scottish Mountaineering Press duly arrived in a smaller and softer format than expected. Gone is the hardback with its black & white plates including the Pools of Dee on the front cover. Retained are the fine foreword from Tom Weir and the excellent line drawings by John Mitchell. I particularly like the one of the Etchachan Hut with its old storm-porch and Creagan a' Choire Etchachan in the background. The new front cover is a striking illustration of the guided Syd walking through his beloved Lairig Ghru.

Donald Bennet, SMT Publications Manager at the time, asked well-known SMC and Cairngorm stalwart Derek Pyper to review it for the Aberdeen Press & Journal. Donald described it as 'of unusual interest, for it is the memoirs of the blind climber Syd Scroggie and we were lucky to obtain the manuscript.'

Ken Crocket has done a fine job of editing the twenty-first-century version, and he points out at the beginning: 'Some of the social and environmental perspectives in this book are likely to be considered out of step with current thinking. After careful consideration we chose to retain some, but not all, of these viewpoints in order to accurately represent Syd's style of writing and the cultural norms of that era.' Syd was one to shoot from the hip and generally didn't miss the target. The Duke of Edinburgh Award Scheme and our National Outdoor Training Centre at Glenmore Lodge came under fire – most uncharitably and unfairly in my humble opinion. Syd's work obviously predates political correctness and the cancel culture of today.

He had a remarkable life story. In pre-war days he was a distance runner and talented rock climber who knew and loved the Cairngorms. On leaving school he worked with publishers DC Thomson in Dundee as a sub-editor at *The Hotspur*. During the war he reached the rank of lieutenant in the Lovat Scouts, and before joining the allied forces in Italy he spent the winter training in the Rockies, making a first winter ascent of Mount Columbia, Canada's second-highest peak. Sad to say, a fortnight before the end of the war, Syd was blown up by a land-mine and lost a leg as well as his sight.

Not deterred in the slightest, Syd reached out for someone who would act as a pair of eyes and made many trips back into the Cairngorms holding on to a shoulder and rucksack strap of a trusted companion. Remarkably, he summitted over 600 hills well into his eighties.

His writing captures beautifully the rich wildness of the area and the inspirational and therapeutic powers it offers. He brings to life the bothy culture of Corrour, Geldie Lodge and Luibeg and the characters that frequented these Highland howffs. Bob Scott gets his rightful place as Cairngorm royalty, with numerous amusing anecdotes.

> Bob liked telling stories about the gentry as the gillies find them. This one was about the laird briefing his head keeper about a maharaja. 'Mind ye noo, Willie. He's a big man in his ain country – so ye'll mind and gie him his title and treat him wi' proper respect.' Next day it seems, Willie observed due protocol and was a model of patience forbye when it turned out the maharaja was a poor hand at fishing. 'You will pardon me your Royal Highness if I jist gie ye a wee demonstration o' how to dae it correctly,' he said. There was no improvement. 'Na, na, na, gie's the rod your Royal Highness an' watch mair closely this time.' The maharaja was making a botch of it again when the keeper snatched the rod away from him: 'In the name of God ye ignorant fool!'

One wonders if Bob himself was that keeper in question! On a different occasion,

… we turned across to the bothy and the smell of wood-smoke, whence came a cheery hail in the Aberdeen tongue from that most affable of deerstalkers, the burly Bob Scott. 'I doot ther's nae room in the bothy; it's ower full wi' thae Etchachan loons, I'll let ye into the stable.'

Again referring to Scott's:

Dominating the bothy was a granite fireplace, so massive that it might have taken a day's labour in Rubislaw Quarry to howk it out.

I am told you would know of Syd's presence at Luibeg before entering the bothy. An artificial leg would be draped over the fence with hobnailed boot still attached to the end of it. He was undoubtedly one of the great characters of the day. There is an excellent interview with him and Tom Weir for *Weir's Way* which can be found online and well worth a view.

On a trip to Corrour with two friends, Syd describes

… lounging in this chiaroscuro of candle and firelight when we were joined by a lone walker, a medical student from Aberdeen by the name of Andrew Brockie, as we quickly found out. [Next morning …] Andrew Brockie, a humorous chap with dark, wavy hair, peered out of his sleeping-bag, his head supported by rucksack and folded breeks, and a fag in mouth. In the instant intimacy of bothy life, he had already risen high in our estimation, both by the likeable quality of his character and by the fact, as he complaisantly informed us, that he had fallen a hundred feet practising rock climbing in Rubislaw quarry, Aberdeen, and got away with it.

Other characters of note include Maggie Gruer, who was most hospitable to the men stravaigin' through the Lairig, and Mrs McDougall who had the tiny youth hostel at Inverey. As a child my dad and his cronies took us to the old school at Inverey for weekends in the hills and I distinctly remember seeing Bob Scott in his tweeds holding court in the bar at Mar Lodge. Mrs McDougall was the caretaker of the long closed-down school and would give us the keys on the Friday night on our arriving from Peterhead via the Coilacriech Inn at Ballater.

Throughout the book, which has only 12 chapters, none of which is named, is a peppering of verse, some of which I get, most of which I don't, but this is a lack of appreciation of poetry on my part. Overall, I very much enjoyed the book, which is written in a style that is easy to relate to, and is packed with amusing anecdotes. I feel it is a more compelling narrative of the Cairngorms than for example, Nan Shepherd's *The Living Mountain*, which I have still to get to grips with despite my best efforts. Anyone who has spent quality time in the Cairngorms will get much of Scroggie's musings.

Top marks to the team who have revived this publication and won over folk like me who didn't give it a chance first time around. Donald was right when he said all those years ago, 'it is a valuable addition to Scottish climbing literature.'

Niall Ritchie

Uncoiling the Ropes – the memoir of a trail-blazing Irish climber: Clare Sheridan (Mweelrea Press, 2020, paperback, 198pp, ISBN 978-1-78846-159-7, £18).

This is a good read. The author has written a refreshing account of her climbing life with candour and colour. Climbing, including working as a mountain instructor, has clearly been at the centre of her life, and we get an absorbing story of over fifty years of exploits from early rock to *grandes courses* in the Alps and exploits in the wider ranges. She offers an interesting Irish perspective, charting developments from the 1970s to the present day in traditional climbing, bouldering, sports climbing, training and ethics. Clare Sheridan has many trail-blazing achievements to reflect on. As a woman who has climbed consistently at a high standard for a long time, she gives us additional warmth and a fresh perspective.

The book has an interesting take on many topics such as siege versus alpine-style expeditions, fatalities, training, injury, strength, excelling as a woman in a male-dominated world, and juggling climbing ambitions with the practicalities of parenthood and work. These topics are addressed clearly without fanfare and supported by many anecdotes about characters and climbing trips. In telling of her achievements with both honesty and modesty, including her open admission of fear ahead of big routes, her narrative has a different tone from many other memoirs.

Ireland was a different world in the 1970s from the country we are familiar with now. The north and south were on different paths, but both had plenty of unclimbed rock. The country was deeply conservative. 'Self-control and refinement' were the virtues instilled and admired in girls. The revelation of the first kiss and of leading the first VS are given equal attention as they happened around the same time. Divorce was legalised only in 1996! This mattered for a good Catholic girl cohabiting with a divorced Protestant man. Her lifestyle challenged many norms and threatened her livelihood as a teacher at a time when the church held huge sway in the running of schools. In the 1970s and 1980s it was very unusual for women to climb and lead at a high standard, let alone put up new routes. Sheridan describes her early innocence and her breakthrough to climbing VS and how she had to face questions about whether a woman would ever be strong enough to lead extreme. Later she covers attitudes to climbing and risk as a parent who has continued to climb at a high standard up to the present. The book demonstrates her considerable contribution to Irish climbing and adds perspective to Irish climbing in general. Clare Sheridan and her long-standing life-partner, Calvin Torrans, have shared an enthusiastic commitment to climbing and to each other. They have had a huge part in the development of Fair Head, one of the most extensive and impressive cliffs in the British Isles. This is a most refreshing account of a climbing life.

Stan Pearson

Emilio Comici – Angel of the Dolomites: David Smart (Rocky Mountain Books, 2020, hardback, 247pp, ISBN 978-1-77-16045-67, £30).

David Smart has followed up his excellent biography of Paul Preuss with another *tour de force*. Comici, best known for the first ascent of the north face of the Cima Grande di Lavaredo, was one of the most eminent Italian rock climbers of the inter-war period – although Smart gives credit to many other less well-kent names from that generation; and in the later 1930s the accomplishments of Lecco-based Cassin and his companions began to outshine those of the Trieste climbers such as Comici.

The city of Trieste provides a vital backdrop to Comici's early years, emerging from 500 years of Austrian rule at the end of the First World War, just as Comici emerged from his teenage years. The successful irredentist struggle morphed into

Mussolini's fascism, a movement which fired the young Comici's imagination. While he joined the fascist party, enjoyed the marching and blackshirt uniforms, and later became a minor fascist official, Smart's portrayal is full of nuance in its understanding of the character of Italian fascism, and the changes it underwent in these two decades. Comici's politics were proudly patriotic, anti-German but not apparently antisemitic.

Coming from a poor working-class background, Comici's personal style and his attitude to climbing are contrasted with the bourgeois and gentlemanly approach of mentors such as Julius Kugy. When, however, he moved away from Trieste to become a mountain guide he found his urban values equally at odds with those of traditional local guides: '… he did not realise that their lives were as far from a day cragging at Val Rosandra followed by an evening in the smart bars of Trieste as alpine goat farming was from working in the Magazzini Generali.'

Comici was innovative in his approach to aid climbing. Having been a caver before he took up climbing, he introduced etriers into his climbing, and while 'the deliberate use of pitons that would only support body weight … was unknown … [he] taught himself how to place pitons which would hold no more than his body weight in tiny pockets and cracks … [and] would intersperse these dubious pitons with more solid "base" pitons to catch him if he ripped out the weaker ones.' He was an early user of double ropes for aid climbing, being held on one rope while placing a higher peg. He also used to tow a thin extra line to haul up more pitons if required.

As a guide Comici had some interesting clients, including the wealthy Anna Escher, herself an excellent climber, with whom he climbed in Spain, Greece and Egyptian Sinai – where their ascents prefigured American desert rock climbing. He had other more tragic female friends: Bruna Bernardini who could lead Grade VI but died when her rope broke, and the poet Antonia Pozzi who committed suicide. Being very close to his mother and totally dedicated to his climbing way of life it may not be surprising that he was unable to sustain a relationship with any of the many women drawn to him.

There was much competition for the first ascent of the north face of the Cima Grande. After several false starts, and anxious not to be pipped, Comici and the Dimai brothers from Cortina swallowed their rivalrous reservations and established a 'partnership of convenience' to seize the honours: 'For ten years the lower wall had defeated all comers … on ten exacting pitches they had utilised every known technique and some 75 pitons.' Although their ascent received huge acclaim it produced no material rewards. Comici followed this stunning success with what he considered his most elegant and exposed climb, the great prow of the *Spigolo Giallo* (Yellow Edge), with his friends Mary Varale and Renato Zanutti. However, he was frustrated by weather, poor companions and old injuries in his attempt to make the first ascent of the north face of the Cima Ovest, which fell to Cassin, and by 1938 he was not involved in the famous 'conquests' of the Eigerwand and the Walker Spur.

The year after his ascent of the Cima Grande Comici turned to extreme soloing. He repeated Preuss's extraordinary solo of the east face of the Campanile Basso, and then in 1937 he soloed his own route on the Cima Grande in just over three hours, surviving a sudden ledge collapse that could have obliterated climbers below as well as wiping him out. He died in fact in 1940 in a banal accident on a practice crag when a rope that he had borrowed broke on an abseil.

There is far more than mere climbing achievements in this impressively researched book. We get a picture on a broad canvas of Dolomitic rock climbing in this period of intense national competition, enhanced by references to Comici's sparse attempts at writing and Pozzi's profoundly moving poetry. Smart excels at penetrating the emotional and psychological depths underlying the bare act of climbing while never neglecting the sociopolitical context in which the protagonists lived out their adventures.

Descriptions of Comici's ascents in the Julian Alps and eastern Dolomites would have been enhanced by the inclusion of some maps. I would guess that few British climbers will be familiar with such peaks as the Ago di Villaco, Dito di Dio, Jof di Montasio and Sorella di Mezzo. There are rather small black & white photos of Comici's routes on the Cima Piccola di Lavaredo, the north face of the Civetta and the Sorella, but in general the illustrations have not been used to their best. While many are of great historical interest, they are not arranged in any logical order and several are too small to be appreciated.

It seems petty to point out errors in such a splendid book, but I cannot resist mentioning a couple. On page 135 Smart refers to the 'seven' great north faces, and lists just the famous six, and then speaks again a couple of pages later of 'two out of seven of the great north walls'. To my knowledge it was always just six north faces that were considered the great Alpine challenge. Finally, Cassin's expedition to Gasherbrum IV was in 1958, not 1969.

Geoff Cohen

Crack Climbing: Pete Whittaker, with illustrations by Alex Poyser (Vertebrate, 2020, paperback, 272pp, ISBN 978-1-911342-76-2, £25).

A good book is a like a good climb: it needs to inspire, it should be attractive, and it ought to impart memorable life experiences. *Crack Climbing* by Pete Whittaker is a very impressive book, which successfully combines all of these elements and much more in its 256 pages.

- Inspiring – each time I dip into this book my hands start to sweat, and I get the urge to scrunch them into the coolness of a crack, to learn something new, and to have fun in the process.
- Attractive – this book is beautifully laid out, with spacing, fonts, highlights, call-out paragraphs, action photos, explanatory diagrams, and much more besides, all carefully presented to draw you in. A great deal of thought and expertise has gone into it, and it works beautifully.
- Memorable – the book is memorable in both its technical content, specifically how to climb cracks, and also in the accompanying diagrams, images and stories that collectively get you fired up to go and do it.

Crack Climbing combines clear, comprehensive, well-thought-out instructions, with a coffee-table book of amazing pics, and great stories – a book that is equally at home at the crag or in the sitting room; I cannot think of another climbing book that combines all these elements so successfully. Chapters are logically laid out, covering techniques from the smallest to biggest cracks, equipment and protection, a who's-who of 'meet the master' climbers, and perhaps most importantly of all, how to tape up.

The photos are excellent throughout, covering a vast spread of venues and crack types, and with women well represented too, all with proper 'try hard' faces rather than posed shots, which will hopefully help inspire future generations. The picture of Mary Eden on page 168 is genuinely 'am I looking at this the right way up' arresting, and not simply because of the SMC-baiting route name.

There is a playfulness to the writing which I find engaging, for example asking a series of truly world-class climbers 'What is your favourite colour of climbing pants [trousers]?', which seems to reveal much more of their personalities than standard questioning, some respondents evidently playing with it whilst others are deadly earnest, perhaps lost by the deadpan British humour. And there are some great technique names too, for example *the teacup jam* (helpful for anyone that remembers the Alien Rock off-width? RIP).

Is there a correlation between good climbers and good authors? In Pete's case, the answer is a resounding Yes: *Crack Climbing* evidently benefits from the same focus and attention to detail that has made him such a superb climber, and it has clearly been a real labour of love. He successfully imparts his encyclopaedic knowledge in a manner that can be read cover-to-cover or dipped into like a guidebook, and even the introductory 'Five Rules of Crack Climbing' taught me useful things that I'd somehow overlooked, and in a way that was immediately applicable the next time I went crack climbing.

Who is this book aimed at? Firstly, I meet a lot of climbers professing to know how to hand-jam and finger-lock, who therefore think they can climb cracks. However, 'mid-grade' crack routes in places like Yosemite in California, and Stanage in the Peak District, are excellent at highlighting any shortcomings, and many people come away battered and bruised from their first couple of crack climbs, usually abandoning expensive bits of kit in the process. Consequently many climbers avoid such routes, but the harsh reality of climbing, like much of life, is that improvement often comes by embracing what you're worst at. Secondly, have you lived in one area for a while and climbed all the routes you can do or want to do? This book is a great way to re-inject a bit of what is arguably the most memorable phase in all our climbing careers, specifically where we're trying new things, pushing beyond our comfort zones, and racking up new and memorable life experiences. Thirdly, this book is ideal if you have specific crack projects in mind, and going armed with a copy of *Crack Climbing* is likely to help stack the odds in your favour, and save you a great deal of grunting and skin-loss in the process.

Failings? My immediate response is to say 'None, this book is perfect,' but if pushed hard I'd identify occasionally sentences where the grammar is slightly different from what I expect; but I'm far from an expert in this area, and it is possibly just Pete's way of speaking. The other failing exposed *by* this book (and certainly not a failing *of* the book), is the way cracks are so under-represented in climbing walls nowadays: it's like a vicious cycle – crack climbing is a learned skill which people frequently overlook, meaning they find them hard and avoid doing them, so walls don't provide them – hence climbers continue to have crack-climbing epics outdoors and otherwise miss out on their beguiling charms.

The book is a bargain at £25, and it's hard to see how Pete's considerable efforts will be repaid, but as a minimum it may further cement his reputation as one of the world's leading authorities on crack climbing.

My only regret is not finding this book sooner! Perhaps my roof-crack climbing sessions at the Crack Den and Meggetland bridges in Edinburgh during lockdown would have been slightly easier; but then again, I enjoyed the journey, if not the canal swim.

Olly Stephenson

CORRECTIONS & CLARIFICATIONS

'Yes, I have learned from the mistakes of others, but mostly I am self-taught.'
– Robert Brault.

The following errors occurred in the 2021 *SMC Journal*.

p. 282 A word was truncated in Billy Hood's account of lockdown, which should have read: 'As on small hills all over Scotland, it was ski-anywhere time. The Muirshiel Alps had turned into the Hardangervidda.'

p. 296 Mike Dixon completed a third (not second) round of the Munros in 2020.

p. 366 In Ian Mitchell's review of *The Hunt for Mount Everest*, Raeburn's reconnaissance of Kangchenjunga should have been dated 1920 not 1905.

As always, these errors have been corrected in the archived version of the *Journal*.

ORDERING THE SMC JOURNAL

Members should automatically receive a copy of the *Journal* when it is published. Members wishing to order extra copies or non-members wishing to place a regular order should contact the Distribution Manager, Dave Broadhead, by **e-mail** <journal.distribution@smc.org.uk>.

SMC JOURNAL BACK NUMBERS

Back numbers of the *Journal* may be obtained from Clifford Smith:
16 House o' Hill Gardens, Edinburgh, EH4 2AR.
e-mail: <journal.archive@smc.org.uk>
tel: 0131-332 3414   mob: 07748 703515

The following years are available: post and packaging are extra.

	Year		Year
£5.00	1972	£12.95	2000
	1977		2001
	1978		2002
	1979		2003
	1980		2004
	1983		
		£13.95	2005
£5.50	1985		2006
			2007
£5.70	1986		2008
	1987		
	1989	£14.95	2009
	1990		2010
	1991		2011
	1992		2012
			2013
£6.95	1993		2014
	1994		
	1995	£16.95	2016
			2017
£8.95	1996		2018
	1997		2019
	1998		2020
			2021
£11.95	1999		

SCOTTISH MOUNTAINEERING CLUB HUTS

Bookings can be made to stay at any of the five Club Huts by contacting the relevant Custodian.

CHARLES INGLIS CLARK MEMORIAL HUT, BEN NEVIS
Location: (NN 167 722) On the north side of Ben Nevis by the Allt a' Mhuilinn. This hut was erected by Dr and Mrs Inglis Clark in memory of their son Charles who was killed in action in the 1914–18 War.
Custodian: Robin Clothier.
e-mail <cic@smc.org.uk>

LAGANGARBH HUT, GLEN COE
Location: (NN 221 559) North of Buachaille Etive Mòr near the River Coupall.
Custodian: Bernard Swan, 16 Knowes View, Faifley, Clydebank, G81 5AT.
e-mail <lagangarbh@smc.org.uk>.

LING HUT, GLEN TORRIDON
Location: (NG 958 562) On the south side of Glen Torridon.
Custodian: Patrick Ingram, 119 Overton Avenue, Inverness, IV3 8RR.
e-mail <ling@smc.org.uk>.

NAISMITH HUT, ELPHIN
Location: (NC 216 118) In the community of Elphin on the east side of the A835.
Custodian: John T. Orr, 8 Fleurs Place, Elgin, Morayshire, IV30 1ST.
e-mail <naismith@smc.org.uk>.

RAEBURN HUT, LAGGAN
Location: (NN 636 909) On the north side of the A889 between Dalwhinnie and Laggan.
Custodian: Gordon Lacey, 10 Alder Avenue, Lenzie, G66 4JG.
e-mail <raeburn@smc.org.uk>.

SCOTTISH MOUNTAINEERING CLUB GUIDEBOOKS
Published by SCOTTISH MOUNTAINEERING PRESS

HILLWALKERS' GUIDES
The Munros
The Corbetts & other Scottish hills
The Grahams & The Donalds

The Cairngorms
Central Highlands
North-West Highlands
Southern Highlands

SCRAMBLERS' GUIDES
Highland Scrambles North
Highland Scrambles South
Skye Scrambles

CLIMBERS' GUIDES
Scottish Rock Climbs
Scottish Winter Climbs
Scottish Sports Climbs
Inner Hebrides & Arran
Ben Nevis
The Cairngorms
Glen Coe
Highland Outcrops South
Lowland Outcrops

North-East Outcrops
Northern Highlands North
Northern Highlands Central
Northern Highlands South
Skye The Cuillin
Skye Sea-Cliffs & Outcrops
The Outer Hebrides
Scottish Winter Climbs West

OTHER PUBLICATIONS
Ben Nevis – Britain's Highest Mountain
The Cairngorms – 100 Years of Mountaineering
A Chance in a Million? – Scottish Avalanches
Hostile Habitats
The Munroist's Companion
Scottish Hill Names – Their origin and meaning
Mountaineering in Scotland: the Early Years
Mountaineering in Scotland: Years of Change
The Cairngorms Scene & Unseen

APPS
SMC guides to the Northern Corries and Polney Crag are available on the
Rockfax App <https://www.rockfax.com/publications/rockfax-app/>.

E-BOOKS
Please see <https://www.smc.org.uk/publications/ebooks>

APPLYING FOR MEMBERSHIP OF
THE SCOTTISH MOUNTAINEERING CLUB

The following notes are provided outlining the principles by which climbers may be admitted to membership of the Club.

The Committee does not lay down any hard and fast rules when considering applications but considers each case on its own merits. Candidates must be over 18 and have experience of mountaineering in Scotland in both summer and winter. This experience should have extended over a period of at least four years immediately prior to application and should not be confined to just a single climbing district.

The normally expected climbing standards include:

- Experience of winter climbing including several routes of around Grade IV standard and the ability to lead climbs of this level of difficulty.
- Rock climbing experience including climbs of Very Severe (4c) standard and the ability to lead routes of this level of difficulty. In considering applications, emphasis will be placed on multi-pitch climbs in mountain locations.
- The ascent of at least 50 Munros of which at least one third should have been climbed in snow conditions.

In short, the candidate should be able to show – by producing a detailed list of climbs – that they are competent to lead a variety of outings in the mountains of Scotland in both summer and winter. The technical standards specified refer to applicants currently active and may be varied at the discretion of the Committee for older candidates provided that the applicant's routes reflect a reasonable standard for their time. Climbing in the Alps and elsewhere is taken into consideration. Candidates who do not fulfil the normal qualifications listed above but who have made special contributions to Scottish mountaineering in the fields of art, literature or science may receive special consideration.

It is essential that each candidate, before applying, should have climbed with the member proposing the application. It is also desirable that a candidate should be introduced to a member of the Committee before the application is considered. Application forms must be obtained on behalf of candidates by members of the Club who may not propose or support candidates for election during their own first two years of membership. The annual membership fee is £40.00 (£30.00 for those aged 65 and over) which includes the *SMC Journal*.

A fuller version of these notes for members wishing to propose candidates is available from the Club Secretary who is happy to advise candidates and members on any aspect of the application process. Please contact Tom Prentice, Honorary Secretary at:

e-mail: <secretary@smc.org.uk>

OFFICE BEARERS 2021–22

Honorary President: Neil W. Quinn
Honorary Vice-Presidents: Robert T. Richardson & Robin N. Campbell
President: David J. Broadhead
Vice-Presidents: James D. Hotchkis & Christopher R. Ravey

Hon. Secretary: Tom Prentice, 302 Albert Drive, Glasgow, G41 5RS. **Hon. Treasurer**: Pauline A. Kell*, 81 Queensferry Road, Edinburgh, EH4 3HW. **Hon. Membership Secretary**: Jamie Thin, 35 Ellen's Glen Road, Edinburgh, EH17 7QL. **Hon. Meets Secretary**: David Myatt, Blairhill Gardens, Rumbling Bridge, Kinross, KY13 0PU. **Hon. Editor of Journal**: Graeme D. Morrison, 42 Orchard Drive, Edinburgh, EH4 2DZ. **Hon. Librarian**: John C. Higham, Kaya, 39 Lonemore, Strath, Gairloch, IV21 2DA. **Hon. Archivist**: Robin N. Campbell, Glynside, Kippen Road, Fintry, G63 0LW. **Hon. Custodian of Images**: David Stone, 30 Summerside Street, Edinburgh, EH6 4NU. **Hon. Reporter on Accounts**: John A.P. Hutchinson, 11 Sandfield Avenue, Milngavie, G62 8NR. **SMC Information Manager**: Bob Duncan*. **SMC Website Manager**: Martin McKenna, e-mail <smc@smc.org.uk>. **SMC Website Editor**: Rob Lovell. **Convener of Publications Sub-Committee**: D. Noel Williams, Solus Na Beinne, Happy Valley, Torlundy, Fort William, PH33 6SN. **Convener of Huts Sub-Committee**: Bob Reid, 5 Findon Place, Findon, Aberdeen, AB12 3RS. **Rep. to Mountaineering Scotland**: Stan Pearson, 5 Greenhill Park, Edinburgh, EH10 4DW. **Committee**: Fiona Murray, Christine Watkins, Graeme Morrison, Viv Scott, Timothy Elson and Jamie Thin.

Journal Information

Editor: Graeme Morrison, 42 Orchard Drive, Edinburgh, EH4 2DZ. **e-mail** <journal@smc.org.uk>
New Routes Editor: Simon Richardson, 22 Earlswells Road, Cults, Aberdeen AB15 9NY. **e-mail** <newroutes@smc.org.uk>
Photos Editor: Ian Taylor, 15, Pulteney Street, Ullapool, Ross-shire, IV26 2UP. **e-mail** <itandtf@hotmail.com>
Reviews Editor: Geoff Cohen, 198/1 Grange Loan, Edinburgh, EH9 2DZ. **e-mail** <geoffrcohen@yahoo.com>
Distribution: Dave Broadhead, 17 Drumdyre Road, Dingwall, IV15 9RW. **e-mail** <journal.distribution@smc.org.uk>
Back Numbers: Cliff Smith. **e-mail** <journal.archive@smc.org.uk>

INSTRUCTIONS TO CONTRIBUTORS

The Editor welcomes contributions from members and non-members alike. Priority will be given to articles relating to Scottish mountaineering. Articles should be submitted **by the end of April** to be considered for inclusion in the *Journal* of the same year. Material is preferred in electronic form and should be sent by e-mail direct to the Editor. Most common file formats are acceptable.

Illustrations not relating to an article should be sent to the Photos Editor. All images should be high resolution and have explanatory captions including the source. Books for review should be sent to the Reviews Editor by the end of April.

The Editorial team reserves the right to edit any material submitted.

* Appointment *pro tem*, subject to AGM confirmation.

INDEX OF AUTHORS

INDEX OF PEOPLE

Bold numerals denote an article by the person; *italic numerals* denote an image of the person. Abbreviations: fn = footnote; ff = and following pages.

INDEX OF PLACES & GENERAL TOPICS

Italic numerals refer to a picture. Abbreviations: fn = footnote; ff = and following pages; FA = first ascent; FWA = first winter ascent.

INDEX OF PHOTOGRAPHERS & ARTISTS

INDEX OF REVIEWS
(Reviewer in parenthesis)